WOMEN AND THE IDEAL SOCIETY

WOMEN AND THE IDEAL SOCIETY

Plato's *Republic* and Modern Myths of Gender

NATALIE HARRIS BLUESTONE

THE UNIVERSITY OF MASSACHUSETTS PRESS
AMHERST, 1987

Printed in the United States of America
LC 87–6002
ISBN 0–87023–580–x cloth; 581–8 paper
Set in Linotron Goudy Old Style
Printed and bound by Thomson-Shore

Library of Congress Cataloging-in-Publication Data

Bluestone, Natalie Harris, 1931–
Women and the ideal society.

Bibliography: p.
Includes index.
1. Women. 2. Plato. Republic. 3. Feminism.
4. Political science—Philosophy. I. Title
HQ1206.B48 1988 305.4'2 87–6002
ISBN 0–87023–580–x (alk. paper)
ISBN 0–87023–581–8 (pbk. : alk. paper)

British Library Cataloging in Publication data are available.

For Max Bluestone
In Memoriam

Do you accept the community of the women with the men in education, children, and guarding the rest of the citizens; and that both when they are staying in the city and going out to war, they must guard and hunt together like dogs, and in so far as possible have everything in every way in common; and that in doing this they'll do what's best and nothing contrary to the nature of the female in her relationship with the male, nothing contrary to the natural community of the two with each other?

Plato,
Republic, Book V, 466d.

Christian morality . . . introduced into the world the purest idea of marriage, and the most perfect form of domesticity. . . . Plato's view on the contrary misled him . . . to an utter destruction of both; and this is what every individual of sound mind . . . would gladly erase out of his work, even to the very last trace. . . . [H]ere is concentrated all that was mistaken in the development of the Hellenic mind.

Friedrich Schleiermacher,
Introductions to the Dialogues of Plato

Contents

Preface

I owe an enormous debt to Aron Gurwitsch, George Boas, and Ludwig Edelstein, teachers and mentors, who, in the 1950s when such views were heretical, fostered in me the belief that woman's intellect was in every way equal to man's. These three scholars, although not social radicals, truly believed that the life of the mind, which they valued highly, was in no way gender-connected. It was a time when female undergraduates were being discouraged from continuing their studies, when as a young teaching assistant—then called a "section man"—I could eat at the Faculty Club only on specified Ladies' Days, and membership in the campus literary society was closed to women. It is all the more remarkable, then, that these rare scholars rejected the prevalent wisdom and taught me to ignore Aristotle's dictum, "*Gunai, gunaixi kosmon hē sigē pherei.*" Indeed the present volume is an attempted refutation of this idea that "Silence is a woman's glory." And I can only hope to repay my debt to Gurwitsch, Boas, and Edelstein, now—alas—all dead, by passing on the flame of scholarship and egalitarianism to my own students, and hopefully to my readers.

My aim in this study has been to present a consistent, coherent, logical argument to show that a systematic bias against women philosophers has pervaded scholarly thought. I do not wish to rant bitterly or denounce in anger, for it is my belief that a careful demonstration of my case can encourage men and women of good will, interested in Plato and in the truth, to examine what has been done and what is to be done. My second goal has been to reveal and assess the contribution of recent feminist writers who have brought to center stage for the first time the idea that Plato's *Republic*, and indeed any ideal commonwealth, requires not only Philosopher-Kings, but also Philosopher-Queens.

In my efforts I have benefited greatly from the help of colleagues and friends. Parts of the manuscript have been presented to the Research Colloquium of the Alliance of Independent Scholars, the Radcliffe College Alumnae Board of Managers, and the Graduate Philosophy Colloquium, York University, Canada. I particularly want to thank Judith Amory, Hugh Amory, Michael Bennett and my other friends at HCHP, Nancy Downey, Renate Hanauer, Abigail Housen, Judith Kantrowitz, Eugenia Kaledin, Annette Pringle, Chris Paci, Mary Paci, James Shen, and Nancy Zumwalt. I am especially grateful for the incisive criticism of Mona Harrington, who read the entire manuscript and whose encouragement was indispensable. My greatest debt is to my children, Hanya and Sasha, and most of all to my husband, George Bluestone, whose patience, devotion, concrete help and emotional support sustained me throughout the work.

N.H.B.
Cambridge, Massachusetts

WOMEN AND THE IDEAL SOCIETY

Introduction

COMMENTARY ON PLATO'S *REPUBLIC*, BOOK V AND THE EXCLUSION OF WOMEN FROM THE PHILOSOPHIC LIFE

In Plato's *Republic*, the most influential philosophical work ever written, Socrates proposed an ideal society in which superior men and women would rule together equally. The Athenian philosopher thus became, more than twenty-three hundred years ago, the first advocate in human history of a measure of sexual equality. The guardians of his society were to be true philosophers, passionately committed to reason and trained in its rigorous application. Believing that some women possessed the necessary capacity for reason and philosophy, he introduced the then startling proposal that identical leadership roles required identical education for the most capable members of both sexes.

From Aristotle onward, writers and scholars have explored all aspects of Plato's great dialogue on the nature of justice and the just society. Some commentators had even expressed vague enthusiasm for greater civic participation by women. But until recently only a very few bothered to discuss the advisability or feasibility of identical education from earliest infancy for gifted boys and girls. And not until the 1970s has there been a single commentator who wholeheartedly agreed with the Platonic suggestion of identical leadership roles for both genders. In fact, throughout the centuries, Plato's passage on sexual equality has suffered a singular fate; it has been largely dismissed, deplored, or ignored.

In earlier eras, the excision of Plato's discussion of women rulers was deliberate. Modern awareness of the *Republic* begins in the fifteenth century when Marsilio Ficino reintroduced Plato into the mainstream of Western thought by translating all the known dialogues into Latin. Before Ficino, Leonardo Bruni had translated several of the *Dialogues* and the *Letters,* but declined to translate the *Republic.* He feared that its radical ideas, particularly those on women, would upset his readers. This dedicated classicist at least did not underestimate the importance and subversive character of the Platonic suggestions. He found Plato too searching, unconventional, and disturbing. And at a time when very few in the West knew Greek, he made the decision in effect to suppress the *Republic* because he knew its suggestion of the "community of wives" as he put it, would be offensive to his Florentine audience.[1]

Later scholarship, starting with the renewal of serious interest in Plato in nineteenth-century Germany, dismissed the subject of women rulers in a different way. Scholars in the German tradition did not censor Plato where they found his ideas threatening. On the contrary, beginning with Friedrich Schleiermacher's careful early nineteenth-century translations, scholars made a conscious commitment to strict objectivity. Philosophers and historians of philosophy returned to the actual Greek texts, seeking to distinguish the authentic views of Plato from those of earlier translators and interpreters. Widespread attempts were made to establish the definitive Greek text, to offer the best translations in many languages, to explicate difficult passages. The ostensible purpose of all these efforts was solely to make clear what Plato really meant.

But in the numerous translations, explications, and "companions" that have continued to appear down to our own day, hostility toward the Platonic suggestion of equality persisted. Unsubstantiated views of women's differences and unexamined assumptions about women's limitations occurred repeatedly. Further, despite their stated aim of complete objectivity in rendering Plato's thought, commentators frequently offered their own beliefs that men and women cannot or should not play the same leadership role in society. In short, on this highly charged issue, objectivity faltered and scholars dealt with Plato's radical proposal for equality with a bias they themselves did not recognize.

This bias, although sometimes glaring, was far more often subterranean and subtle. Most of the commentators whose work I examine in this book would vociferously deny any outright contempt for women or their abilities. Such disdain is well documented among the Greeks; traces of it appear in Plato himself.[2] But scholars of the last hundred years are far less likely to avow such feelings openly.

Nevertheless, a pervasive, unexamined resistance to the idea of female rule has characterized most nineteenth- and twentieth-century scholarship. Since virtually all scholars had been male, their attitudes no doubt reflected the age-old fact of male dominance in Western society. However, the assumption that it is right for males to rule, carried into philosophic thought, also helped to sustain and even shape the anti-female biases of scholars, educators, and politicians across the generations. The very students who were most likely to speculate freely on fundamental questions and criticize prevalent social practices received no encouragement from the Plato scholars to examine freshly what came to be known as The Woman Question. By downplaying or disregarding Plato's provocative proposals for women rulers, philosophers, whose task it is to question the dominant assumptions, instead reinforced the tendency of the "educated gentleman" to ignore the matter of sexual equality as an important element of justice.

With the advent after 1960 of a new feminist movement and the entry of more women into the field of philosophy, Plato's argument for women rulers has been revived. The commentators of the 1970s and 1980s have made a significant contribution by successfully focusing attention on the long-neglected passage calling for Philosopher-Queens. They show that Plato's admirers failed to see the inconsistencies in his beliefs about women, and some even expressly desire to dethrone and discredit Plato. Many also recognize the hostility of previous commentators to the suggested reforms. For generations of commentators have perpetuated attitudes, often despite protests to the contrary, which have kept women excluded from the realms of reason, philosophy, and civic authority.

But there are problems also in this revisionist effort. In many cases, feminist commentators use the Platonic text as a mere pretext for making sectarian points. Instead of explicating the relevant passages, they devote themselves only to praising Plato for a total egalitarianism he did not in fact profess, or to condemning him for not having gone far enough. Some feminists—primarily women, but also male enthusiasts—plunge into analyses which betray a painful lack of preparation for scholarship, a disregard of the original Greek text, and little or no acquaintance with Plato's other works.

On occasion they even outdo male misogynists in suggesting that women need not rule since they have other intuitive gifts to contribute. Some feminist scholars condemn reason itself. They do not, like Luther, denounce it as a whore. But they do not value it as a true mistress, nor, like C. S. Peirce, urge that we cling to logical method like "the bride we have chosen from all the world."[3] Instead, reason becomes a false master foisted on us by a male establishment, by a tradition which begins with the ignoble paedophilic Plato. In the eagerness of feminist commentators to re-evaluate female contributions to history and validate women's role as homemakers and emotional foci of family life, they downplay the worth of intellectual activity and call for separate but somehow equal standards for evaluating human achievement.

The new Plato scholarship, therefore, while providing a corrective for the male biases of the past, has added biases of its own. In some cases it has also produced an odd alliance between scholars still writing in the misogynist tradition which denies that women are equal to men in their capacities to reason and to rule, and a feminist school which denies the importance of reason and political leadership, and thus minimizes the need for women's participation in public life.

In my view, denigrating intellectual activity as a game not worth playing is ultimately self-defeating. There is little to be gained from undervaluing the rich, varied humanistic tradition of great books, great scientists, great artists, theologians, and civic rulers. And, we must face the truth that women have contributed far less than men to this heritage. Rather than denying the importance of public effort and achievement, the message should be the one Socrates forced on his reluctant audience. Women must now participate in these activities fully.

It is of crucial importance now to assess rationally the proper role of women. In this study, I seek to show the continuing relevance of the questions and arguments first formulated by Plato. Starting with the original text, I trace the interpretation over the past hundred years of the passage on women guardians, seeking to separate objective comments on its meaning from those reflecting the prejudices of particular scholars.

In setting out on this enterprise, I acknowledge fully the extraordinary complications surrounding the problem of bias in philosophy. Throughout this book my assumption is that no interpretations can be independent of their social context. Like many post-Renaissance, post-Kantian thinkers, I see all truth as "the daughter of time." We can only base our beliefs on the evidence available at a given time, and the pursuit of certainty is a hopeless quest. Scholars must endlessly seek objectivity or, as Huntington Cairns has said, their enterprise is not philosophy. "When ideas are manipulated for class or group interests, the name for this in Plato's day was sophistry."[4] Similarly, one of the most distinguished of the British Plato scholars, A. E. Taylor, declares, "The last thing I should wish is that the reader should see Plato through my spectacles."[5] Still, the objectivity Taylor calls for is only relatively possible to achieve, no matter how scrupulous and vigilant the interpreter. In the end, one can only see ancient writers through one's own experiences, convictions, and assumptions.[6]

Nevertheless, even if distortion of vision is ultimately inevitable, it is still possible to avoid some of the blind spots which distort and obscure the meaning of a text. That is, while no one can be wholly free from the biases of a particular culture and time, other forms of bias *are* avoidable. These are sometimes personal and idiosyncratic, sometimes the result of group partisanship of which scholars can and should be aware. And they can and should minimize such departures from objectivity by realizing and declaring where their allegiances lie in such controversial areas as that of sexual equality.

The undeclared, underground anti-female prejudice that has marked much of Plato scholarship until recent years has been as damaging to a clear discussion of sexual equality as overt discrimination. As American blacks discovered, it was in some ways easier to fight the Southerners' outright exclusions and declarations of racial inferiority than the more subtle prejudices of

Northerners. If there are philosophers today who genuinely believe that women's training and role should not be identical to men's, that women can never be true philosophers, they must not be prevented from arguing their case freely and openly. Few of the commentators that I consider in the pages that follow have been willing to state forthrightly that half of the human race was automatically disqualified from the pursuits of reason. Even the professor who aggrandized Hitler's *Mein Kampf* did not see himself as anti-female. Instead, he declared that the Nazi program was actually implementing Plato's egalitarian aims for women in the *Republic!*[7]

The persistence of subtle bias against women arises partly from the very ambience of classical scholarship. The atmosphere of Plato's *Symposium,* with its gathering of men who through their erotic attraction for each other will reach a higher love of truth and beauty, has for centuries had its appeal. Whatever their sexual preferences, many young men have found that male-bonding genuinely fosters intellectual growth. The picture of beloved teacher and brilliant youth that we find in the Socratic dialogues has had a powerful influence. Victorian Englishmen openly admired this ambience of ancient Greece, and even repressed and homophobic Germans valued discipleship and quasi-father/son relationships in university circles. The presence of a large number of females might well have disturbed this growth-enhancing atmosphere.

Scholars have made varied use of the *Symposium* in their interpretations of the egalitarianism of the *Republic.* These uses will be discussed later at length. But it is important to note at the outset that no necessary connection exists between homosexuality and misogyny or any prescribed attitude toward women's ability or societal role. Homosexual males have on occasion displayed particular sympathy for, and understanding of, women as victims of discrimination. But in some intellectual circles, the existence of an all-male homoerotic atmosphere has tended rather to inhibit and discourage female students.

The intellectual excitement of such circles as that around Ludwig Wittgenstein at Oxford undoubtedly was conducive to the mutual exploration of philosophical issues. But despite a few exceptions membership in the circle was predominantly and pronouncedly all-male. Even at mid-century the linguistic usage of British scholars reflected this exclusion of females. In his influential book, *The Concept of Mind,* Gilbert Ryle talks repeatedly of the "lad who thinks" with no consciousness that some of his readers might be female. Thus, even at mid-century the linguistic formulations of British philosophers reflected this exclusion of women. From the fourth century B.C., when one of the few women said to have attended Plato's Academy was reputed to have worn men's clothes, to anecdotes about the economist Keynes' and other famous professors' willingness to accept female assistants only so long as they appeared indistinguishable from men, women have found, and still today continue to find, scholarly doors closed to them.[8] Well into the last quarter of this century, the full participation of women in the life that philosophers have always told us is most worth living, the life of rational decision-making, is far from accomplished.

Women have made advances, however, and the historical moment may finally have arrived when for the first time there is a genuine possibility of joint leadership in the society as a whole and of genuine exploration of the question of equality between the sexes. At such a juncture, it becomes all the more important to explore the ways in which avoidable bias on the subject still persists, particularly in the institutions of learning. One classicist has suggested that unfortunately democracies discourage research into unpalatable or unpopular truths like the essential inequality which he himself believes to exist between the abilities of men and women.[9] In my view, such suppression is indeed unfortunate. Those who maintain unpopular opinions must be encouraged to bring them out into the open where they can be scrutinized, supported, or refuted.

As part of this scrutiny, I aim, in the intellectual history of Plato scholarship that follows, to reveal the preconceptions and inconsistencies that have through the years distorted commentaries on Plato's proposal. I do not embark on this enterprise in the spirit of those post-revolutionary Chinese women taught to "speak bitterness." Nor do I wish solely to add to the litany of anti-female references in Western thought, an exercise which one theorist has aptly described as "tedious and depressing."[10] My aim is rather to correct the record so that future readers of the *Repub-*

lic and its commentaries will be particularly wary of unconscious bias and special purpose and will return to the text itself, engaging with it in the spirit of inquiry championed, if not always followed, by Socrates himself.

In the dialogues Socrates describes himself as a midwife who assists others in the delivery of ideas. If he had been female, able to function literally, not only figuratively, as a midwife, he might well have noticed further unexamined assumptions in his audience. But the enterprise of discovering the nature of the just and virtuous life through rational analysis would ultimately have been the same.

Much of the feminist commentary I deal with in the second part of this book extends this inquiry. Although the writers I cover would not all claim to be Plato scholars, many of them make significant contributions to the on-going discussion. I shall try to show, however, that in the process some have undervalued "the greatest philosopher that ever lived" and overemphasized the emotional excellences of women.[11] If I am sometimes harsh in my criticism of female colleagues it is perhaps because one is often hardest on one's own. My object throughout has been not rancor, but rather the restatement of the value of careful scholarship and the importance of continuing the tradition with a passionate, and ultimately gender-free, commitment to ferreting out the truth.

DETAILS OF THE PLATONIC PROPOSALS FOR SEXUAL EQUALITY AND SOME EARLY INTERPRETATIONS

Plato's proposal to include women among the true philosophers appears in Book V, from 449c to 473e.[12] There, Plato's teacher, Socrates, protagonist of the dialogue, presents his listeners with three paradoxical features of his proposed "city of speech." These he describes as the Three Waves of his argument in defense of the arrangements for an ideal *polis.* The First Wave which threatens to drown his listeners is his suggestion that just as male and female sheep dogs are equally responsible for guarding the flock, so female and male rulers will guard the city, protect it in war and rule it in peace. The fact that there are differences between males and females, that as Plato puts it, the "female bears and the male mounts," is not a difference relevant to the governing of the state.[13] Just as the bald and the long-haired are opposite in one respect, but that respect does not affect their ability as shoemakers, so the differences between men and women are not differences with respect to any art or practice connected to the organization of the city. For Plato, it is true that the class of men excels that of women in all practices; however, many individual women are better than many men in many things. Plato puts it, "There is no practice of a city's governors which belongs to woman because she's woman, or to man because he's man; but the natures are scattered alike among both animals; and woman participates according to nature in all practices, and man in all, but in all of them woman is weaker than man."[14] Since women and men have the same natures in regard to ruling, they must follow the same practices in preparation for ruling. They must be equally trained in gymnastic and music; this would be what Plato calls "according to nature," whereas the Athenian practice of highly dissimilar education he considers "against nature." For Plato, to reach truly just practices we must understand what is natural as opposed to what is merely conventional, legal, or customary. Women's participation in the gymnastic training that will ensure the necessary physical strength and discipline requires that female guardians must exercise naked in the gymnasium as men do. Although initially this will seem laughable, the practice can be seen to be beneficial if it is properly considered. In fact, Plato assures his listeners that in the last analysis his entire proposal of equal opportunity for both sexes is both possible and advantageous for the society.

The Second Wave of the Platonic scheme is that male and female guardians are to live communally, eliminating private marriage arrangements and also abolishing what we would call the nuclear family. Children will be raised communally with parents and offspring unaware of the biological connections between them. Marriages are arranged by the state with periodic festivals where temporary unions are consummated. Subtle lots must be fabricated, one of Plato's "noble lies," to assure that citizens will blame chance rather than the rulers for each union. As the offspring are born the task of caring for them will be taken over by the male and female officers designated for this job. With the help of wetnurses and governesses the women will be spared the "wakeful watching" and other labors connected with infancy, making for what Glaucon, Socrates' interrogator, calls an "easy-going kind of childbearing" for the women guardians.

The offspring must be born of those in their prime, which is between twenty and forty for women, twenty-five and fifty-five for men. When the women and men are beyond the age of procreation they are free to have intercourse with whomever they wish with certain exceptions. However, the partners in these unofficial pairings must be especially careful to avoid conceptions. And they must understand that should a fetus force its way into the light of day, "there's to be no rearing for such a child."

Plato believes that the abolition of private property and of the family will keep the usual causes of dissension, the fighting over money, children, and relatives, from disturbing the tranquillity of his ideal state. His arrangements will promote very strong ties among the rulers. And although they will live simply, they will be rewarded by seeing the preservation of the whole city as well as by the support, prizes, and honors given them by the public.

The Third Wave, the final paradox of Socrates' argument, is that these guardians, men and women alike, must be true philosophers, reaching knowledge of the good through reason and dialectic. Only the rule of such philosopher-guardians can guarantee the welfare of the State. Plato thus calls for Philosopher-Kings, and—if the terminology be properly extended, as it rarely is—Philosopher-Queens to rule. For, as he puts it: "Until the philosophers rule as kings or those now called kings . . . genuinely and adequately philosophize, and political power and philosophy coincide in the same place . . . there is no rest from ills for the cities . . . nor I think for human kind."[15]

These are the bare outlines of the Platonic plan. My aim in this book is to trace the history, from roughly 1870 to the present, of the treatment of these passages on women guardians. Before the time at which this study begins, there was a period of a thousand years, from Proclus in the fifth century until the flourishing Platonism of the Italian Renaissance, in which we hear almost nothing of the *Republic.* Although the text may have been available to the medieval churchmen, there is no extant commentary in the West on the dialogue. Surprisingly, some later commentators have suggested that the medieval Church itself was an embodiment of Plato's ideal republic. The noted classical historian Ernest Barker, although making no claim for a direct influence, thinks the Church's own principles make it *naturaliter Platonica.* He compares the papal monarchy to the Philosopher-Kings. And he suggests that the hierarchy of priests, monks, and laity correspond to the three classes of Plato. For Barker's analogy to hold, he must overlook among other aspects Plato's insistence on female guardians. The medieval Church—and for that matter the Catholic Church today—had no women equal in ruling power to the male leadership.

The argument for an "unconscious debt" of the Church to the *Republic* is convincing only if one judges the call for female rulers to be peripheral. In discussing views of Plato's scheme, Ryle makes a related point about the connection between the interpreter's interests and his judgments. Plato's view of the body politic as an organism, Ryle drily remarks, is apt to appeal less to those who are told that they are constituted by nature only to be the body's feet. The appeal, he points out, is bound to be greater to those who are assured that their role is that of the body's eyes or brain.[16] Likewise, the omission of women from the dominant group can be expected to be of more concern to female commentators, most of whom do not appear on the scene until late in the 20th century.

Any direct influence of Plato's utopia on medieval thought would probably have had to come from the *Timaeus,* which is the one book of the Platonic corpus that we know was extant. That work, which contains a brief summary of the ideal city of the *Republic,* is notorious for its misogyny. In it, Plato warns that a man who lives an ignoble life will be demoted after death, condemned to live as a woman.[17] Misogyny of this sort is more characteristic of the attitudes of the early Church than is any program for identical roles.[18] Of course, all that can be said of the contempt for women that appears in the *Timaeus* as well as in most other Greek writers is that it coincided with the prejudices of the educated man of the Middle Ages. And, despite that much-noted Christian emphasis on equality of souls in men and women, it is hard to see how the structure of the Church exemplifies a belief that women's and men's natures are qualitatively identical.

There was, however, a direct Platonic influence on the philosophy, if not the practice, of Islam. From about 800, Islamic thinkers were translating Greek philosophical works into Arabic and attempting to harmonize them with Islamic theology. In the tenth century, al-Fārābī proposed a theory of a philosopher-caliph based on his reading of the *Republic.* But he, too, in keeping with the Islamic assumption of the inferior status of women, takes no note of the egalitarianism of Plato.[19]

On the other hand, Averroës, the last and perhaps greatest of the Islamic philosophers, wrote an extensive three-part commentary on the *Republic* in which he discusses the proposal for sexual equality with sympathy. We have only a Hebrew translation of his work, but if it is a faithful rendering of the original, then Averroës' support for sexual equality is astounding. There are no biographical or sociological details available that would account for the fact that this Arab thinker, although a committed Muslim, seems to have been far more open in the twelfth century to the idea of female guardians than some American university professors are in the late twentieth.[20] As in William James' definition of the true philosopher, Averroës on this issue is able to "fancy everything different from what it is . . . to see the familiar as if it were strange, and the strange as if it were familiar."[21] And even if, as I believe, he was somewhat less consistent and less completely egalitarian in his acceptance of Plato's program than some assert, he was nevertheless remarkably openminded.[22]

Averroës finds it deplorable that in his own states women who are not being fitted for any of the human virtues often resemble plants. He writes: "In these States the *ability of women is not known* because they are only taken for procreation" (*my emphasis*).[23] This stands out particularly when compared with the views of scholars I present in this book who are quite certain they do know what women's abilities are. As we shall see, some are even sure that Plato actually placed women among the guardians solely for their role in procreation. Averroës' belief that for Plato "women are essentially on the same level with men in respect of civic activities in the same classes" makes his agreement with the

Greek philosopher even more striking.[24] Since he seems mistakenly to have believed that Plato clearly intended that men of *every* class would have intercourse only with women like themselves who had training identical to their own, what the egalitarian Averroës approved was even more far-reaching than what Plato actually proposed. Such enthusiasm for the Platonic proposals is unmatched so far as I can discover in the Western tradition.

Although we hear of the *Republic* from the Italian humanists, extended commentary does not appear again until the eighteen-hundreds. There are a few translations and paraphrases earlier in the century, but the period I shall explore in this book begins with the important publication in England in 1871 of the first English translation of Plato's complete dialogues by the distinguished scholar Benjamin Jowett. The *Republic* was the subject of Jowett's first course of lectures at Oxford. His notes to the Greek text and the portions of his projected but uncompleted analytic essay have been of interest to scholars. But it is his translation which has had the most significant influence on generations of students and general readers.

Concurrent with Jowett's work, notable Plato scholarship also flourished in Germany and a rich cross-fertilization took place between writers in both countries. And from that time on, new translations and interpretations have appeared in numerous countries and continue to be published in books and journals throughout the West. One of my main aims in the chapters that follow is to analyze the presuppositions of the voluminous commentary from 1870 to 1970 on the egalitarian proposals in Book V.

My second aim is to focus attention on the feminist writers of the last decades who have at last entered the dialogue. When a new class or group is finally empowered to participate in scholarly endeavors, previously overlooked meanings are bound to emerge. Just as labor historians viewing the documents of the industrial revolution from the vantage point of the factory workers have come up with new interpretations and evaluations, so too women writers have seen new implications in Plato's ancient text. They have turned to the *Republic* in the process of rethinking the perennial questions about the nature of the complete life. In asking how women, as well as men, can best participate in a society geared to the well-being and fulfillment of all, they have reexamined the plan for male and female guardians of the state.

The outstanding classicist-philosopher Martha Nussbaum clearly articulates the questions involved. Understanding Plato, she believes, will aid us in deciding what kind of education women should have and what they will become as a result. Will the idea of a separate women's sphere disappear? Will women still love and care for their children as before, or is some radical change in the structure of the family like that proposed by Plato for his guardians necessary? Plato valued both gentleness and assertiveness. Nussbaum reminds us that in thinking about the ideal society, we still need to ask what kind of emotional attachments are compatible with public and private gentleness. She sees that the most important question about women's upbringing and education is still whether they will and should "become free and autonomous citizens just like men."[25]

Plato's text has frequently served as the jumping-off point for disagreement among feminists in their answers to these questions. In the second half of this book I shall survey and evaluate these recent examinations of Book V. In order to show exactly why the text has supported varying interpretations, it will sometimes be necessary to dwell on small details. The general reader may want to scan these quickly, although I believe that only by examining many trees can we legitimately make generalizations about the forest.

One of the purposes of my analysis of details and nuances in the new feminist explication is to show certain dangers implicit in contemporary rethinking of the *Republic.* My aim is to steer a course between the Scylla of sexism and the Charybdis of separatism. Just as I reject the anti-female bias of the great Plato scholars I also regret some recent writers' underestimation of the human accomplishments of the past, simply because they are the work of the dominant male culture. I consider it a mistake to elevate the supposed female virtues over the worth of logical analysis and rational principles.

An alarming trend among feminists in general appears clearly in some of the scholars' condemnation of Plato. Many consider current educational methods and ways of thinking about morality to be defective because societal practices are wrought in a "masculine mold." They consider competition a masculine trait and the disregard of loving affiliations a masculine failing, and consider both the source of much of the world's ills. But there is no convincing evidence that cooperativeness or the valuing of emotional life is sex-linked. Plato advocated unifying affiliations, and his true philosophers were meant to be *lovers* of truth. Religious moralists, almost all of them male, have always stressed the affective side of human existence. In the Platonic ideal of the examined life, the kind of reason advocated requires both logical operations and the intuitive thinking he called "direct vision."

In the pages that follow I shall try to show that some feminist writers in their zeal to validate the emotional strengths and family contribution of women through the centuries have unwisely minimized the importance of rationality. They have unduly praised women's separate virtues practiced in a private sphere. Fearing that women will become "just like men" they lead us away from the truth that indeed *identical* traits should be valued in both.

This is not to side with those writers who wholeheartedly embrace the Platonic proposals and seek to sweep under the carpet the inconsistencies in Plato. The Athenian philosopher, although a great thinker and a great artist, was also a purveyor of the biases of the ordinary Greek male. And in the fifth century BC the ordinary Athenian was guilty of an extraordinary degree of misogyny. Even in Book V Plato speaks disparagingly of the beliefs of a "small, womanish mind" (469d). "Imitating a woman" in sexual encounters, that is assuming the submissive position, he considers humiliating (395c, 397c). In the *Apology* he reproaches those who plead when they are condemned to death as "no better than women" (35). Within the framework of the *Timaeus* myth, as I have mentioned, to exist as a woman is to be in an inferior state (42b–c). In the *Laws* he describes women as secretive and crafty, less capable of virtue than men (780e–781b).

Besides such evidence of misogyny, he also exhibits the bias of most ancient Greek philosophers against democracy. As often noted there are elitist and authoritarian elements in his social planning, elements which it is doubtful would produce the eudaemonia he envisaged. Plato was concerned with gender equality only for the best and the brightest. If he intended similar changes for the class of manual workers as his own theory of justice would require, he said nothing of plans for such changes.

Nevertheless, his work deserves repeated attention. For even though the contradictions in his thought cannot be reconciled, the fact that he was the first to raise the crucial issues puts us in his debt. Without worshipping him uncritically we still should admire his wisdom in concluding so long ago that the physiological differences between the sexes must not affect their participation in civic life.

In my conclusion I shall argue that sociobiologists are still addressing the same questions about the relevance of biological differences that Plato formulated. Scientists seek evidence for inevitable female disadvantages as well as special excellences. But their recent attempts to prove that there is a male human nature and a separate female human nature are no more convincing than the arguments Socrates expected from his listeners. Nor can the ethical questions be turned over to the biologists as the founder of sociobiology has suggested. Scientific research, the very questions we ask, involve assumptions about value. Male and female philosophers are needed to examine these assumptions. Genetic investigations cannot themselves tell us how we ought to live. Those who proclaim that the diversity desirable in human communities is, and therefore ought to be, determined by gender are mistaken. They are promulgating myths, not in the neo-Platonic sense of illuminating stories which provide otherwise unreachable insights, but myths in the vernacular sense of unwelcome distortions of the truth.

Besides my examination of these distortions I have one further aim which underlies this entire study.

I want to underscore the value of the scholarly enterprise and pay tribute to that activity of explicating the texts of others which is so often disparaged or underrated. Through the traditions of interpretation, new generations of students are helped to learn about the past and acquire the resources to shape the future. As intermediaries between the readers and the ancients, commentators perform a great service. By reinterpreting in the light of their own world views the meaning and relevance of the thought of the past, they help to determine which works will be influential in the future. These scholars surely deserve much gratitude for the crucial role they play in keeping valuable texts alive.

1

The Prevalence of Anti-Female Bias in Plato Scholarship, 1870–1970: Seven Types of Hostility

EQUALITY AS A NON-ISSUE: NEGLECT OF THE PROPOSALS

In an extensive survey of commentaries written from 1870 on in many languages, including French, Spanish, Italian, Russian, Hebrew, German—and English, and composed in Hong Kong, Canada, England, and the United States—I find an overwhelming antipathy to the proposal for women guardians in the *Republic.*[1] One of the most striking features is the complete neglect of what others in the same period have termed Plato's "radical, even revolutionary" proposals.[2] Very few give any serious attention to the central role Plato himself claims for the First Wave of his argument for a just society. Commentators often completely ignore the proposal for sexual equality while discussing the other two elements—abolition of property and the family—at length. Many of the writers, almost all of whom are male, are particularly concerned about the elimination of the family. Since even those who have no wives nor any interest in women's roles are or were part of a family, one can see how this idea of Plato's might be of more direct interest to them. But whatever the reason, there are a large number of writers who, while occupying themselves with minutiae of Greek religious practice and obscure literary allusions, do not even mention the complexities and contradictions in the Platonic text on female equality.

The prominent logician who has translated and annotated the chief Russian edition of the *Republic* is not averse to commenting on the contemporary relevance of the Platonic scheme and points out that the holding of property in common is not to be compared with the Marxist view. Plato's schemes are utopian rather than scientific. He takes the trouble to explain this Soviet sense of "scientific" but he does not have a single word to say on the subject of equality of male and female guardians.[3] Since the Russian Revolution paid lip service to egalitarian reforms for women similar to those Plato proposed, one might expect comment not only on property relations but also on equality of leadership roles. But none is forthcoming.

Likewise, the author of an annotated Hebrew translation ignores the proposal of sexual equality both in his introduction and in his notes on Book V. It is, of course, unfair to expect a commentator to be objective and then condemn him for not interjecting his own opinions as to what is important. But as with the Russian, so, too, the Hebrew translator is not in fact averse to connecting Plato's views to contemporary realities. Writing in the early 1930s, this Israeli socialist refers in his introduction to the current importance of Plato in the face of the "sinking of human culture" reported in the European newspapers.[4] But he makes no comment on the suggestion for equality of the sexes despite the fact that the kibbutz system was founded on just such joint leadership. Nor does he bother to note any similarity between the original settlers' provision of communal child care and the Platonic proposal for communal child-rearing.

Immediately after the war, Karl Popper published an opposing view which sees Plato not as an antidote to European irrationality but rather as himself a dangerous authoritarian. In *The Open Society and Its Enemies,* Popper seeks to combat the idealization of Plato and condemn his anti-liberal, anti-humanitarian attitudes. He calls Plato one of the founding fathers of racism and denounces the deceit the philosopher recommended to keep the masses subservient. According to Popper, there would be no room in Plato's ideal state for an independent thinker like Socrates. In Popper's attack on Platonic "totalitarianism," he accuses the Athenian of wanting to return "to the tribal *patriarchy* of the time before the Fall" (*my emphasis*).[5]

Popper supports his conviction that in ancient Greece there was a humanitarian "equalitarian movement" by citing Democritus, Pericles, Antisthenes, even the historical Socrates, as proponents of an open society. He discusses their anti-slavery, anti-nationalist beliefs, their creed of "the universal empire of men." In order to contrast Plato with this tradition and show what a thoroughgoing, unmitigated "reactionary" the philosopher was, Popper might be expected to attempt to reinterpret or explain away the seemingly egalitarian statements in Book V about women's capacity to rule.

In fact, Popper makes absolutely no mention whatsoever of Plato's views on women. In his praise for the more democratic Socrates, Popper might well have tried to minimize the importance of the *Republic*'s suggestion of sexual equality, perhaps attributing the views to Plato's teacher, as others have. But Popper makes no such attempt. In hundreds of pages of texts and references, Popper buries only a single example from the *Theatetus* of Platonic humanitarianism which he admits is difficult to reconcile with the thesis of Plato as totalitarian enemy. He assumes that the passage in which Plato equates masters and slaves, Greeks and barbarians, must have been written before (rather than, as is commonly held, after) the *Republic*. The *Republic* itself he finds wholly without any redeeming humanitarian features.

Popper's own definition of the essential features which would allow any doctrine to be considered humanitarian do not include a single mention of the female half of the human race, which has been persistently oppressed throughout history. As a spokesman for the downtrodden, Popper completely ignores Plato's advocacy of women rulers in a time when women were widely viewed as property. What in Popper's day and before was repeatedly called Plato's "feminism," has no role whatsoever to play in Popper's analysis. Even if there is justice in his denunciation of the aristocratic, anti-individualist bent of Plato, it is clearly not correct to accuse the philosopher of advocating a patriarchy. And it shows at the very least an insensitivity to a major egalitarian issue to write a lengthy accusatory volume without granting his ancient opponent some slight credit for the proposal on women guardians. Popper might well have been able to show that joint male and female aristocrats still involved a closed society; but he did not even consider the issue important enough to discuss.

It is equally surprising that there is no mention of the issue of female equality in a companion to Plato's *Republic*, published as late as the 1980s.[6] There was some reason to wonder how works appearing in England in the years immediately following Mill's historic *On the Subjection of Women* could ignore Plato's discussion. But then Mill's voice was a relatively isolated one in scholarly circles. It is far harder to understand how this current guide for students appearing in a world where a strong women's movement exists in many countries, and where serious readers will undoubtedly include women, can ignore the issue entirely.

WOMEN *ARE* DIFFERENT: THE PROPOSALS AS UNNATURAL

The most common reaction among those who do consider Plato's proposals is to contend that in fact the equality, which Plato claims is "according to nature," is on the contrary "unnatural." Critics offer a variety of reasons to support their position. The argument takes many forms, from the well-meaning paternalism of Jowett to the blatant sexism of the American translator Allan Bloom. A few, like Ernest Barker, are aware of the pitfalls of trying to determine what is "natural." Barker admits that though his aim is to interpret Plato *sub specie aeternitatis,* despite the political crisis of the time in which he is writing, his efforts may be only *sub specie temporum suum.*[7] That is, he is aware of the difficulties of eliminating cultural bias. Nevertheless, the learned Oxford scholar explains that although many may sympathize with the emancipation of women, the fundamental argument which underlies Plato's scheme raises doubts. If the basic difference between men and women is that one begets while the other bears children, it produces a number of other differences "which cut deep."

> The fact of her sex is not one isolated thing in a woman's nature . . . : it colors her whole being. She is by nature the centre of the life of the family. . . . She has by nature a specific function of her own, which she will always refuse to delegate to a crèche, and the long period of growth and the need of nurture of her children (which finds no parallel in the children of "the other animals") will always make the discharge of this function the work of a lifetime. The unmarried woman may enter into the open field of the

> world's activities; the married woman has her life's work ready to her hand.[8]

Thus, what is really natural to women is a lifetime of motherhood. He concludes that the state ought not to abolish maternity but rather to recognize it as a function and a contribution to the community. Through child-rearing the woman will take "her station in the common life," and by doing the thing which pertains to her station she will attain to Justice.

In another work, Barker tells us that it is not possible for men and women to come together merely for sexual intercourse as Plato proposes.[9] Given the current divorce rate and the statistics on multiple partners for both sexes in today's America, we can only conclude that his view of what is possible needs alteration. Barker finds Aristotle's more sympathetic treatment of marriage preferable to that of Plato, who he says failed to appreciate "the real nature" of the marriage tie. Aristotle's view of marriage, it will be recalled, is based on the natural domination of the male, as in the master-slave relation. Aristotle considers the female by nature inferior, born to obey and without the ability to be virtuous in the same way as a man.[10] Barker does not, however, allude to this aspect of Aristotle's admittedly more enthusiastic support of private marriages.

Benjamin Jowett also finds Plato's view of what is natural mistaken and offers his own idea of the natural differences between men and women in character and capacity. Jowett's views are not always easy to ascertain, since they are only hinted at in the periodic summaries and paraphrases in the margin of his translation of the *Republic*. They can also be inferred from the vagaries of his linguistic usage, as I shall discuss later. But in an interpretive note in his edition of the Greek text, he spells out his ideas about equal education for women and offers a theory about women's true nature.[11]

First, he details four aspects of Plato's proposal which are worthy of attention, that presumably should be considered sympathetically. He phrases them carefully so as to avoid offending his readers and to persuade them that although Plato's views differ from modern, that is, Victorian English ideas of education, they nevertheless have merit. The meritorious aspects he finds are: 1) the consideration of the subject independently of existing practice and with reference solely to sexual differences; 2) the implication that bodily health and strength and the training by which they are achieved are equally necessary for males and females; 3) the belief that both sexes have the same interests and duties and are capable of the same occupations in a degree greater than that allowed by social practice; and 4) the contention that false delicacy is a poor foundation for manners and morals.[12]

But despite the value of these considerations, Jowett decides that Plato has actually made a major error. The error "seems to arise" from the Athenian's failure to consider the other differences "to which the differences in sex give rise"; these are differences "in mind and feeling."[13] The problem is that Plato has forgotten a crucial fact. Jowett quotes with approval from an unidentified source that "women's best education is the training of their children."

Furthermore, Jowett finds that Plato has lost sight of the fact that education is relative to character, and the character of women is necessarily formed by the universal opinion of mankind. Evidently, Jowett loses sight of the fact that Plato considered character only in connection with capacity regardless of the opinion of the multitude. That is, one human being learns quickly, the other less so; one female has the capacity for medicine, another does not. This is the only sense of character relevant in Book V. And it is on the basis of such judgments of individual character that Plato believes the opinions of mankind *ought* to be formed. Exactly what Jowett himself means by the "universal opinion" which forms the character of women is not clear. Throughout history there have been a few who held the opinion that women have the capacity for an education identical to men's, and such opinions have increased markedly in recent years. Presumably, then, Jowett would have to admit that as views of women's nature changed, so too would the resultant character itself change.

But Jowett does not seem to allow for this possibility. Difficult as it is to be sure of his precise position, one aspect is entirely clear. Jowett assumes that his view and that of "modern philosophy" is preferable to that of Plato. Women in fact have "equal powers of different qualities" rather than the unequal powers of the same quality that Plato ascribes to them. Woman is not "undeveloped man" as he interprets Plato to have said. Her nature is diverse from man's, and it is therefore natural that she be educated differently.[14]

Unlike Barker, Jowett does not specifically comment on the unnaturalness of the prescribed mating arrangements for the guardians; but he does point out that the prohibited unions would no longer rest on any natural or rational principle.[15] In the interpretations of both thinkers two distinguishable but related issues regarding what is natural arise. There is 1) the question of "woman's nature" and its necessary consequences, and 2) the question of whether the monogamous (or perhaps more accurately, moderately polygymous, or "double standard") family is "natural." On both issues, the view of the eminent classicist K. J. Dover, who in his work has taken the issue of Greek homosexuality out of its Victorian closet, has much appeal. Dover declares himself unwilling to engage with any enthusiasm in debates about the naturalness or unnaturalness of human behavior. He observes that any community encourages behavior which it regards as possibly conducive to an eventual situation of a kind desired by that community. It discourages behavior which seems likely to hinder the development of such a situation.[16]

I agree with Dover that the absence of any clear correlation between "natural" and "desirable" is self-evident. Rape and homicide are species-typical in men and orangutangs; in the sense that they occur regularly, they might then be described as natural to these species, but not to other "lower" animals where such behavior never occurs. Few, however, would argue that rape and homicide are therefore desirable. Nor could Plato's commentators defend their use of "natural" as meaning "descriptive of a statistical majority of known cases in man's history." The majority of male humans that have lived thus far have died before their seventieth year; this too cannot be seen as *ipso facto* desirable.

Despite obvious ambiguities of the term, commentators throughout the period under discussion have automatically assumed that their readers would understand what they meant by "natural." They have repeatedly attempted to equate the natural with the desirable, or at the very least, by labelling a situation "unnatural," to convince us automatically of its impossibility or undesirability.

A typical example of this procedure occurs in the work of the well-known Victorian Platonist, Walter Pater, who opposes Plato's views on both issues, that of women's nature and of marriage. He forthrightly opposes the Platonic view of women's leadership role and informs us that such modifications of married life would "deprive mothers of that privacy of affection regarding which the wisdom of Solomon beamed forth." On the one hand, he complains that Plato would be dealing with humans in the same manner as a breeder of birds or dogs. The plan is a "strange and forbidding experiment," or so it should seem to us from the vantage point of "laws now irrevocably fixed on these subjects by the judgment of the Christian church."[17] Pater does not even attempt to answer Plato's contention that, despite the conventions of the day, the sharing of rule by men and women actually preserves the natural relations of the sexes. Instead, he merely states without argument that female equality and identity of role are "altogether out of harmony with the facts of man's nature."[18] (By "man's nature" he of course means "woman's nature," i.e., man in the generic sense.)

A later English philosopher, Bernard Bosanquet, is more sympathetic in principle than Pater to the need for similar education for males and females. He writes that the fact that the Greek household was almost Oriental in its seclusion of women makes Plato's revolutionary demands for women understandable.[19] Bosanquet doesn't find it surprising that Plato wanted to put an end to the Greek family because it was, he says, "a wretched institution." But his final word on the subject is the familiar refrain. On the matter of the lack of difference between the sexes except for the fact that one is weaker, he writes with careful phrasing that "we may be disposed to think that in this he was blind to essential facts of human nature."[20]

A. E. Taylor agrees that Plato is unaware of the true nature and purpose of human sex differences. He explains Plato's blindness by suggesting that Socrates' treatment of sex in the *Republic*, like that of all non-Christian moralists, involves an underestimation of the significance of sex for the whole of the spiritual life.

Taylor assumes that the impulses of sex and family affections are for humans intrinsically, that is, naturally, connected. Natural sexual impulses, Taylor concludes, are subjected to much severer restraints in Plato's state than in any which has ever been adopted by a Christian society.[21] The intolerable severity and self-denial are the chief reasons that Plato's scheme is unfeasible. (As a male Christian moralist, Taylor's interests, unlike those of the present writer, cause him to overlook entirely that Plato grants almost complete sexual freedom to women over forty.)

Taylor makes no attempt whatsoever to compare Plato's proposals with the actual sexual satisfactions of the upper-class Greek wife. Demosthenes' often noted view of fourth-century Greek women, even if it is only one possible account of their status, is relevant here: "We have *heterai* for pleasure, concubines for our day-to-day physical well-being, and wives in order to beget legitimate children and have trustworthy guardians of our households."[22] This clearly does not present a picture of extensive physical and consequent spiritual satisfaction for wives to be contrasted with the self-denial of Plato's ideal society. Unfortunately our knowledge of women's thoughts and experiences at this time comes almost entirely from literature written by men. Therefore, it is difficult to make reliable comparisons between the sexual satisfactions open to women in classical Athens as compared to those offered by nineteenth-century Christianity. Nevertheless, we have little reason to believe that throughout the centuries the ideal of Christian marriage has guaranteed more sexual satisfaction, for women at any rate, than actual Greek practices or Plato's reforms.

Taylor is also sure that the view of differences between the sexes which cause Plato to extend the duties of warfare and statesmanship to women is erroneous. He says Plato is wrong about sexual distinctions affecting the individual only in respect to procreating and—what Taylor includes as Platonic—to rearing a new generation. Here, this careful scholar actually and uncharacteristically misreads Plato. In the *Republic,* only the bearing is admitted as a relevant sexual distinction. The *trophe,* rearing, or upbringing of the children is alterable; and as Taylor surely knows, the raising of new generations will be communal in the ideal state. It seems to have been hard for him to accept that

Plato did not automatically assume, as he himself does, that children's upbringing is by nature a female task. For Taylor reproduction and child care are both natural to women, and these distinctions profoundly affect the rest of their functioning. Women cannot be soldiers or political leaders because sexual distinction "goes deeper and modifies the whole spiritual life profoundly."[23]

It is striking that scholars whose interpretations make the Platonic text vital and comprehensible in many respects are so much less careful when dealing with matters of female equality. It has been suggested that there is no topic in classical studies except that of homosexuality on which a scholar's normal ability to perceive differences and draw inferences is so easily impaired. Only on the subject of homosexuality is a writer "so likely to be thought to have said what he has not said or to be charged with omitting to say something which he has said several times."[24] But I contend that the subject of women's nature and role provides as great a tendency to misread, misquote, and suspend the usual standards of evidence.

Taylor, like most other commentators, feels no obligation to offer evidence for the way in which sexual differences necessarily alter women's consciousnesses or consciences. In general, none of the commentators find it necessary to offer biological, historical, or anthropological data to support their view that, in the modern vernacular, "anatomy is destiny." Even men writing in the 1960s and 1970s do not attempt to provide evidence. Nor do commentators entertain the possibility of suspending judgment on women's true nature until more information is available.[25] A scholar as intent on objectivity as Taylor proclaims himself to be in his Preface might in 1926 have called for more investigations on the actual connections between sexuality and psychic characteristics. He suggests that the historical Socrates was influenced in his views on female emancipation by the existence of women like Pericles' mistress Aspasia, who was famous for her intellectual attainments. However, he does not seem to have been influenced by the attainments of Queen Elizabeth I. Nor do most of the other writers who disparage women's abilities for leadership find it necessary to account for modern female parliamentarians and even heads of state who somehow, contrary to female nature, manage to display equal aptitude for statesmanship.

One of the most blatant distortions of Plato's view of what is natural occurs in the comments of a Canadian rabbi, Solomon Frank, in his study of Plato's theory of education. Like Pater, he makes the unself-conscious assumption that what he approves will be generally accepted as both desirable and natural. Frank uses as his chief source for Plato's theories the *Laws,* which contain the modified views of Plato's later years. These views constitute advantageous regulations for an actual Greek state rather than a description of what would be best in an ideal state. Although even in this latter book Plato advances reforms which would provide for more equitable treatment and use of the resources of half of the human race, his radical plan for complete equality is not sustained.[26] But even in discussing the arrangements in the *Laws,* Frank superimposes his own opinions without even a minimal attempt to guard against seeing Plato through the presuppositions of a twentieth-century conservative Canadian religious educator. In his paraphrase, he speaks of the stages of a girl's life as "maid, wife, mother, and matron" with no prototype for this division in Plato's texts at all.[27] The main emphasis of his discussion, which largely ignores the topic of education in the *Republic,* is on the contrast between expert and amateur in male and female training. Plato, he tells us, believes that women should learn some of the same things boys do, but always in an "amateurish spirit" in distinction from the boys' expertise in such matters, e.g., military drill. I am not suggesting that there is absolutely no basis for this distinction in Plato's *Laws.* However, to write as if this were all Plato had to contribute to the subject of women's education is to downplay the ideals of the *Republic* to such an extent as to distort Plato's total views.

It is worth quoting in its entirety the footnote in which Frank attempts to deal with what he admits might be considered contrary to his interpretation of Plato's sole view of the connection between women and warfare. This footnote is a striking illustration of the way in which prejudice can interfere with our reading of important philosophical texts, as well as with the disinterested consideration of what is best for society. Frank writes: "It is thus only women with a natural turn for warlike pursuits who are to be selected and educated for this function; and *at that,* they are allotted the less heavy duties of military life (457) and are 'never to violate, but always to preserve, the natural relation of the sexes' " (466).[28]

Frank intends this final quote from Plato to convince us that the "natural relation" for the Athenian philosopher, as for Rabbi Frank, is that even if girls did participate in war, they must be protected, as nature dictates, by their superior, expert menfolk. The reference given is to line 466d in the *Republic.* In fact, in that line Plato says exactly the opposite of what Frank intends. Having based his entire argument on *physis,* what is genuinely natural, rather than *nomos,* the merely conventional, Plato in this passage (only part of which is quoted by Frank) clearly restates that men and women should pursue the same tasks. Both when they are staying in the city and going out to war, they must guard and hunt together like dogs. He then puts it unequivocally that *by* doing this (Bloom translates "in doing this," but the meaning is the same), they are doing nothing contrary to the nature of the female in her relationship to the male, "nothing contrary to the natural community of the two with each other."[29]

The generous interpretation of Frank's misreading is that in his zeal to preserve the conventional relation of the sexes, as formulated in Jewish law and custom, he finds it hard to face that Plato genuinely stated the contrary. The fact, however, is that in this passage Plato is asserting precisely that since other animals share in aggression and ruling, such joint participation is in fact natural.

Later English and German commentators have not missed this point. Instead, they reinforce the oft-stated objection that Plato is mistaken in his view of female nature. There is no need to discuss at length the position of R. C. Crossman. He certainly cannot be accused of any concealed attempt to use the original text for a hidden agenda of his own. For the aim of his *Plato Today* is stated explicitly; his specific intention is to update Plato's views for the twentieth-century reader. This British scholar and politician considers himself to be in agreement with what he calls Plato's "feminism." But it is not complete identity of role that he finds desirable, for he fears that much will be lost if egalitarianism "goes too far."[30] As we shall see, there are many others who echo this cry.

One highly influential commentator who does not even profess sympathy with egalitarianism is Leo Strauss, who is a frequent target of feminist attacks in the 1970s. Like the feminists, Strauss attributes crucial importance to the proposal for gender equality. However, he views it in a diametrically opposed way. It is not a forerunner of modern equalitarian programs, but instead Plato's way of showing us that the just city could never come into being. Regardless of what Socrates actually says, Plato's real intention was for us to recognize that his utopia was ultimately unrealizable.

At least Strauss sees that a revolutionary change would be required to fulfill Plato's scheme. And he finds that, no matter how desirable, in the final analysis such reforms are unnatural; therefore, a just society in Plato's sense is impossible. Strauss himself accepts Plato's framework for discussing the good of societies and concludes with a realization that is intended to move us with its tragic overtones. The just city cannot come into being because absolute communism and the equality of the sexes—and that is the precise phrase he uses—"are *against* nature."[31]

Allan Bloom, whose translation contains an extended interpretive essay, follows Strauss in his reasoning on the unnaturalness of the proposals. Since Bloom, too, is the target of much criticism and controversy, and since many of his objections to female equality recur in his defense and rejoinders to these attacks, I shall postpone the bulk of discussion of his views until later. It is important to point out here, however, that he joins the voices of those like Taylor and Strauss who condemn Socrates for "forgetting the importance of the body."[32] Only on the precondition of such "forgetting" could Plato have made such a proposal. For if he had considered the body and its needs correctly, he could have seen that the differences between men and women are far more crucial than Socrates allows.

Bloom also finds Plato's abolition of the family unsatisfactory. For the family, by which he evidently means our current Western notion of a nuclear family, is "surely somehow natural."[33] The father, if he is anything, is the one who engenders the child. The strength of what Anna Freud has called "psychological parenting," so that in her view the parent is not necessarily the one who contributes the sperm but the one who nurtures the child emotionally, is not even considered. Nor does he consider animal evidence. We know there are biological species where there is no parental investment in the offspring, as well as animals where the young are cared for by what we would call foster parents. I am not suggesting that animal data is ultimately decisive.[34] However, any commentator in the 1960s who wishes to pronounce on the naturalness of parental feeling, and therefore on the impossibility of communal rearing for males at least—he mentions only fathers—might be expected to adduce anthropological or biological information to support his view. Instead, his assumptions are baldly stated; he appeals evidently to "common sense."

An interesting contrast to Bloom written at approximately the same time is a little-known commentary written in Hong Kong. I include this study because the fact that it is addressed to students culturally different from the audience of the other commentators requires a less dogmatic approach to the naturalness of any given kind of family. N. E. Fehl's *Guide to the Study of Plato's Republic* is addressed to Chinese students at Chung Chi College to whom he declares, "Plato is our contemporary here within these green hills so close to the boarder [sic] of China."[35] His analysis revolves much less around what is natural and relies much more on the varying arrangements that have actually existed. He discusses how the family types in ancient China differed from those of fourth-century Athens and points to the similarity between the Greek schema and the Hindu caste system. He also describes the varying foundations of marriage in what he calls tribal and religious societies and the differences between the Catholic and Protestant views of the purposes of sexual union.

Fehl's own view is hard to determine because of the question and answer format he uses to stimulate students. The importance of his discussion, however, is that unlike Taylor, Strauss, Bloom, and others, he cannot call upon an assumed unanimity or self-evidence for his own views about mating, incest, and the importance of the body. He can still, however, assume certain shared assumptions about the preeminence of the male sex. So he tells his Chinese theological students at a Christian college that just as Eve was an after-thought of Yahweh, so women and the family are dealt with in a parenthesis in Plato's dream of the ideal society.[36] This disparaging of the issue no doubt has as much to do with Fehl's own bias as it does with a correct interpretation of the text.

On the other hand, his anthropological perspective, with its emphasis on the typology of family structures, leads him to consider seriously Plato's alternatives. Fehl distinguishes three types of family: the consanguine, the conjugal, and the communal. The first, which Plato took for granted, consists of a large family which includes not only parents and children, but grandparents and the male descendants of the grandparents and their wives and children. This was also the structure of ancient China and was in fact an obstacle to the development of a strong central government. Fehl sees Plato as suggesting another kind of family which he calls the communal. The third alternative, what he terms the conjugal family, where the structure is centered in the ego-spouse relation, he seems to agree with contemporary radical feminists is undesirable.

This conjugal family is the modern urban family in which frequently both mother and father are employed away from home. This type may be a necessity of urban industrial society, he states (using Hong Kong, I assume, as his model). Fehl asks whether this urban nuclear family is not worse than Plato's suggestion.[37] He thus implies that no one kind of family is more "natural" than another. As we have seen, this is not the view of the majority of the commentators from 1870–1970. The pervasive attitude is rather the one expressed by Desmond Lee in the introduction to his frequently reissued translation. He tells us that both the desirability and the very possibility of exact similarity of role are questionable. "To sweep aside the physiological differences as unimportant and ignore the psychological differences they *entail* is to be in danger of ignoring women's special excellences" (*my emphasis*).[38] He warns that if you merely expect women to do the same things as men, they are likely, as Plato in effect said, to end up as inferior men. Is it not better to recognize the difference rather than pretend it does not exist? he asks.

This solicitous concern that women might "end up" as lesser men, a concern shared by Jowett and others into the 1980s, will be discussed later. The important issue here is the dogmatism of Lee's final formulation. For the chain beginning with the suggestions that differences "cut deep," are profound, alter women's entire being, and several other metaphorical expressions alluding to women's diverse abilities, ends with a conviction of logically entailed consequences of biology. Lee gives us no hint of what those special excellences are which Plato denies women to possess. Nor does he expand on how female physiology inevitably produces psychological differences, nor why these differences exclude women from a leadership role.

The commentators we have been dealing with all share the assumption that women's nature is ascertainable and that it is other than Plato describes it. They all find the proposals of Book V in some sense unnatural and use this either as an automatic justification for the undesirability of gender equality or at the very least as strong evidence against its advisability.

WOMEN HAVE BETTER THINGS TO DO: THE PROPOSALS AS UNDESIRABLE

Several commentators who deem Plato wise in many other respects find that his proposed changes in the relation between the sexes are clearly undesirable. These writers do not discuss the plan primarily in terms of its naturalness. When they do, they may even grant that some features of the arrangements in Book V are more natural, generally meaning more analogous to animal practice. Nevertheless, such changes would be bad for women and for society.

Chief among the influential scholars arguing for the undesirability of equality of role is the noted British scholar Richard Nettleship. Nettleship's Oxford lectures of the 1880s were reproduced from notes and published just before the turn of the century. His *Lectures on the Republic of Plato* have been continuously reprinted and have thus influenced students for over a hundred years. In many areas, his commentary is incisive and helpful, but on the matter of equality for women his arguments are suspect. He does make a contribution by pointing out, more than seventy-five years before the identical "discovery" is made by the twentieth-century feminists, that Plato is not concerned at all with the *rights* of women. For Plato, equality is solely a question of women's duties to the community. Socrates does not make his proposal in the interest of women as a class whom he supposes to be wronged, but in the interest of the state.

According to Nettleship, it is doubtful whether Socrates' plan would have struck an Athenian as favorable to women. "It might," he writes, "very likely have seemed to be dragging them out of a position in which they would rather be left."[39] Nettleship's phrase how it would strike "an Athenian" is unclear—does he wonder about the reaction of males or females or both? He does not address this question, but he does seem to imply that the austerity of the guardians' lives would have kept Athenian women from choosing it freely. But Nettleship surely knows that Plato was himself well aware that it would not be easy to convince his guardians, either male or female, to accept the austere life he outlined. Both males and females might rather be left in their ordinary positions, and this is why Socrates introduces his complicated measures of deception and rewards to motivate them.

Probably Nettleship believed that Athenian women would have found the life of leadership and equality even more distasteful than the men, would have resented being dragged out of the positions they occupied even more than the Athenian heads of households. He is expressing the view stated much more openly by an historian who contrasts the life of modern "emancipated women" with the advantages of Athenian wives. Although the former have more personal freedom, the Athenian women had all the advantages of being well-protected.[40]

The crux of the matter lies in how one evaluates the position of fourth-century Greek women. Some have stressed that they led a life of idleness and subjection. No male would willingly trade the absolute lack of control over marriage partner and choice of pursuits for such legal protection. Although other historians and commentators have in fact bemoaned the subject condition of women, Nettleship, here at least, does not seem to share their concern. In my opinion, Greek women might well have preferred to become rulers rather than remain the property of their husbands. At the very least, there seems no reason to believe that it would be any more difficult to persuade a woman than a man to enter the guardian class.

Nettleship thinks that hardly anyone would dispute Plato's

assertion that it is the real good of the community that ought to prevail. He agrees, too, that this good involves as much cooperation as possible between the sexes so that they can make the greatest contribution to the common life. But Plato's view of cooperation between the sexes Nettleship calls "narrow." Plato was mistaken in thinking that cooperation involves participation in deliberative, administrative, and military functions. He writes: "[A]s it might be put now, there are thousands of ways of contributing to the service of society besides being a member of Parliament or a soldier. One has, then, to distinguish between Plato's principle and the particular application he makes of it, which is to a certain extent determined by the circumstances of his time."[41]

Nettleship interprets Plato as having said that the more cooperation there is between men and women the better. But Plato does not speak of cooperation between the sexes in general, but only of identity of function among the superior. Nettleship clearly prefers the Victorian British idea of women as helpmates. He says he agrees with Aristotle that the difference between men and women is one which fundamentally affects their social functions. They ought not to do the same things, but to supplement each other. He seems to agree, too, that the analogy of the lower animals proves nothing. For even if some male and female animals are not so widely differentiated in character, this is due to the fact that animals are not so highly developed as man. In man, the most highly developed animal, the differentiation of the sexes is greatest.[42]

Nettleship does not offer any reasons why this differentiation is the most beneficial arrangement for society as a whole. He certainly makes no attempt to view the question of access to leadership from the point of view of the women then beginning to agitate for change. He simply assumes paternalistically that the many ways women could do service in his society were satisfactory for them and best for the common good. There are many other examples of commentators who believe the Platonic proposals would be highly detrimental. Their arguments are forcefully put by the great German scholar who proclaims that the arrangements suggested in Book V are "altogether intolerable and most corrupting."[43] All of these writers prefer the *status quo,* the relations between the genders in their own societies, to Plato's innovations.

PLATO DIDN'T REALLY MEAN IT: THE PROPOSALS AS UNINTENTIONAL, UNWELCOME, OR COMIC

One minority view is that Plato himself never really meant—or at the very least was less than wholehearted about—his suggestion of female and male guardians ruling equally. Although other writers have asserted adamantly that there is no point on which Plato speaks with more decided conviction, these commentators insist that the entire proposal was never intended to be taken seriously. While some attempt to justify the arrangements by showing that they would not have seemed as paradoxical to the Greeks because of the presence of the Spartan example, the commentators that I shall now discuss find the plans not only paradoxical but basically amusing, absurd, ironic, and intended as a joke.[44]

The mildest version of this view consists only of a weak doubt about Plato's own faith in his argument. Since Plato was clearly mistaken, we must look for some logical or psychological reason to "explain away" his strange ideas. Thus, Constantine Ritter tells us that Plato himself "did not quite trust his proposal." This is Ritter's "impression," but he does not offer any internal evidence on which he bases his impression.[45]

One of the strongest expressions of this argument which recurs throughout the German tradition appears much earlier in the commentary of Karl Nohle, published in 1880. He writes that Plato "has to admit" that there is no complete equality between men and women. Furthermore, "he cannot deny" that the difference in their biological share in reproduction "hinders women from playing as great a part in the governing of the state." There must, then, have been other reasons that made the philosopher overlook these basic defects in women.[46] He assumes that Plato would have thought the governing classes much better if they consisted only of men and so undertakes his reforms only with great reluctance.

The problem, Nohle thinks, is that if only males governed

there might be fear for the children of the guardians. Since the mothers would be inferior to the fathers in education of mind and body, future guardians might be dragged down to the level of the industrial class. To prevent this, "wives of guardians" must also be admitted into the circle of rulers. But when there, they can find nothing to do because the communal arrangements abolish all housekeeping and separate married life, and the State takes over child rearing. Therefore, since no possible occupation remains for women, he must assign them the same work as men, in spite of their lack of qualification for it.

For one who admires Plato as much as Nohle does, it seems strange that he finds Plato guilty of such a major logical inconsistency. If the whole concept of justice is based on each person's doing what he is best suited for, the existence of rulers who were basically unqualified would seem a major discrepancy. I should think Plato would be reluctant indeed! As the earliest feminist commentator phrases her objections in 1913 to what she generously terms Nohle's "interesting attempt to account for Plato's wish, "[I]t seems extremely arbitrary to attribute so torturous a mode of reasoning to Plato, in the face of his express and repeated affirmations that a State is only half a State if its women are allowed to run to waste."[47]

This idea of Plato's dissatisfaction with his own proposals surfaces again years later in the commentary of the eminent German classicist U. v. Wilamowitz-Moellendorff. He tells us that the very logic of Plato's own thinking forces the philosopher to conclusions which he himself does not welcome. Plato knows that woman is the object of man's strongest desire and man wants her as his property more passionately than anything else. This knowledge forces Plato into a conclusion which is "*sehr unwelkommen*" to him.[48]

Like later feminists, Wilamowitz believes that it is the idea of the abolition of property which logically precedes the abolition of marriage for the guardians. Since such a result is a logical requirement, Plato tries to resign himself to the consequences. But, as Wilamowitz puts it, "There is evidence that he manages this resignation only incompletely."[49] Since Wilamowitz realizes that the *rule* of women is logically independent of the elimination of private property, he looks for some other logical requirement that led Plato to this further undesirable but unavoidable proposal.

He decides that it is Plato's belief that women possess immortal souls and are therefore receptive to virtue that forces the unwelcome conclusions. It is virtue that determines their place in society, and as far as they are receptive to philosophy, they must rule. Wilamowitz does not explain why Plato himself fails to make this argument in Book V. Nevertheless, this commentator concludes that such reasoning must actually account for the unwelcome proposal.

Throughout the discussion, Wilamowitz talks of "*Weiberregimente*" and "*Weibe ans Staatsruder,*" that is, "women at the helm" rather than the joint rule of equally capable men and women which Plato actually calls for. This is partly because he has begun his discussion with a consideration of the connection between Aristophanes' *Ecclesiazusae,* or "Women in the Assembly" and Plato's proposals. The confusing terminology probably stems from the fact that in this comedy the theme *is* actually what would happen if a role reversal were to occur and women were to take over leadership of the state. The connection between these two works has been controversial for well over a hundred years. In the last decade, as we shall see, an evaluation of this connection becomes crucial to whether Plato's proposals are also intended as comic. But although Wilamowitz would like to minimize the importance of the reforms, he is adamant that they must not be compared to the worn-out theme chosen by Aristophanes which is only a pretext for entertaining his audience with a few dirty jokes. It is "ineradicable nonsense" that Plato was influenced by the *Ecclesiazusae,* for the two views do not have anything in common. The important point, for Wilamowitz, is that Plato really knew nothing about women, whereas Aristophanes knew the "*Hausfrau die in ihrem Reiche wirklich herrscht.*"[50] Evidently Plato's lack of knowledge of the housewife who rules in her own home is responsible for the proposals that he was so reluctantly led to make.

Thus, all those who believe Plato to have accepted his own conclusions only reluctantly still assume that they are the result of serious, if misguided, considerations. However, there is a contrasting view which even more effectively minimizes the importance of the ideas. With varying degrees of insistence, some commentators have announced that the whole discussion was intended as a joke.

One of these is I. M. Crombie, who thinks Plato's thoughts on sex relations, marriage, and the family "should be read by connoisseurs of *a priori* absurdity." He says that the most charitable comment to make on the reforms is that Plato intends "to pull the legs" of those who attach undue value to family ties.[51]

A later scholar, Paul Friedlander, also suggests that Plato introduces his paradoxes and plays with them "*pour épater le bourgeois.*" By having the women exercise naked with the men in the gymnasium and by elaborating on the institution of communal marriage, Friedlander considers Plato to be introducing amusing and even grotesque details.[52] Another interpreter, H. Gauss, objects to Friedlander's making the proposals playful. But in doing so, Gauss distorts Plato's text; and Friedlander later defends his own view by pointing out this distortion. Gauss evidently considers Plato's demands for the same educational opportunities to be straightforward. Unfortunately, he writes of them that Plato went so far as to demand "*Frauengymnasia,*" women's gymnasiums, where they, like their male colleagues, devote themselves to physical exercises after having shed their clothes.[53] But Friedlander is right that Plato does not specify such sex-segregated facilities. Gauss's attempt to make the idea more respectable is reminiscent of the French commentator who describes the Greeks as exercising "*presque nus.*"[54] Such reticence, however, does not alter the basic point that Plato makes. Just as the barbarians laughed at the Greeks when they first exercised nude, Plato assures his audience that the strangeness of the practice would eventually wear off. Many writers have pointed to the fact that Spartan women exercised along with men as a possible source for this idea. Although we do not know exactly what Spartan women wore for their gymnastic training, it would not doubt have shocked some Athenians if even the Spartan practice was instituted at Athens. We know that in most Greek cities, women were not even allowed to eat at the same table with a male not related to her.[55]

We also know from mosaics in Sicily that Roman women

engaged in sports in very brief costumes startlingly like our bikini bathing suits.[56] Almost nude is, of course, not completely naked, but a convincing case can be made for the fact that the former can be as distracting as the latter or more so. The important point, I think, remains that the requirement of joint nudity (not unlike the nude bathing that takes place on many beaches today) is hardly enough to discredit the seriousness of the proposal of equal education in *musike* and *gymnastike* for both sexes.

Despite his introduction of possible comic intention for Plato, it is important to indicate that Friedlander's own view differs from the major proponents of the "joke" theory. For he, unlike them, believes that Plato is in fact deeply serious behind the jest. In support of later feminist commentary, he states that it is not the institution that matters, but the principle represented by it. In principle, as many as possible should be able to share in the education provided by the state. He thinks that education in "our own society" has moved much closer to adopting Plato's paradox. He does not, then, accentuate the comic aspect solely to highlight the impossibility or undesirability of female equality.

However, the views of Leo Strauss and Allan Bloom do exactly that. Strauss describes Plato's dialogues in general as "slightly more akin" to comedy than to tragedy. And the *Republic* he finds "manifestly akin" to Aristophanes' *Assembly of Women.*[57] Bloom says that he relies heavily on Strauss' "authoritative discussion" for his own interpretive essay. And, in his notes to the text, he points out the probable allusions to *Ecclesiazusae* in Book V.

In Bloom's discussion, the judgment that the three paradoxical waves are primarily comic is inseparable from his contention, introduced above, that the proposals violate "our understanding of human nature." The first paradox of female equality he finds laughable and ridiculous, whereas discussion of the second proposal emphasized the comic element less. With the idea of philosopher-rulers the laughter and indignation reappear in a more intense form. The whole book, he writes, "*can only be understood* as Socrates' response to his most dangerous accuser, Aristophanes, and his contest with him. . . . In Book V he tries to show the superiority of the philosopher . . . by producing a comedy which is more fantastic, more innovative, more comic . . . than any work of Aristophanes."[58] In stressing the absurdity, he echoes

Strauss' vague and archaic adjective, calling Socrates' comedy "akin" to *Ecclesiazusae* in that they both propose emancipation of women and communism.

Strictly speaking, as I have said, what *Ecclesiazusae* actually proposes is role reversal with women ruling while men stay home. Praxagora, the heroine of the play, introduces a bill into the assembly for the "putting down of men."[59] This has a modern ring, evoking the excesses of some radical feminists; but there is a major logical and practical difference between gynecocracy and the identity of the role proposed for the guardians. Most of the commentators who discuss the connection of the two works, regardless of their views on the independence or reciprocal influence, do judge the theme of female equality to be similar. They fail to stress what I would consider this striking dissimilarity.

Bloom thinks that Book V surpasses and radicalizes the reforms of the Athenian women in the comedy. In the play, the women's reforms, he says, are *just,* but politically impossible. In my view, what Aristophanes has Praxagora and her comrades suggest in their gynecocracy is certainly not just, for it involves the arbitrary rule of one group over another. The misuse of male resources may in fact be possible, though it is true that contrary to the wishful thinking of some feminists, no female-dominated society has ever existed.[60] But it is surely not just in Plato's terms. And I doubt very much that Bloom actually considers most of the comic suggestions (such as the requirement that the young man sleep with the "old hag" before he can have intercourse with the young woman he desires) to be just.

The radicalizing to which Bloom refers lies evidently in the outrageousness of suggesting that men and women exercise naked together. I shall confine myself here to those arguments he offers in his original essay. As mentioned before, his views have been attacked by male and female feminists in the 1970s and I shall discuss their objections and his response to them later in that context. The important point here is that Bloom finds the public nudity of men and women to be nonsense as a political proposal.[61] The full equality of the sexes, what Bloom calls "sharing the same locker room," could not possibly work even on Plato's own terms. Men can be naked together because it is relatively easy to desexualize their relations with each other. I assume

Bloom speaks only of the relative ease since he is well aware that the sexual desire of many Athenian males was at least as strong for other nude males as it would have been for nude females.

But the difficulty comes according to Bloom because the mutual attraction of men and women must be fostered rather than discouraged if the city is to be preserved. This mutual attraction evidently could not be maintained if women exercised naked alongside men. Bloom ignores such practices as nude swimming beaches, and nude family bathing in Japan (where reproduction seems to continue despite the supposed difficulties). Nor does the increased licentiousness that Bloom thinks would inevitably result "because civilized men need some mastery over their sexual appetites" occur in all societies with different attitudes to nudity than ours.

For Bloom, however, the entire prospect of nakedness in the gymnasium is both 1) impossible in itself, and 2) symbolic in its contradictions of the impossibility of equality and ultimately of the entire foundation of the ideal State. Such a State would be impossible because its law would "at the same time encourage and forbid the mutual attraction of the sexes." In my view, what would actually be required would be the State's discouraging action on the attraction at one time, and encouraging it at another. This is perfectly possible, and in fact goes on all the time. Plato himself encourages male-male attraction as a means of understanding the desire for the good, though he discourages action on the attraction most of the time. Repression will be necessary in the just city, but then some kind of repression *is* necessary to female equality. But repression of sexuality has been and probably always will be necessary to all forms of civilization. If the city, as Bloom himself says, can, and has, forbidden homosexuality, then law and custom have also sequestered women and forbidden "undesirable" unions. The 1977 execution of Saudi Princess Mishaal for adultery is evidence of the extent to which the State can still forbid mutual attraction.

Bloom, however, finds the whole proposal of sexual equality preposterous. The erotic improprieties will be so extensive that their complications only reinforce the lack of seriousness on Socrates' part. It is not usually thought possible, Bloom tells us, to make the sexual passion respond only to those objects chosen by the city, in a way and at a time deemed fitting by the city. Although he finally grants that some training and repression of sexual desires is possible, the Platonic suggestions are outlandish. Many anthropologists would suggest that the erotic impulses of women have frequently been just as rigorously regulated. From the practices of ancient China to those of many religious sects today, extensive regulation of sexual behavior has persisted. Both Moslem fundamentalists and orthodox Jews rigorously control women's sexual behavior. Religious authorities even determine on which days of the menstrual cycle intercourse is permissible. According to reports from modern China, in order to encourage birth control, charts of the menstrual cycle of women residents were publicly posted in neighborhood health centers. Premarital sex was ostensibly almost eliminated at the same time as the age for marriage was raised.

Bloom seems to forget that the "sexual passion" of most women throughout history has been restricted in its expression to the partners chosen by fathers or male relatives, if not by the State. The way and time have been decided primarily by the wishes of the husband. I am not commenting on the desirability of State-regulated temporary unions nor supporting the view that male, female, or joint nudity is necessary to the cultivation of human physical excellence. What I am suggesting is that the variety and severity of extant customs might have given Bloom pause in his considerations of what is humanly possible.

On the whole, Bloom's account of the necessary relation between shame and sexual attraction and his total account of human sexual desire seem idiosyncratic. He certainly makes no attempt to support it with any currently available psychological data. He tells us that incest taboos are accepted without question and hardly need to be taught. Recent evidence in the United States suggests that incest taboos are frequently violated, that more than twenty-five percent of females are reported to have been sexually assaulted by male relatives. Researchers believe that young boys are also more frequently involved than is reported in sexual encounters with related females. Since reporting such incidents is still considered unmanly in this culture because of the belief that males should always desire intercourse regardless of the circumstances, we probably do not have accurate statistics on such unwanted incestuous relations. Evidence of voluntary violations of incest taboos is of course far less reliable. Although sociologists today believe that incest taboos are natural in the sense that they have been evolved as adaptive for our species, evidence still suggests that the specific forms the taboo takes has much to do with convention. Bloom says that Socrates speaks as if he were talking of regulations no more important than rivers and harbors. Bloom is surely right that the matter is generally regarded as far more important than that. However, in the matter of incest, it does seem that justice, that is, unfair exploitation, is the modern issue rather than violation of the natural.

According to Bloom, Plato has a hidden agenda. The real reason women are placed among the guardians is not because they possess the same capacities as men, but precisely because they are different. Socrates needs women guardians because they can bear children and men cannot. Why Socrates does not tell us that he is "fabricating a convention about the nature of women" when he tells us at many other points when a myth or a noble lie will be necessary to gain his aims for a just society, Bloom does not explain.

He does, however, recognize the contradiction in Plato's comments on women, which becomes a major issue in the feminist commentary of the 1970s. Aware that Plato finds the best women always inferior to the best men, Bloom goes so far as to assert that it would be highly improbable that any women would even "be considered for membership" in the higher classes.[62]

Thus, he would seem to agree with Nohle that Plato would have greatly preferred to have all-male rulers. The argument is basically the same, although Bloom goes even further than Nohle. It is not only that the guardians might be inferior if their mothers were inferior, but rather that female guardians are necessary if there are to be any future guardians at all. The same objection applies to both commentators. For if Plato actually did not believe women capable of ruling, his placing them among the philosophers would undermine his whole theory of justice, in which each person does what he is best suited for. Although Nohle does not seem to have noticed this lack of logic, Bloom thinks it adds to the general absurdity and comic irony of the project. But if what Plato has created is a society in which women perform jobs for which they are basically unsuited, he has created a state which is not comic, but rather fundamentally unjust. And so, Bloom, like Strauss before him, must see that a decision about the capacities of women is essential to a plan for an ideal society, and therefore, despite his protestations, no laughing matter.

OTHER WAYS OF "EXPLAINING AWAY" THE PLAN FOR GENDER EQUALITY

Other writers also look for ways of explaining why Plato came up with his paradoxical reforms. These explanations tend to minimize the legitimacy of these reforms. The line between "explaining" and "explaining away," of course, is not always easy to draw. One example of such speculation on Plato's motives is the account of the scholar-psychoanalyst, Bennett Simon. Unlike many of the previous classicists, Simon's intentions are surely not anti-female, and when not discussing the *Republic,* he explicitly expresses pro-feminist attitudes. Unfortunately, however, psychoanalytic theorizing about the underlying psycho-sexual conflicts of long dead literary figures often tends to reductionism. That is, it leads the reader to focus on the "neurotic" reasons for a theory, rather than on the possible logical and philosophical validity of the claim. Thus, Simon's account, whatever his intention, has the effect of casting doubt on the objectivity, and therefore the validity, of Plato's arguments for that abolishing of family life which makes it possible for women and men to rule equally.

Simon writes that an important aspect of Plato's design for his ideal state is the wish to protect the elite and the guardians from "primal scene trauma" and its consequences. On the basis of biographical detail, he tries to show that the arrangements Plato makes for his guardians are intended to spare them the damaging experiences of parental intercourse, which he speculates the philosopher must have witnessed in his own childhood. This hypothetical trauma led Plato to prescribe practices for the guardians which require "ordered and regulated intercourse, not 'in the dark,' . . . and as far as possible intercourse should be dissociated from biological and social parenthood." The motivation for Plato's proposals is his unconscious belief that only new modes of sexuality and birth that eliminate parents copulating in the dark can eradicate the whole host of evils that disrupt societies.[63]

Simon also sees the "Allegory of the Cave" as a primal scene fantasy. This is not the place to try to evaluate the possibility of using ancient texts to reveal the psychodynamic issues of their authors, and to assess the particular difficulties involved when little or no direct biographical information is available. However, I do wish to point out that such analyses, regardless of their authors' intentions, tend to obscure and trivialize these central visions of Western philosophy.

Simon has little to say about the specific connection between identical roles for women and primal scene trauma; but he does seem to consider the minimizing of biological differences inherent in such equality as all part of the philosopher's wish to deny the importance of male-female intercourse. It is not clear if Simon himself accepts the orthodox Freudian position on the importance of those biological differences that Plato underplays. The original psychoanalytic view would characterize a woman trying to do the same job as a man as denying her femininity, fantasizing a male body, being unwilling to accept her biological deficiencies.[64]

Simon does not raise these issues, but concentrates instead on what Plato hopes to achieve by minimizing the primal scene. This leads him to a mistaken reading of what Plato actually says. According to Simon, fraternal love can replace fratricide only by minimizing the primal scene. But it is not rivalry that Plato wishes to eliminate. Plato does not abolish the family in order to keep brothers from killing each other, but for precisely the opposite reason. It is the family loyalties that are divisive to the State. And, of course, it is only among the guardians that he specifically abolishes marriage, though Plato himself does speak at one point as if fraternal love would be fostered throughout the city by his new arrangements.[65] As some commentators have noted, Plato's failure to provide a motive for the artisan class to feel loyal to their guardians is a major drawback to the possible success of his city. At any rate, it is inter-family, rather than intra-family, strife that Plato fears. He wants to create one big family whose mythical mother and nurse is Mother Earth, and whose members are fashioned as gold, silver, or bronze by a male god. If such a fiction is evidence of the avoidance of a primal scene, then the creators of hundreds of similar myths in many cultures may well have been equally traumatized.

This is not to suggest that Simon is wrong to raise the issue of the Greek male's fear of the female and of female sexuality. He is wrong, however, in stating that in societies in which males are considered superior, female sexuality is seen as non-existent or inferior.[66] The Greeks at any rate did not see women as without sexual appetite. K. J. Dover, who has made a careful study of the subject, notes that in contrast to the curious beliefs propagated in the English-speaking world during the last hundred years or so (conditioned by the Victorian presupposition that absence of sexual response is morally praiseworthy), the Greeks were inclined to think that women desired and enjoyed sexual intercourse more than men.[67]

The major point for our purposes is that Simon's entire discussion detracts from the significance of Plato's proposal of equality of role. One could advocate the abolition of private families, substituting male rulers and well-regulated female slaves, and avoid primal scene trauma equally well. Why Plato went to such lengths as to have male and female philosopher-rulers is not illumined by Simon's psychoanalytic speculations.

A contrary explanation of why the *Republic* advocates the emancipation of female guardians is offered by A. J. Taylor. He believes that it was the historical Socrates, Plato's teacher, rather than Plato himself, who actually advocated such reforms. In other words, it is Socrates' early childhood and not Plato's that we would have to search for explanations. Taylor says that the proposals are no personal development of Plato's thinking, but rather only the "necessary consequences" of the position of the actual Socrates.[68] Taylor cites Aeschines' work *Aspasia,* of which we have only a fragment, as evidence of Socrates' pro-female leanings. We have, of course, very little historical information about Socrates apart from Plato's portrait of his mentor. But Taylor notes that the Socrates described by Aeschines thought that the goodness of woman was the same as that of a man. Socrates supposedly supported this belief by pointing to the political abilities of Aspasia and the military achievements of the Persian "Amazon," Rhodogyne. This thesis of Taylor's is not altogether convincing if we assume that earlier Platonic dialogues like the *Apology* contain the views of the historical Socrates, while later ones are more purely Platonic. For in the *Apology*, Socrates dismisses his wife as he is about to die, preferring the rational conversation of his young male friends to the "womanish wailing" of Xanthippe. (It is, I suppose, possible to believe in the need for sexual equality and yet find one's own wife inferior. However, the situation does suggest a certain misogyny which is discussed at length by the commentators of the 1970s.) At any rate, Taylor has not proven his case that the proposal for gender equality is merely the logical outcome of Socrates' own views which Plato felt constrained to follow.[69]

We now come to the final way of explaining away or minimizing the novelty and need for Plato's reforms. This is to assert that such reforms were indeed admirable and have in fact already been accomplished. The French commentator, Maurice Croiset, writing in the 1930s, expresses sympathy with the offering of equal education to men and women. He says that this aim of Plato's has actually been accomplished in the France of his day. Considering that there were fewer women than men in higher education and that French women were unable to vote at the time he was writing, his claim seems at best premature.[70]

One of the most bizarre expressions of this view occurs in a book published in Germany in 1933, comparing Hitler's political program and Plato's *Republic.* Joachim Bannes writes that the aims of the National Socialist "freedom movement" were identical to Plato's in creating equal education and social roles for women.[71] He refers us to Hitler's *Mein Kampf,* which he assures us shows the ideological influence of Plato and demonstrates Hitler's plan for equality for women.

The only relevant reference to be found in *Mein Kampf* would seem to be a statement about physical training. Hitler writes that the emphasis on physical education must be the same for men and women, although "the aim of female education undoubtedly has to be preparation for motherhood."[72] There were, of course, no women in the elite schools of Germany in the 1930s and early 1940s. And in fact, Hitler was so irrational in his opposition to the participation of women that he avoided mobilizing them for forced labor until very late in the war. This was clearly contrary to his own interests and to the practice of both Britain and the United States. Even Socrates in fourth-century Athens is said to have suggested to Aristarchus that women be put to some productive work when an unusual situation necessitated it. When Aristarchus fled with fourteen relatives from Athens to Piraeus during a political disturbance and was left with no means to support a large household, Xenophon tells us that Socrates advised his noble friend to set the women to work, contrary to the usual Athenian practice.[73] Furthermore, Hitler in his anti-Semitism took over the idea of the Jews as a principle of femininity, demonstrating a pervasive misogyny.[74]

BIAS IN LANGUAGE: THE CONSEQUENCES OF HIDDEN ASSUMPTIONS

There is a distinct category of commentators whose disapproval of Plato's views involves no overt statements, but nevertheless reveals a marked unconscious bias. This bias is apparent in their choice of language to state what Plato said, or in questionable translations from the Greek, or in what seem unwitting misreadings. C. H. Hoole's "brief summary of the arguments and doctrines of the *Republic* expressed as far as possible in the words of Plato" supplies an example. His renderings are expressed in the language of the Victorian gentleman. He writes: "*Woman is the weaker man;* for both sexes have the same capacities for the performance of the active duties of life, the same in kind though existing in higher degree in the male" (*my emphasis*).[75]

The striking feature here is the unconscious irony in the phrase "woman is the weaker man." It is possible that Hoole means to convey that woman is *a* weaker man, but he clearly knows that Plato admits the reproductive differences are genuine. Instead, what Hoole probably intends is only the accepted vernacular of the time. As one would say on the playing fields of Eton that Jenkins was the weaker man, that is, the less able, Hoole is here using "man" in the generic sense. His all-male students evidently found no difficulty in understanding what now appears to us as the awkwardly androcentric "*woman* is the weaker man."

Jowett's phrase, "the female sex in man," is equally awkward.[76] Many of the phrases in his translation are even more unconsciously amusing and revealing. The high comedy of Victorian euphemism appears in his rendering of the line, "then the wives of our guardians will have a fine easy time when they are in the family way."[77] Even when there is meant to be no family, Jowett still cannot bring himself to describe the women as "pregnant," but persists in using "in the family way." Regardless of what stand one takes on the importance of linguistic habits as embodiments of sexism in need of change, it would be hard to deny that this use of "in the family way" is not only unintentionally ironic, but actually misleading. At the same time as John Stuart Mill was calling for radical changes in family structure, Jowett was describing women who produce children from temporary unions and live communally as equal rulers without private families as "in the family way."

It is not surprising that Jowett uses such formulations in what has been called his idealization of Plato and his desire to make his views comfortably acceptable to his Victorian audience.[78] His "cover up" of homosexual references so that he translates *erastes* and *eremenos* as "lover" and "his beloved," in hopes of downplaying pederasty, has been criticized.[79] But the distortions that result from his attempts to obscure the radical nature of Plato's views on women are equally important. When he writes of the mating arrangements of the guardians, he assures us that "they cannot be allowed to live in licentiousness." But Plato is not here concerned with the limitation of sexual indulgence, as is indicated by the fact that men and woman outside the regulation age for breeding can do as they please. But for centuries what was called by an earlier translator "the delicate question of the community of women" has prevented writers from seriously considering the justice of equal education and social roles for women.[80]

The most flagrant example of attempts to square the Platonic view with that of Victorian Christian sexual morality is in the translation of *Republic* V, 457 as "let them strip, clothed in their *chastity*."[81] This translation of *arete* as "chastity" is clearly unwarranted since what is intended is the connotation of excellence, which stems from the proper development of both mind and body. Although the Greek gentleman, like the Victorian Englishman, would also value sexual purity and fidelity, it is precisely a new social order with different conventions that Plato seeks. The translator's reluctance to face the idea of identical standards for both sexes surfaces there. Even Cornford's and Bloom's choice of "they will clothe themselves in virtue instead of robes," does not sufficiently eliminate overtones of the old sexual morality. J. Adam, who is himself more enthusiastic about equality of opportunity for "gifted females," translates "they will clothe themselves with excellence instead of garments."[82]

T. H. Warren compares this line to Tennyson, who says of Lady Godiva, "Then she rode forth, clothed on with chastity." But Plato's meaning differs markedly from that of Tennyson, who specifically intends to praise the sexual fidelity, rather than the physical superiority, of the heroine.[83] The problem is compounded by the fact that throughout history an excellent woman has usually implied a virtuous woman in terms of sexual morality, that is, a chaste woman, whereas "an excellent man" carries no such connotation. This notorious "double standard" has been eliminated in Plato's state.[84]

Like Jowett and Warren, Cornford, in his freer translation and summary of Book V, also tries to square the Platonic proposals with prevalent English morality. Besides attempts to defend Plato against the charge of advocating infanticide, he tries to make the sexual encounters in the ideal state more palatable through his choice of words. Thus, he writes that "wives" must strip for exercise.[85] Although the Greek *gyne* means both "woman" and "wife," the choice of the latter here is misleading. Many of the commentators persistently describe these unions which would not last for more than a month as "marriages." They refer to the women guardians throughout as "wives." Plato himself does call the three-day mating sessions "sacred marriages." But he certainly does not intend, as F. M. Cornford puts it, that good warriors will be rewarded with more liberal opportunities "to sleep with a wife."[86] The crucial point is the persistent lack of symmetry; it is not "husbands" who strip in the gymnasium, but rather, men.

Alexandre Koyre, in his *Discovering Plato,* assures us that we must not imagine this communal status of women as synonymous with sexual promiscuity. He writes that "marriage exists, but is of short duration."[87] This does seem to be stretching the accepted use of the word when you remember that a woman might have as many as twenty of these "marriages" while she was of breeding age. If you were to reward her excellence as the male guardians are rewarded, she would have even more of these "marriages." Of course, as has been pointed out by commentators in the 1970s, Plato himself does not mention rewards for the women.

Nevertheless, Cornford, in his eagerness to make the Platonic arrangements less revolutionary, tells us that the unofficial unions might be permanent. And the rewards for valor are "not to have several wives at once, but to be admitted at more frequent intervals to the periodic marriage festivals, not necessarily with a different wife each time."[88] Cornford neglects to mention that in introducing this idea of more intercourse for the heroes in war Plato says that "if a man happens to love someone, either male or female" the fact that neither may refuse to kiss the hero will provide incentives for valor. Nettleship, too, tries to make Plato's views palatable to his audience. His assertion that as part of the austere life of the guardians they cannot "keep mistresses" evokes the companionate marriage of the English upper class much more than it contributes to helping the student visualize the possibility of a new order.

As we have seen, Wilamowitz speaks of *Weibergemeinschaft*, *Weiberregemente*, and *Weibe ans Staatsruder*. Thus, to say "women's affairs," "women's rule," and "women at the helm of the State," he uses the older form "Weibe," which refers more to wives than to females in general. Unlike the Greeks, he had separate terms at his disposal. Since the term *Frauenemancipation* was in common usage when he wrote, he might well have chosen the more neutral "Frau." Jowett speaks of the women guardians as "helpmeets," thus accommodating the independent guardian women to the Christian idea of Eve. But these women are not "wives," not auxiliary or ancillary, and the novelty of their status is obscured by these seemingly harmless word choices.

Besides the question of distortion of meaning, there is the related but separable issue which I discussed in my introduction and which needs to be repeated here. The female student who is confronted with the pronouns "he" and "his" when reading about the guardians and their education can add "she" and "hers." But the cumulative effect of the commentators' failure to include her in their terminology created a subtle feeling of exclusion. At the very least, it fosters among women readers the sense of the unimportance of the entrance of females into the guardian class. The choice of pronouns de-emphasizes the plan for "Philosopher-Queens." The term itself as a coordinate with the ubiquitous "Philosopher-King" has only recently been used at all.

Almost exclusively, we find such formulations as that of Charles Bakewell. After telling us that Plato is in advance of his time in including women, he goes on to describe the guardians as "these best of men."[89] Bakewell, while stating that Plato does not appreciate that abolishing the family would at the same time be destroying virtues fostered in family life, mentions female guardians. But he then describes this ruling circle as a "very small group of carefully chosen men." He summarizes the character and ability of the guardian with the description, "a man of quick mind, . . . gentle and just in his dealings with men."[90]

I contend that more than linguistic convenience is at issue here. For it is striking that Bernard Bosanquet, who is more enthusiastic than most for what he calls the "violent revolution" which Plato demanded in advocating an equal share for women in the pursuits and the education of men, makes some effort to alter his terminology. Among books and articles focusing solely on the theory of education in Plato, he alone writes that the reforms would produce "a hearty, active, and disciplined young *creature*" *(my emphasis)*.[91] Instead of Nettleship's and others' talk of educating the young lad, "the public school boy," Bosanquet's language incorporates the realization that ideal education was also for the best women. Here, the failure to alter the linguistic convention may not involve any intentional distortion. But it surely perpetuates that omission of half the human race from serious consideration that, almost 2,400 years ago, Plato wanted to rectify.

AS LONG AS THEY DON'T GO TOO FAR: THE WARNINGS OF THE SO-CALLED FEMINISTS

We now come to that category of commentators who, at least in expressed intent, eagerly desire some kind of equalization. There is no sharp differentiation between some of these writers and the ones I have already considered. In their work, a few lines will appear that express enthusiasm for female emancipation or what they sometimes call feminism. One is then lulled by a false sense that there, at last, is a scholar who believes that women are capable of the same tasks as men. However, on careful reading it soon emerges that such a conclusion must be carefully qualified. The final word is that equality is a good idea, as long as women don't make excessive demands. Even those who openly and repeatedly express enthusiasm eventually warn that equality is desirable only so long as women (as we would now put it) "know their place."

Thus, Richard Crossman professes himself an advocate of women's rights and on the whole approves what he terms Plato's "feminism." But, as we have seen, he fears that much will be lost if egalitarianism "goes too far." Most typical of this view is the argument to be found in the one book devoted entirely to the subject of Plato's ideas on women. In *Les idées de Platon sur la condition de la femme,* Jean Ithurriague repeatedly expresses his feminist sympathies. He quotes with approval an 1866 statement from the suffragist Susan B. Anthony that "equality of intelligence and virtue between the two sexes is indisputable; why make a difference between them?" Ithurriague sees Plato as only one in a long line of feminist advocates, far from a revolutionary or an "illuminé." Such ideas he tells us were in vogue in Athens in Plato's time in poetry, the theatre, and among philosophers. Practices in Egypt and Sparta led the way to reforms favorable to women. He even goes so far as to contend that "if the Orient made women into an inferior type, Egypt and other primitive peoples placed her on the same level as man and conceded her the same rights and privileges." But Plato was the precursor and "*le plus grand des féministes.*" After him, Ithurriague tells us, women will no longer be thought of as she was before him. And despite the vicissitudes of an unequal struggle, the basic idea of the equality of women and men will make its way, taken up again later and illumined with a new light by Christianity.[92]

In this supposedly linear progress, he devotes three short paragraphs to Aristotle. He admits only that the Stagyrite was without Plato's "largeness of spirit and liberalism" on questions of women's role. Reinterpreting what few, if any, commentators today would deny was a disparaging attitude toward women, Ithurriague defends Aristotle. Although Aristotle reasons like many ancient and modern conservatives (*"hommes prudents"*), he safeguards the dignity of women and adopts the moral equality of men and women. This is not the place to discuss Aristotle's views, but it is worth noting that Aristotle did not in fact believe that a woman could be virtuous in the same way as a man. He believed rather in woman's natural inferiority and natural role as subject to her husband. The relevant point here is that Ithurriague's sanguine view that progress has been constant beginning with Plato and that prejudices are "fading away" is unwarranted. Even if one were to accept his view of Plato as an unambivalent proponent of female equality, we would then have to say that it is the counter-influence of Aristotle that has prevailed until fairly recently.[93]

Ithurriague's own view in the 1930s was that we were not far from complete equality. It becomes clear, however, that the equality he approves is not the position of Book V of the *Republic,* but the assigning of tasks "fitting to their sex" which he finds in the *Laws.* In his final summation, he pronounces Plato's doctrine to be unequivocally that the actual inferiority of women is due solely to the defects of their education. Ithurriague overlooks the contradictions in Plato and is unaware of any inconsistency in his own opinions. One must give women an education identical in all respects to that of men. By nature she is the equal of man, and capable like him of performing *"offices les plus délicats et . . . fonctions les plus difficiles."*[94]

At the same time, a certain crucial qualification on his part emerges. He finds Plato to have been "preaching wisdom" when he urges the legislator in the *Laws* to confide to women only the functions conforming to their character and their sex. He writes, "The great philosopher of Athens has generously opened the road to liberation for women while pointing out to her her duties and without hiding from her the *boundaries that the weakness of her sex sets* to her claims" (*my emphasis*).[95] Thus, Ithurriague, after tracing the origins of Plato's views describing the subjugation of Oriental women and the oppressive situation of women in classical Greece, concludes his noble sentiments with a note of caution. In woman's attack on behalf of her just claims, he puts it, one may fear that she will go beyond her objectives and "call down on herself, by abuse or excess, legitimate reactions." Ithurriague fears that unreasonable ambition might lead women outside their natural paths, "estranging her from the duties that belong to her alone, from the functions that nature and reason reserve for her." One would not dream of haggling with her or refusing her this right which she obtains by her intelligence and her energy. This self-proclaimed feminist ends his study by informing us that woman is entitled to her rights so long as "she knows how to remain within the limits fixed by a sound equity, if, in short, she knows how to remain a woman, mother, wife."[96]

Once again there is the unsupported appeal to the truly natural. But of more concern is the paternalism and warning of a possible backlash from this professed champion of women's rights in the early 1930s. Such a double message can surely do as much harm as the outspoken anti-egalitarian views we have considered.

The final self-proclaimed feminist to be considered is F. A. Wright, whose work ends with even more virulent judgments. This English scholar, author of a book on "feminism" in Greek literature, finds both strength and weakness in Plato's feminism. The weakness, as we have often heard before, stems from Plato's inclination to disregard some of "the invincible facts of human nature."[97] Wright calls Plato "essentially a masculine genius." Like Wilamowitz, he believes that Plato's feminism and his educational reforms are weakened because they stem from ideal theory, rather than any actual experience. Nevertheless, Wright is enthusiastic about certain aspects of Plato's feminism.

He approves Plato's treatment of the question of military service for women. According to Wright, if a man is unwilling or unable to defend his country, he certainly has no claim to citizen rights, nor does a woman. Therefore, he writes in 1923 that it may reasonably be argued that the qualification for a vote is neither property nor sex, but the proof that the individual has passed through the period of training necessary to qualify him as a defender of the fatherland. A soldier needs only courage, strength, and skill, all three of which Wright believes women to possess. In fact, in the passive courage which a modern soldier chiefly needs, women possibly "have a slight advantage over men and they usually recover more quickly from wounds." Modern warfare requires chiefly endurance: the power to stand exposure to the weather, insufficient food, lack of sleep and comfort, marching capacity. He writes: "No one who knows the vagabonds and strollers of our English roads will say that women are not capable of supporting all these hardships as well as men. The female tramp is every whit as sturdy and hardy as her male companion."[98] Even the skill to handle a gun and the power of shooting straight are matters almost entirely of training. And he believes that the natural qualities that facilitate such training, a steady hand and a sharp eye, are by no means predominately male characteristics. It is a picture of female physical prowess worthy of the most militant contemporary feminist. Unfortunately, there is always the danger that such generalizations, based on the flimsiest of evidence, can easily be turned against women's aspirations.

Another aspect of Plato's program which Wright approves are the reforms in feminine education which he believed strongly were in the process of being realized. He notes that the educated woman was even being allowed to become herself a teacher and rank with male colleagues. His enthusiasm is so excessive that he writes that in the inner circle of Plato's Academy, "the first University College of which we know, *men and women met on equal terms and shared responsibilities and privileges*" (*my emphasis*). This singular view he supports only by referring to the two non-Athenian women reported by Dicaearchus to have attended the Academy. Considering that there is no evidence of other female attendance and that not a single Athenian woman appears as a participant in any of the dialogues, this conclusion is highly suspect.

So, too, is Wright's belief about the source of Plato's contempt for the society of his native city. According to Wright, Plato correctly saw that "the main cause" of the unfortunate condition of his state, was "the indifference to women and children which the ordinary Athenian prided himself on displaying."[99] How sharply this view contrasts with the opinions of those commentators who believe Plato's reforms for women were a mere unwelcome afterthought!

Such undiscriminating zeal often turns out to be a mixed blessing. And such is the case with Wright. He concludes his chapter by declaring that although Plato is sometimes wrong about women, he clearly hits the truth about one of the natural weaknesses he ascribes to them (in the *Laws.*) Plato is on target when he tells us that *secretiveness* is the one quality which is peculiarly a woman's, and not a man's, characteristic. This quality is the result of many centuries of self-suppression and gives a certain "aggravating charm" to the female mind and usually does no particular harm.[100] One might suggest that if it is the result of the habit of centuries, then its innate naturalness would at least be questionable, but Wright does not raise this issue.

On this shortcoming of women, he is unrelenting. In his adamance, he even seems to desert the subject of Plato in order to inform us that women's secretiveness is the chief reason for their comparative failure in literature. It is "sincerity in writing" which is literature's saving grace, and if a book is not frank, it should never be written. Most women, he says, fail in frankness toward themselves and their readers. He writes: "George Eliot, Ouida, George Sand . . . dissemble their facts as much as they dissemble their names. Like ostriches, they hide their faces under a cloud of words."[101] This judgment, which implies that like the children of irregular unions in Plato's ideal State, a book like *Middlemarch* "should never see the light of day," comes from an avowed and enthusiastic feminist. One can only rejoin: if these are our friends, God save us from our enemies!

THE EXCEPTIONS: EARLY GENUINE ENTHUSIASM FOR THE EGALITARIAN REFORMS

In all this litany of hostility to identical roles for women, feminists do possess some genuine friends. Two male scholars stand out as notable exceptions. One of them, the distinguished historian and pupil of Bentham, George Grote, was born in the eighteenth century and thus belongs chronologically more to the earlier tradition of great German scholars from Schleiermacher to Ast whose major focus was on establishing the exact text and the authenticity of the corpus. The first edition of Grote's *Plato and the Other Companions of Socrates* was issued before the period under consideration, but his comments were still influential when Pater was proclaiming the superiority of Christianity over the Platonic reforms.[102] The thrust of his lengthy discussion of Book V (along with a thorough, accurate paraphrase) is to convince his readers of the "extraordinary variety and discrepancy of approved and consecrated customs" that have existed in the world.[103] He takes a cultural relativist position throughout, giving examples of actual practices in ancient times which would seem even stranger to his readers than the suggestions for Plato's commonwealth.

Grote considers Plato to "dissent altogether" from the common man's opinion that women are naturally unfit for ruling. He points to Plato and Aristotle's opposing views on the subject. Then he uses the discrepancy between them to illustrate the uselessness of arguments based on the word Nature. Grote believes that when we see two such distinguished thinkers completely at issue as to what Nature indicates "in this important case," we realize that "each of them decorates by that name the rule which he himself approves."[104] The same might be said of the conflicting views on women's natural capacities that have appeared in the more than one hundred years after Grote's pronouncement.

Grote makes an effort to talk about the "distinguished persons in the regiment (*male or female, as the case may be*)" (*my emphasis*). He writes of the education of boys and girls, using pronouns carefully and emphasizing repeatedly how strongly Plato was attached to his doctrines about the capacity of women.[105] He even uses the modified views in the *Laws* as evidence of how unchanged Plato's opinions were about "the mischief" of separating the training and function of the two sexes, and of confining women to indoor occupations, to what is called in the later book, "a life of darkness and fear." In Grote's enthusiasm, he deemphasizes the traces of misogyny which commentators in the 1970s find not only in the *Laws* but in Book V and other places in the *Republic.*

He does not, however, try to gloss over the fact that in the ideal State, as he interprets the text, the best women will be on a level only with the second best men. The heaviest and most difficult duties, "those which require the maximum of competence to perform, will usually devolve upon men."[106] But he is eager to understand where Plato got the idea that even in cooking and weaving men were superior to women. In Greece, weaving was generally a woman's occupation, though we cannot be sure whether it was exclusively so. In Egypt, however, weaving was done by men; Grote wonders whether Plato perhaps saw finer Egyptian webs. If so, he would use this knowledge as ammunition against those in his audience who might claim that women have special aptitudes for certain occupations.

He wants also to show that there were precedents in the ancient world for extremely competent women. He regrets that Plato probably didn't know of the exploits of the brave and skillful Artemisia who, according to Herodotus, distinguished herself in the expedition of Xerxes against Greece. Plato could have strengthened his argument by the pertinent example of the "courage, vigor, and prudence" of Zenobia if he could have quoted the original letter addressed by the Emperor Aurelian to the Roman Senate.[107] Plato turns to contemporary factual examples of the Scythian and Sarmaritan women to show that women are capable of efficient military service. But, according to Grote, he might well have used ancient legends which abounded in tales of aggressive women. The goddess Athene, patroness of Athens, was the very impersonation of "intelligent terror-striking might," constraining and subduing Ares himself. In a statement as forceful as any combative contemporary feminist, he reminds us that the goddess Enyo presided over war as much as did Ares. He points to Artemis who, though she only fought wild beasts, was equally formidable—"indefatigable as well as rapid in her movements—and as unerring with her bow, as Athene was irresistible with her spear."[108]

The point throughout is to show that there were abundant examples to embolden Plato in his affirmations of the female's capacity for warlike enterprise and laborious endurance. Grote, again like certain overzealous modern feminists, even recalls the legendary Amazons as examples that Plato might have seen as supporting his views. Although we know the Amazons to be legendary, Grote reminds us that the ancients believed their existence to be historical fact. They were thus influential on the Greek imagination, particularly because they were so familiar to the public through paintings and sculpture. The Amazons were in fact an extremely popular subject for sculpture. We learn from Pliny that since all the most distinguished sculptors executed versions of them, this was the only subject upon which a direct comparison could be made. Grote argues that the idea of women performing traditionally male roles would not have seemed outlandish to Plato. Although feminists today might interpret the statues as embodiments of the masculine fear of female power, Grote sees mythological examples as suggesting rational possibilities to the philosopher.[109] Grote points to a passage in the *Laws* to show that Plato complains bitterly of the repugnance felt even to the discussion of his modified proposals for sexual equality. Although it was contrary to current Athenian practice, Grote believed there were numerous reasons why it seemed both possible and desirable to the philosopher.

The chief purpose of Grote's discussion is to explain why Plato thought women could participate in active pursuits and why he might indeed be able to convince the more open-minded of his hearers. Grote goes to great lengths to show exactly how the usual relations of the sexes would be combated by Plato, giving the proposals the serious attention they deserve. He describes enthusiastically the muscular development and the rough and unadorned bodies of the female guardians. He speaks of the indiscriminate companionship, with perfect identity of treatment and manners between the two sexes from earliest infancy, the training of both together for the same public duties under constant supervision. The possibility that neither Strauss nor Bloom can countenance as anything but an ironic joke, Grote goes to great lengths to make convincing.

He concerns himself with the reforms in sexual practice that Plato suggests. He even tries to render imaginatively, through colorful descriptions, the way the strict regulation of exercise and diet, combined with monastic censorship, would place the sexual appetite under the ruler's control. He reminds us that in their proposals for social change, not only Plato, but Xenophon and Aristotle, looked to the example of Sparta. The Spartan way of life, strictly controlled and markedly different from the Athenian, was much admired by all the Greeks. Grote even discusses the question of abortion and infanticide, a practice we know existed in Sparta, without making any attempt, as many commentators have, to cover up what both Aristotle and Plato considered acceptable treatment of undesirable infants. Without condoning the specifics of the philosophers' views on the subject, Grote wishes to show the rational intent behind them. In doing so, he uses language consonant with that of current pro-abortion advocates. The rationale behind the philosophers' proposals is that "procreation ought to be a rational and advised act."[110] It should be governed by a forecast of the consequences not only to personal happiness, but also to the good of society.

Thus, Grote, unlike the overwhelming number of other commentators, 1) summarizes Plato's views sympathetically and accurately; 2) chooses his language carefully to avoid minimizing the novelty and importance of the proposals; and 3) disparages any appeal to what is "truly natural" as a legitimate ground for denying identity of role to women. His final conclusion is that a more egalitarian society is possible, but he finds a major difficulty with such utopian views. The problem is where will the motive, the demiurgic force, for instituting such reforms come from? Plato does not provide any source which will give such reforms their first impetus.[111] And, in my view, this question must still be of primary concern to feminists today.[112]

There is also one other commentator who presents an unbiased account of the proposals in Book V and in fact expresses even more outspoken enthusiasm for the "emancipation of women" than Grote. This is the viewpoint of Theodor Gomperz, whose four-volume work, *Greek Thinkers,* first appeared in Leipsig in the early 1890s.

Gomperz is not blind to Plato's prejudices and discusses the "mere pride of birth and rank" which influence him in the contempt for the lower orders which Gomperz, like so many of us, disapproves. Prophetic of the attack on Plato's overvaluation of unity, he notes the fact that Plato is free of the anxiety that has troubled some of the best men of the nineteenth century. That is, he underestimates the dangers of uniformity, of what Gomperz describes as "the Chinese ideal of making all people alike."[113] But, unlike Jowett, he does not use our Western liberal preference for individualism or diversity as an apology for maintaining separate and distinct occupations for women.

Instead, he stresses, like Grote, the examples known or believed to have existed of "community of women" and emphasizes that the paradoxes of today are the commonplaces of tomorrow. He calls for empirical tests of social reforms. With a refreshing sense of possibility lacking in all those writers who find it a violation of women's nature to perform certain tasks, Gomperz alone calls for empirical trials. He says that we require of deep-reaching innovations that they shall establish their viability and usefulness not solely by reasoning, but by actual experiment.[114]

Furthermore, he criticizes the argument of Aristotle that the world is now very old and had the realization of reforms like Plato's been possible they would surely have already occurred. With extended ethnographic and historical perspective such an argument is now far less appealing, Gomperz thinks. But he was writing about human possibilities at a time of great optimism; such optimism has undoubtedly been tempered in the twentieth century. Nevertheless, his warning against Aristotle's position on social change still applies. Such reasoning, he writes, is "the standing and staple argument of all conservative minds against subversive innovations."[115] And here again, Gomperz was prophetic. In Plato scholarship, such denial of female possibilities became dominant in the century following his work.

Unlike most commentators, Gomperz judges that the rationalistic utilitarian element is only an afterthought for "the aesthetic and ethical preference" which supplies the real motive power for the Platonic reforms. It is hard to resist the conclusion that it is Gomperz's zeal rather than Plato's that makes him overrate the Athenian's profemale sympathies. Gomperz writes that Plato desired the full and many-sided development of women's talents. He dreamt of their elevation from profound ignorance and subjection, bordering on servitude, to the power of knowledge and proud independence. Plato "felt the charm of the ideal type of woman which he had in his mind's eye," and which was rudimentally exhibited by Spartan women with their fine physical development and celebrated beauty. The proverbial boldness that came of Spartan semi-emancipation Plato wished to ennoble by a better education and to transfigure into "self-conscious dignity."[116] Gomperz imagines such considerations outweighed the rationalistic considerations Plato uses to support his proposals. Gomperz has perhaps imagined too freely. Self-conscious dignity and a dream based on a guiding vision of women is hard to reconcile with those traces of misogyny which are exhibited throughout the dialogues, or with the breeding arrangements, which some find "repulsively utilitarian."[117] Glowing statements about the physical and mental virtues of women simply do not exist in Plato.

To the modern-day feminist, Gomperz's enthusiasm is welcome with all its excesses. In considering the emancipation of women, he describes himself as turning from critic to eulogist. In following in Socrates' footsteps, Plato "has given utterance to the pure and complete truth, almost without admixture of error."[118] As we shall see, that small reservation that Gomperz sustains becomes the major complaint against Plato of the critics of the 1970s. Gomperz's own enthusiasm for Plato and for the idea of equality for women is almost unbounded. Gomperz does not gloss over the fact that the female is described as the relatively weaker sex. However, he explains that this relative weakness only appears on striking an average, since an arrangement of all men and all women by order of capacity would yield a highly diversified series. And qualitative differences that would affect roles do not exist.

Gomperz then launches into what can only be seen as a much needed corrective to this aspect of Plato's view. He writes:

> Even in respect of that average inferiority, it cannot as yet be regarded as established that, where intellectual gifts are concerned, it is an ultimate unalterable fact. On the other hand, the possibility is not excluded that a free field for the development of women's talents might bring to light average differences of even qualitative order. Only so much is certain, that these differences could never suffice to justify the limitations of callings for one half of the human race.[119]

I quote at length, because this is a view which does not surface again for close to eighty years.

Gomperz provides an eloquent reply to all those who have doubted women's capacity for genuine accomplishment. His answer to those who have observed in the past that intellectual creations of the first rank which demand exceptionally sustained concentration—in poetry, music, philosophy, or history—have not been produced by women, is convincing and still relevant to those who persist in such opinions today. This empirical rule, he says, has merely provisional validity and may at any moment be broken through by a brilliant exception. In narrative literature, he insists, women have in the last decades of the nineteenth century produced works that rival their male counterparts.[120] Further, women's presumed inferiority may well be due to the pressure of unfavorable circumstances rather than to any deficiency of talent.

Gomperz has his own vision of the charm of the new woman: "Their cheeks are bronzed with sport, they deliver lectures and take part in public meetings, they paint pictures and write books; many professions, in North America almost all, are open to them; and they are leaving farther and farther behind them the stage in which they were banished to the washtub and the needle, the kitchen and the nursery."[121]

In the light of "the feminine mystique" of the later forties and fifties, Gomperz's optimistic appraisal of developments in the United States turned out to be unwarranted. In his own country, the later acceptance by many of the Nazi view of women's role—"*Kinder, Küche, Kirche*"—show that he was far too sanguine about women's prospects.

Gomperz did see the interconnection between the retention of private families and the possibility of realizing Plato's ideal.[122] Unlike later feminists, however, he makes no suggestions for changing roles within the family, nor does he discuss the possibility of eliminating the nuclear family. Instead, he accepts the fact that, given the modern way of ordering the family, the division of labor which Plato generally supported but rejected in regard to the sexes is likely to obtain in most—though not necessarily in all—cases.

Therefore, though he applauds the bronze-cheeked lecturers, he explains that "nothing can be more natural" than that mothers, being kept at home by the care of their children, should devote themselves to household duties and other tasks like nursing which are suited to their degree of physical strength.[123] The naturalness to which he refers seems to mean only that such arrangements are reasonable; his words lack those overtones of biology with which we are now so familiar. For he stresses that in the highly civilized nations at the time he was writing the development was in the direction Plato desired. Like Ithurriague, he considers that a considerable part of Plato's demands have actually been fulfilled. But he does not accompany his rosy picture of progress with any such admonition to women not to overreach themselves. It is true that his view gives a sense of the inevitability of certain family arrangements. He makes no visionary prediction of men sharing in child care; nor does he suggest communal care of infants or the ill aged. Still, his voice is rare in a chorus of nay-sayers. (Even John Stuart Mill, whose pedigree as an early feminist is strong, has no greater confidence in the possibility of married women with children performing exactly the same tasks as men.)[124] In his Plato commentary, Gomperz may not proclaim the likelihood of complete realization of gender equality, but he at least allows for the possibility. And his message throughout is that women have done good work and achieved notable success in many spheres, whenever the accident of birth or the play of circumstances has presented them with the opportunity.

The last commentator I shall discuss is Adela M. Adam, the *only female* to write about the relevant section of Book V before the New Wave of commentators in the 1970s. Like Gomperz and Grote, she does not describe herself as a feminist. She does not even express an enthusiasm or crusading spirit comparable to theirs. But in her little-known book, published in 1913 to satisfy a demand she sees for "a clear account, intelligible to the plain man, of what Plato did in the moral and political sphere," she clearly favors many of the changes Plato proposes.[125] She shares with later feminists the belief that, despite the philosopher's intense conservatism in some respects, on the question of the education and duties of women "he was perhaps the most daring innovator the world has ever seen."[126]

For the first time, she calls attention to a discrepancy between Plato's professed program and the automatic bias of the Greek male. No previous commentator had noted this, nor does it become a major issue until sixty years later. A. M. Adam puts it forcefully: "It is easy to see that his intellectual conviction outruns his instinct." In discussing the *Laws,* she indicates that Plato "whenever he remembers his principles" actually means women to take a wider share in government.[127] This shows her awareness of the tension between Plato's professed desire for reform and other competing assumptions.

She also concludes, as does the most recent feminist writer on Plato's theory of education, that as the philosopher progressively developed his scheme he was plainly thinking of men guardians only in the *Republic.* He only remembers women when "he sharply reminds himself . . . that the fair images of Philosopher-Kings that he has been making represent also Philosopher-Queens."[128] To my knowledge, this is the first use of that corresponding form, "Philosopher-Queen," a term which might well have appeared earlier had there been many women scholars commenting on the text.[129] To guarantee the intended joint rule, such an expression is surely necessary, but so far as I can determine, the phrase, or its precise equivalent in any other language, does not occur before 1913. Various points of A. M. Adam's interpretation will be questioned later. She accepts that in Plato the best women are excelled by the best men; she doesn't even reserve the doubt expressed by some that it is only "highly unlikely" that the best *individual* could be female. In her attempt to garner enthusiasm for Plato's educational reforms, she may exaggerate in stating that women are to share with men the exact same responsibilities for bringing up children. But in general, she describes Plato's views in the *Republic* and the *Laws* more accurately than many of her male counterparts, and she repeatedly emphasizes their importance.

Nevertheless, Adam is not a feminist in the same sense that most of the commentators of the 1970s and 1980s use the term.[130] For her final word is that Plato's "half-unconscious" reservation of certain duties for women foreshadows very nearly the course that events are likely to take. And she makes no objection to this course. As the State takes over more and more the care and education of children and the morality of the sexes, women will increasingly take these positions. Nursing and social welfare are the kind of jobs that will always absorb the energies of most women "who have time to spare from their own families." It is only "when a woman *shows a special aptitude* for serving her country in some other way" (*my emphasis*), that Plato's claim that her power should be used is triumphantly vindicated. In other words, A. M. Adam does not call for the employment of women in non-traditional occupations, nor does she believe that this is the path women's struggles ought to take. She expresses no concern that Plato spoke of equality only for an elite group. She, too, assumes that only "gifted women" (as her better-known scholar husband first described them) would be interested in roles equal in status to men. But despite her reservations and her own modest ambitions, her views stand out against those of most of her male counterparts. She stresses that whatever gifts a woman has Plato rightly wishes to be turned to account for the common good. And she states unequivocally, "He sees that the work of bearing children to uphold the State in the next generation cannot possibly occupy a woman's whole life."[131]

2

The Resurgence of Interest in Philosopher-Queens

THE QUALITY OF THE NEW SCHOLARSHIP

After years of neglect and hostility to the proposals in Book V, a sudden interest developed in the issues. From 1970 onwards, numerous articles appeared in diverse publications. The contrast between the previous marginal treatment and the new attention and recurrent discussion is striking. No doubt this new interest is partly attributable to the appearance on the scene of female commentators. There *were* isolated women classicists writing on the *Republic* earlier, but unlike Adela M. Adam, these few women scholars, like their male colleagues, paid little or no attention to the question of female equality. Thus, for example, in a 1950 book concerned solely with Plato's theory of Philosopher-Kings, Rosamond Sprague never even raises the question of the possible effect on the theory of the presence of Philosopher-Queens, nor even acknowledges their proposed presence.[1]

The cause of the flurry of interest, then, is not only the advent of female scholars. More important is the development of an organized women's movement with vocal representatives within universities and the concomitant desire by feminists of both sexes to understand past inequities and redress previous wrongs. Today, it is more difficult for scholars, regardless of sex, to reveal anti-female bias without a defensive posture. Women scholars who previously might have preferred, whether consciously or not, to ignore the issue so that they would in no way stand out from or alienate their male colleagues, are today freer from such concerns. The new climate for younger scholars has eliminated some of the need for such unconscious self-censorship and protective coloration.

An interest in the history of feminism has arisen and such investigations have become more respectable. Unfortunately, concern with women's issues has also become more fashionable in some circles. People sometimes chose to write on the topic because it was timely whether or not they had any background or preparation for such studies. Consequently, there is a great discrepancy between the thorough, painstaking works of past scholars and the open partisanship of some current discussions of the *Republic.*

One serious failing which I find in many of the post-1970 articles is their discontinuity with the work of the past. Many display a basic a-historicism in their approach. At the same time, they also fail to refer to the efforts of their contemporaries on the same topics. Without investigating, many write as if they have suddenly discovered what no one else ever noticed. This stance is markedly different from that of previous commentators who, when dealing with most issues in the *Republic,* foster the sense of a continuing dialogue. Earlier scholars usually show great respect for the work of others, even when they disagree sharply.

Along with the disadvantages of ignoring past scholarship, there are undeniably also certain advantages. Writers can no longer presume their audience to have a general acquaintance with Greek, Latin, ancient history, or even major Western literary works. They therefore have a chance of reaching more readers if they eschew footnotes and other scholarly apparatus. Thus, even when the writer herself has not looked into previous work, her popularization of the issues might still be beneficial. Some of the articles of the 1970s, though adding little to the on-going scholarly enterprise, have no doubt provided a service to interested readers who have neither the background nor the inclination to deal with the details of previous interpretations. A further advantage for the young scholar of today who is willing to ignore past views is the elimination of that paralysis which can result from being overwhelmed by the best of, or at any rate the bulk of, what has already been thought and said.

Whatever the advantages, the danger remains of producing work representative of two unfortunate extremes. Much of the publication of the 1970s alternates between two opposing shortcomings. One the one hand, we find large-scale conclusions which in effect amount to "rediscovering the wheel," and on the other hand, narrow logical analysis which is trivial, will be read by few, and has no influence. Among the articles I shall now examine in detail are pronouncements made as if they were original discoveries, when in fact they are only restatements with a history in the scholarly literature of rebuttal and reinforcement. Others offer narrow linguistic analysis which, even when correct, adds little to the understanding of Plato or to the discussion of the best deployment of women. Scholarship which avoids these extremes, which shows familiarity with previous work in many languages and sheds new light on important issues, is relatively rare.

Besides the a-historicism, there is also a tendency to use language far less precisely than do the scholars of the previous hundred years. Of the commentators I have already discussed, few, with the notable exception of Walter Pater, can be accused of general vagueness of thought or language. The great Germans—Zeller, Ritter, Friedlander—on the whole reason clearly and use concepts with admirable precision, except perhaps in those few instances where unconscious prejudice intervenes. Many of the committed feminist commentators use language imprecisely and do not carry through on the philosophical and logical implications of their assertions. Admittedly, a delicate balancing act is required to avoid pedantic trivialization, to offer important new insights, and yet to use language, logic, and factual detail carefully.

This ideal of scholarship has been difficult to meet in the last ten years. Some of the reasons for the difficulty relate directly to two important issues Plato himself addressed. The first involves that democracy he deplored, for, along with the enormous benefits democratization has conferred on those of us of the lower bronze class, it has also necessarily weakened the structures which supported the great scholarship of the past. The second issue is that of the equal education for qualified women, which Plato was the first to advocate. It, too, has had an indirect, but nonetheless, negative impact on the former conditions for scholarly excellence. No matter how imperative and just these two connected reforms, their increasing realization has involved certain "trade-offs."

The learning of the great classicists was primarily acquired at elite schools. The time required for their scholarly pursuits was provided by institutions which did not demand that the scholar meet classes and deliver prepared lectures several times a week, as is often the case in the universities of today. In the more hierarchical pre-1970 societies, professors were accorded respect and recognition in many segments of the community. Now, scholars often must work without strong institutional support, with the threat of "publish or perish," or more pointedly, "tenure or trauma." The community's evaluation of the scholar in America, at any rate, has measurably changed. Whereas being a professor was considered among the top status jobs in polls of the 1950s, recent studies show the public's rating of the university teacher has dropped markedly.

Formerly, a scholar could count on his wife to tend to his needs, protect him from interruptions, and value his work, whether she understood it or not. Far fewer scholars today can claim such a devoted spouse. A scholar's wife, even if her inclinations in this transitional period were to follow the older pattern, has been influenced by the media and other social pressures to consider it undesirable to live vicariously through her husband's work. Thus, even if she is not economically constrained to work, nor motivated toward an independent career, she is still unlikely to perform the old jobs as willingly as the "helpmeets" whom Jowett praised. (The female scholar, of course, has always had to function without such a wife.) Such helpmates formerly played a crucial role in providing the atmosphere for scholarship. The value of a spouse's services and support, whether provided without enthusiasm or freely offered, cannot be overestimated.

There are other problems specific to the female scholar who is beginning to attain a greater measure of equality in the university. Side by side with her new status is a new psychological burden. Women in the United States, at any rate, are influenced by the myth that they can "have it all." They are led to believe that they can enjoy the satisfactions of child-rearing, domestic activities, and some of the leisure activities of an earlier middle-class mother while excelling in intellectual pursuits. All of this is assumed to be possible without any cataclysmic changes in the social structure.[2] British and American female scholars, hoping to produce a body of work like Taylor's or Bosanquet's, also experience other strong pressures. They are expected to provide for the emotional and intellectual needs of 2.2 children, maintain their sexual attractiveness, succeed at work so that the laurels of the guardians in Plato's scheme will be awarded to them, and perform at least half of the manual labor necessary for maintaining a household.[3]

Nor do single scholars, male or female, often have the same background of support and intellectual conversation once available in the rooms at college or dinner at High Table. The trusty servant and university-connected amanuensis are not available. Scholars may have the compensations of computers, typewriters, and interlibrary loan facilities, but they rarely have a partner of the same or opposite sex who is willing to take on the chores which would leave him or her free for months of uninterrupted study.

Still, in some fields, first-rank scholarship has been produced in the 1970s, and it is surely unfair to juxtapose the life work of a Victorian scholar against a brief article in a little-known journal. Furthermore, even if the proliferation of periodicals and low-cost editions has resulted in a "rush to print" and a lowering of standards, these results must be balanced against pronounced benefits. For we cannot forget that such changes have also been responsible for the possibility of participation in the life of the mind by a far larger percentage of the population. Concurrent with this broadened participation has been that equalizing of opportunity and expectations for females which has led to the raising of new questions for the first time in twenty-three hundred years about the Platonic proposals.

THE FIRST AWARENESS OF PREVIOUS BIAS

An important characteristic of the post-1970 scholarship is the dawning realization of the previous hostility to the idea of sex equality in the *Republic*, along with attempts to account for this hostility. Christine Pierce opens up a Pandora's box—to use the misogynist myth for my own purposes—by calling attention to that hostility for the first time in print. She finds that much Platonic scholarship has been a set of "variations on the theme of women's essential inferiority." Commentators have faulted Plato for failing to consider the necessary consequences of that inferiority in developing the social, economic, and political structure of a society. Pierce notes that few have been aware of what an ingenious critique Book V offers of the main assumptions used repeatedly in arguments against equality. Pierce focuses on this Platonic critique of the ideas of "women's place" and "man's competence," introducing a new theme which, with its variations, appears repeatedly in the scholarship of the next ten years.

Covering approximately ten scholars who have been hostile to Plato's proposals, she begins the process of countering their incredulity and disapproval. Pierce is particularly effective in answering the arguments of Leo Strauss. Her aim is to undermine his contention that Plato wished us to realize the impossibility of the creation of a just city and used the clearly false notion of the equality of the sexes as one of the indications that the *Republic* is indeed an impossible abstraction.

Like most feminist commentators after her, Pierce also finds the interpretation of Allan Bloom (who accepts the Strauss thesis) particularly offensive. Opposition to Bloom is likely to continue, particularly if he persists in defending and expanding his objections to sexual equality, as he has been inclined to do in the fifteen years since the publication of his highly influential "Interpretive Essay." Pierce marshals several arguments against Bloom's belief that Plato in fact did realize women's inferiority, but merely fabricated a view of their competence to cover up the truth that women are placed among the guardians only for reproductive purposes. Without realizing that Bloom is not alone in this view, she offers an interesting rebuttal, one not stressed by scholars who have tangled with Bloom after her.

Instead of the more basic argument I have outlined above against Bloom (that Plato's entire concept of justice would be undermined if women were allowed to do work for which they were not suited), she suggests another line of reasoning. She says a myth to support assigning the same social role to women would not only have "devastating social consequences."[4] By subverting competence, it would run counter to the obvious and, to her, plausible purpose of Plato's other myths. She correctly observes that the allegory of the metals is designed to help people face up to an accurate assessment of their abilities. But a fabrication about women's nature would have a very different function, since it would lead people to believe women are capable, when they are not.

In criticizing previous commentators, Pierce reminds us that philosophers have often been accused of defending as eternal truths the customs and assumptions of their own societies. Plato and Aristotle argued in defense of slavery, and Kant considered Euclidean space a logical necessity. She offers tentatively that this same tendency may pervade philosophical scholarship, "the tendency to superimpose the mores and beliefs of one's own society on figures of philosophy's past."[5]

Thus, Pierce effectively introduces the idea that an examination of previous views on the *Republic* may show the extent to which beliefs about the intrinsic inequality of the sexes has permeated our own society. She also issues an important *caveat.* She warns that anyone who thinks the solution to current problems in sex equality can be worked out mechanically, i.e., "without changing hearts and minds," can be seen to be mistaken if they consider Plato commentators. She writes, "The length to which 'pure' scholars, rational men are driven shows that accepting women as persons requires more than philosophical justification."[6]

In the final analysis, Pierce considers the passages in the *Republic* about men and women having identical natures and meriting identical roles to be "clear and straightforward." Therefore, the commentators' questionable interpretations *may* be due to the intrusion of their own outlooks. On the other hand, my contention is that the passages themselves are not entirely clear and consistent, as the discussions of commentators after Pierce amply show. In my opinion, these very inconsistencies and ambiguities foster the projections of scholars' own attitudes onto the work, a practice as characteristic of the feminist commentators who follow Pierce as of the hostile interpreters of the past hundred years.

INCONSISTENCIES IN PLATO: WAS HE A FEMINIST?

A second major characteristic of the new scholarship is the focus on the web of previously unnoticed inconsistencies in Plato's total view of women. Commentators distinguish at least four different ways in which Plato's views are inconsistent or contradictory. And they take their stand on whether Plato can accurately be described as a "feminist" depending on how they view these inconsistencies. Those who see the inconsistencies as trivial embrace Plato as their champion. But there are many others who find the contradictions irreconcilable and adamantly reject any classification of Plato as a woman's liberationist.

For the first time, commentators call attention to the sharp discrepancy between the misogyny scattered throughout the dialogues and Plato's claim that both sexes have the same nature. This discrepancy they find even within the *Republic* itself. They also note the contrast between arrangements for women in the ideal city and those in the second-best (or more correctly, third) actual city of the *Laws*.[7] This contrast, unlike the others, has been mentioned frequently by previous scholars. To a man, they have, of course, preferred the arrangements in the *Laws*.

Feminist commentators discover a third pattern of inconsistency between the attitudes revealed in the myths of the *Symposium* and the *Timaeus*, when contrasted with the strain of relative egalitarianism of the *Republic* and the *Laws* taken together. Establishing this inconsistency involves an exploration of that question, which has long been of interest to scholars, of the relation of the Platonic myths to the philosopher's actual views. Here, the issue is his true view on women's nature; and a consideration of the myths in this connection becomes important for the first time in the commentary of the 1970s.

The final ambiguity writers deal with is the more subtle, but equally troublesome, question of how to reconcile Plato's belief that men and women are equal in nature and yet women are always inferior in capacity. The adequacy of the previously propounded solution that the two sexes are not different in kind, but only in degree, becomes a major point of controversy in current scholarship. The problem becomes how one can speak of Plato as a feminist—as most previous commentators have—when he proclaimed the class of women inferior.

By the mid-1960s, H. D. Rankin had already introduced the question of troubling inconsistencies, although feminist commentators do not seem to be aware of his efforts. In his book on Plato's treatment of the individual, Rankin does not specifically identify himself as a feminist, and speaks more dispassionately than later writers. But he notes with regret that there is "little stability" in Plato's attitudes and focuses on several kinds of inconsistencies, including the fact that throughout the dialogues places exist where women are classed as natural inferiors, with children, slaves, and foolish people in general.[8]

Rankin supports Plato's purpose, which he sees as the attempt to make the women guardians independent and as free as possible, "subjects" rather than objects. He refers to Simone de Beauvoir's idea that relations between the sexes suffer because women have seen themselves both as "subjects" and as "objects" and regrets that de Beauvoir did not discuss Plato's ideas on the topic. He writes that "it is not surprising, and not at all undesirable, that they should seem temperamentally similar to men." I am assuming that he means here that neither Plato nor Rankin regrets the loss of sharp distinctions between the personality traits valued in men and those valued in women. This contrasts markedly with Jowett, Wilamowitz, et al., who deplore the loss of "femininity" in the guardians. Rankin, using existentialist terminology, instead applauds the great advance of the idea of female guardians over previous notions of "women's situation in the world." He laments (as some later enthusiasts neglect to do) the sad discrepancy between the *phylakes* and the traditional subservience which Plato evidently imagined for the lowest grade of women in the *polis.* Although he says we should not overlook the inconsistencies, Rankin finds that Plato's ideas, on the whole, compare favorably with twentieth-century attempts "to rationalize the balance of rights" between the sexes.[9]

In the commentary of the 1970s, the inconsistencies take center stage, with writers falling into two opposed camps. There are those who defend Plato vociferously and others who see him as just another woman-hater, part of a chain of philosophers from the pre-Socratics to the mid-twentieth-century metaphysician

Paul Weiss, who advises in his book on the philosophy of sport that women be viewed as "truncated males."[10]

In the first group are writers like Abigail Rosenthal who declare that the feminism of Plato is exemplary and unparalleled in philosophy or political theory.[11] Martha Lee Osborne also falls into this group. In her title, she unequivocally states that anatomy does *not* spell destiny in Plato. Biology, she says, is irrelevant to Plato's views because he is a metaphysical idealist in whose work "the soul is celebrated at the expense of the body."[12] Therefore, one would expect that in utopia the destiny of women as well as men would be determined by their sovereign souls. Plato's view of the place of women in an *ideal* society did not change at all.

One of Osborne's chief aims is to refute the dubious attempt of Anne Dickason to explain the differences between the *Republic* and the *Laws* on the basis of the alleged biological views in Plato's myths.[13] She justifiably objects to the use of the famous myth on the origin of the sexes advanced by Aristophanes in the *Symposium*, as if it were Plato's own view. And she likewise rejects Dickason's use of the speech of Timaeus on women's inferiority, showing that here again one cannot ignore the dramatic nature of the dialogue or neglect the possible relevance of the fact that the speaker is Pythagorean. In the end, Osborne insists that what is remarkable about the city of the *Laws* is not how far short of the ideal it falls, but how close it comes.

Christine G. Allen also argues that Plato was "thoroughly consistent in his theories on women."[14] She finds a single view underlying all this work, but contrary to Osborne she thinks one can use selected myths to resolve any apparent inconsistencies. Her theory is that Plato always believed not only in the equality of souls, but in their pre-existence and immortality. Her argument rests on the evidence of certain "central" myths, though she is aware that some of the myths must be disregarded. That is, she takes over the idea of "levels of myths" from Friedlander, borrowing his tripartite scheme in which the higher levels "render intelligible the mysterious aspects of life" and "create a new kind of truth."[15] But she then takes the *Timaeus* myth of incarnations and upward striving of the soul *literally*, to show what Plato "really thought" about women. In my opinion Allen's belief that

Plato's consistent view was that women are equal to men in their immortal souls but only an "inferior kind of incarnation" presents great difficulties. Statements in the *Republic* that the *physis* of men and women is the same, and that some women have natural aptitudes superior to some men for some jobs, simply cannot be reconciled with her theory.

The classicist Dorothea Wender also belongs in the Plato-as-feminist camp, but she does not attempt to reconcile inconsistencies. Instead, she tells us that although Plato was indeed a paedophile and a misogynist, he is also a feminist whose proposals are "delightfully radical!"[16] In order to describe Plato as a feminist, she must, however, arbitrarily adopt a definition which differs from that in most dictionaries, or from what I consider a general understanding of the term.

For my purposes in this study I have assumed that a feminist must at the very least 1) consider it an important and disturbing fact about all previous social organization that women have been oppressed, and 2) propose that henceforth complete gender equality should prevail. I have intentionally not attempted to formulate any more complete definition here, choosing instead to focus on how recent writers on Plato have construed the term. The various shades of opinion among feminists have been well categorized by Alison Jaggar, who describes the different programs embraced by liberal feminists, radical feminists, Marxist feminists, lesbian separatists and Socialist feminists.[17] All of these would find Wender's definition unsatisfactory.

In her otherwise informative and amusing article she chooses to define a feminist as anyone who believes that women should be given a better place in society, legally, politically, or professionally. To be a feminist, one need only profess that women are entitled to a position which "more closely approximates that held by men of the same class." A feminist, according to Wender, need not necessarily believe that women are equal to men "*in any way*" (*my emphasis*).[18] This seems an odd use of the term. One can hardly deny that it is often used vaguely, although rarely I think to refer to the indefinite, and even contemptuous, meliorism that Wender allows. For she describes Plato as a feminist, even though she maintains a view echoed by later commentators: "Plato does not promise that women are equal to men—he cannot; it seems to him they are not."[19] Nevertheless, she describes him as a feminist since he does propose complete equality of opportunity. In fact, with the abolition of all domestic work, he goes even further in this direction than many feminists today would go. Although he weakens the feminist program in his second-best state, the treatment of women still remains the most radical part of the proposed constitution. There is also evidence for feminism in the other dialogues. In short, Plato did not like women, but he favored their emancipation.

In examining what might be called the New Wave of Plato commentary, it gradually becomes apparent that, like the proverbial glass of water that can be seen as half full or half empty, Plato's proposals can legitimately be viewed in opposing ways. Those who stress the egalitarian strain see the glass as half full. That is, though now aware that the philosopher's proposals are incomplete, they believe we ought to accentuate the positive. Thus, W. W. Fortenbaugh, in reacting to the denunciation of Plato by a fellow classicist, offers a warning. He writes that we can only obscure the significance of Plato's approach by "an excessive concern with the possibility of latent misogyny."[20] It is important to remember that in the previous hundred years of commentary not a single word has been said about *any* anti-female attitudes in Plato. Although some writers did refer to the unequal status of Athenian women, they judge Plato to be admirably aware of female suppression and even excessive in his zeal to remedy their deprivation. Thus, the sudden pointing to what has always been there to see, like the revelation of the ruler's nakedness in the tale of the emperor's new clothes, has much value.

Brian Calvert is a feminist who wisely takes this dual possibility into account in his interpretation. In the end, he believes that Plato was primarily pro-female and reads the passages in Book V as the strongest expression of Plato's sympathy with the feminist cause. Writing in the context of the new scholarship, Calvert sees the need to refurbish Plato's image. He attempts to clarify how we should understand those passages which cast doubt on whether Plato should be regarded as a champion of the equality of the sexes. Plato, he says, was operating on two levels at the same time. In the dialogues, these two become "unconsciously mingled." It should not be surprising that someone who is trying to formulate and give moral justification for a revolutionary idea should find it difficult to liberate himself from the traditional views. Calvert finds that on the rigorous and philosophical level Plato is completely egalitarian. There is "a lot of backsliding," however, in which he is guilty of the most obvious male chauvinism.[21]

This defense strikes a completely new note in the history of Plato studies. It is a view which could only have surfaced at a time when the Freudian notion of unconscious motivation is a commonplace and when agitation for women's rights and "consciousness raising" for men had already occurred. Although I would argue that even on the philosophical level the description of female nature as "equal in kind but not in degree" is not rigorously egalitarian, Calvert surely deserves enormous credit. As a male philosopher in a field which has systematically excluded women for centuries, his awareness of and desire to explain inconsistencies is highly praiseworthy. I wholeheartedly applaud his recognition of the difficulties men face in freeing themselves from pervasive sexist attitudes absorbed, as it were, with their mother's milk!

Besides these serious attempts to defend Plato and argue for the strength of his feminism, numerous well-intentioned, but poorly argued and confused pronouncements on Plato's glorious advocacy of women's rights have appeared. Among the excesses are the statements of the editor Joseph Ghoughassian who says that feminists may rejoice in what Plato said about their fortunes. In fact, it is his work that has kept the feminist program alive and is actually *responsible for* our current ability "to rethink the roles and images of the sexes." If it weren't for Plato, the Aristotelian view would have eclipsed "the rebellious consciousness of the feminist movements that surfaced throughout the centuries."[22] No attempt is made to show any causal influence for Plato's work on such movements. In fact, I have been unable to locate any evidence whatsoever that the passages in Book V to which Ghoughassian refers had any influence at all until quite recently on the thinking of men or women, except perhaps the negative one of keeping the *Republic* from being translated.

Ghoughassian thinks we should excuse Plato for thanking the gods that he wasn't created a woman because he left a "vast literature on women" to later generations. Of course, Ghoughassian is misinformed. We have no record of Plato expressing gratitude for not being born a woman. He is probably referring to the account of Diogenes Laertius of a story attributed by some to Thales, but by other biographers to Socrates. Furthermore, there is of course no vast literature on women left by Plato. There are numerous other confusions and misstatements not worth dwelling on except to point up the dangers of searching for confirmation in ancient thinkers for currently fashionable views which coincide with one's own.[23]

At the same time that Ghoughassian is touting Plato's influence, another editor is including him as an *unsung* champion of women. Noting that Xanthippe is practically a synonym for a shrewish wife, Mary Cohart finds it particularly ironic that Plato attributed his own ideas on equality to Socrates.[24] She makes no attempt to assimilate any of the scholarship on the actual views of the historical Socrates. This lack of concern for accurate historical research reaches absurd heights in a popular book called *The First Sex.* In the author's attempt to show that a matriarchy once existed, she distorts history to a bizarre extent by making it seem that the projected city in the *Laws* actually existed. She cites the Platonic proposals for female guardians, magistrates, and priests as if such a society had actually existed in the ancient world.[25] Such disservices to scholarship are all the more alarming since, unlike most of the scholarly articles I am considering (which are on the whole accurate and carefully reasoned), these textbook introductions and popular works of propaganda are more likely to reach a wide audience.

In opposition to this group of informed and misinformed writers who applaud Plato's feminism, is an equally diverse and vocal group of dissenters. These range from those who consider Plato among the worst of male chauvinists to others who would grant him some credit, but believe that on balance he does not deserve the accolades he has been receiving in the last ten years. The scientist Richard C. Lewontin, who has devoted much thought and energy to women's rights, even describes Plato's discussion in Book V as the earliest one in which intellectuals explain to one another why affirmative action just doesn't work in the academy.[26] He says that Plato ran an academy even more male-biased than its modern equivalent. As a means of highlighting the faulty arguments of male academics today, Lewontin says of Plato, "I suppose he searched for women candidates but none were suitable."[27] With admirable intentions, he misinterprets the nature of "marriages" between the guardians. Unfairly, but probably only half-seriously, he tells us that in reading the description of guardians and their wives he is reminded of his housemaster and his wife, "an educated and cultured woman who presided at the tea table while talking of Michelangelo."[28]

Behind the sarcasm, Lewontin clearly considers it important to claim Plato as a forerunner of those contemporary academics who, while paying lip service to meritocracy, continue the present discriminatory situation and mistakenly believe it to reflect the actual lack of merit among women.[29]

Martha Nussbaum, though she is well aware of current discrimination, defends Plato eloquently. She says that Plato did not favor "affirmative action" only because Athenian society was so profoundly unequal that women could not be expected to overcome their disadvantages. Republic VII, she points out, contains a devastating indictment of this society "not least of the way in which it neglects and/or corrupts the capabilities of its women." The only way to rectify the situation would be to rear human beings *de novo* in a way in which they had never been reared before. Then the remaining differences in physical function would no longer be judged as linked to intellectual capacity. And in working toward such a society today she thinks women can demand consideration on an equal basis, "asking those who assess our credentials to 'look to that city and constitute themselves as its citizens,' Rep. 592B." But Lewontin still prefers to see the glass as more than half empty and refers to Plato's use of the "sex-biased form 'guardian's women' " as an indication of the asymmetry Plato assumed between the sexes.[30]

Another of those who disparage Plato is Elizabeth Janeway, the author of a popular feminist book intriguingly titled *Powers of the Weak.* On the subject of Plato, she is a purveyor of misinformation. Unlike Lewontin, who shows an impressive knowledge of the *Republic,* she seems to have no direct acquaintance with Plato's work at all, but nevertheless describes him as a major villain. Without referring to any Platonic text herself, she quotes a secondary source on slavery and political power, offers an out-of-context paraphrase, and evidently finds Plato virtually indistinguishable from Aristotle in calling for the obedience of the masses.[31] She mentions the concept of Philosopher-Kings. But then, although her book is about the age-old powerlessness of women, she completely neglects to mention that Plato wanted to include an equal number of women among the powerful.

In contrast, the knowledgeable classicist Sarah Pomeroy bases her dissent on careful textual analysis. She concludes that although Plato may seem revolutionary in comparison with the prevailing Greek misogyny, scholars who have hailed him as a believer in the equality of the sexes are mistaken. The truth is that he never intended women to be equal in status. In fact, one can tell from Plato's diction that he is "incapable" of seeing women as equal. In elaborating on what she refers to as Plato's lack of capacity, she states that "he could not, or did not wish to free himself from the Athenian prejudice which treated women legally as perpetual minors."[32] Pomeroy offers no further clarification of the distinction between incapacity and unwillingness or disinclination. According to her, Plato "couldn't conceive of women living without male tutelage." Furthermore, Plato "tends to" classify the women with the children, since in seven out of nine passages, possession of women and children are considered simultaneously.

In Pomeroy's eagerness to emphasize the anti-feminist aspect, she downplays the evidence for the existence of contradictory tendencies in Plato. She does not allow for Plato's being in two minds on the subject, as he was on other issues.[33] She does not emphasize the possibility of a philosopher consciously and genuinely choosing one attitude toward women, while unconsciously clinging to an alternative view. In short, she seeks no explanation like Calvert's for Plato's wavering and ambivalence. She seems unaware that her claim that Plato *could not conceive* of complete equality requires stronger evidence than she presents. Her mere indication of contradictions, which show that Plato in fact *did not* consistently maintain a plan for complete equality throughout the relevant passages, is insufficient to support her charge.

This is not to deny the existence of those contradictions that male commentators overlooked for hundreds of years. In the 1970s, several commentators have found many residual inequities which escaped previous writers. For example, Pomeroy is not alone in pointing out that Plato nowhere describes the predictable consequences of wife-sharing, which would be the "sharing of husbands." Many now notice, too, that rewards of more frequent intercourse are offered solely to the bravest men, displaying unequal treatment. But of course none of these anomalies demonstrate that Plato could not conceive of another kind of woman. As many of the earlier commentators pointed out, he had legendary models in Amazons and goddesses who lived without male tutelage. And the fact remains that he actually did conceive of the idea of women guardians who perform the same tasks as men.

Much of Pomeroy's argument turns on the use of the Greek word *koinōnia,* a term which refers to common, or public, affairs, property, or acts. She chooses to stress that Plato describes the common holding of women as *koinōnia,* which is the term used for property in Athenian legal documents.[34] Although this legal use is undoubtedly frequent, Pomeroy perhaps overstates her case. The adjectival form appears at the outset of the discussion in the proverb used by Euripides and others: *koina ta philōn (Republic,* V, 449c), which translates as "common are the things of friends." As is the case with *ktesis,* and for that matter "acquisition," "having" or "possessing" in English, you can both acquire and possess knowledge as well as objects. Ideas, as well as property, can be common to friends. Aeschylus says, "Fortune is a common thing."[35] Fortenbaugh, who challenges Pomeroy's view, is right that there are many kinds of *koinōnia,* and that Socrates must make clear what sort of commonality exists between male and female guardians.[36]

To be entirely fair, Pomeroy would have to admit at the very least that Plato uses the term in more than one sense. As Fortenbaugh says, the sense of legal possession does not appear in Socrates' important final summary. There, he is clearly referring to the *koinōnia* of men and women to education, children, and guardianship. Women will watch and hunt together with men, generally sharing (*koinōneia*) all things in every way. This does seem to be a *koinōnia* of partnership rather than an arrangement of captive property.[37]

My point is not that Plato never lapses into language and policies which countervene his plan for complete identity of role. I am not even sure what it would mean to say that such backsliding was inevitable, that he was "incapable" of doing otherwise. Nor do I wish to detract from the credit due Pomeroy for pointing out the pervasiveness of misogyny in the classical philosophers. I want only to suggest that Pomeroy is overzealous in her attempt to discredit totally Plato's praiseworthy attempts at equalizing the roles of the best and the brightest of both genders.

Marylin B. Arthur is equally eager to combat the idea that Plato's proposals are an example of liberated thinking. The equality of the sexes really "entailed" the very different idea of "holding wives and children in common." Women, she says, were to be held in common by the men of the class as a whole; they are thus "the exchange objects." Like Pomeroy, she refers to the idea of *koinōnia* and tells us that the proverb "friends' possessions are held in common" refers to a system of free exchange within a restricted group. Arthur compares such a system of free exchange unfavorably with Homer's picture of married life in the *Odyssey.* She describes Penelope and Odysseus as sharing their thoughts as they share their household.[38] I cannot see how the relationship of Penelope, who sat spinning and warding off suitors while Odysseus roamed, can serve as a prototype for any kind of desirable marriage. As the historian M. I. Finley reminds us, more often than not, Penelope was omitted from Odysseus' image of the home he longed for. According to Finley, Homer fully revealed what remained true for the whole of antiquity, that women were naturally inferior and therefore limited to producing offspring and performing household duties, while meaningful attachments took place between men.[39] The relation between Odysseus and Penelope is certainly not a relation between equals. For me, the Platonic plan of men and women ruling equally, studying and exercising together, still seems preferable to the model of Penelope waiting patiently while Odysseus wandered.

Julia Annas also tells us that it is quite wrong to think of Plato as the first feminist. His arguments are unacceptable to a feminist and the proposals made in Book V are irrelevant to the contemporary debate. She is not satisfied with Plato's assertion that there is no civic pursuit belonging to a woman as such, or to a man as such. Since he offered no trace of an argument against the existence of "specifically male competences," his presentation is decisively lacking.[40] For a feminist, this issue must be uppermost.

Annas' view is that anyone acquainted with the modern literature will realize that those objecting to the idea that men and women should share all roles are "not very worried" about whether there are some jobs that only women are suited for.[41] Since these are less well paid and less prestigious jobs, the antifeminist is not concerned with them. Opponents of feminism are interested solely in those jobs for which only men are suited. But Annas neglects the fact that in hard economic times men *are* interested in jobs traditionally held by females, and furthermore, many females need and desire blue collar jobs. A feminist emphasis, it seems to me, must involve the breaking down of all gender designations as guarantees of or barriers to job competency.

As we have seen, Plato's discussion is directed toward showing that women have no special competence in, for example, cooking. In the modern world, cooking at the professional level has been traditionally male and feminists are still working to open up opportunities in this field. The decisive issue does not seem to me to be the need for arguments against special competences for either group. It is true that Plato offers his male audience empirical examples to show that women have no monopoly on ability in any area. One can sympathize with Annas' perceptions, since Plato's tone of "men can do anything women can do—better" (to invert the heroine's claim in the musical comedy song) is undeniable in Book V. Nevertheless, she undervalues the importance of his overall attempts to demonstrate that biological differences are irrelevant to all but reproductive activities.

In my view, the question of whether women have innate special excellences is very important indeed; the fact that Plato denied the existence of such excellences has great significance. For the history of Plato scholarship shows how frequently the argument of women's special abilities has been used as a justification for keeping them out of traditionally male fields. Whatever the logical weaknesses of such arguments, their repetition has had a deleterious effect. A condescending insistence that women are specially endowed for jobs connected with child care or nurturing has conveyed the message that since ladies do these things so much better than men they ought to stick to those areas. Plato's attempt to disqualify such arguments is therefore more important to feminism than Annas allows.

She believes that historically the main objections to attempts by women to enter hitherto male professions, or obtain allegedly male rights like the vote, have been based on the argument that there are certain activities for which only men are suited. The argument today is that the difference in men's intelligence militates against women having serious careers comparable to men's. But in my view, the argument also still revolves around whether women have special abilities.

Anthropologists, sociobiologists, and other social scientists continue to assert that women are biologically primed for nurturing roles. They should therefore choose careers which will utilize their allegedly innate skills in interpersonal relations. As I shall discuss in my final chapter, some modern thinkers now call for the placing of women in roles where their supposed collaborative style and special peace-keeping abilities are essential. Thus, the assertion of special competencies is used to suggest that women in positions of power would perform better in solving national and international disputes and even be more effective in preventing nuclear war and guaranteeing the survival of the human race. Whether or not one finds such arguments convincing, the discussion is certainly relevant to feminism. Although Annas is correct that claiming specific competences for men undermines women's demands for equality, Plato's arguments against specific competences for women are surely equally relevant to the continuing debate.

Many current feminists would insist that fathers must be seen to be equally competent for the task of caring for children. The suggestion that women are biologically, psychologically, or intellectually better suited to raising children is an important stumbling block to the restructuring of family life which many feminists see as essential to their gaining full equality.

Annas' article is carefully argued and, unlike many others, draws on the work of previous commentators, carrying on the tradition of scholarship as a continuing dialogue. But in the end, her demand that Plato, in order to be a forerunner of women's liberation, must have precisely the same concept of justice as fairness as she (and many, though not all, contemporary feminists) seems to me unreasonable. Annas says that Plato is not at all concerned with women's desires or needs. He doesn't care whether their present roles frustrate them "or whether they will lead more satisfying lives as guardians than as housebound drudges."[42] Plato's arguments are authoritarian rather than liberal and far from the arguments that women should have equal opportunity because otherwise they lead stunted and unhappy lives and lack the means for self-development.

But this is to say that, given Plato's views of justice for human beings, Plato *a priori* could not have been advancing feminist aims. It is to define feminism so that only the moral aim of "self-development" or her own view of justice as fairness is compatible with it. This is not only far from Wender's extremely broad definition of the term, but also contrary to other more limited, but equally valid, concepts of feminism, including those compatible with various versions of utilitarianism.[43] Plato does not directly address the question of whether women will be happier as guardians, any more than he asks directly whether men will be happier. In fact, he knows that, given conventional views of what provides satisfaction, a good deal of persuasion and reinforcement will be necessary to convince men to embrace such an austere existence. Plato assumes that if all citizens of the *polis* are doing what they do best, they will, by being useful and living harmoniously, attain the highest happiness.

Why can't genuine feminists base their convictions on the belief that the subjection of women is wrong because in the long run it is harmful to all humanity? Surely feminists *can* hold a consistently utilitarian morality. They can maintain that the ultimate reason it is wrong to deny any group the development of its talents depends on the consequences produced for society as a whole. It is consistent with feminism to maintain that unequal treatment of the sexes is harmful, not only because of its effect on women, but equally because the oppressor suffers from a diminishing of his human possibilities and the deprivation of the benefits of a truly equal sexual mate. The black American writer James

Baldwin argues similarly against racism when he stresses what is lost by whites, and thus by society as a whole, through racist practices.

Annas' charge that on a utilitarian argument as soon as more efficient means to the desired end are found "women can at once be thrust back into the home" is not justified.[44] Plato's metaphysics is grounded in the very different belief that developing one's nature to the utmost will alone provide for the best state. So that a woman not using her natural capacity would necessarily produce a less desirable state than one in which all act according to their nature. It could not then be true, as Annas puts it, that the moment the state "did not need extra women public servants, there would be no grounds for letting them have the jobs." Instead, new jobs which use their capacity and further the purposes of the state would have to be found.

Annas raises the question of the fate of the many potters' wives who might want to be potters in the ideal state. "Presumably," she writes, "the Guardians (male and female) would only tell them to stay at home and learn *sophrosune* in carrying out their appointed tasks."[45] But such a presumption cannot be based on an attempt at sympathetic understanding of Plato's view of justice. Plato's disdain for the artisan class is lamentable, and he surely tells us little of the arrangements for the lower classes. It is true that he only mentions women's abilities in connection with those who would be Philosopher-Queens. But if we are "presuming" on the basis of his total view, we would have to presume that potters' wives would also have to do whatever their nature fitted them for. If they had an aptitude for pottery and instead did only weaving, this, in Plato's view, would be unjust.

There is no doubt that Annas is correct that Plato's argument is not couched in the modern terms of "women's rights." But the granting of what we call "rights" would be considered by him to be ultimately justifiable only in so far as it ensured the smooth running of the whole. And it strikes me as still a meaningful question to ask any moralist what the ultimate justification of a right is. That is, the question still remains of what arguments justify the statement that it is wrong *in itself* to deny women equal rights. The superiority of Annas' own doctrine of fairness over Plato's concept of justice is not self-evident.

Another feminist, Lynda Lange, also joins the camp of those who deny that Plato deserves the appellation of feminist. She focuses on "the inadequacy of his views from the standpoint of feminism today." Plato did not intend that the guardian class be equally divided by sex. She even claims that Plato's recommendations do not "necessarily imply" that *any* of the guardians will be women.[46] Like many of the writers in the 1970s, Lange's main interest is to show, as the title of the book in which her essay appears indicates, the "sexism of social and political theory." In the process, she ignores the historical importance of Plato's enterprise and misinterprets his philosophical aims. For surely to understand the *Republic* is to realize that the philosopher-rulers, who alone see the truth, must be born of the best-endowed and the best-educated of both sexes. How, then, could there be no female guardians?

Lange is also guilty of neglecting the previous scholarly literature, so that she announces, as if it were her own discovery, that Plato uses the language of property relations for the common "ownership" of female guardians. In fact, she even states that Plato does so "consistently." She does not refer to the Greek text nor to the problem of the translation of *koinōnia.* Nor does she allow for any of the contrary formulations discussed by Pomeroy and Fortenbaugh (and apparent even in translation). Her aim throughout is to outdo Annas in her condemnation of the Athenian philosopher for not basing his discussion of women guardians on the fairness of the matter. Lange's discovery of the obvious, that Plato's recommending equal education is ultimately derived from his concept of justice, seems sufficient to automatically discredit him. That he followed his own agenda and not that of the contemporary women's movement dismays her. "If Plato were a feminist but merely inconsistent, it strikes me as unlikely that the inconsistency would be quite that gross . . . " she writes.[47]

Another representative of the view that Plato is no friend of women is the strangely muddled position of Arlene Saxenhouse. Her approach is different from all others, however, and I think few would describe her own argument as feminist. It contains, without specific acknowledgement, several of the strands of the Bloom-Strauss position. She gives her own version of the argument that Plato actually wanted to show that the *Republic* is unrealizable. Plato's recommendations for women were not intended to foster their emancipation, but rather to forewarn of the injustice that politics imposes on "the philosopher himself."[48] And the injustice of Socrates consists of his disregarding the sexual qualities of the female. In a restatement of Bloom's charge that Plato "forgets the body," she writes that women guardians are "almost without body" and free from eros. She conveniently ignores the fact that Socrates gives the eros of women over forty free rein, and that he makes careful provisions for the development of women's bodies in the gymnasium.

But Saxenhouse intertwines the argument of Plato's lack of appreciation for women's unique physiology with the contention that he wanted to show the impossibility of the just state. Her own view of women's physiology is a version of the belief we have seen expressed before by male commentators, the belief in "special excellences." She deplores Socrates' neglect of the peculiar biological qualities "that women alone have and that make them superior" in their ability to bear children.[49] She tells us that even women least skillful in this task do it better than men! I shudder to think how she would describe all those women today who either do not possess or do not exercise this skill in which their superiority supposedly lies. For she objects to Plato having reduced motherhood to a "bare minimum," to nursing. This reduction ultimately accounts for his judgment of their inferiority. The actual purpose of Plato's proposals is, she tells us in a confusing metaphor, "to cast a philosophically significant shadow" over the whole enterprise of the ideal city. Evidently, politics is fundamentally imperfectible, always to be plagued by conflict. And the implication is that women ruling, rather than being mothers, is against their nature.

It is the process of giving birth that she wishes to glorify. She tries unconvincingly to unite the female with the philosopher because of the "generative powers" of both. Without any references to the text, she argues that both the female and the philosopher are cast uncomfortably into a political community that concentrates on war. By forcing women into politics, Socrates turns them away from the generation of life to a concern with death. She wants us to see the pursuit of knowledge, rather than its attainment, as feminine or generative. Why pursuing is parallel to giving birth eludes me. In general, Saxenhouse fails to make her case for the equation of the masculine political world with death and the feminine philosophical world with life in the *Republic*, despite her reliance on metaphors of Socrates as midwife and philosophy as giving birth to ideas. In Plato's just society, the philosopher-rulers of both sexes must wage war effectively against their external enemies. And the arguments of Book V are advanced, not through metaphors, but by clearcut discursive statements comparing male and female dogs to male and female human beings.

Like many of the earlier male commentators, she stresses that males need females in order to give the city sons. But she offers her own addition that the female needs the male in order to fulfill her nature as the bearer of children. Of course, it is Saxenhouse and not Plato who confines women to this function. She thinks that Plato intends for us to find laughable the attempt to turn a female into a male, just as it would be laughable to turn the philosopher into a politician. Both would be perverting the natural.[50] Thus, she ends up with that view of some previous male commentators that the mainstream feminists have so vociferously denounced, the view that Plato's proposals are not intended seriously. She does not even acknowledge that the text itself states that it is precisely treating women differently from females of other species (in which leadership is shared) that "perverts the natural." Her fear of androgyny, what she calls the "de-sexed female," leads her to join those who doubt Plato's seriousness.

It is tempting to compare Saxenhouse's position to that of the well-known female opponent of the Equal Rights Amendment in the United States. This political figure advocates that all women stay home with their families, while she herself makes a career of traveling extensively, giving lectures designed to convince women that it is their nature to strengthen the family and avoid public life. Like the Cretan who says that all Cretans are liars, Saxenhouse works in political philosophy, attempting (though perhaps unsuccessfully) to argue abstractly and combatively while maintaining that it is women's nature to be gentle and generative of children rather than ideas. What her case surely demonstrates is that gender, even in a society where the sexes are still raised very differently, does not determine (even when gender-based self-interest might be expected to operate) one's position in a given controversy.

PRIVATE WIVES AND SEXUAL EQUALITY

Susan Moller Okin takes another view of Plato's intentions. She attempts to prove that Plato's plan to abolish private wives left him no alternative other than to provide for gender equality. Her analysis includes an admirable discussion of the inconsistencies of Plato's views within the *Republic*. But to make her case that abolition of the private sphere is prior to the instituting of Philosopher-Queens, she concerns herself more with the discrepancies between the *Republic* and the later *Laws*. She gives an excellent account of the arrangements for women in the latter, pointing out that women there perform in positions "not of the highest rank, all those domestic, nurturing, child-oriented tasks to which women have always been assigned."[51] Needless to say, she notes this assignment with none of the enthusiasm expressed by Rabbi Frank, who made the identical observation, but lauded Plato's return to common sense.[52] She, on the other hand, decries the philosopher's failure to institutionalize what he has proposed for women in general terms.

Contrary to the usual view, she surprisingly concludes that Plato's general aims actually grew "increasingly radical" from the *Republic* to the *Laws*; the Republic itself she has previously termed an "extremely radical dialogue."[53] She finds Plato's "general proclamation" in the *Laws* to be that boys and girls should have the same education and training, that women should share with men in the whole of their mode of life. But, she objects, Plato then "fails to apply these precepts in many of the most crucial instances."[54] And for this failure Okin has her own dubious explanation.

To understand her position, it will be necessary to include some discussion of the arrangements in the *Laws*, although they are not of direct concern in the present study. Despite the incisiveness of much of Okin's account, I believe she is mistaken in dwelling on a supposed necessary relation between the abolition of the family and private property and the establishing of gender equality for the guardians. She is quite right in that the discrepancy between the expressed egalitarian aim and its actualization is most pronounced in the *Laws.* According to her, the difference between the two works in regard to women's role hinges entirely on the question of the family in each. In the *Republic,* the abolition of property and the family for the guardian class "*entails* the abolition of women's traditional sphere" (*my emphasis*).[55] Only because Plato has eliminated the family does he reduce the differences between the sexes to their role in procreation. But in the *Laws,* the reinstatement of property requires monogamy and private households. And this restores women to their role of "private wives" with "all that this *entails*" (*my emphasis*).[56]

This question of the logical relationship between the two reforms has been discussed far more often than Okin realizes. She does see that by following her reasoning we end up with strange bedfellows, for she finds herself agreeing with the notorious misogynist Rousseau about the connection. In *Emile,* he wrote, "Having dispensed with the individual family in his system of government, and not knowing any longer what to do with women, he [Plato] finds himself forced to turn them into men."[57] For Okin the relation between the two innovations is as Rousseau saw them, but with an important modification. Rousseau, she says, should substitute that Plato has turned women into "people," rather than into "men." For Rousseau "in many important respects only men were people."[58]

As we have seen, not only Jowett, but even Saxenhouse and the Italian feminists have taken Rousseau's objection seriously, worrying whether Plato has in fact done women a disservice by turning them into men. The relevant point here is that Okin agrees with Rousseau about the causal effect of one reform on the other. Though she seems aware of only a very few, she notes that those commentators who have considered the connection disagree with her. Pierce stresses the independence of the two proposals, whereas Strauss finds a causal link, but doesn't declare himself on the direction. The third scholar she mentions, A. E. Taylor, she correctly notes finds the connection to occur in the reverse direction.

However, her understanding of Taylor is based on a serious misreading. She is right that he sees the desire to emancipate women as leading to the abolition of the family. But she is unfair to this great scholar in insisting that Taylor asserts this "rather dogmatically," without giving any reason.[59] For on the very page to which she refers, Taylor states his reasons clearly. As we have previously discussed, Taylor believes that it is the historical Socrates who is the original feminist. He writes: "[T]he general principles which underlie the treatment of the position of women . . . are no personal 'development' of Plato's; they belong to the actual Socrates. . . . Hence the thought that the duties of statesmanship and warfare should be extended to women must be regarded as strictly Socratic, and the rest of the proposals . . . are no more than necessary consequences of this position."[60] In Taylor's view, then, Plato was saddled with the liberationist philosophy of the actual Socrates and therefore required to make the other accommodations.

Okin is also mistaken if she believes her own view of the matter has been neglected since Rousseau. As we have seen, Karl Nohle views the connection as she does, though he draws other conclusions from it. He, too, thinks as she does that Plato was constrained to concede equality to women, having instituted the other reforms to assure the unity of the state and the moral excellence of the guardians. Because women of excellent quality were needed for breeding, they were placed among the guardians. And once there, women had nothing to do, so they had to be given the same work as men.[61] Thus, he claimed long before Okin that abolition of the family, both logically and psychologically, preceded the proposals for equal role.

The major difficulty of Okin's position is that she never sufficiently clarifies the precise nature of the causal link between the two ideas. Most of the time, she implies that a relation of logical necessity obtains. But she equivocates, and occasionally it seems that she is referring only to some kind of psychological constraint. It is not easy to understand exactly what she intends when she writes, "[I]t was his dismantling of the family which not only enabled Plato to rethink the question of women and their potential abilities but *forced* him to do so" (*my emphasis*).[62]

In response to her earlier article outlining the same position, William Jacobs had pointed out that the connection cannot be a strictly logical one.[63] But her only concession to his decisive objection is a slight change of wording in one instance in her later book. When speaking of one of the other commentators, she changes "entails" to "leads to" and refers to Jacobs.[64] But this is hardly sufficient. She fails to see that what is necessary is a complete rethinking of her position. However, she never clarifies further in what sense family and property abolition "require" equalization of role.

It is obvious, of course, that the proposed plans for superior males still leave open a wide range of logically possible arrangements for women. Male rulers and a colony of female acolytes would suffice. A corps of celibate rulers who adopted the gifted sons of traditional families in order to perpetuate themselves would satisfy the logical requirements. This might even seem far more feasible to the Athenian audience. For Greek heads of households often adopted sons when they were without male heirs. Even in our own time, the American sect of Shakers consisted of celibate men and women who relied on adoption to continue the group.

Perhaps, however, what Okin really intends is "psychological inconceivability" rather than logical entailment. Maybe she means only that he was "forced" in the sense that it would have been very difficult for him to reconsider women's abilities as long as he continued to think in terms of the Greek family. Okin is eloquent in her condemnation of the family arrangements Plato knew best. She stands solidly among those who interpret the available evidence as incontrovertibly indicating that women were thoroughly and indefensibly oppressed in ancient Greece. Her description of what she calls "the Greek family," with its enforced seclusion and rigorous restriction of women to home and child care, is accurate as far as it goes. But she fails to mention that it applies only to the upper classes. She neglects the fact that some citizen women worked in the fields with their husbands and plied retail trades. Below a certain point on the social scale, in families with few or no slaves, it is unlikely that women were segregated. According to Dover, lower-class women would have had to go on errands and sell in the marketplace. He also concludes that attitudes and beliefs about women's moral capacity and responsibility must have varied between social classes.[65]

There is no reason why the visionary Plato could not have

independently conceived of another kind of family. Despite the conventional connection between women and property, and women and inferiority, a man whose genius produced a work that has remained vital for centuries could surely envision a family different from that existing in a city many of whose practices he deplored. If by family we mean only a male, a female and their offspring, forming a social unity (as families are now minimally defined by anthropologists), a great thinker like Plato, even though male, would not necessarily be forced to accept a single kind of family with a fixed set of property relations.

My own view of the proposed reforms is that they are inextricably intertwined. There is a danger that speculation about which of the Two Waves came first will distract from our consideration of the justice of each. For although the co-equal proposals are connected as Plato presents them, the justice of each can be considered separately; and Plato does so. Okin herself seems somewhat uncertain of her ground, despite her twice-published, lengthy argument. For at one point, she writes, "to the extent that a causal relation exists."[66] In ordinary language a causal relationship either exists or it does not, and it is hard to ascertain what she means by degrees of causality. Her statement that once the family is abolished, "there seems to be no alternative" except for Plato to consider women as persons in their own right, would indicate a definite causal link, as does her usage of "entailment" and "forced." But she also states that "*if* they [women] are to take their place as members of the guardian class," then they must have equal natures.[67] I would agree that the operative word is "if," and that Okin's reasoning is therefore circular and begs the question. The loss of their role as private wives does not require women's elevation to guardianship. And *if* Plato plans for them to be guardians, then he must have been *independently* committed to the equality of their natures.[68]

A consequence, as we have seen, of judging the elimination of family and property to be prior, either logically or psychologically (i.e., in Plato's thought processes), is that it fosters the view that the emancipation of qualified women was of relatively little importance to him. Okin seems to be aware of this herself, and thus, like many of the feminists, she fluctuates in her assessment of the degree of credit he deserves. It is always tempting to search, as she does, for unexpressed reasons for a philosopher's theories. Okin is right that Plato's lack of respect for women, as they were in the Athens of his day, is "understandable."[69] Even her allusion to speculation that he had personal psychodynamic reasons for wishing to minimize the anatomical differences between the sexes cannot be rejected. The fact that Plato nowhere shows that he understood the essential inequality of the upper-class Athenian family nor the unfairness of women's position is bound to detract from the enthusiasm a modern feminist can feel for his reforms.

However, in the end all Okin's attempts to show that he himself thought his proposals for women less important than the abolition of the family and property are unsuccessful. She surely overstates her case when she writes that it is *above all* the elimination of the "passion to acquire" which is "the road to virtue."[70] Here, she misunderstands Plato; for it is unity he desires and not an end to acquisitiveness *per se.* Her contention that private interests are to be abolished to eradicate selfishness and divisive interests in the ideal state is not entirely accurate either. They are, after all, only to be abolished for the guardians; we have no reason to believe that the majority would not own property. (We also know nothing about their family relations, nor does Plato tell us how he intends to reconcile identical male and female natures among the third class.)

This retention of property by the bulk of the members of the state makes that frequent usage of the term "communism" for the reforms a misnomer.[71] But even the possession of goods in common by the guardians does not involve the complete renunciation of acquisitive instincts. The entire "military establishment" of the auxiliaries is designed to protect what is theirs against the stranger-barbarian. This contrasts sharply with the Roman Church's requirement of poverty for monastic orders. Okin thinks that to Plato the greatest danger was, in her words, "the fatal preference for material possessions" over the welfare of their souls.[72] But this is to superimpose a Christian view which does not express Plato's intentions. As Okin herself noted at one point, the goal is for all to say "my own" about the same things. Thus, Plato's aim is to redirect the natural desire for ownership so that it can be used for the benefit of the group as a whole.

In sum, Okin is wrong that the threat of acquisitiveness is uppermost among Plato's concerns in the *Republic.* Nor does the reintroduction of the family in the *Laws* have the "direct effect" of putting women firmly back into their traditional place. The standard scholarly opinion for the reversion to convention remains convincing. As Plato grew older and legislated for an actual, rather than an ideal, city, he became more willing to make accommodations to traditional practices.

But what then is it that makes so many commentators sense that Plato's program for sexual equality, even in the *Republic,* is relatively unimportant to him? He is surely less consistent and less eloquent about this reform than about the others. Many commentators must sense that Plato's chief desire is to enlighten his audience about the nature of the true philosopher. He seeks rulers who will know the good, distinguish truth from falsehood, and guide the society wisely. I see his reforms as essentially interrelated. Good guardians come only from good stock and good stock can only be produced from good mothers and fathers. Plato's main concern is to produce guardians who, after emerging from the cave, will see the light and recognize and uphold the principle of unity behind all appearances. In a society in which the utmost unity is possible, able women must do what their nature fits them for. Otherwise, the *kallipolis* will not exemplify perfect justice. But the feeling remains that Plato's dearest aim—the existence of true philosophers—might still be attained without equality of roles. It might still be possible for some men, i.e., males, to escape from the shadows of the cave.

It is then the culmination of the three paradoxical waves which has the effect of overwhelming all of the other reforms and perhaps making gender equality seem less important. By focusing on the final wave, commentators for hundreds of years have succeeded in ignoring the startling wave that precedes it. And it may be this that causes some female commentators to realize that Plato's chief desire is not the one they would make uppermost. This realization, along with the recognition that Plato undeniably had no interest in equality for the sake of what we would call women's individual fulfillment, has perhaps led Okin, as well as many other feminists, to conclude that Plato's commitment to sexual equality was relatively unimportant.

EDUCATION, ENVIRONMENTALISM, AND THE CONCEPT OF *PHYSIS*

In the understandable objection of many commentators to Plato's lack of concern for what we think of as self-development, they sometimes underestimate the strength of his conviction that doing what one's nature warrants is the source of human happiness. To understand this, one must explore thoroughly the ancient Greek and specifically the Platonic idea of "*physis.*" Both Okin and Jane R. Martin, another writer on Plato's theory of education, are aware of the importance of the idea of innate abilities to the Platonic, as well as to the modern discussion of gender equality. I shall deal first with the views of Okin, since here again I believe her interpretation has serious flaws. She is admirably aware that *physis* is a complicated notion, but in my view, her understanding of it involves a misapprehension of Platonic metaphysics which vitiates her analysis of the reforms for women guardians.

Okin speaks of Plato's "environmentalism," a judgment she can make only on the basis of what I consider a faulty understanding of *physis.* Plato, she tells us, believes in education as the *chief* determinant of character. One assumes she classifies him as an environmentalist in the same sense that we would today so describe thinkers who decline to evaluate the potential of individuals unless they have been exposed to the same opportunities. Presumably, environmentalists in this sense believe that early environment, socialization, and education are far more important than genetic considerations in human development. Okin says that Plato places "the greater weight" on education over heredity, but unfortunately falls short of applying his own convictions. In trying to convince his skeptical audience that women should be trained for the same civic functions, he misses out by failing to employ his best weapon. She concludes that Plato "almost entirely fails to apply" his alleged environmentalism.[73]

Here, Okin seems to have succumbed to the temptation, as have many before her, to report not what Plato did say, but rather what he should have said. I am sympathetic with her desire to praise Plato for realizing the importance of education. But she misleads her readers when she writes of the philosopher's belief in the "influence of the environment" over what translators variously render as "inborn dispositions," "innate tendencies," or "natural capacities." In a book on such a topical subject, with an audience unlikely to have much acquaintance with classical literature, her first obligation is undoubtedly to clarify what Plato actually did say in the Greek text.

Okin tries to support her view that, far more than most commentators have acknowledged, Plato "strongly opposed the prevailing emphasis on the immutability of the innate."[74] It would take us too far afield to try to determine what the prevailing emphasis actually was in classical Athens. Suffice it to say that even Euripides, to whom she refers, did not believe that ability and character were completely unchanged by experience. In fact, the view of many Greek writers compares with a prevalent common-sense outlook of today. The assumption is that a person is born with certain capacities which limit how far he or she can develop; but events can and do affect how the innate capacity is expressed. Our modern version of the "immutability of the innate" occurs in current idioms taken from computer technology. People speak of human beings as "programmed" in a given direction. And in explanations of personality style, some say "that's just the way he's wired," unexaminedly referring to presumably fixed neurological patterns which somehow determine temperament and character traits.

The relevant issue here is that Okin misunderstands the Platonic concept when she tries to set up an opposition between the innate and the acquired.[75] She attempts to establish that some elements of "what Plato calls nature are by no means innate, *but* have been developed by training and habit" (*my emphasis*).[76] Such an opposition, however, is Okin's and not Plato's. She is well aware that Plato's distinction between *physis* and *nomos* is complex and difficult, but she makes it even less intelligible by removing it from its metaphysical context. She obscures the fact that for Plato an entity possesses a certain trait which under proper conditions will be exhibited in the course of its natural development.

The example Okin chooses to show that "we must look closely at the environment" to determine the *physis* of a thing illustrates her misunderstanding of the Socratic view. She refers us to the *Phaedrus,* where Socrates is seeking the true nature of the soul.

But she is mistaken in thinking that the interchange between Socrates and Phaedrus supports her view; precisely the opposite is the case. Socrates intends no recognition of the efficacy of the environment when he says they must reflect on how the soul "acts and can act on other things."[77] Socrates is here searching for what is the *same* in all instances of the soul. One discovers this by a dialectical method which disregards superficial appearances and discovers what is identical "behind" the varying actions and interactions.

Socrates' search for the *physis* in this dialogue has no relation at all to environmentalism. No alleged emphasis on the primary importance of training or outside influence appears in this dialogue on the soul. On the contrary, the Socrates-Phaedrus exchange exemplifies rather that search for the invariant which is the key to Platonic metaphysics. The philosopher believed in an *eidos* of individual things as well as of classes. It is precisely this emphasis on immutability which his twentieth-century opponents have deplored as a dangerous essentialism.[78] In the *Phaedrus*, Socrates is interested in how the soul changes *only* as a basis for a logical analysis that will lead to what is identical in all souls. He likewise assumes that all classes possess an identical attribute, that all men, all women, and all sheep dogs possess an identical nature which constitutes them as a class.

Thus, the changing entities of the world have structure. But he also uses *physis* not only for the concrete *eidos*, but also for the tendency and striving which this form *determines* in every actual entity. As John Wild points out, in Plato there is a ubiquitous factor of "unfinished tendency."[79] Many scholars have attempted to clarify this dual usage. But the distinction between the two senses of *physis*, the static and the dynamic, which Okin takes over from Cornford does not help her case. Cornford rightly makes a distinction between 1) the constitution, structure, essence of a thing, and 2) the way a thing grows.[80] But this latter sense of a thing's development is *not* a distinction, as she would have it, between a fixed element and the partly unpredictable effects of what we call environmental influence.

The crucial point is that for Plato a thing's development is part of its nature. Those with musical natures show an early aptitude, and if their ability is developed they play well into old age. Plato says that each of us is naturally not quite like anyone else, but rather differs in his nature and is apt for the accomplishment of different jobs. Okin considers Shorey's translation of *physis* here as "nature from birth," an overinterpretation.[81] But in my view, the scholar-translator, unlike Okin, correctly interprets Plato's intention, as does Cornford himself, who translates "innate capacity."[82] As Jowett stresses, the point is that all do not have the same "natural aptitudes."[83]

The issue here is more than a trivial argument about the proper translation of a single word. It is rather that any attempt to present Plato as having believed that the different natures of people result primarily from their different environments cannot succeed. Such an interpretation, though it may link Plato with current reformers, leads to a misunderstanding of the chief point of the *Republic* and its concept of the just state. We may wish that he did not find the capacity to be a carpenter or a physician a matter of inborn abilities. But if education and rearing were the decisive elements, then why divide people into classes at birth at all? Why not simply select people at random for different kinds of training, assigning Job A to the first thousand born, Job B to the second, etc.? The principle of each one doing what he is fitted for by nature, which is Plato's definition of justice, might then mean each one doing the job for which he was trained. The myth of the silver, bronze, and gold classes would then be unnecessary, and one could always decide that he did not like his present job and would prefer to be trained for another. But Plato's state could allow for no "mid-life career change." His belief is rather that just as silver has a fixed nature and is not suited for cooking pots, the farmer has certain aptitudes and is not suited for learning the art of medicine.

But Okin persists in maintaining that Plato's predominant stress is on nurture, and that the nature of a thing is "unknowable as long as that thing is the recipient of discriminatory training and treatment."[84] This is her view and not Plato's. Okin speaks from the vantage point of a twentieth-century scientific outlook, from a world of controlled studies where "truths" about natures or what we would call capacities, aptitudes, abilities are supported by experiments in which attempts are made to perform identical operations on like materials to secure highly probable conclusions.

But this is not Plato's universe at all. Plato does not say that the nature of our two hands is unknowable in the metaphor Okin cites from the *Laws*, any more than he says that the nature of women is unknowable. Instead, he declares that "our two limbs are by nature balanced." It is by bad habit alone that we create differences between them. In de-emphasizing Plato's misogyny in the *Laws*, Okin omits to note that the source of these bad habits is, like the source of so many other evils, "the folly of nurses and mothers."[85] Plato has deduced by his dialectical method that the left hand is equal in capacity to the right, just as he has deduced that women are by nature twice as bad as men. Given our different methods of establishing truth, we conclude on the basis of neurological research and empirical observations of moral behavior that both of these Platonic deductions are in fact fallacious.

Okin wants to give credit to Plato for his desire to offer women the chance they did not have in Greek society, the chance to see if they would measure up to male achievement. But we must avoid recasting Platonic thought in the terms of our pragmatic, scientific world view. On our terms, it is only after a long trial period that we could know for certain what women can achieve. To Okin, the result of equal treatment is genuinely unknown. With admirable fairmindedness, she insists that if women have not succeeded thus far in certain areas we cannot at this time prove beyond a doubt that the reasons are purely "environmental." Her belief that equal socialization and education will produce equal results is thus only a highly probable hypothesis which awaits future confirmation. To superimpose such a view on his own—even to suggest that on the basis of the very arguments he presents he could have seen the light—is more than anachronistic. It renders his entire opus unintelligible, so that we lose far more than we gain.

It cannot be stressed too often that Plato's method is to decide through reasoning what the nature of a class is and then to proceed from there. His conclusions are never intended as tentative in our post-Renaissance sense. Okin tells us that from the total context of the Platonic dialogues we can see that it is "the rational" *rather than* "the natural" which is their author's central standard. But here again, she is mistaken in setting up such an opposition. For what Plato means by *physis is* ultimately the rational. In a century which takes "an event" as its basic unit, Platonic metaphysics is perhaps difficult for us to grasp. But it is surely still to a large extent built into our language. When we say that a circle *is* round, or that women *are* nurturant, we employ the Greek metaphysic of substance and attribute and of class membership. That is, what characterizes a circle is its roundness, a given woman her ability to nurture.

Admittedly this geometric model has its drawbacks, and it clearly landed Plato in inconsistencies and outright contradictions, particularly in dealing with the human and animal world. But our aim should be to understand the legacy he left us, in connection with thinking about women's nature, as well as in other respects. To understand the advantages and disadvantages of his essentialist metaphysics, we must take all possible steps to guarantee that we do not distort what Plato actually said.

Unlike many recent commentators Okin does make a genuine attempt to deal with the text. But her conscientiousness is undermined by a desire to mitigate the fact that Plato is inconsistent both in the *Republic* and in the *Laws*. No amount of effort—and Okin certainly works very hard at it—can dissolve the inconsistencies. The very example she chooses as the "most significant passage of all . . . relating to the nature of the female sex" demonstrates how ineradicable they are.[86] Once again, I think her example demonstrates the exact opposite of what she attempts to prove.

The passage she refers to concerns the aesthetic education of the two sexes which, as she rightly points out, Plato considered enormously important for the formation of character. In the *Laws*, the Athenian stranger proposes that different words and music should be assigned to boys and girls because of "the natural differences" between the sexes. Okin admits that such a pronouncement certainly "seems at first" to be hard to reconcile with the conclusion of *Republic*, Book V. But she tries to convince us that the statement is in fact *not* a description of the natural differences between the sexes, but rather a *prescription* about what are "to be regarded" as the natural differences between the sexes for the purposes of that society. It is, she tries to convince us, solely a ruling about how the two sexes must come to think about themselves and about each other.[87]

But neither Plato nor the legislator are practicing any deception here. Once again, Okin has superimposed the modern ideas of self-image and sex-stereotyping instituted for a hidden purpose. Plato, however, clearly intends that the legislator prescribes only on the basis of what is natural and rational. He makes no distinction here between the prescriptive and the descriptive. His meaning is exactly as construed by Glen Morrow, whose interpretation of this passage Okin rejects (although in other respects she says she has relied heavily on his analysis). Morrow rightly states that Plato is here referring to "the specific differences between the psychical nature of women and that of men."[88] Taylor's translation captures Plato's unequivocal meaning well: "[W]hat music should be assigned to females is indicated by the actual natural distinction of sex, which should therefore be our basis for discrimination."[89]

Okin gives us no plausible explanation of why the legislator should prescribe on a basis which Plato himself knows to be false—or even questionable. If such were the case, wouldn't Plato reveal that his proposal is actually based on an expedient falsehood? Morrow's interpretation is the correct one, and we have every reason to believe that as Plato wrote those lines he was expressing his belief in a fixed female human nature. It is evidently difficult for Okin to think herself into the position of one who wants the political order to reflect, be based on, be in tune with a "natural" ontological order which exists independently of what anyone legislates. But such was Plato's belief. And what Okin calls "apparently contradictory" conclusions about the nature of women in his two societies are not in fact only apparent. No enthusiasm for Plato or for equality or for her thesis that the reinstatement of private wives necessitates a betrayal of his increasing egalitarianism can reconcile the inconsistencies.

Unfortunately, however, we are not dealing only with outright contradictions such as the opposition between the clearcut statement in *Republic,* Book V that women and men have identical natures and this passage in the *Laws* that there are psychic differences between them. The issue would be clearer if Plato always used the word *physis* in its strictly metaphysical sense. But we must admit that he sometimes uses it in a less precise vernacular sense, much as we today might talk of someone having, for example, a disagreeable nature, indicating traits or qualities, but making no definite commitment to their permanence. That is, sometimes we cannot ascertain whether Plato means that a trait he describes is, as contemporary sociobiologists might put it, "irremediable." Although more often he uses *physis* in the technical sense, clearly implying necessity, he sometimes, both in the *Republic* and the *Laws*, falls back on the common sense usage still current today, which blurs the distinction between the habitual and the inevitable.

Because of this variability in usage, translators have found it necessary to vary according to the context the expressions they use to translate "nature" and "natural." Sometimes the personal concerns of the translator affect the choice he makes. Okin cites Bury's omission of "nature" from his translation of "women are twice as bad as men by nature." She admits that Plato's statement "seems grossly inconsistent."[90] I suspect that Bury knew very well that this was a use of *physis* denoting a fixed attribute. Most likely, he desired to soft-pedal this no longer acceptable idea. Jowett faces the issue head-on and unself-consciously translates "in proportion as women's nature is inferior to that of men in capacity for virtue."[91]

Understandably, Okin would have preferred Plato to state that women's true nature was unknowable. And although he says no such thing here, there are occasions when it is difficult to tell whether a human trait he describes is not only inborn, but immutable. Immediately before his declaration in the *Laws* of women's twofold inferiority, he has stated that women are prone by nature to secrecy and stealth because of their weakness. This weakness is surely intended as biological. Plato's statement then might generously be interpreted to mean that, in this instance at least, women's deprivation causes their depravity. In most places, women cannot endure to have the truth spoken, "but in this state they may," he tells us. As we have seen, a twentieth-century self-styled feminist considers women's secretiveness to be a natural rather than a cultural trait.[92] The elder Plato probably believes that extra-strict legislation would always be necessary to counter this inborn defect, but that perhaps the flaw could be remedied. But however we interpret it, there is no chance that women's moral weakness and tendency to hide "in dark places" is purely environmental.

Nor does the example she adduces from the *Republic* show that Plato ever thought that environment alone could shape a person's nature. Socrates does say that education will produce, engender, create, implant good natures or constitutions, using the word *empoiei.*[93] But even here the analogy is with breeding stock and the assumption is that, although you can improve the breed, you must start out with the best materials. In another example which Okin thinks will illustrate that *physis* indicates abilities which are not innate she also errs. Quoting again from the Bury translation of the *Laws,* she cites the lines suggesting that women may participate in horsemanship although it is not compulsory for them: "But if, as a result of earlier training which has grown into a habit, their nature allows, and does not forbid, girls or maidens to take part, let them do so without blame."[94] In this more acceptable context, Bury does translate *physis* as "nature."

However, no opposition is intended in this example either between a girl's nature and her training. What Plato says is that if a girl has had the earlier training to prepare her, she may take part. That is, a girl may ride if, as Jowett puts it, she is strong enough and desires to do so. It is clear here, as elsewhere, that what Plato intends is that some women may be born with physical ability which can then be sufficiently trained. That is, some women may have enough innate capacity to perform the same tasks as men. But women's native ability is in general always inferior to men's.[95]

So much for the theory that Plato's views have grown increasingly radical! Okin is surely mistaken that in the earlier *Republic* he may have chosen to present "the less radical line of attack" as a sop to the misogyny of his audience. She proposes tentatively that, although Plato himself actually believed that environmental changes alone could show what women were capable of, he purposely advanced a different argument because it was more persuasive. But we cannot possibly ignore the great importance of the actual line of attack that he chose. In demonstrating that there are no differences between men and women relevant to the job of ruling, he establishes the value of the dialectic method over the eristic. Socrates' desire to illustrate the superiority of his analytic method, as has often been noted, is crucial at this point in the dialogue. For in order to reach the highest Good, rulers must be adept at the use of this analytic technique. Would Socrates really choose to show us faulty conclusions resulting from the use of his method, conclusions which Plato himself (and presumably Socrates) knew to be erroneous, but which his misogynous listeners accepted? I can see no value in entertaining the hypothesis that the argument for sexual equality in Book V involves "a convoluted route" which Plato takes "in spite of his own beliefs."[96]

Instead, we must accept at face value that Plato in the *Republic* clearly maintained three connected propositions. 1) The capacity to perform certain tasks is innate and can be detected very early. 2) Such capacities or aptitudes are in general not, as we would now say, "sex-linked." 3) These innate abilities in all areas, even given optimal conditions for development, will always produce lesser results in most women.

Plato then does not consciously use "according to nature" more as a sanction for decisions he has already made than as a standard by which to make decisions. It is true, as Okin says, that the philosopher frequently exposes what is commonly regarded as natural as merely alterable convention.[97] But his own view of the natural is surely meant to approach the eternal truths of an intelligible universe rather than the mere *doxa* of the many. If Plato believed, as she asserts, that what is natural is only what the philosopher-ruler tells his citizens, he would surely say so.

Nor did Plato's view of the natural capacities of women become more egalitarian as he grew older. The traditional explanation of why the reforms are less far-reaching remains more plausible. The society of the *Laws* was designed to be an actual realizable state rather than an ideal city of speech. In both works, Plato expresses some ambivalence about women's abilities. To summarize, the *Republic* contains two kinds of statements. There is: 1) a strong argument that women as a class are equal to men in capacity, although on the whole, weaker in all pursuits; and 2) other overt statements and intimations that women are more cowardly, less trustworthy, innately worse than men. The same mental split occurs in the *Laws.* There are strong declarations that women are capable of pursuing the same tasks as men, alongside statements about women's natural moral inferiority and secretiveness. Even in the strongest statements in both works, the qualification of complete equality appears. The metaphor of ambidexterity, which alludes to the need to train both sexes, contains the same reservations about total equality as in the *Republic.* For the limbs, he says, should be trained equally "as far as possible."[98] So in both the *Republic* and the *Laws,* as earlier commentators have gleefully noted, women should do what men do only "so far as possible."[99]

In conclusion, I believe that Okin is mistaken not only about the increasing radicalism of the *Laws,* but also about Plato's alleged "environmentalism." Nonetheless, she has undoubtedly made a valuable contribution, for she has countered the view that the *Republic* ignores biological differences. She has shown that Plato, unlike some of his interpreters and millions of others throughout history, "very rationally" avoided the mistake of assuming "that the entire conventional female sex role follows logically from the single fact that women bear children."[100] Okin has called attention to the significance of Plato's radical ideas, to the possibilities for building on these ideas, and to the need to counter the hostility of earlier commentators. She has placed Plato solidly at the head of a long line of thinkers whose work students must assimilate (and on many issues overcome) as women move into new positions in society and begin to get the equal education they need, desire, and deserve.

Let us turn now to the opinions of Jane R. Martin, who addresses the same questions of the importance of education in Plato and also considers the issue of innate ability. Unlike Okin, she argues that equal education is not enough. She agrees with those feminist commentators who praise Plato for favoring equal opportunity. But, in sharp contrast to Ithurriague, that alleged feminist of the 1930s who, as we have seen, lauded Plato's emancipationist views, but feared that in the philosopher's enthusiasm "he went too far," Martin thinks Plato's reforms did not go far enough to produce the results he desired. She openly admits to using Plato only as a "point of departure" to help us understand what is required if sex equality is to be achieved in our own society." Like Crossman, she is writing about Plato today. Thus, she differs from most of the other commentators who, in the guise of clarifying what Plato said, in fact tell us rather what he should have said. Martin, however, informs us at the outset that her objective is less to interpret the *Republic* than to show how assumptions about education have implications for a theory of women's societal role. She concludes that given Plato's assumptions he would have failed to guarantee sex equality. But it is not her aim "to condemn him for doing less than he should have for female guardians."[101] She wants rather to show us how we can learn from the shortcomings of what she calls his "Production Model of Education." This view of education as preparation for pre-assigned functions in society has unfortunately dominated Western thought and still has an unwholesome influence today.

Martin's effort suffers from the drawbacks of all such attempts to juxtapose modern terminology and assumptions on theories formulated in very different historical periods with very different presuppositions. She does not offer an interpretation of Plato's aims nor present the total context of the earlier thought, nor does she give us an explication of her own educational theory. Therefore, readers only superficially acquainted with Plato are likely to come away with serious misunderstandings. Their views of what equality would entail today might be reinforced, but they would not be prompted to examine their own presuppositions. Thus, there is a cost to Martin's failure to clarify the thought of the *Republic* in its own terms. The likelihood is that she ends by preaching solely to the faithful. This, of course, has some merit, but it is not the usual aim of the "modern philosophical discussion" as the volume in which her article appears describes its contents.[102]

Martin believes that Plato would provide equal "role opportunity" for female guardians, but it is her tentative assumption that he *might* not provide what she terms "equal role occupancy." What she means is that there is no guarantee that identical education will yield identical results, though evidently she allows that it *might* do so. The fact that people with "similar talents" often learn in different ways requires different modes of instruction. Unfortunately, Martin never clarifies what she means by "similar talents," giving us no theoretical model or operational definition of them. Plato, of course, had no concept of genes. But anyone speaking today of natural talents presumably refers to genetic inheritance, or to a hypothetical, if still unverifiable, similarity of brain structure or chemistry. Despite these presumed similarities, Martin maintains that some people *start* with handicaps having nothing to do with natural ability. In fact, if the early socialization of females in the ideal state parallels that of girls today, let alone of girls in Plato's Athens, "it is unlikely" that an identical education would produce equal numbers of male and female guardians. The likelihood is, she says, again tentatively, that without special treatment female warriors and rulers would not be able to finish the required curriculum in physical skills and abstract thinking.[103]

She believes that when Socrates proposes that men and women with the same talents should have the same education, he is extending to women a kind of education which has been designed for future male guardians, what she calls education in the male mold. The passage she cites from the text can only be used to support her case if you already believe that educational content and methods are intrinsically sex-linked. In Book V, Glaucon says there will be ruling men who are morally good and noble (*agathon*). And Socrates immediately corrects him: "And ruling women, too, Glaucon, I said. Don't suppose that what I have said applies any more to men than to women, all those who are born among them with adequate natures." But this does not satisfy Martin for "there is no reason at all" to assume that "male-based educational methods" will transform most females who are potential guardians into actual ones.[104]

Like Adela Adam more than sixty years earlier, Martin interprets this passage as showing that women are only an afterthought to Socrates. Martha Nussbaum takes a much more positive view. She considers this statement in which Plato uses *archousas*, the female present participle of the verb "rule," along with the masculine form *archontas*, to be "a very important passage." She describes it as the first known argument for linguistic feminism. In it, she says, Socrates implies that Glaucon's failure to use both forms will obscure from his imagination the genuine possibility that some women will meet the test not only of guardianship, but also of philosopher-rulership.[105]

Martin, however, uses the passage as evidence that Plato and his recent commentators have failed to see that a property or a characteristic which doesn't make a difference to the performance of a role "might in fact" make a difference to the learning of that role. The differential socialization which she evidently thinks would persist in Plato's state "might make a difference" in the ways females learn. There "may" also be physiological differences relevant to how they learn.[106] She does not clarify whether she considers these differences to be solely environmental. She is, of course, eager to avoid "biological determinism."[107] But some, at least, of the sources she cites on sex differences do claim that biologically based differences in learning exist even if they do not completely determine achievement. Martin herself hedges on this question. She prefers to focus on the purported differential socialization in Plato's state, which would affect females' motivation to learn and "readiness" when their formal education for ruling begins. But Martin here underestimates the consequences of significant social change. As the mother of the first female candidate for the vice-presidency of the United States put it, the assumption from birth that every little girl could become president will surely make a difference.[108] Martin underestimates the effect the possibility of being chosen as a guardian would undoubtedly have on female motivation.

In a sense, Martin ends up voicing, almost in spite of herself, the same objections to the Platonic proposals that most of the earlier male commentators had raised. The unavoidable conclusion to her line of thought is that ultimately biological differences *are* relevant to the ability to learn and accede to the guardian class. But she equivocates. Her tentative formulations allow for the possibility that some females will not be impaired by early training or "sex-related physiological and psychological differences."[109] In Plato's scheme that is all that is necessary.

For, as she well knows, Plato's intention differs from her democratic ideal of developing the multiple abilities of every individual to their fullest. Plato wishes to make the earliest possible selection of those who learn most easily. For those of us committed to complete egalitarianism, sympathy with Martin's principles should not obscure the contradictions of recruiting brain surgeons and

Olympic athletes on the basis of democratic rather than Platonic assumptions.

It is clear that Martin does not clearly face the problems raised by the existence of differing innate characteristics. In fact, her chief example, designed to buttress her case against the same education for both sexes, contains a fatal flaw. Her discussion presupposes familiarity with current psychological and educational research. Modern educators have shown that there are varying methods of teaching basic mathematical, verbal, even musical and drawing skills. Such methods will produce a degree of proficiency, despite differing abilities. Martin chooses to discuss proficiency at the game of tennis. But it is not proficiency at which Plato aims, but the highest possible degree of skill. And therein lies the rub.

Martin explains that a tennis instructor will tell students to watch his racquet in order to learn how to serve the ball. But she confesses that since she is not visually oriented, the instructor's method will improve the serve of her colleagues, but will have no effect on her own. It is only when the instructor analyzes the serving motion verbally, introduces a meaningful metaphor or actually takes her arm and puts it through the correct motions, that her game will equal that of the others. She thinks that although some of the "fast learners" have more aptitude for the game, it is not true that all of those whose serve is improved quickly by the visual method actually have more innate aptitude. "Where education is concerned natural talent is only part of the story."[110] But in my view, this is wishful thinking if what you are trying to do is to produce superior tennis players. For the best tennis players must have visual acuity; they must be able to learn orally, kinesthetically, *and* visually. Extra effort and high motivation, as well as varying training methods, may produce the outstanding, superior competitor who has all those benefits *plus* the natural ability to learn easily by any method. Without the natural advantage of the ability to learn visually, I fear Martin will never make the guardian-class tennis players!

Unfortunately, although Martin has told us that she opposes Plato's "Production Model of Education," she has not made clear what she herself considers the purpose of education to be. Nor has she offered any arguments to refute Plato's idea that only the best must rule. We can probably assume, however, that in so far as she is interested in a just state, she would be satisfied with producing "good enough" citizens.[111] If, however, excellence or superiority is what one seeks, the use of tennis as a paradigm carries great dangers for a feminist. The problem is not only one of discrepancies in natural ability which may include learning styles (which, in turn, may or may not be themselves "natural.") Nor is it the handicap Martin mentions of some female players' difficulties in acquiring serving skills because of their inadequate practice in throwing balls. This obstacle has been overcome, and many women now throw balls competently and can beat many men in many sports.[112] But no alterations in educational methods can successfully compensate for the fact that tennis also requires physical strength and upper arm development. And this would seem to be the sticking point.

The evidence that the surge of testosterone at puberty produces the specific male physique with its greater muscle mass and upper arm strength seems incontrovertible. The ideal tennis player then must have overcome any personal obstacles and be visually and kinesthetically acute. And although I am doubtful that Martin can currently assess the presence and precise degree of natural ability in herself and others, let us grant that the best players must have superior aptitude for the game. But part of this aptitude, no matter how you construe it, must include great strength. This is undoubtedly why the top male players repeatedly defeat the top female contenders and few would deny that they will continue to do so.

This is precisely Plato's view of the differences between women and men in all activities. If all functions *were* like the game of tennis, then his view that men are inevitably better at all pursuits, even though some women can do them very well, would indeed hold universally. The point made by some commentators that specific females might still excel even under Plato's class inclusion model, would not even apply. If life *were* like tennis or football, then there very well might not be enough women to go around to comprise the partners for the guardians.

At least Martin bases her account on a sounder interpretation of *physis*. She refers to Socrates' assumption that for all pursuits a person has a natural aptitude which is both "fixed and unchanging" and also capable of being developed (or thwarted) over time. She seems to accept this Platonic view when she asserts that, although she does not learn quickly visually, she nevertheless has as much aptitude for the game as some of the fast learners. I am not myself so sanguine that such convictions can be translated into the language of verification of our modern scientific world view.

One final objection remains to be made to Martin's evaluation of *Republic*, V. In her praiseworthy eagerness to promote an end to sex stereotyping in our own society, she underestimates the revolutionary character of Plato's ideas about what she calls "socialization." Martin is not satisfied that Plato's abolition of the family will eliminate differential socialization. Her disapproval of the "genderization of traits" prevalent today clouds her vision of how different the values of the *Republic* were to those of the Athens of Plato's time.

For the purposes of changing our images of male and female characteristics, Martin believes that Plato's provisions for censorship do not go far enough. She says that aggression in females might still be differentially valued. But the image of Spartan women riding to war was admired by the Platonic circle. Furthermore, gentleness is to be a valued attribute of all guardians, and the very nature of the philosopher is to be a lover of beauty. The description of the true lover of wisdom in the *Symposium* and elsewhere is hardly the macho image of the ruthless businessman or philandering athlete she fears. Plato's choice of desirable human characteristics and his ideal of "manhood," though still more bound up with physical courage and ability in war than we might desire, nevertheless differ markedly from those of the mass of mankind throughout history. They are far from those of the Americans who have provided the data she quotes to show "the genderization of traits."[113]

Because Plato himself is aware that his proposals are shocking, he finds it necessary to convince his audience that recommendations like naked physical exercise for females will at first seem laughable. But they must see beyond the conventional and realize that what promotes society's goals is in the end beneficial. And that is why children in the city will be sent away so that completely new rearing and education, new forms of what we now call socialization can occur. The guardians will then take over: "[T]hey will rear them—far away from those dispositions they now have from their parents—in their own manners and laws. . . ."[114] And we must remember that in striking contrast to current practice, the creators of the manners and the laws will be both males and females working together. Women will be equally responsible for formulating and enforcing the laws and establishing which traits are to be valued.

Martin's thesis, that Plato's educational reforms may not produce the results modern feminists desire and will involve a "masculine mold" of education, has two drawbacks. First, her efforts to update Plato are likely to distract from the value of what the philosopher actually said. And in addressing the modern issue, she may shift the focus from what I believe is the most important aim, that of planning for, as one female primatologist put it, "getting the job done."[115] This was Plato's goal, and I consider it still uppermost. In my view, if the traits required for a desired result happen to be those historically valued as "masculine," it is more important to re-evaluate them as "human" than to try to change or eliminate them. Undoubtedly, some of the traits Plato valued are inappropriate for our democratic society. But even in modern terms, for many reasons, including the importance of cooperativeness, it is inaccurate to describe his philosopher-ruler as cast in a "masculine mold." Plato's primary aim, the loving pursuit of reason, was then, and seems to me still, to be a truly androgynous goal.

DOWN WITH PLATO—DOWN WITH THE LIFE OF REASON: THE FAMILY AND NEW THEORIES OF WOMEN'S SPECIAL VIRTUES

In Jean Elshtain's book on women in social and political thought, she includes a section entitled "Divine Plato, Down to Earth."[116] In it, she denounces Plato with sarcasm and vituperation for his excessive rationalism.[117] Her discussion is lively and provocative, clearly deeply felt rather than an academic exercise. She enters the debate as if she were arguing with a contemporary opponent.

By stating her case forcefully, she reinforces the vital nature of the questions and invites her audience to participate in an ongoing discourse.

Before considering her view of the *Republic* and her suspicion of reason, I wish first to call attention to the pronouncedly a-historical character of her scholarship. Despite her strong protests to the contrary and her avowed aim of judging individuals and issues in their historical context, she often isolates Plato's thought from the philosophical problems of the day. She does not mention the major commentators of the last hundred years, nor give credit to those who have already raised all these issues, which she discusses in a tone of debunking discovery. As I have mentioned previously, many current feminist commentators exhibit this same lack of reference to their fellow workers in the field.

Elshtain also displays a certain hubris. She tells us, for example, that Plato just did not have the "conceptual adequacy" to deal with the concept of human nature.[118] Whereas some writers have declared that it is impossible to determine what is or isn't "natural," others have suggested that Plato had a coherent concept of nature, but nevertheless reached the wrong conclusions about women's nature. Still others have told us what he should have meant by nature on the basis of consistency with his own premises, but Elshtain is the first to suggest that he was simply inadequate to the task.

The a-historicism of her approach is apparent in the fact that, although she quotes or refers to over fifteen secondary sources who have commented on Plato or whose comments can be applied to Plato in her text of over twenty pages, not one of these sources is a classicist, philosopher, political scientist, or other thinker *writing prior to 1967*. That is, in making use of the thought of others, she neglects the vast amount of earlier scholarship that might shed light on the problems she discusses, referring only to that published in the fourteen years prior to her work.[119] There is one exception to what might be considered this shortsightedness. She does mention Freud in a footnote, suggesting that Plato may have been one of those the psychologist had in mind when he observed that philosophy frequently "goes astray in its method by overestimating the epistemological value of our logical operations."[120] This speculation on what Freud might have had in mind is not convincing if we refer to what Freud actually wrote about Plato. The founder of psychoanalysis greatly admired Plato, and, unlike Elshtain, valued him as a forerunner in the recognition of the power of hidden emotions and the presence of psychic conflict.[121]

Elshtain's general tone is of one bent on dethroning a figure too slavishly worshipped, despite the fact that she expects that there will be feminist readers who do not believe that "patriarchal theorists" should be given the sympathetic consideration she presumably intends.[122] But in order to maintain this view of general adulation, she must omit entirely the great disrepute Plato fell into after World War II. She seems unaware of Fite's condemnation of Plato's homosexuality and "the Platonic legend" in general, and does not even mention Popper's notorious attack on him as an enemy of the open society. Almost forty years earlier, in his frequently reprinted *History of Western Philosophy,* Bertrand Russell derided Plato's totalitarianism.[123] Since then, there have been many who have attacked Plato as authoritarian and elitist, as well as many who have come to his defense. Most feminist scholarship is a continuation of this tradition of attack and defense; and even the search for unconscious motives has been present for a long time.[124] The idea that Plato remains on a pedestal simply does not square with the facts.

Elshtain, however, sees herself as setting Plato's "feminist defenders" straight, though she would be hard put to find a single writer of the last ten years who is not well aware of the presence of anti-female sentiments in his work. At least half a dozen writers, as we have seen, make the pointing out of this misogyny their central concern, though Elshtain does not allude to this fact.

Take, for example, the controversy we have discussed over the use of *koinōnia* in Plato's statement that the guardians will have all things in common, including wives. She assumes this to be the quintessence of the Platonic position, without considering the total discussion or the use of the concept in the Athens of the time. Taking the translation as unproblematic, she insists that what Plato really meant, despite any internal evidence to the contrary, was that women were to continue to be the property of men. Neglecting the articles written dealing with the intricacies of Greek usage, she offers the Pomeroy position as if it were original and makes no attempt to explain any apparent contradiction.[125] She fails to put the question in terms of the language and customs of the time. Nor does she give any credit to those who, in far greater depth, have already explored the territory she covers. Much of Elshtain's lack of sympathy comes from her mistrust of reason; she warns against the consequences of overvaluing "rational thought, dear to the heart of Western philosophy."[126] Along with what is by now the standard opposition to Plato's "intellectualism," Elshtain fosters what I consider an even more alarming tendency. There is in some current feminist thought an attempt to polarize male and female ways of being, suggesting that women are primarily concerned with care, responsibility and attention to relationships, while cold, abstract, logical reasoning and concern with universal principles is the male mode.

In Elshtain's case, this de-emphasis of reason is accompanied by a search for emotional, i.e., unconscious in the psychoanalytic sense, motives for Platonic doctrines. Thus, although she professes herself to be against reductionism, her repeated descriptions of politics as a "defense" and of Greek, particularly Platonic misogyny as based on "fear of Mother," are specifically designed to reduce the importance of Plato's conclusions.[127]

Elshtain deplores not only Plato's continued search for the unchanging, but she resents even more his devaluing of everyday affairs, which she sees as directed more against women than men. Her own conclusions on the public and the private, the point toward which all her researches into women in social and political thought have been converging, are diametrically opposed. Her view is what she herself terms "a perverse version of the Platonic epistemology." She describes herself as "calling for the redemption of everyday life."[128] It is not easy to ascertain precisely what she means given the difficulties of her telescoped and imprecise phraseology.[129] But it is clear that she agrees with the view that a major concern of feminists must be "caring about what seems to be of no importance, to be the insignificant, . . . the well-known, the familiar" details that make up human private lives.[130] Evidently these, rather than any abstract principles, nor what current psychologists call peak moments, the trances and visions and mythological meanings that lead Socrates to transcendence, must be the starting point of political theory. In fact, they turn out not only to be the starting point. At base, the individual concrete experiences of women, which she accuses feminists of having heretofore neglected and which must be taken into consideration when deciding as Socrates would say "how we are to live," assume major importance. For Elshtain they become the chief value of her entire world view, or as she puts it "epistemology." Whereas Plato is searching for what she calls "Extralinguistic Truth," she is searching for some infinite variety of meanings that come out of dialogue like that of the psychoanalytic encounter whose truth, she tells us, is "created" in the encounter.[131]

Reason is characterized repeatedly as "cold," exercises in formal logic are contrasted with lived meanings. The purported enemy is always "the absolute, the universal." But Elshtain is not the first thinker to find it difficult to maintain such a position consistently. She recognizes that in writing political theory others will charge her with employing abstractions. Clearly, she herself cannot escape some acceptance of that quest for a "one in many" that Plato taught us to undertake. Nevertheless, Elshtain both rejects the Platonic emphasis on the rational and the conceptual, and deplores the liberal and "liberal feminist" belief in "abstract individuals."[132]

But she is in the trap of the Cretan who protests that all Cretans are liars. A political theorist, anyone who writes books, even, in the last analysis, anyone who uses language, is dependent on reason. Humans, she tells us, are not distinguished by their capacity to reason, but by "their imperative to create and find meaning."[133] Let us leave aside the epistemological distinctions between "creating" and "finding"—that is, between making what has not existed and discovering what is already there—with which she does not deal and which might, if developed further, vitiate her anti-rationalism. Here, the important point is that Elshtain writes as if you could have meaning without truth and a criterion of truth. In another place, she offers, almost parenthetically, a criterion for sound political theory, speaking of internal consistency and coherence. It is as if an adherent to a "Coherence," rather than a "Correspondence Theory of Truth," could eschew the workings of reason. In actuality, any criterion for the truth of theory requires concepts, words that name those concepts that can be used by many to describe what is the same in many instances, many experiences, many private lives.

Thus, Elshtain emphasizes the aspect of Plato she sees as most dangerous, the Plato for whom differences between individuals do not ultimately make a difference. She sets herself in opposition, particularly so, one presumes, from her vantage point as a woman, a mother-scholar, to Plato's eternal forms. She rejects those other aspects of the Platonic corpus, embraced by many who have read and been inspired not only by the reasoning, but by the dramatic and lyrical force of the dialogues. She fails to appreciate Plato's skill in creating concrete characters; the aging Cephalus, the drunken Alkibiades, even the rounded portrait of the snub-nosed, barefoot seeker after Truth, his beloved teacher, Socrates. She finds only that Plato is wrong about the value of the life of the mind. She denounces his call for participation in what is everywhere the same and the source of certainty, that search which has always characterized religious thought.

To this one-sided, incomplete picture of rationalistic abstractions, she opposes an equally one-sided construction of her own. The view presented by Elshtain and others, whom she quotes approvingly, is that it is not reason, but care, concern, connection, embodied private existence that is important and valuable. Furthermore, Elshtain obfuscates the issue by telling us that it is also "interesting." Diversity and conflict are what provide interest. Plato's ideal republic, in eliminating these, will be "joyless and tedious."[134] Although she contradicts herself at various points, there is a sub-theme that because what is different about people—their biological distinctions and personal connections—is what is interesting about them, maintaining these differences is therefore a positive good. Presumably, she would not want to retain class distinctions, divisions between the rich and the poor, because they, too, are interesting. (Tolstoy begins *Anna Karenina* with the idea that all happy families are happy in the same way, and each unhappy family is unhappy in a different way. This makes the latter more interesting, no doubt, but neither she nor Tolstoy would argue for the perpetuation of unhappy families.)

It is interesting diversity, rather than the Platonic emphasis on the examined life, that Elshtain values. She scathingly attacks "liberal dualisms" in this book and elsewhere, rejecting distinctions between mind and body.[135] But nevertheless, though she presumably would deny it, it is a surprisingly "liberal" emergence of diverse opinions in the free marketplace of ideas that turns out to be a major value. In fact, it is the vision of many concrete experiences of individual women in myriad private households that must be the cornerstone of feminist theory. The incorporation of diapers and diversity into a total view of the relationship between the public and the private is the theoretical aim which she opposes to what she sees as Plato's "social engineering."

Another of her chief complaints about Plato enters here. It is not only his emphasis on abstract reason, but his abolition of the family, that she denounces. Here again, she is caught in a dilemma of her own making. Having disavowed abstractions, she is forced to talk about "the family" which has existed transculturally. She writes: "What we call human capacities could not exist outside a familiar mode; for human beings to flourish a particular *ideal* of the family is necessary. . . . [T]he family's status as a moral imperative derives from its *universal*, pan-cultural existence in all known past and present societies" (*my emphasis*).[136] She even quotes Stuart Hampshire's view that "language constitutes the essence of man as a species" and it is the family setting that humanizes him. How surprisingly Platonic to hear her talk of the *ideal* family!

Although she is aware that some will object that what has always been is not necessarily beneficial, she proceeds to build her argument against those who would change family arrangements on the basis of the fact that to be human is to have a family. Theorizing, she thinks, must focus on our current concept of the family as an ideal. Nor should we be swayed by any of the evidence that a large number of Americans, at any rate, no longer live in a nuclear family, evidence which she considers skewed. Families are undeniably preferable to any communal alternatives. This is undoubtedly one of the chief reasons that she is so unwilling to give Plato any credit at all for the suggestions in the *Republic* that others have seen as alarmingly or happily egalitarian.

Plato's abolition of the family is disastrous. She is as sure as

Bloom that the philosopher did not have women's welfare in mind. In fact, she adopts, again without crediting him, though she is clearly familiar with his writing on the subject, the *exact* view of Bloom. Plato only included women among the guardians because he needed them for their reproductive function, not because he genuinely entertained the possibility of their having the same natures as men. She even goes further than Bloom in imagining that the women would soon realize this themselves.[137] For reasons of his own, Plato mistakenly wanted to change basic family patterns. She brings the force of selective psychoanalytic thinking on early childhood attachments to show that we violate at our peril the mother-child bond which is crucial—and presumably always has been crucial—to developing a secure, empathic adult citizen. Children of the American communes of the 1960s make bad citizens presumably because of the inherent impossibility of communal child care. Likewise, children of the kibbutz supply an inordinate number of army officers, which, needless to say, is not seen as an admirable devotion to the general welfare.

Most disturbing of all in this anti-communal diatribe is the fact that even the day care arrangements advocated by the most moderate of feminists turn out to be fraught with menace.

> To advocate and provide full-time public day care for children from the age of two (or younger) would allow some women to stride full-time into the public arena much sooner than if they had to wait until their children reached school age, but the take-over of child-rearing by public institutions would also denude the private sphere of its central raison d'etre and chief source of human emotion and value.[138]

For one who espouses diversity, this is a curious devaluing of the variety of private arrangements that exist and have existed in human lives, including the lives of those who bore no children or whose pre-school age children occupied less than one-tenth of their life spans. Now that human life expectancy is more than seventy years, the idea that *no private life* can meaningfully exist apart from a specific type of early child connection and rearing, seems at best unsubstantiated.

Just as Elshtain sees politics as a "defense" against the lure of the private, those who rail against reason and against Plato's and some recent feminists' undervaluing of the family might be seen psychoanalytically as a defense against the genuine lure of hard thought. One could speak of the temptation to neglect one's family that must be overcome by many modern scholars. Women still teaching in predominantly male establishments often feel the conflict between family and public duties more acutely and might well need to guard ("defend") against a desire to minimize family concerns. All such speculations, however, particularly when unsupported by biographical information and actual associations, shed very little light on the validity of a position.

Part of a defense against the lure of the world of work is a syndrome that might be characterized as "whistling in the dark" or the "Sour Grapes School of Female Differences," which I touched on in my introduction. The position is not unlike the condescending theory of "special excellences," which earlier Plato scholars have used to justify the exclusion of women from politics. It, however, is intended as a feminist argument and proceeds slightly differently. The discussion of Carol Gilligan's version of women's differences will take us somewhat afield from interpretations of the *Republic* and anticipate the conclusions in my final chapter on the continuing vitality of the questions Plato raised. But it is important to discuss her argument here, because it is currently influential in feminist circles and is quoted approvingly by Elshtain.

On the basis of her psychological research, Gilligan describes what she considers the "different voices" of male and female thinking about morality. She attempts to establish that women take the feelings of others into account and act so as to maintain relationships and social networks, whereas men do not. Females, she believes, employ "a moral language profoundly at odds with formal, abstract models of morality defined in terms of absolute principles."[139] To Elshtain's credit, she does see the implications of such a conclusion, rather than remaining with Gilligan's presumed view that these voices are merely "different." Commenting on an earlier article which appeared before Gilligan's book-length study, Elshtain urges, "*if* it is the case that women have a distinct moral language," then we must preserve that private sphere that makes such a morality possible and "*extend its imperatives to men*" (*my emphasis*).[140]

Officially, Gilligan tables the question of the origins of these alleged differences in moral reasoning. She says that she is making no claims about either the origins of the differences nor their distribution in a wider population, across cultures, or through time. She is aware that these differences arise in a social context, "where factors of social status and power combine with reproductive biology to shape the experience of males and females." The origins of the greater sense of connectedness that she finds in her interviews with women discussing both hypothetical moral dilemmas and actual decisions about abortions might then be solely cultural, but she does not stress this. Instead, despite her disclaimer, there is some sense throughout the book that "reproductive biology" may be crucial, that the distinction is so pervasive that more than socialization is surely at work. For example, she believes the fact that the female does not have a primary task of separating herself from her mother since her body and biological role will be identical, plays a decisive role in shaping female morality. The developmental task of separation-individuation that leads men to think in terms of individual achievement is different because of this body-based difference.[141]

Whatever the reasons that women deviate from a standard model of ethical thought founded on abstract justice and rule-following, the feminine mode is different, more empathic, and compassionate. Gilligan finds women's truths "contextual," rather than abstract. What she neglects is the fact that, even if we assume that in making moral decisions many factors in a given context must be considered (factors which are peculiar to each individual situation and include the feelings of the agents), some decisions are *better* than others in that context. And what makes them better is an objective matter. In other words, contextual relativism in ethics must be distinguished from subjective relativism. Gilligan would not wish to advocate that all thinking about morality is equally valid, that "right you are if you think you are," or even, like twentieth-century emotivists, that there can be no genuine moral judgments but merely expressions of preference. She clearly thinks that women do well to consider feelings and the furthering of relationships. If this is the case, then some "abstract" standard of truth is involved. Contextualism in ethics involves logic just as any thinking or "moral reasoning" does. If there is such a thing as "maternal thinking," as Elshtain suggests, then it leads to correct decisions based on factors neglected by non-mothers, but used logically as premises to support a conclusion. Otherwise, it is not thinking.

In my view, Gilligan has in fact set up a "straw person" in her contention that previous ethical thought has been based on a sex-linked concept of right action. Her criticisms may have some validity in connection with the contemporary developmental theory of Erikson and Kohlberg, whom she specifically attacks.[142] But what of the Biblical injunction, also presumably devised by males, to "Love thy neighbor"? The morality of Jesus, which emphasizes care and concern for the least of humans, for the one sinner who strays from the flock and is more important than the entire herd, is also morality devised and promulgated by men. The Roman injunction that "*summa ius, summa inuriam,*" that following the law slavishly can be harmful and morally wrong, is a male position as well. The very phrase Gilligan uses to describe the female as opposed to the male mode of thinking about morality, "justice tempered with mercy," is an ideal invented by men. The "*Eyl maleh rachamim,*" "God filled with compassion," is as powerful an impulse in Judaism as is the rule-following an "eye for an eye"—supposedly "male" thinking, exemplified in other passages on the Biblical Jehovah.

Gilligan also neglects twentieth-century existentialist statements about morality. Although invented by men, it is a morality based strongly on care, on what Heidegger calls *Mit-sein,* or being-with. It involves evaluating each existential situation on its individual merits and is about as "contextualist" an ethic imaginable. In the version of Martin Buber, the I-Thou connection must be the main consideration in all choices. Thus, for atheist existentialists like Sartre, Catholic thinkers like Marcel, and Jewish existentialist moralists, all male, care and concern for others always take precedence over rationality and any abstract sense of justice that supposedly characterizes the male mode.

It is the idea of a hierarchy of moral values that both Gilligan and Elshtain reject. In discussing the responses of eleven-year-old boys and girls to moral questions, Gilligan emphasizes that we should not "scale differences from better to worse."[143] But, although Elshtain, like Gilligan, is in principle against hierarchies, she sees that a value system including considerations of responsibility rather than rights alone must be extended to men, i.e., is preferable.

Thus, in the end value judgments must be made, and some kind of hierarchical order cannot be avoided. It would seem that a morality which includes a synthesis of logic and concern for others' feelings is in some sense "higher." It is not simply a matter of a different voice. If women have fears of achievement because it involves isolation or an unwanted standing out, such fears must be alleviated. Either the society must be changed so that women do not end up any more isolated than men, or women must be ready on occasion to choose isolation or personal loneliness for the sake of realizing their ambitions and developing their gifts to the highest degree possible.

To my mind, no studies to date conclusively prove that women are in fact always more likely to take the feelings of others into consideration when thinking about moral issues. But even if this were to be convincingly demonstrated, the reasons cannot be shown to be biological. Further, I consider thinking in general a human, not a male trait; there is no reason to undervalue it, nor to characterize a particular kind of thinking as "maternal." And if women are or have been less effective at logical reasoning, then it would be better to socialize them so that any such discrepancy was eliminated. It would also be equally crucial to educate males to include emotional factors and the maintenance of human connections in the principles they use in ethical thinking.

To return to Elshtain's interpretation of Plato, I want to say a word here about her use of what she calls "depth psychology" to explain away much of what Plato says, as well as to show the importance of the emotional as against the rational in philosophical thought. Elshtain's approach is to "look for clues" in the writing of all her political theorists that they are fending off some idea, fear, or desire they find incompatible with their self-concept, or their vision for society, or their understanding of the world.[144] Unlike Bennett Simon, Elshtain only hints darkly about what Plato's motives for eliminating private life for the guardians must have been.[145] But evidently, her view is that Freud has taught us to see metaphysical systems as "defenses" against perceived threats and dangers.[146] In my own view, an equally important use of Freud is as a reinforcement of the importance of reason, of the search for a rational method to understand what otherwise appears to be irrational behavior.

Elshtain wants to exonerate the true Freud from those feminists who have vilified him. But just as I have tried to show the many contradictions in Plato so that there can be no "true Plato", so, too, there is no true Freud. However, Elshtain's very undertaking of such an enterprise is further evidence of the power of the Platonic model. Like so many other theorists, she still searches for what a body of work "really means." One can find in Freud numerous statements about the importance of the emotions, the irrational, what has come to be called "being in touch with your feelings." There is no doubt that one can also find a devaluation of the female, despite Elshtain's attempts to ignore this aspect.

There is clearly a strain in Freud that advocates what Gilligan describes as a male model of morality. Elshtain does not mention the Freud who considers genuine conscience and the ability to make just and impartial decisions as having their roots in castration fear. Since women, for him, are in a sense already castrated, they do not have this need to internalize authority. Freud therefore believes, unlike Plato, that women's relation to justice will inevitably be different.[147] Although the Freudian theories that Elshtain values are those that emphasize the importance of bodily difference, presumably she does not champion this particular instance of that emphasis.

Surprisingly, however, she does quote approvingly the fact that, although Freud knew the truth about the symptoms of one of his female patients, he decided it would be unwise to enlighten her. She was married to an unsympathetic husband and burdened with marital and parental responsibilities. Since Freud believed the woman to be objectively constrained by her economic and emotional dependency on her husband, he "found it better to allow the woman her 'escape into illness' than to confront her with the self-serving nature of her periodic incapacity."[148]

Elshtain finds this a model worthy of emulation. Freud's example is one we should follow in listening to the voices of women today, in treading carefully before we attempt to rid them of their illusions, even illusions fostered by commerical interests encouraging them to spend time and money to increase their seductiveness.[149] No doubt Elshtain's motives for not wanting to disturb the lives of the mass of women, who she thinks are unlikely to attain most of the goals fostered by the women's movement, are sincere. Her aim is the genuine one of avoiding the inflicting of unnecessary pain. But in my own view, fostering such "paternalism," or perhaps in this case, "maternalism," rather than taking on the Socratic task of shaking people from their complacency, is more harmful in the long run.

What makes her advocacy of protecting women's illusions particularly surprising is that she condemns Plato most strongly of all for a similar belief. In the *Republic,* Plato tells us that the mass of mankind need their illusions and therefore the guardians must invent stories that will keep them from knowing the truth. Her vociferous condemnation of Plato does not acknowledge the fact that the matter of when to reveal and when to conceal the truth is not always such an easy decision to make. My own view is that in the long run, truth-telling—seeing the good, formulating it rationally, and relating what one believes—will bring more value into the world.

This presumes the environmentalism and some version of that ultilitarianism she deplores, a utilitarianism characteristic of the currently out-of-favor liberal view. It assumes that, even if individuals are not blank tablets (as Elshtain wishes to convince us), they can nevertheless be taught to recognize the truth, as Socrates believed they could. For Freud to decide beforehand to deny his patient the possibility of seeing the meaning of her illness and perhaps finding an alternative, despite her limited options, does not seem praiseworthy. At the very least, it would seem Freud might have offered his patient the opportunity to refuse to accept his truth with all the force of that human capacity for denial that Freud himself made us aware of. Neither the Plato of the Noble Lie, nor Freud, nor Elshtain have sufficient faith perhaps in that poster slogan, "The truth shall make you free although first it will make you miserable."

Thus, one can stress many different aspects of Freud. But there is certainly a dominant strain which advocates reason-infused-with-feeling as the best basis of human choice. Plato, too, is an advocate of what Georges Grube calls "intellect . . . vivified by a stream of deep emotion." I agree that the third and fourth books of the *Republic* present us with a picture of human functioning such that "the accusation of anti-emotionalism, or at least of cold intellectualism so often levelled against Plato no longer holds."[150] In discussing Plato's theories on the nature of the soul, Grube concludes, "[W]e have here a carefully propounded psychological theory which combines the uncompromising intellectualism of the *Phaedo* with the magnificent defense of emotion which is the *Symposium.*"[151]

A proper understanding of Plato, as has often been pointed out, includes the realization that his belief that "knowledge is virtue" is not the naive intellectualism of one who blindly assumed that abstract knowledge of morality would automatically produce moral behavior. Freud admired Plato precisely because the Greek philosopher was aware of the subterranean force of feelings and because his concept of knowledge involved what today would be called authentic "insight." It is only when we genuinely understand what is right, what is the best life we can live, what is in fact in our self-interest in the long run—only when we know it with the combined force of thought and feeling, that we will behave morally. Isn't this the therapeutic goal of that psychoanalytic encounter Elshtain values? The aim of psychoanalytic practice can be seen as the attainment of insight, the fusion of knowing and feeling, that enables us to behave as our best selves. And this was also Plato's goal. To see him as a thoroughgoing rationalist committed only to abstract principle, is to misconstrue his purpose and undervalue his contribution.

HOW IMPORTANT IS THE BODY? HOMOEROTICISM, HUMAN NATURE, AND ANDROGYNY

Many feminist commentators deplore the atmosphere of Plato's famous and eloquent dialogue on the nature of love, the *Symposium.* Elshtain takes the extreme position that this dialogue shows that Platonic metaphysics *in its very nature* excludes women.[152] The passage advocating equality in the *Republic* cannot possibly be taken seriously because the ambience in which Platonic theory was developed was one in which women did not, or even could not, participate. Even though *hetarai* did on occasion participate in male conversation in classical Athens, and although a few women probably attended Plato's Academy, Elshtain is clearly correct that there are no women present at the symposia or other events described in the dialogues. The atmosphere was indeed generally uncongenial to women.

There is no doubt that one of the ways Plato uses to show the path to his eternal Forms is through the use of that erotic feeling that his male listeners felt for the beauty of other males. But Elshtain misunderstands both Plato and K. J. Dover, whom she quotes in this context. In my view, she is mistaken in her belief that homoeroticism is the only, or the chief, or in any sense, an essential element in the doctrine itself.

She writes:

> The good man . . . comes into being through a process of private speech from which women . . . are excluded. . . . His debarment of women from the search for wisdom can be explained both by the social milieu within which the search occurred, including its sanctioned homoerotic attachments between older and younger men, as well as the particular *nature* of the truth at which Plato aimed. That is, a particular homosexual ethos . . . fused with what we call the Platonic metaphysic.[153]

Elshtain actually goes so far as to say that the *process* of reaching the Forms, as she puts it, "infected" the substantive conclusions.[154] But surely generations of neo-Platonists, modern Platonists, and advocates of various aspects of Plato's metaphysics, epistemology, and ethics have seen themselves as followers of a doctrine essentially separable from the "infection" of Athenian homosexual practice.

It is not my intention to underplay, as other commentators frequently have, Plato's use of homoerotic attraction as a method of making the search for ideal prototypes of earthly particulars intelligible. But Dover describes the situation accurately and incisively when he says that Plato *exploited* the homosexual ethos for his own purposes. Contrary to Elshtain's interpretation, Dover concludes that, although the sexual behavior of fifth-century Athenians influenced the *form* in which Socratic philosophy was realized, it did not influence its basic assumptions.[155] In other words, the existence of a world of Being, the accessibility of that world to reason, and its dependence upon Good are *not* dependent on the homosexual ethos.

It is true that in the Socratic ambience, intense eros was experienced more often in homosexual than in heterosexual relationships. Such attractions also made more sense as instances of the desirability of restraint from bodily gratification. Dover reminds us with that combination of scholarly mastery and common-sensical detachment that is characteristic of his work, that "it was after all the prescribed role of women to be inseminated," whereas popular sentiment romanticized and applauded the chastity of an *erōmenos* and the devotedly unselfish *erastēs.*[156] Plato's main point is that true eros is not a desire for bodily contact, but rather "a love of moral and intellectual excellence."[157] If there is in fact a special applicability of the analogy between a man's love of one *like him,* but more beautiful, to the idea of the attraction of beauty in its purest state, Elshtain's conclusions still do not necessarily follow. For one could then effectively substitute the unconsummated attraction of a woman for another woman to approximate his meaning. This was evidently done by literary women in the eighteenth century, who based their theories of friendship for each other on what they considered the Platonic ideal. And, of course, heterosexual eros has often been seen as a stage on the path to higher beauty. As Erich Segal reminds us, there is a distinct parallel in Dante's love for Beatrice, a love which inspires his ascent from worldly error to the pure light of Paradise.[158]

Surely anyone, regardless of gender, can understand the erotic attraction of ideas. Bertolt Brecht has his Galileo say he loves "old wine and new ideas," reminding us of the sensual excitement of intellectual activity. But here again, Elshtain does not attempt to understand Plato, but rather to discredit him, to disenthrall Plato's feminist defenders.

To accomplish this end, she uses any ammunition she can muster, and even makes an error in her reference to one passage in the *Symposium* to demonstrate Plato's incorrigible misogyny.

Her accusation is that Plato speaks of the heavenly Aphrodite, inspirer of sacred love, as having no female strain in her; practitioners of such love value the male sex as stronger and more intelligent.[159] But this is not Plato (or his spokesman, Socrates) talking at all. The mythic description is offered by the notorious homosexual Pausanius from whom one would expect exactly such a speech. One of the major points of the *Symposium* is that the speakers preceding Socrates do not have the true picture of love. Even if we assume that Socrates does not see his own speech as directly contradicting each of the others, but grant that there is meant to be some validity in each of the preceding versions, it is still a distortion to assume that every voice in a dramatic dialogue represents the author.[160] In her eagerness to show Plato guilty of even more than the ordinary Greek misogyny, she distorts what Plato actually said so as to invalidate the passage on equality in Book V. Although we need not be enthralled by his granting the best women a place along with the best men, one must take greater care in any attempt not only to knock Plato from his pedestal, but to grind him to the ground.

As we have noted, Elshtain is not alone in objecting to the homoerotic atmosphere of the dialogues, and it is important to understand the anger generated in many contemporary feminists by their feeling of being excluded. Wender's objectivity toward the fact that Plato did not like women although he favored their emancipation is unusual. In my view, further analysis of the precise connections between homoeroticism and misogyny are more useful at this point than outrage.

These connections are not clear-cut. Through the centuries, some homosexual males, but surely not all, have combined their sexual preferences with a distaste for women and a general disparaging of their capacities. The question of whether homosexual males are more guilty of anti-female attitudes and exclusionary practices than heterosexuals is an empirical one that we do not have the data necessary to answer. From my study of Plato commentary, it should be clear at least that scholarly husbands have displayed a goodly share of misogyny, while Plato himself, though partial to young boys and wifeless, did suggest females rule equally. Plato puts the egalitarian proposals in the mouth of Socrates who, in Plato's portrayal, was constantly attracted to young boys. But the historical Socrates was also twice married and later tradition even describes him as "actively involved with women."[161] Thus, in the long run, it is not only possible, but advisable, to consider Plato's theories independent of his or Socrates' sexual preference.

It is worth pointing out that scholars particularly enthusiastic about the ideas in the *Symposium* (where being "pregnant in body only" is disparaged) have been guilty of particularly flagrant male chauvinism. I shall digress briefly from Elshtain's views to show how disparaging attitudes persist today in those inspired by Plato. For example, the classicist Thomas Gould who, in his book *Platonic Love,* makes a case for its superiority to Christian and modern Romantic Love, also makes a case for the general inferiority of women. Gould found the world in the 1960s just as much a man's world as it was in Plato's time. Artistic, scientific, and civilizing activities he judged still to be carried on, on the highest level, almost entirely by men. "In all this time there has still not appeared a great woman philosopher, mathematician, painter, composer, tragedian, or physicist—and poets, novelists, and scholars only of the second order. Nor can muscular inferiority or time lost in pregnancy and suckling really explain this fact in modern times." He tells us that we must probably assume that there is some additional difference between men and women. Although he grants that there is no evidence for a difference in intellectual ability, he is certain that "there must be something" which causes men to develop a more compelling sense than women of what he calls an "urgency in abstract standards."[162] This urgency (which he covers himself by saying, at one point, "usually" is not developed by women) is what causes personal feeling to fade by comparison and is at the root of all the major accomplishments of Western civilization.

He expects his readers to agree that "the most splendid achievements are realized in masculine society."[163] He respectfully considers Freud's theory on the anatomical explanation for women's lack of reason for internalizing authority and abstract standards, the famous castration anxiety explanation of male achievement. He believes that women are less subject to ideas of justice and patriotism and assumes that only a genetic or biological explanation will suffice. He ignores the fact that despite differential socialization throughout history, many women have professed and acted on abstract loyalties. Queen Elizabeth I was as loyal and effective a ruler as any that England has had. She clearly displayed the capacity, in Plato's terms, for "the most efficient possible pursuit of what is most worth having" for her subjects. In the twentieth century, many political opponents would insist that Indira Gandhi, Golda Meir, and Margaret Thatcher somehow seem to have internalized all too well that "threatening authority" whose wrath, according to Freud's anatomically-based theory, only men fear. Whatever the reasons, these women have been as uncompromising on abstract concepts such as national sovereignty, the imprisonment of political opponents and the undesirability of compromise with opposition parties as any men.

Furthermore, many would disagree that the highest level of accomplishment has been carried on throughout history only by men. Gould classifies George Santayana as a first-rate philosopher. But presumably George Eliot (Marian Evans) must by his standards be considered only a "second-order" novelist. The most generous conclusion to be drawn is that Gould has not made his standards clear, nor would his judgments be widely accepted. For he even seems to believe that the production of only second-rate, rather than first-rate, *scholars* is somehow genetic. Gould might convince some that poetic, painting, and musical geniuses are born, not made, and that outstanding artistic ability is carried through sex-linked genes, or is an inevitable result of physiology. But few, I think, would accept that the differences between a first-rate scholar and a lesser one can really be anatomical. Nor is his rewriting of history to show that in fact wives have not inspired men to great deeds convincing. "The will to write great novels or symphonies would have had to have been there before marriage and might just as well have been realized in celibacy," he writes.[164] Women have thus neither written great books nor been responsible for them vicariously. With such attitudes still abroad in classical studies among Plato enthusiasts, it is no wonder that Okin and Elshtain connect love in the *Symposium* with the belittling of women.

It is troubling to Gould that the view that immortality is better achieved through the production of great works than through human offspring is offered by the female Diotima. Those annoyed with Plato's homoeroticism do not even mention this fact. It is indeed hard to give a satisfactory reason for the fact that a speech on the central concept of Platonic metaphysics is pronounced by a woman, albeit a foreign and unusal one. Can it be that not only in the *Republic,* Book V, but even in the *Symposium,* Plato was not as convinced as this contemporary twentieth-century professor that women are incapable of making first-rate speeches and articulating important ideas?

Gould thinks one cannot simply substitute boy-girl or conjugal love for the erotic attraction between older male lover-and-mentor and beautiful young man. He is right about this if we consider the *Symposium* solely as literature. For to make such a substitution is to detract from the particularity of a special ethos and moment in time. But as philosophy, the appreciation of the beauty of, and passionate desire for union with, another human being can and has been used making just such a substitution. Logically speaking, erotic attraction can provide a "way in" to the Realm of Forms for all true philosophers, including the female guardians of the *Republic.*

In my view then, Elshtain is mistaken that the use of homosexual eros is a fatal infection. It is, in fact, only one device among many. It is surely of no more importance than the Allegory of the Cave which, unlike the exposition of eros, appears in the very work which claims female equality. In that allegory, both men and women are chained and both must find their way into the light of true Being.

The analogy of homosexual attraction to the relation between particulars and universals has a metaphorical function similar to the device that Wittgenstein uses to make his opposing position about the existence of universals clear. Wittgenstein uses the notion of "family resemblance" as a way of clarifying the connections between members of a class designated by the same word. He believes, contrary to Plato, that such particulars do not have a common element uniting them, do not participate in or serve as examples of any real form, but are merely a "network of overlapping relations."[165] These relations he likens to the family resemblances we observe in related individuals. This theory based on his analogy has captured philosophical imaginations as has Plato's analogy of the ascent of eros. But in the end the espousal of Wittgenstein's non-essentialist position does not depend on whether one accepts this particular analogy or not, on whether one notes that members of a family *do* have a common element, though it is not an observable feature. The theoretical position is distinguishable from the analogy used, one might say exploited, to clarify it. In the same way, Plato's metaphysic is distinguishable from the analogy used to help his listeners understand it.

The theory of ideas in fact appears in many other dialogues where it is not explicitly connected with homoeroticism. It seems wrong to say that because these other dialogues also describe an all-male atmosphere that the conclusions reached cannot be shared by women, or do not apply to, or automatically "disbar," women. If this were true, then all metaphysical or epistomological positions expounded by any philosopher in a work describing an atmosphere *sans* women would be equally suspect. Hume's skepticism and Berkeley's idealism might be seen as equally infected in substance, since their dramatic dialogues also occur in all-male atmospheres. In general, such a species of the genetic fallacy might ultimately lead us to reject all views formulated in or addressed to groups that excluded women. This would of course involve the rejection of most previous philosophical and scientific truth.

The surprising fact is that far from discrediting Plato for all time, Elshtain must rely on the very Platonic doctrines she deplores in her own ethical stance. The feminist theory she propounds in her final chapters, long after she has brought the divine Plato down to earth, involves a rejection of current ethical subjectivism. She denounces the twentieth-century separation of fact from value, basing her own "moral imperatives" solidly on her assessment of truths about human nature. Thus, without acknowledgement, she returns to the presuppositions of Plato who was perhaps the first philosopher to maintain that human beings are possessed of a fixed nature, and that it is only on the basis of this nature that we can decide how we ought to live. As we have seen, Elshtain stresses that the family is a universal element of our humanity. She finds evidence of this in reports that prehistoric man was found buried with flowers. She assumes these tributes were obviously left by family members.[166] It seems feasible to me that these tokens of the value of human life and its aesthetic significance might have been left by companions in the hunt rather than blood relatives. But the point here is that she adopts the basic premise that humans have certain *universal needs* that unite them as a species. Although, unlike Plato, this leads her to emphasize the importance of the private sphere, the relevant issue is that in this assumption of common human characteristics, she follows the lead taken by Plato.

In the context of her condemnation of him as the villain who is responsible for the Western undervaluing of our animal nature, she quotes the English philosopher Mary Midgley. Midgley, in her book *Beast and Man,* also urges an appreciation of tendencies, feelings, and behavior that we share as a common biological heritage. She advocates the rethinking of concepts used by ethologists to describe animal species, so that they can be employed for understanding human nature. But Midgley, even if she rejects Socrates' facts, sees merit in his approach. She is in general less disparaging of Plato, less eager to save us from what Elshtain calls our filiopiety. Unlike Elshtain, Midgley credits Plato with basing his morality on his idea of human nature, which is the method she also thinks we ought to follow.[167]

Midgley seems to accept that there are "natural differences of emotions" between the sexes, though she also maintains that sex-linked moralities cannot really be of much use. It is not only that their potential efficiency would be halved by the fact that fifty percent of people belong to each sex. She writes: "More important still, we all have the emotions of both sexes within us—not enough to realize them fully, but enough to need more, enough to make a single sex world a poor one for anybody."[168] She apparently finds some validity in Plato's description, taken over by many others, notably Spinoza, that pity is "womanish," whereas courage is manly. But her contention here, like my quarrel with Gilligan, is that "splitting the human race like that is not rational at all" and should not be fostered. A man without pity, she tells us, is a monster, as is a woman without courage. If there is something specifically wrong with the kind of pity normally felt by women, then it can be stated, and ought to be, in other ways than just by mentioning the sex involved.[169]

In my view, this is precisely the meaning of the passage in the

Republic on women's nature. But Midgley, despite her appreciation of Plato for wisely giving the central role in his philosophy to the concept of the Good, objects strenuously to his arrangements for women in Book V. And it is this aspect that Elshtain quotes approvingly. Midgley, like so many commentators before her, finds the family arrangements proposed for the guardians hopelessly unnatural. Although writing in the late 1970s and clearly conversant with Freud, she does not, however, look for unconscious motives for Plato's distortions.

She accepts that Plato hoped to get rid of private property, "most of all in what he rightly saw as its central case," attachment to one's own family. Midgley's concern is that, although man is indeed a political animal, he cannot possibly become merely that. She finds that there is a natural balance of private and public which defies distortions as extreme as Plato's. She admits that sacrifices of the private can be made, as in religious communities and kibbutz life. But, like the sociologists I discuss in my final chapter, she, too, stresses that these sacrifices have inevitable costs. Although the price can be paid, provided that the goods secured really seem worth it to all concerned, it will be paid with effort. The bargain, she says will need constant attention and there will be special dangers of emotional stunting and self-deception. She believes that "natural feelings like our strong and special affection for our children" could only be replaced with something that would be worse.[170]

Plato, of course, was aware of the fact that sacrifices would be involved for his rulers and knew that most people would see such sacrifices as unbearable. His aim was to convince his listeners that specific rewards of status and added pleasures, and ultimately the intrinsic rewards of the philosophical life, would compensate for the sacrifices. Midgley points out with a generosity that Elshtain cannot muster that the experience of religious and other specialized communities should by now have shown us "what Plato, when he wrote the *Republic*, could not know."[171] She believes that the experiences of the intervening centuries have shown the difficulties of a way of life which overrides the natural balance of human feelings.

The violation of that balance she finds most apparent in two features of the Platonic proposals, at which she tells us even the most drastic reformers quail. Actually, although Bloom objects to expecting a man to feel fatherly emotions for the child he did not "engender," Midgley is unique in objecting to the provision that mothers be expected "to suckle, indiscriminately and without continuity, any baby that on any given occasion is handed to them."[172] Unlike the commentators of the previous hundred years, Midgley's vantage point as a mother may well make her particularly sensitive to this point.

Midgley shares with many other writers, as we have seen, her objections to the state's requiring citizens "to be ready to leap into sexual activity each time that the state confronts them with a breeding partner, but to be abstinent all the rest of their lives."[173] It is not clear exactly what she intends by this latter phrase, but she would surely seem to be mistaken if she forgets that Plato is providing only for what might be considered a short period of adult sexual life. It is important to recall that not only adolescents, but also older men, as well as women over forty, are free to follow their inclinations. In the end, Midgley thinks that tackling the quite tough problems of women's lives with the concept of equality is like trying to dig a garden with a brush and comb. She wishes to reconcile the idea of our having a specific nature, a capacity to do "what each of us has it in him to do," with the possibility of freedom and ameliorative social change.[174] Thus, she does not object to the use of the word "unnatural" to describe treating men and women altogether in the same way. Nor does she mind anyone saying that Plato's idea of abolishing marriage and "the family" is unnatural. She differs from those of us who find the concept of "the natural" vacuous; she finds it useful in so far as we make clear its double sense. Things, she says, can be natural in the minimal sense—widely practiced, emotionally seductive, hard to eradicate—and yet do not have to be so in the strong sense in which we are called to approve them. But will people be willing to give up the advantage of the positive connotations of calling something natural, of the emotive force of such a usage? In our modern secular society, few would be inclined to say "that practice is natural but very bad." The danger is far greater that thinkers will continue to capitalize on what Lovejoy termed "the metaphysical pathos" of words like "natural," just as Elshtain calls Plato's reforms "social engineering," but would never describe the radical changes she might propose in such terms.

Because Midgley desires a better world for all, she declares it "hard to take much interest" in the question of whether the few at the top are male or female. Understandably, she is more worried about the majority of men and women left in what they regard as outer darkness, even if all sex barriers were removed. Elshtain, on the other hand, is concerned with gender equality, but asks what woman would accept parity on Plato's terms? She believes that the vast majority of individuals, both in Plato's time and today, would prefer to remain in their unjust societies.[175] I myself am not so sure that the circumcised wife in modern Sudan or even the elderly impoverished American widow whose family lives thousands of miles away might not well prefer the life of one of Plato's female guardians to their own existence. This is not to deny the extreme nature of Plato's reforms, but only to reiterate that the family arrangements that have existed and persist in many parts of the world have surely not been any more consistent with that human flourishing that Elshtain desires. There is a certain lack of sympathy for this fact in her vituperative attack on Plato's attempt to find a more just ordering of society.

Elshtain's diatribe against Plato also includes a rejection of the mind-body split underlying his metaphysics and of his consequent devaluing of the body. In rejecting the idea that men and women do not differ in their fundamental nature, she tells us that her being a woman is the "essential and interesting bedrock" of her identity. (Presumably, a commensurate formulation is true of men, too.) She speaks of the "bio-social" and "psycho-social and sexual identity" of women that is "stripped away" in Plato's scheme.[176] Doubtless, our physiology is a component of our identity; nevertheless, at the risk of feminist and modernist heresy, I would still suggest that de-emphasizing the body has some value. One need not commit oneself to oldtime religion or repressive psychological theories to advocate less preoccupation with the body. Women have suffered for a long time from the persistent emphasis of the world's thinkers on the anatomical differences between the two sexes. The great paintings of the Renaissance show graphically the belief that the evil temptations of women's anatomy keep humankind (or men at any rate) from entering the

Kingdom of Heaven. Plato at least saw that deeply felt moral knowledge and scientific excellence were attainable regardless of one's sexual anatomy. Women have suffered greatly from being taught to focus on their bodies, enhance their physical charms, minimize their so-called anatomical imperfections, and use their bodies to barter for advantage. Even today, among the best educated women, there is alarming evidence that females continue to be more preoccupied with their bodies than males. Researchers and clinicians find female college students troubled by body-related concerns. These show up in obsessional concern with clothing, constant dieting patterns, and acute disturbances in eating behaviors. College counselors describe women as caught up in an unending struggle to reshape their bodies, change their faces, and clothe themselves in expensive and often uncomfortable clothing. One researcher notes, "This consistent societal emphasis on a woman's body leads women to use their bodies as a primary source of validation."[177]

Such negative results of emphasis on the importance of the body do not decisively prove that Plato was right to de-emphasize anatomical differences. But it does suggest that there may be some merit to Socrates' minimizing of the importance of female anatomy for his guardians. Numerous studies have concluded that, although more than half the undergraduate students in the United States today are female, women's growth in general competence and knowledge in college does not match that of men. Research shows that this is attributable at least in part to women's continued obsessions with their bodies.

Nor does Plato de-emphasize the body in the way that some feminist scholars would have us believe. Bodily excellence is a great value to Plato; it is only anatomical differences that he wishes to minimize. His program of rigorous physical activity is crucial to the development of male and female guardians alike. In contrast, today the competitive sports that colleges support to foster individual achievement and collaborative effort among men are, in the words of one educator, "only grudgingly being opened to women." An American judge, in ruling on a case of sexual discrimination in education, stated that athletic competition builds character in our boys, echoing the ancient Platonic view.

But, he adds, "We do not need that kind of character in our girls, the women of tomorrow."[178]

In my view then, Elshtain is wrong in condemning Plato so vociferously for minimizing bodily differences between individuals. Her own accentuation of diversity, spontaneity, plurality, the concrete uniqueness of the way each individual as Heidegger puts it, "stands in" the world, has merit. Nevertheless, for the task of shaping political theory, the ability to reason clearly, and use language precisely is crucial. And if we are committed to discourse, we must employ the laws of logic, laws to which one's "psycho-sexual identity" is ultimately irrelevant. Even for those of us who prefer the twentieth-century view shared by existential-phenomenologists and British linguistic philosophers, that we are not separable bodies and minds, but beings who as Sartre phrased it, "exist" our bodies, aspects of the Platonic view remain useful. There is still a sense in which, for the purposes of thinking, femaleness or maleness remains as she puts it contemptuously, merely "contingent."[179] Even if it could be shown that my experience of the public and private sphere will always differ from male experience, regardless of how egalitarian societies become, the fact remains that in order to understand any descriptions there must be intended meanings whose referents are the same for both sexes. Otherwise, Elshtain writes only for women, or for those who have had similar, or even somehow identical, experiences to hers.

Elshtain's attack on androgyny also seems to me mistaken. She rejects this movement toward identifying traits which have been socially stereotyped for one sex and fostering their development in the other sex. Elshtain says that although equality can be used as a political rallying cry, androgyny cannot.[180] But in fact many have already put their energies into such a movement, and we have already seen the resulting changes in social behavior even at the elementary school level in the United States, changes for which we can and must continue to agitate. Plato, as we have seen, was aware that his guardians must combine the traits of gentleness and spiritedness. Elshtain finds little value in this call for an amalgamation of traits made twenty-four hundred years ago. In my view, however, such wisdom is one of the many reasons why the text of the *Republic* has had such enduring vitality and will continue to merit admiration despite her attempts to disenthrall us.

THE PERSISTENCE OF SEXISM IN RECENT COMMENTARY

Most of the writers in the 1970s have chosen to examine the Platonic proposals primarily because they are themselves interested in the achievement of gender equality. Allan Bloom is a notable exception among them, and I shall therefore conclude my analysis of recent commentary with a discussion of his views. As a well-known classicist and translator, his chief interest is in explicating the text; and his sympathies do not lie in the direction of changing the traditional relation between the sexes or equalizing opportunity. His earlier remarks in his "Interpretive Essay" have been widely attacked. In the 1970s and 1980s, he has chosen to defend his position and even to expand and reinforce those assertions which have caused him to be repeatedly termed "sexist."

He is not only courageous in maintaining his unpopular position, but adamant in his interpretations of the text. He maintains that the consequences of Plato's assumption of the inferiority of women as a class would inevitably mean that the best women are always inferior in capacity to the best men. Recent commentators challenge this interpretation, demonstrating that Bloom's logic is fallacious. All that is implied is that on average women are less capable than men. Logically speaking, the most outstanding *individuals* could still turn out to be female.[181]

As an example to dramatize this point, I offer the biological fact that in living mammals, the class of males is on the whole larger than the class of females. However, many species do exist in which females are larger than males. Relevant to a refutation of Bloom is the fact that females are the larger sex in the blue whale, the largest species which has ever lived on earth. The biologist Katherine Ralls points out that, therefore, the largest *individual* animal was or is undoubtedly a female.[182]

Thus, the most competent individual in the *kallipolis* might well have been a female and among the best (as among the biggest) there might well be a great number of females. We have no way of knowing whether Plato thought out these implications. But at the very least there seems no reason to believe with Bloom that there wouldn't be enough females to go around if education and earliest training were identical, just as today at elite traditionally male universities we have reason to believe that if only test scores indicating scholastic ability were considered, entering classes would be at least half female. As we have seen, Bloom contends that females are needed only for their difference, for their ability to reproduce the guardian class. But this rejection of the idea that their nature warrants their participation remains unsupported.

The argument of Bloom's which receives most attention in the new commentary is his repeated insistence that the proposals are offered in jest.[183] Several writers attack this claim that in Book V, Plato is trying to outdo Aristophanes at his own game. Dale Hall attempts to prove that Bloom is wrong about the seriousness of Plato's intent, and thus about the desirability of equality for women as well as the possibility of the combination of philosophy and ruling. He charges Strauss and Bloom with pursuing an approach which is "anachronistic and unhistorical."[184] Like the other critics of Bloom, he suggests that nudity in the gymnasium is not such an absurd impossibility. Even if there is a connection between *Ecclesiazusae* and Book V, Hall finds no convincing reason to accept Bloom's speculation on a comedic rivalry. Barker's view that Plato was seeking to meet the current satire or Adam's conclusion that Plato is taking seriously Aristophanes' parody of views with which Plato himself sympathized, is every bit as plausible.[185]

An extended discussion of the probable relation between Aristophanes' *Assembly of Women (Ecclesiazusae)* and the implications of that connection is necessary, and I shall consider the matter shortly. First, however, it is important to refute the view of the *Republic* as irony on general grounds. I wish to cast doubt on Bloom's total account of human sexuality and its relevance to gender equality. Hall's charge that Bloom's views of gender are "anachronistic" is probably mistaken. For the proposals would undoubtedly seem as strange to fourth-century Athenians as to even the most biased of modern professors. As Bloom himself says, Socrates was well aware that he was wounding the "dearest sensibilities of masculine pride."[186] In general, however, Hall's attack is well aimed and his objection that Plato gives us no evidence that Socrates' intentions are ironic as he does in the other dialogues, is cogent.

To this, I would add other crucial objections. Bloom accuses his opponents of not paying attention to the text.[187] But if we pay close attention to the text, we must find a convincing interpretation for the oft-quoted statement that the useful is beautiful and the useless ugly. Even if we read Plato as Bloom would have us do, as primarily a dramatist in the *Republic,* rather than a metaphysician offering serious arguments, we still have only two possibilities for giving the statement meaning. Either Plato is totally ironic here and does not mean that only what is useful is beautiful, or he in general believes this, but in this particular case, thinks it doesn't apply. If Plato is being ironic about the value of the useful, then his banishing of the poets because of their detrimental effect on the state is based on some kind of satirical falsehood. This would be true of many other of the major tenets of the work, making the whole enterprise a kind of doublespeak, a conclusion it is not clear whether Bloom himself is willing to support.

The other possibility is that Plato usually believes this, but is showing us how such "utilitarianism" doesn't always apply. Plato would then be taking seriously the opinion of the masses that women exercising naked alongside men is laughable and, though useful, nevertheless absurd. His argument (which we have no reason to doubt) that non-Greeks originally laughed at that Athenian practice which his audience accepts as useful, would be invalid, somehow underscoring the alleged comedy. Our knowledge of the text of the *Crito,* where Socrates explicitly demonstrates that it is not the opinion of the many which is to be considered, must also be ignored. Here, the opinion of the many is correct and Socrates is suggesting an absurdity.

Either possibility does not seem satisfactory. We can concur with Bloom that "senses of humor . . . do differ."[188] Nevertheless, he has not succeeded in proving his case, neither in his original essay nor in his rejoinders to his feminist opponents. He has not demonstrated that Plato only jested about equal training for women, nor has he shown that the proposal is, was, and always will be, laughable.

I do not wish to belabor further the point about the hilarity of female nudity, for the focus should be on equality of training, rather than on the clothing worn (or nor worn). But it is worth pointing out how very idiosyncratic Bloom's sense of humor is. He writes that imagination suggests that "the external signs" of erotic attractions on the playing fields "might provide some inspiration for tasteless wits." And, when reminded about Athenian homosexuality in connection with the need to control eros, he states that homosexual intercourse can be consistently forbidden, but not heterosexual intercourse.[189] But wouldn't the tasteless wits have had just as much of a field day watching men attracted to men, if there were no way of controlling the physical signs of attraction? Socrates is clear about such physical signs as in the passage from Kharmides (155c–e), when the philosopher is inflamed by the sight of the sexually aggressive Kharmides' provocatively open cloak.[190] Of course, when men are concentrating on another important activity, the erections to which I assume Bloom is referring can presumably be controlled. On Bloom's own terms, such control would have had to be exercised in the Greek gymnasia in order to avoid constant comic outbursts.[191]

The issue is only important because it helps show that Bloom's entire view of sexuality is askew. He says we need freedom from a moralism which forbids us to see what in nature defies convention in order to read a Platonic dialogue. But Bloom fails to appreciate that human sexuality is a much more complicated phenomenon than his assumption of a fixed natural condition allows. Plato did not believe that *desire* for same-sex intercourse was unnatural. The Catholic Church does not find total sexual abstinence "unnatural," but rather both possible and admirable for its elite. Masturbation, on the other hand, it does judge "unnatural." Regulation of sexual expression has always existed; and if gender equality really entailed the elimination of that shame which he considers natural, then it seems to me that revisions of what we consider shameful both can and ought to be undertaken. The burden of proof remains on Bloom to demonstrate that the connection between shame and eros is unalterable.

To Bloom it is completely absurd for Socrates to found his argument on the assertion that the difference between male and female is no more to be taken into account than the one between bald men and men with hair. The proper question here is: taken into account *for what?* My answer is to support a functional view of human beings. Such role-oriented arguments are still tenable despite the opposition of many feminists who would like to abandon a functional approach because it has worked against females in the past. It is true that male philosophers have traditionally asked "What are women useful for?" and come up with only one answer. But the question itself does not entail that women are solely for childbearing any more than men are solely for inseminating. But if the aim is to increase the size of a family or a total population, then the sex of the two people engaged in the activity is relevant, whereas their baldness is not.

Thus, certain qualities are relevant to certain tasks as Plato clearly pointed out, and it does not make sense to say that these qualities are never sex-linked. For the task of incubating a human infant, as opposed to a bird embryo, having female reproductive organs is relevant. For the task of nurturing children—which I assume to include unselfish and affectionate concern for the infant's welfare, investment of time and energy teaching the child skills and guiding thc child's values, as well as provision for the material well-being of the child—I cannot see that the nature of the reproductive structure or function is any more relevant than the amount of hair. If this point of view is absurd, then it is an absurdity being maintained by an increasing number of otherwise intelligent people. At the very least, the absurdity is not self-evident. The question of what women are for is not different from the question of what men are for. To be human is to be capable of choosing certain goals, and it is always relevant to ask which capacity and which action, whether by female or male, can best realize a particular desired goal.

The accusation that feminists make against political thinkers that they ask "what is man's nature?", but "what are women for?" cannot be legitimately leveled against Plato. Instead, he asks in general "what are men and women for"? He believes that some men and presumably some women (although he does not so specify) are equipped for carpentering—as we would say, have the genetic talent for it. Some men and some women, on the other hand, are suited for doctoring, an activity he does mention for women, although we have no other account of the existence of any female physicians in ancient Greece. He believes education can foster excellence in medical practice, but basically one either possesses the ability to learn that function more easily and therefore ultimately better than another, or one doesn't. Each person thus has a natural function suiting him or her to a particular task. And Plato's whole concept of justice is based, not in jest, but seriously, on the idea of each one "doing what comes naturally."

Bloom's judgment of his own belief in the vast importance of the differences between the sexes is probably correct. He judges that his view is "not due solely to his ethnocentrism." Unless ethnocentrism has become a code word for male chauvinism, the charge against him must be broadened. His sexism no longer pervades our entire culture. For today, in electing a leader in some countries, as well as in the selection of a professor of Greek or philosophy by some of those academics whose pedantry he derides, reference to gender has indeed become as irrelevant as Plato suggested it might be. This is not to claim that any modern culture has achieved the total disregard of gender. Some argue that the choice of a female prime minister in England was made because she was the best qualified individual; whereas, in the United States the appointment of a female to the Supreme Court, as well as the selection of a female vice presidential candidate, was based precisely on the candidates' femaleness. Such strategic necessity has arguably influenced the appointment of female professors. But the point behind such choices is that it has now become wise strategy for justice to be seen to be done. And the answer to Bloom is that when female appointments are made, his "masculine pride" must cope with the fact that the gender of the candidate will eventually turn out to be no more relevant than the baldness of the cobbler is to his performance of his trade.

This brings us at last to that connection which Bloom has persisted over the years in maintaining is absolutely crucial to a correct reading of the *Republic.* The fact that Socrates refers to the *Ecclesiazusae* he considers "too evident to need discussion."[192] It will be remembered that the great German classicist Wilamowitz, author of numerous books on Plato and on ancient literature, asserted precisely the opposite, in the same impatient tone.[193] But Bloom summarily dismisses all those, and the number is great, who have denied any connection between the bawdy comedy—in which women dress up in men's clothing, take over the assembly and impose their will on their husbands—and the proposals in Book V.[194] The most recent editor of the Greek text, R. G. Ussher, points out that chronology can support either the view that Aristophanes guys the views of Plato, or that Plato builds (with "*reproaches for his levity*") on the principles put forward by the playwright. Neither dating nor similarities of language and expression prove that Plato is referring to the play. Ussher leans toward the view that the model for Plato's political views is "some now unknown thinker, prominent at the period . . . of the play, but later ignored by Aristotle. That Plato copies Aristophanes is very unlikely, whereas the possibility that both rely on an earlier philosophy is not only likely but attractive."[195]

Ussher points out that as early as 1811, Book V had already been seen as an answer to Aristophanes' travesty of Plato's already known views. I assume Bloom would consider Ussher's position merely another in a long line of inventors of "schools of thought the existence of which has no basis in historical fact."[196] But, of course, his own interpretation also has no basis in historical fact, but must rely largely on his idiosyncratic reading of both texts.

Ussher is clearly correct that any statements about the relation of the two texts *must be tentative,* given our current state of knowledge. Is Bloom's absolute certainty then based on some ulterior motive? Ussher's argument that the play itself does not even prove that Aristophanes himself is rejecting either the rule of women or communism in the last scenes, but rather "playing for laughs," is convincing. The last scenes are not chapters in a textbook as they have sometimes been misread to be. I think, although I am not certain, that Bloom's view of their vying for comic effect also involves that both Aristophanes and Plato actually rejected the idea of equality for women. Bloom hints on several occasions that his view of the *Republic* would all come clear if we understood the Platonic view of the relation between poetry and philosophy. But while we await his promised clarification of the subject, it is hard to ignore the fact that Aristophanes was clearly writing the former.

Even if we grant that Praxagora's speech about the lot of women and the fact that parents would not know their own children bear pronounced resemblances in content (and perhaps in style, although this is less certain) to passages in Book V, this hardly proves that Plato, too, is playing for laughs. Praxagora is married to an offensive old man who, it is hinted, has difficulty satisfying her sexual needs. A consequence of the reform she demands involves a beautiful young man being forced into intercourse with an ugly old woman. Bloom describes this as an instance of what is "most private and most unequal by nature" being subject to the public sector. It shows "the absurdity of trying to make politics total, of trying to make an equal distribution of all that is rare, special and splendid. . . . It reveals the tension between *physis* and *nomos,* nature and civil society."[197]

But what of the unnaturalness of Praxagora's union, or of any beautiful young woman, like the fourteen-year-old described in Xenophon's *Oeconomicus,* forced to take over the running of the household and the duties of the marriage bed of a man twice her age? Are we to assume that this is merely one of the natural inequalities which Bloom considers "necessary concomitants of any political order"? If erotic choice is rare, special, and splendid, surely it is so as much for a beautiful young woman as for Bloom's beautiful young man. Aristophanes himself perhaps has some idea of the purely conventional nature of such arrangements.

At any rate, to take Plato comically assumes that he knew only too well that all the equality of training which he proposes could never make women men's equals. Bloom believes the "actualizable regime" of the *Laws,* where "women are educated differently and lead very different lives," is the political result of the inquiry of the *Republic.* But even in the *Laws,* Plato proposes an education far more similar than that current in Athens. Why does he bother, if the pronounced inequalities noted in *Ecclesiazusae* are simply natural and necessary? Why propose women magistrates who make important decisions if a state in which even the best females have no voice in the assembly is somehow natural?

I shall not dwell here on the rest of Bloom's idiosyncratic interpretation of the relation between philosopher and city in the *Republic,* for he says himself that he is only offering a series of hints about the permanent human problems involved in Socrates' "playful competition with Aristophanes." I applaud this rare expression of the seriousness of the issues of erotic choice and gender equality. The reader must decide, however, whether Bloom is convincing when he asserts that the focus of the issue of political reform for both Praxagora and Socrates is sexual affairs, and the reason that philosophers must rule is also chiefly a matter of sexual activities. For according to Bloom, the philosopher-guardians are "primarily matchmakers or eugenicists who have to spend a great deal of time and subtlety . . . to get the right people to have sexual intercourse with each other."[198]

At the risk of laying myself open again to that charge of the "stiff pedantry" of academics which Bloom deplores, I would suggest that sexuality as a means to other ends is Plato's intention in Book V, as it is in the *Symposium.* There is no way to know for certain whether Plato, if he in fact knew the *Ecclesiazusae,* would have shared the Athenian acceptance of Praxagora's copulation with the flatulent Blepyrus as natural, whereas a young man copulating with an old woman would be judged unnatural. We know only that in his ideal city, he found no reason to advocate such a reversal. The unions proposed were not laughable in the Aristophanean sense. The best were to be mated with the best, presumably the young and the fair with the young and the fair. (Among the guardians, theoretically, a fifty-five-year-old man could mate with a twenty-year-old woman, and a forty-year-old woman with a twenty-five-year-old man.) I cannot see that such arrangements would seem outrageously comic even on the basis of the Athenian categories of "the natural" versus "the conventional." How much less so to those of us who find such categories ultimately unworkable. In this case, I do not even think senses of humor differ all that much. In this, as in most of the other issues, we have reason to believe that Bloom's certainty about the permanent inequality of the sexes is gradually becoming a minority opinion.

3

The Continuing Importance of Plato's Questions

Enthusiasts and disciples of Plato have repeatedly claimed that he had already raised in the 5th century B.C. all the fundamental questions of philosophy, that subsequent discussions, as Whitehead remarked, have all been merely "footnotes."[1] In respect to what used to be called The Woman Question, that claim is no exaggeration. For all the major contemporary issues of sexual equality are touched on in the arguments of *Republic*, Book V. And even the order in which Plato raised the questions still remains cogent. For decisions about the roles desirable for males and females today still must be based on a general theory of what kind of society we want. That is, some answer to the question of what society best promotes the welfare of all underlies all current demands for change in the position of women. We cannot ask what is best for women without inquiring, with equal urgency, what is best for men.

Further, in this process of deciding what makes a society desirable for all, we still need to ask if there are any innate biological differences between the sexes that must be considered. The search for "natural differences" now leads us to research in genetics, biochemistry, and neurology. But there is also still an interest in ethology, in observations and theories about the behavior of animals and its relevance to the roles the sexes ought to assume in human society. Plato referred his listeners to the behavior of guard dogs. Contemporary sociobiologists point instead to the apes and other primates, terming them "our closest relatives," and referring to their "fixed action patterns" in discussing possibilities and norms for human behavior. So, too, Plato's discussion continues on whether current sex roles are conventional, that is, primarily (or entirely) the result of culture. Reformers and anthropologists are interested in what the evidence of other societies can teach us. Just as Plato pointed to Sparta and to practices in legendary societies, modern anthropologists make statements about the feasibility of change or the "stubborn resistance" to change in sex roles on the basis of cross-cultural studies.

The connection between the family, private property, and women's role is also as vital an issue today as it was when Plato proposed the abolition of private families for his philosopher-rulers. Plans to liberate women, or to keep them in their traditional place at the hearth, still depend on choices between the creation of new family patterns or the retention of the old husband-as-breadwinner-and-protector of his own family unit. Radical feminists charge that capitalism and female obedience with its stultification of women's possibilities are intertwined. And advocates of women's primary role as helpmate and mother wish to retain the economic *status quo* with fixed family and property relations. Those who do not want to throw out the baby with the bathwater and who hope to retain romantic love, companionate marriage, and the exclusive affectional bonds of nuclear families still must consider the question in Plato's terms. They still have not solved the question of how these values can be maintained if women are to have exactly the same opportunities and responsibilities as men.

While we are in the process of deciding what the just society ought really to include, and to what extent the roles of the sexes should be identical, we continue to face decisions on educational policy. Once again, the progression is the same as it appears in Book V. Given our aims, what kind of education can best produce the results we seek? If equality of role is best, then should the education of the sexes be identical? If women have always been at a disadvantage, should current educational practices be designed to compensate for this fact? What if the "slight disadvantage" is biologically based, as Plato himself believed and some contemporary scientists also conclude? In other words, current thinkers, in asking whether the discrepancies in attainment are merely the result of age-old differential socialization, are asking the same questions Plato raised. Plato thought in very broad terms about what we now call the "socialization" process. He wanted to control the music and dance his *kallipolites* learned, and to censor the stories they heard. So, too, today's reformers see the need to change media images of the two sexes. They wish to alter the forms of address and restrict publication of sexist language.

Even the final question that Plato asks and never really answers decisively continues to plague us. Is a society ruled by reason and committed to gender equality genuinely possible? Can androgynous lovers of wisdom really accede to leadership in a modern state? Some thinkers describe democracy as threatened constantly by the discrepancy between the myth that all men are created equal and the reality that biology produces unequal and irreversible distribution of crucial abilities.[2] For the same reason, some classicists believe that the basic innate inequality between the sexes makes Plato's egalitarian proposal an unrealizable goal. A current educational strategy of using different methods for different "learning styles" presupposes some possibility of roughly equal attainment. Plato, of course, entertained no such democratic notions and the success of such contemporary efforts to equalize results is still questionable. We cannot prove that a just society which provided equal opportunity not only for its rulers, but for all its citizens, would result in the virtuous happiness of all. This irremediable inequality is what the distinguished scientist E. O. Wilson considers the basis of "the tragic contradictions of human existence."[3] As a sociobiologist, he deals with the same questions that Plato raised; but he answers with certainty that, given our biological heritage, the ideal society of the philosophers could not come into being.

I shall deal at some length with Wilson's views and those of other sociobiologists. For although they are researchers trained in scientific disciplines, they are also the thinkers in contemporary society who, like Plato, have combined their empirical observations with speculation about human social organization in an effort to explain why human societies are as they are. Many of them consciously intend to supplant the philosophers and prescribe, as Plato did, how society *ought* to be, given its biological basis. It is true that some of them equivocate on whether their findings have implications for social policy. As we shall see shortly, one researcher, who insists that there is a distinctive male human nature and a pronouncedly different female human nature—thus contradicting the Platonic view—nevertheless, argues that his conclusions have no policy implications whatsoever.[4] Such an assumption is naive, "wildly unrealistic," as one critic put it.[5] Undoubtedly, all those commentators we have discussed who, through the centuries, have assumed without evidence that there are profound biological differences which invalidate the Platonic reforms, would have welcomed such "scientific" conclusions. They would surely have considered such sociobiological theories about the radical differences between the sexes as decisive support for their own views.

In fact, many of the practitioners of this new scientific discipline, which attempts to build evolutionary theory by showing the interaction between genes and culture, explicitly ask both of the Platonic questions in regard to sexual equality. Leading proponents have addressed both issues: 1) what is the best arrangement for human welfare; and 2) what is biologically possible. And they have assumed these questions to be related in exactly the way Plato did. We must think through what is just, but the possibilities are limited by what ethology and empirical observations about actual practices teach us.

Writers often try to divide those theorizing about the best society into opposing camps, positing a Nature Versus Nurture debate. David Barash, a leading sociobiologist, thinks that Plato, unlike Aristotle, maintained that human beings were "the products of society."[6] Such an interpretation has two flaws. A persistent complaint against the *Republic* is that it would result in a class society in which those who were biologically superior would always remain on top. Whatever else can be said in Plato's defense by egalitarian thinkers who would stress his emphasis on the importance of education, there can be no doubt that his commonwealth is based on a belief in innate merit. In fact, as we have seen, his ideas about the breeding of human beings in the manner of race horses would place him more likely in the camp of the "naturists," were such clear-cut divisions ever workable. The truth, however, is that few have ever seriously argued for the existence of such mutually exclusive alternatives. As Stephen Jay Gould, one of the most vocal and most convincing of the scientific opponents of sociobiology, puts it: "Every scientist, indeed, every intelligent person, knows that human social behavior is a complex and indivisible mix of biological and social issues. The issue is not *whether* nature or nurture determines human behavior, for they are truly inextricable, but the *degree, intensity, and nature of the constraint* [*my emphasis*] exerted by biology upon the possible forms of social organization."[7]

Indeed, the question now, as it was in Plato's time, is precisely whether there are any "constraints" limiting the possibilities of women's participation in society. Wilson, the founder of sociobiology, informs us that ethical questions (and presumably, by extension, questions of the best organization of society) should be removed from the hands of the philosophers since they have insufficient knowledge of biology and evolutionary theory.[8] Let us turn then to the pronouncements of several sociobiologists, ethologists, and primatologists who have used their superior biological knowledge to supplant the philosophers. In my view, they shed less light on the relation of biology and society than did Plato more than twenty-three hundred years ago.

Wilson's own view of sex differences is that the current role distinctions have only "a slight biological component." At birth, he tells us, "the twig is already bent a little bit."[9] A feminist disciple of his defends his use of this metaphor, judging that it indicates only a slight deviation from the desired norm, a minor constraint that need concern us little in deciding what women's role ought to be.[10] In my view, the formulation is neither helpful nor quite so innocuous. It carries the overtones of deformity which have historically appeared over and over from Aristotle to Freud in discussions of women's sexual differences. Furthermore, the implications of Wilson's image are ambiguous. For with careful treatment, bent twigs can be straightened; and for some construction at least, bent twigs might be as good as, or better than straight ones. The real question is what the implications for human societies are of Wilson's "modest predisposition" toward the sex-role inequities which are an "inconvenient and senseless residue" of our biological legacy.[11]

The problem is that the oft-used metaphor of a biological "inheritance" does not help us in assessing the *degree* of constraint. For we can always renounce a legacy, give up an inheritance. And if we attend only to the literal meaning of Wilson's pronouncements, ignoring their tone and the uses some of his followers have made of his views, this biologist is no more anti-egalitarian than Plato himself was. Wilson concludes that biological evidence alone cannot prescribe an ideal course of action, but only help us to define the options and assess the price.

He sees the options concerning sex roles as limited to three possibilities. We can 1) condition members so as to exaggerate sex differences, as is done in most societies; 2) train members so as to eliminate all sex differences; or 3) provide equal access to opportunities, but take no further action. This last option he dubiously calls a *laissez faire* course of making *no choice* at all. This last possibility he finds internally inconsistent and unworkable; in his view, this has been demonstrated in the Israeli kibbutz.[12]

Plato's proposed state is closest to the second alternative. The philosopher assumed his proposals to be based on exactly the sound biological knowledge Wilson accuses philosophers of neglecting. He deemed further action necessary to eliminate sex differences, but such action was designed only to re-educate the upper echelons and change the previous sexual divisions which were based solely on convention. Although he judged men to be biologically more competent as a class in all activities, he did not think any extraordinary methods were necessary to correct women's slight disadvantage.

For Wilson, however, although women's disadvantage is also considered only slight, more strenuous measures will be required. For it is not a matter of degree of competence alone. There are what we would have to call biological differences *in kind*. The discrepancies Wilson finds will require quotas to correct the socially induced disadvantages, but also will require what he calls "sex-biased education" to compensate for biological differences. If we institute both measures, it will then be "possible to create a society in which men and women as groups share equally in all professions, cultural activities and even athletic competition." Although such a society would require the blunting of early predispositions, "the biological predispositions are not so large as to make the undertaking impossible."[13] Both the modern biologist and the ancient philosopher agree that such control over society would result in a much more productive and harmonious society.

Wilson, however, notes the cost of such regulations. Personal freedoms would be jeopardized and some individuals would not be allowed to reach their full potential, he warns. Most commentators in the last hundred years have expressed concern over the first cost, the loss of personal freedom. But since Plato did not call for compensatory measures, none of his interpreters have needed to worry about what we have come to call "reverse discrimination." So whereas they have been outraged at the human cost of solidifying a class system, no commentator has consciously noted that if you promote female guardians, some capable men might be prevented from entering the guardian class.

Commentators have noticed a possible loss of human potential in the Platonic state. They have worried that women's potential for fulfillment through nursing their children and bonding with them would be lost; and some have even remarked about the loss of family affections for men. Although Wilson does not address the question directly, we can assume that his judgment on a state in which neither men nor women are involved in the care of their own children would be that it hinders that "complete emotional development" he desires for both sexes. For Plato, freedom from child care is entirely positive. Wilson, however, states only that abstention from participation in child rearing "might" stunt men's emotional growth. (Presumably, then it would also stunt woman's growth, as so many commentators have noted. Wilson perhaps thinks this so obvious as to be unnecessary to mention as he considers possible alternative societies.)

In Wilson's third possible society, where no action is taken to offset the differences of the bent twig, the provision of equal opportunities and access, he says, will not suffice. If identical education is provided, but no heroic measures are taken, men will continue to hold a disproportionate representation in political life, business, and science.[14] Evidently, he assumes a separable phenomenon called "identical education" could occur. Men have often taken this view, as if equal exposure to the same subject matter were all that was involved in education. But surely all aspects of the educational process cannot be identical unless there are concomitant changes in the roles of the adults that students see in the world around them. Without changes in the subtle gender expectations of teachers, there is no way that education can be truly identical. It is a curiously abstract notion of education that allows Wilson to assume that we could provide truly equal access to all professions and yet make no choices about sex differences. Plato knew better and realized that even the music and body motion of very young children presupposes a theory about their future roles.

Wilson sees the Israeli kibbutz as an example of the workings of an egalitarian ideology without the necessary strenuous compensatory measures. The desired equity has not occurred. His attitude toward the current regression toward traditional roles in the kibbutz is ambiguous. On the one hand, he thinks that "inadequate regulation" has kept gifted women from developing their potential for commercial and political leadership and has also denied men the emotional rewards of involvement with children. On the other hand, he emphasizes much more forcefully that, "despite being trained from birth in the new culture," Israeli women have opted for the development of their emotional potential.[15] He does not stress that they have thereby given up the emotional satisfactions of guardianship. Instead, we are back into a framework where women's "nature" leads them to fulfillment through family rather than leadership.

The Israeli kibbutz *is* the community that most comes to mind when we seek modern examples of Plato's planned society. Like Plato, the original founders of the kibbutz movement sought to eliminate sex differences, traditional family arrangements and property ownership for the good of the community as a whole. The ideology of the original pioneers was designed to establish a special subgroup which, although not composed of philosopher-rulers, was intended to provide an inspirational example for the larger society. Melford Spiro, one of the foremost authorities on gender in today's kibbutz, has come to believe that the lack of sexual equality in today's kibbutz is the result of certain "precultural" factors. Chief among these are sex-based differences, what he calls "motivational dispositions," which he has clearly come to consider as, in some sense, biologically innate. He writes that "even if it were the case that the only natural difference between males and females is one of sexual anatomy, this one difference apparently is not as trivial as had been assumed."[16]

Spiro tries to show that all the provisions he once believed would make for complete gender equality in the kibbutz have failed largely because for the female "the parenting need was the most powerful of all their needs."[17] He tries to show, too, that the free associations of male kibbutz toddlers proves that the degree of aggression they exhibit is biologically programmed, despite efforts of caretakers to treat male and female children equally. Furthermore, even the nudity encouraged between youngsters of the kibbutz (reminiscent of the nude exercises Plato prescribed for both sexes) has not had the desired effect. At puberty, adolescent girls experience shame despite the official views.

Like his fellow anthropologists, Fox and Tiger, he finds support in the reversion to more traditional roles for the view that we must seek equivalent, but not necessarily identical, roles for both sexes in a society. He sees the enhancing of female charm, or as he puts it, "femininity" in beauty parlors, a new development in the kibbutz, as a positive value.[18] However, in my view, the new arrangements have clearly not produced gender equality either in the identity or the equivalence sense. Spiro admits that women no longer hold leadership roles and that many of those involved in early child care are dissatisfied. He even puts it (somewhat grudgingly) that these female caretakers "claim" they don't have the temperament for it. The important issue is that a society in which women choose not to take leadership roles and yet are strongly affected by decisions made by all-male governing boards cannot be a society fostering separate but equal roles.

The key question is why women no longer choose to rule jointly, but have returned to the laundry and the nursery. Plato was well aware that it would not be an easy task to motivate unpaid rulers. And Spiro points out that men, too, are not enthusiastic about taking on the committee work involved in kibbutz management. Presumably, women prefer having the time for their children and grandchildren. But is it really for biological reasons that men do not express the desire to take time for their children, rather than for onerous committees? Can Spiro really show by means of psychological testing of three-year-olds that men have no "internal" interest in the early care of their offspring?

Feminists and others have sought alternative answers for why the original egalitarian kibbutz ideology failed.[19] Surely the fact that early caretakers of Israeli children have always been female suggests the possibility of differential treatment of infants even in the critical pre-verbal years. Nursery workers would be likely to handle (literally and figuratively) little future soldiers differently. From the beginning, Israel was a society geared to military preparedness which—despite female conscription and a nominal role for women in the army—always needed and lauded male warriors. Such a society can hardly be expected to have fostered completely equal leadership roles.[20]

Wilson himself worries that there may be a genetic link between valued qualities like cooperativeness toward groupmates and obsolete, destructive ones like aggressivity toward strangers.[21] Plato, without the benefit of any theories about pleiotropism, the control of more than one phenotypic character by the same set of genes, clearly also thought such a combination natural. Wilson fears that in the planned society, whose creation "seems inevitable" in the coming century, the valuable cooperativeness might be lost if we try to steer people away from the aggressiveness which once provided our "Darwinian edge." Such inevitable social control, he says, would rob man of his humanity in the ultimate genetic sense. In other words, to tamper with the linked phenotypes of cooperation-aggression is absolutely crucial for survival, and yet the results of doing so would be completely disastrous. Evidently, in order to flourish cooperatively, we cannot give up our aggressive traits. But if we continue to act aggressively toward enemies a nuclear war may result. The dilemma is unresolvable, and Wilson thus ends his book with great foreboding. Plato, of course, did not have to deal with our current mutual capacity for total annihilation, and so could allow his guardians to be gentle with each other and fierce toward the barbarian.

Wilson is well aware that cultures can be designed rationally. Like Plato, he believes we can teach and reward and coerce. But like many of the anthropologists who note current changes in the kibbutz and almost all sociobiologists, he stresses the costs rather than the benefits of trying to straighten the twig of sexual inequality. His sympathy is for those whose natural bent has been violated. Thus, he expresses great concern for the cost in personal suffering that homosexuals are paying in a society that does not realize the value of their innate dispositions and mistakenly judges heterosexuality alone to be "natural." But in his role as wiser-than-philosopher biologist and ethicist, he expresses no compassion whatsoever for the thousands of years of oppression and stultification of the possibilities of women which, unlike the persecution of homosexuals, has characterized every known society. Nowhere does he lament the cost paid by women in ancient Greece and China, nor the fate of female infants in modern Asia. He does not consider the widows encouraged to immolate themselves on their husband's funeral pyres well into the twentieth century as worthy of mention alongside his justified horror at Hitler's treatment of homosexuals. Like so many of the earlier Plato commentators, the force of Wilson's social theory, despite his protestations, remains that society as a whole will probably benefit and women themselves be happier if they surrender to their biological constraints.

Even among sociobiologists there are disagreements about exactly what women's innate dispositions are. Melvin Konner accepts the current evidence, rudimentary as it is, that there are marked biological differences between the sexes and judges that these differences will inevitably affect their functioning. He does admit that there is still too little information to make responsible inferences about human behavior. But he clearly finds most telling the fact that there are differences in the male and female rat brain visible to the naked eye and that data on eighteen individuals with a defective gene demonstrate that androgens, and not solely environmental or sociocultural factors, contribute to gender identity.[22] However, the problem for Konner in drawing implications for social policy on the basis of biological research is the reverse of that of Plato. Plato's audience was likely to find the possibility of equal participation of women laughable and highly improbable. Examples of women engaged in desirable occupations were completely non-existent. Proving that a woman ruler was not impossible was the very difficult task that Plato faced. In many intellectual circles today, proving that women are constrained by their biology from performing important societal roles has become the more difficult task. Since females are increasingly moving into leadership roles, it is harder to support the view that traditional sex-role differentiation is inevitable, or even desirable. Sociobiologists find themselves on the defensive. So while Konner, as a biologist, is absolutely convinced that the genetic differences between the sexes result in behavioral differences in degrees of aggression and nurturance, he is eager to assure his audience that discrimination in societal role is not warranted.

Once again, however, although the avowed position is an egalitarian one, hidden biases, conclusions not warranted on the available evidence, emerge in Konner's popular book, *The Tangled Wing.* He expresses sympathy for the women scientists whom he describes as having found gender differences to be "in part biological" and as "uncovering and reporting" that the "sexes are irremediably different."[23] He sees their position as one of "complexity, even anguish." At this stage of research, it is surely impossible for any scientist to "uncover" the *immutability* of gender differences; how could a biologist ever state definitively that a "remedy" for differences could never be found?

Most important, however, is Konner's automatic assumption that the female scientists that he praises for their intellectual courage in facing unpalatable facts, have "sacrificed more than the average brilliant man" to get into problems that trouble them intellectually.[24] Men often worry about the sacrifices women will have to make to pursue a career. Konner is admirably aware of the "oppression . . . bulwarked and bastioned by theories of 'natural' gender differences" that women have suffered. But in speaking of women's sacrifices, he merely assumes, like the male Plato scholars and his fellow sociobiologists, that female researchers have had to sacrifice their emotional potential, presumably the loss of the joys of family life, of carefree leisure and male protection.

But almost all the distinguished women scientists he mentions, ranging from those born early in this century to this current generation, were married and most have children. Their sacrifice is undocumented. When he describes Margaret Mead as "enduring hardships rare for a woman in any era," his description is surely ahistorical and ethnocentric. For millions of women have, and still do, endure far greater hardships in daily toil, forced infanticide, clitoridectomy, psychological abuse—no matter what the loneliness and intellectual courage of a scientific trailblazer. The truth is that the life of a twentieth-century woman scientist, as the lives of women go, is probably among the most satisfactory. In fact, a recent study has shown that far from being victims of great sacrifice, married women in the United States with high status jobs consider themselves and can be objectively rated as having the highest sense of well-being.[25] Since most of his scientists have experienced the satisfactions of rewarding work as well as some of the satisfactions of family life, it is certainly unwarranted to assume that they have sacrificed more than men, and doubtful indeed that they have sacrificed more than the average non-brilliant woman.

Plato, as we have seen, has been accused of making female guardians sacrifice their greatest joys in addition to the general sacrifices that the "average brilliant" male guardians would have to make of family and material goods. In stressing genetic differences, this contemporary biologist might seem to be giving additional support to this view.

He himself is eager to make clear that he does not want to be allied with traditional arguments restricting women to particular societal roles. In discussing gender differences, he calls attention to the finding that women's mood cycles can be predicted from the menstrual cycle, but that men also have the same number of days per month of physical discomfort. Therefore, he assures us that anyone who believes that menstrual distress disqualifies women from such positions as airline pilot and president must consider whether they would want their plane—or their country—piloted by someone who has a few days a month of distress that are completely predictable, or someone who has the same number of uncomfortable days arriving randomly.

Arguments about the negative effects of women's physiology are still with us in public life. In 1982, the United Nations representative from Argentina, when faced with Prime Minister Margaret Thatcher's aggressive stance over his country's invasion of the British-owned Falkland Islands, publicly referred to the "fact" that women were subject to the whims of their hormones. Suffice it to say that the influence of hormones in post-menopausal women has not been adequately studied and that the Argentinian's infuriating comments were based no more on empirical evidence and no less on prejudice than those of his Athenian counterparts. Aristotle, for example, considered the very state of femaleness to be a deformity, since women were unable to concoct or cook their menstrual blood to the final stages of refinement, the fertile stage reached only by male semen.[26]

In fact, Aristotle's belief that there is more difference between women and men than between females and males of other species would undercut Plato's argument from analogy with other animals for opening all societal activities to women as well as men. Most direct evidence of hormonal effects on social behavior have at this point been demonstrated only on animals, rats and songbirds. Even the studies of the effects of the menstrual cycle, which Konner uses to support his view that women should not be limited in their jobs, involve the subjective reports of women describing how they feel rather than direct neurological data.

Subjective factors are, of course, impossible to eliminate in the reporting of all information about sex differences. Konner himself, under the guise of presenting biological information, is guilty of introducing highly speculative theories based as much on wishful thinking as on solid evidence. For he offers us his own version of the Special Excellences argument raised by Plato and rejected by him. As we have seen, many of our commentators believe Plato to have been mistaken; and claim, though without advancing any empirical evidence, that women do have special characteristics that make them ideally suited to certain roles, though not the public high status roles. Konner, however, on the basis of what he considers a growing body of empirical evidence, concludes that women are specially qualified *to govern* at this moment in history. It is his "guess" that in the very near future, objective observers will agree that women differ in the degree of violent behavior for reasons that are in part physiological. And this part is sufficiently important to justify the policy implication that serious disarmament may ultimately necessitate an increase in the proportion of women in government.

Konner discounts the record of past female rulers because such women have invariably been embedded in and bound by an almost totally masculine power structure, and have achieved their positions by being "unrepresentative of their gender."[27] He does admit that some women are as violent as almost any man, but does not note that as cultural roles change, there has been a steady rise in the number of violent crimes committed by women. It is perhaps one of the shortcomings of sociobiological explanations that we cannot be certain that women of the future will not be selected for the presence of aggressive behavior tendencies, causing a more violent female to evolve.

The view of Konner's is currently fashionable and sometimes advanced—equally without definitive evidence—by feminists who point to the so-called gender gap in American politics and to the strength of women's participation in nuclear disarmament movements. Unfortunately, women's tendency to vote for less militaristic candidates, in so far as such a tendency can be substantiated, may as well be the result of women's current role as primary caretaker of sons and her powerlessness, as of any genetic predisposition to pacificism.

Konner nevertheless believes that, since what is required at this historical moment is a tendency to non-violence, given the statistical tendencies of women, "we would all be safer if the world's weapon systems were controlled by average women instead of by average men."[28] Eager as I am both to foster disarmament and to increase the number of women in government, Konner's argument remains more worrisome than convincing. I can see no reason to believe that men advocating disarmament do so because they have a biologically less violent nature. There is no evidence that political peacemakers, past or present, differ in brain structure, have a lower than average level of testosterone, nor even initiated fewer violent interactions in their everyday functioning. There is no guarantee that a political dove would necessarily be less aggressive in his private interactions. The average female that Konner's fellow sociobiologist, Sarah B. Hrdy, describes as highly competitive might well be just as inclined to follow what she saw as her self-interest as the average male. I cannot see that biological factors would guarantee any clear-eyed and possibly unpopular assessment of the need for disarmament. Observation of women in competitive sports who are bound, not by a "masculine power structure," but rather by the desire to win the game in question, use their intelligence and skill with a high degree of aggression, which should not be underestimated. The rulers we need are not those dependent on biological priming, but those capable of overcoming biological constraints, heritages, legacies, etc., in favor of making rational choices. We need representatives of both sexes who are able to reason clearly about alternatives and feel acutely the horrors of war, regardless of their biological predispositions. The presence or absence of hormones, like the reproductive differences Plato discounted, are today just as they were then, irrelevant to suitability for guiding and guarding the flock.

Plato's example of the equality of role in sheep dogs was chosen selectively to buttress his argument. But contemporary sociobiologists, despite their vastly increased knowledge of animal diversity, continue to use their information selectively. Thus, a leading female primatologist and sociobiologist has produced much data that contraverts Konner's optimistic belief in the pacifist nature of females. Sarah B. Hrdy points out, for example, that among all marmoset monkeys studied, fights between females are more frequent and fiercer than those between males. Wild dog and chimpanzee females murder the offspring of subordinate females.[29] She aims to demonstrate that, in general, the prevalent view of the greater competitive potential of males is incorrect. Her years of observation of primate societies convince her that the previous emphasis on the importance of males in structuring the society and the apparent inability of females to maintain stable social structures is inaccurate.

Instead, Hrdy offers a picture of assertive, dominance-oriented females. The primates she has studied exhibit, beside their commitment to reproduction, an equally powerful and universal commitment to compete, and in particular, to quest for high status. She concludes in fact that the central organizing principle of primate social life is competition between females. Although such a picture of the potential of women would have satisfied Plato as equipping them well for their task of guardianship, it does not jibe with Konner's wishful assumption that biology shows that women should rule because they will make better peacemakers.

Over and over again, we see researchers and the social scientists who rely on their work using selected observations primarily to support views they undoubtedly hold for other reasons. Hrdy speaks of the androcentric fantasy of certain primatologists. The physical anthropologist, Donald Symons, whose work has been with Rhesus monkeys, exemplifies the extreme when he assures us that there is a separate male and female human nature based on their vastly different, genetically determined sexual feelings. Symons' position is based on much dubious pre-1960 primate data and highly selective anthropological research as well as impressions gathered from fiction and accounts of female acquaintances. Although it would take us too far afield to attempt a refutation of the many questionable statements Symons makes on the "profound differences in psyche" between the sexes, it is worth discussing one of his contentions which is relevant to the Platonic arrangements.[30]

According to Symons, the male sex drive is critical in human evolution, whereas sexual desire in the female is merely vestigial, a by-product of the masculine phenomenon. Most sociobiologists are inclined to believe that men are always more likely than women to desire sex with more than one partner. Hrdy, on the contrary, questions the pair-bonding hypothesis, which Symons offers, as an explanation of the inevitable differences between the sexes. According to her, recent observation of monkeys and apes make it highly unlikely that the human female's concealed ovulation, non-reproductive sexual activity, and female orgasms are unique. In many primate species, females exhibit aggressive sexuality with numerous mates. Hrdy herself, though she admits that more evidence is needed, believes that there is a selective importance to females of an active, promiscuous sexuality, and that enjoyment of sex could also serve the female's interest at the expense of the male's. She speculates that Western scholars, reluctant to de-emphasize the values of monogamy, may well have overrated its biological importance to the human female. This may explain why, like the Victorians, male biologists assume a lack of sexual feelings in women.

The Greeks did not hold this view at all. In fact, far more prevalent throughout history than the Symons view of the maladaptiveness of promiscuity for women has been the widespread belief in and fear of female sexuality. As Hrdy points out, the majority of the world's cultures have made some efforts to control it. Many deplorable practices, including the surgical alteration of twenty million women today to ensure their faithfulness and the legitimacy of offspring are based on a belief that women are "naturally" every bit as likely to be promiscuous as men. Neither Socrates nor his listeners seemed to have worried about women's unwillingness to engage in sex with multiple partners, though some of his nineteenth- and twentieth-century commentators have been concerned about it. In eliminating monogamy, Plato did not see himself as violating any biological predisposition for either sex. Given recent data on the sexual fantasies and practices of women in the 1970s and 1980s in countries where their activities are relatively less regulated, there seems to me to be less and less support for a belief in the wide discrepancy between males and females in sexual desire.

What is far more convincing is Hrdy's concern that the absence of cooperative effort, the inability to work for the advantage of the entire group rather than that of the individual, may be the biological dispositions that must be overcome by both females and males. Plato's view of the cooperative behavior necessary for successful guardians conforms far more closely to what another primatologist describes as the female "communal" rather than the male "agentic" pattern of social interaction. In discussing sex differences, this researcher points out that "the evolution of self-awareness and language makes much of what we have learned about our primate heritage somewhat trivial."[31] She also points out that females are taught to define their well-being in terms of relationships rather than in terms of self-concern. Presumably, this results from the fact that men, who in every society have more power than women, have succeeded in institutionalizing what is to their advantage, despite any contrary biological disposition of females. But Plato quite correctly realized that both male and female guardians will have to learn to put the welfare of the whole before their own selfish interests.

The question that Plato faced remains as cogent as ever—how what these biologists call "altruism" is to be promoted in a society, since it is crucial not only for survival, but for the maximization of the welfare of all. The philosopher Midgley suggests that as an intellectual position, egoism is perhaps a male "sex-linked doctrine."[32] But few sociobiologists would accept the possibility that women are not only less aggressive, but also more altruistic. Wilson describes only homosexuals as true altruists. While believing women less competitive and less promiscuous, Wilson has founded the entire discipline on the principle that underlying both men and women's social behavior is their "selfish" need to maximize the chances of their genes appearing in the next generation.

Some feminist psychologists, as we have discussed, have sought to demonstrate that women speak in a "different voice," that is, are more concerned with the feelings of others. They do not always declare themselves on whether this is solely culturally induced. Generally, however, they imply that change of social role or education might not eradicate women's greater concern with relationships, since the tendency is in some way tied to their reproductive function. In my view, such speculation on who is programmed to be altruistic has not progressed at all beyond Plato's description of how we can decide what nature an individual has. In the *Republic,* Socrates says that if one learns something faster, then he has a natural bent for the activity. If women can be taught to consider others "more easily" or seem to do it more often without being taught any differently than men, then they're "naturally" less egoistic. But women aren't socialized in the same way as men—we know that—and they never have been. No contemporary social science research can possibly demonstrate that were the identical moral values and emphasis on personal relationships inculcated in both sexes, heterosexual men would nevertheless remain less altruistic. Nor am I sure that Wilson's view of the altruism of homosexuals in the evolutionary sense has much to do with our ordinary usage. The speculation that homosexual males have been selected for helping others rather than competing to get their own genes into the next generation deviates from our usual sense of altruism which includes placing the general welfare of society above one's own immediate self-gratification.

Plato clearly did not believe that women or the avowed homosexuals in his circle were constitutionally more pacifistic or altruistic. Aristophanes can be seen as believing women less ready to support war, but only because it was not in their self-interest to do so. But there seems no empirical evidence nor need for the assumption that one sex is "primed" to be less egoistic. If altruism is a value, we dare not take it for granted that one sex needs less reinforcement to practice it. The task exactly as Plato saw it is still to determine how a society can best promote this quality in all its citizens.

Even among sociobiologists there is a range of opinion about the relations between biology and values. Socrates wanted to demonstrate that the values he sought were at the very least in no way "contrary to nature." If Symons talks as if the fact that "the double standard" in sexual behavior has a biological function, makes it not only understandable, but inevitable and perhaps not undesirable, others are more careful. David Barash wishes to defend his scientific discipline against charges of sexism. Thus, he writes that, although there is a "potential biological basis for the double standard," he is not suggesting that what is biological must also be ethically right or unavoidable. He grants that with the current changes in social tradition and the perfection of birth control, there are sure to be "dramatic changes." He says, however, that we can afford equality of sexual behavior only when the biological consequences of such behavior are equal. And "so long as women, not men, get pregnant, some differences can be predicted."[33]

Presumably, women will always be better at getting pregnant than men, but it is not clear to what extent this makes the "double standard" of male promiscuity and female fidelity inevitable. Plato himself attempted to make allowances for the fact of women's pregnancy, ascertaining that the cost of pregnancy and early child care would be as minimal as possible for his Philosopher-Queens. He evidently saw no particular difficulty that might arise in motivating females to participate in multiple matings. In fact, he assumed that guardian women over forty should be free to handle their sexuality exactly as they pleased so long as no children resulted. Kinsey's statement, that "among all people everywhere in the world, the male is more likely than the female to desire sex with a variety of partners," is often quoted by sociobiologists.[34] But Plato seems to have believed, as did most Greeks, that females were every bit as interested in sex as men. Dover believes that except for the Victorians, it has been widely assumed that women were highly desirous of coitus, presumably not only with one partner, though Dover doesn't explicitly specify.[35] In teaching a wide range of female students from eighteen to seventy-five, my own informal research would suggest that female *desires* are no more monogamous than males. The Hite Report and the Cosmopolitan survey would seem to confirm this. At the very least, sociobiological accounts of female desires surely suffer from lack of adequate evidence.

What needs to be considered is that among all people everywhere, the male has on average been better able to express his desires and choose his encounters, so we really don't know what the female desired or desires. Plato himself stressed the diversity of behavior in different cultures, believed Spartan women to behave in all ways more like men, and no doubt was reinforced in his conviction that women would consent to his mating arrangements by the stories of the promiscuous sexual behavior of Greek goddesses.

It is hard to believe that promiscuity for men and fidelity for women must persist as long as women bear the children. Barash himself states that "humans have achieved liberation from reproduction's tyranny over sex."[36] He does maintain that there is a biological basis for the alleged fact that female politicians have almost invariably been "desexed," that is, less physically attractive than male politicians have been allowed to be. But if this was previously so, it is no longer true in the mid-1980s. Barash would then have to attribute previous choices of unattractive females to the surmountable "influence" of biology rather than to any inescapable constraint.

Barash sees this influence operating in the fact that men are less disposed than women toward "investing heavily in the well-being of their children."[37] Because males of all species must have less confidence in their paternity, "women can be counted on to take care of the kids." That is, the differing reproductive strategies account for why women have almost universally found themselves relegated to the nursery, while men derive their greatest satisfaction from their jobs. Can we expect then that since conclusive proof of paternity will soon be possible, that this age-old unwillingness to participate in child-rearing will disappear? The women's movement of the 1980s has come to realize how crucial it is both to the development of the child and to the very possibility of equality that males be ready, willing, and able to care for children from infancy on.

For Plato, both male and female guardians were to be free of the details of early child care, but both were to participate equally in the later education and rearing. Of course, only genetic relatedness within the group mattered in Plato's society; all children born at the same time were to be considered siblings. Sociobiologists might still not consider this maladaptive, since only a small subgroup would be involved. And for both Barash and Wilson, kin selection—and we would eventually be dealing with an interrelated group—is connected to altruism. And it is exactly such altruism that Plato wished to promote.

Barash not only allows for the possibility that changes may occur in what is adaptive sexual behavior. He even softens the determinist element in sociobiology by attempting to allow for the possibility of free will: "Evolutionary biology is not deterministic. . . . Free will may actually be greatest when everyone is able to behave in accordance with his or her inclinations."[38] Thus what amounts to the determinist view of the majority of the commentators on the Woman Question in the *Republic* might not be warranted on the basis of his answer to the Free Will Question. Presumably, gifted women could freely choose to renounce the influence of their genes and accept their place among the rulers.

This question of whether anatomy is destiny remains as alive today as it was twenty-four hundred years ago. In an item in a respected popular scientific journal reporting on recent discoveries of certain tissue differences in the male and female brain, the writer concluded that this "may be the first indication that anatomy, after all, *is* destiny." These first indications of an anatomical difference between the brains of men and women, they speculate, "may" be linked to the controversial finding that men outdo women at visual-spatial disciplines, such as architecture and geometry. The research by two physical anthropologists who dissected the normal brains of nine men and five women—that is, a total sample of fourteen—found the splenium (the rear portion of the corpus callosum) of the female brain to be larger and more bulbous than in the male brain. This, they suggested, might give women richer communication of visual-spatial information between the two hemispheres and somehow—though they admit it is still a mystery—have the paradoxical effect of limiting women's visual-spatial abilities.[39] But why should such research be seen as an early indication of women's *destiny,* or even as an inevitable limitation on their ability to be outstanding architects or geometricians?

The only answer is that one already presupposes biological

determinism and the inevitability of women's inferiority. Plato, of course, had no knowledge of modern scientific method, no means whatsoever of investigating hormonal and brain chemistry. It is clear that he chose to minimize any possible biological differences other than reproductive ones for his own purposes. But so, too, has the research of the last century and a half into "sex differences" often reflected the unconscious purposes and prejudices of the researchers.

It is now well-known that Victorian scientists argued that if women used their brains excessively, they would impair their fertility by draining off blood cells needed to support the menstrual cycle. (Given the acute need to restrict the birth rate, it is perhaps unfortunate that this "finding" could not be substantiated. Colonies of women working at Greek and algebra might have helped us attain zero population growth throughout the world!) Nineteenth-century scientists stated that it was the smaller brain size that made women less intelligent than men. Then, when craniologists thought intellect to be located in the frontal lobes, autopsy reports showed frontal lobes in females to be smaller. And when researchers decided the parietal lobes were the source of intellect, they found millimeter differences in cadavers whose sex they already knew.[40]

Social scientists, too, have "discovered" sex differences which have not held up upon further investigation. The conclusions of the psychoanalyst Eric Erikson in the 1950s were influential for decades, but have turned out to be highly questionable. He tested eleven- to thirteen-year-old children and concluded that their ways of building and thus of thinking were determined as his mentor Freud had theorized, by their genital anatomy. He found that boys' spatial constructions were dominated by thrusting height and downfall, girls' by static enclosure.[41] Such purported differences in perception and presentation of inner and outer space conformed to early psychoanalytic views of the role which, in Plato's terms, "according to nature" each sex must play. The sanction for Erikson was not the good of society, but rather the psychological aim of avoiding psychic pathology in women. Erikson's conclusions have now been shown to have been based on a very loose interpretation of his own data. And when younger children were tested, thus reducing the effects of socialization, no differences were found in the number, size, or type of towers (the supposedly male construction) built by boys and girls.[42]

Research into sex differences continues today and it is popularly believed that significant differences are emerging through more careful, unbiased investigations. But even those who expect that striking innate differences will eventually be discovered have to admit that so far no important structural differences have been observed between the brains of males and females. And none would deny that differences between men and women have been narrowing over evolutionary time and that this process has recently been accelerated. Furthermore, scientists, social scientists, and philosophers on both sides of the controversy on the existence and relevance of biological differences other than reproductive between men and women all accept one fact. That is that differences among members of the same sex are far greater than average differences between the sexes in all those features that Plato considered relevant to the guidance of an ideal society.

The real danger, then, is not the one so often expressed; the problem is not that we ignore biology at our peril. Instead, what we must guard against is the tendency to accept too quickly whatever the current scientific view of the "natural," the biologically inescapable, happens to be. Even if early cross-cultural research, showing that boys in all societies run in packs, whereas girls do not, has not held up, this does not mean that we should abandon attempts to discover if there are any biological sex-linked behavioral dispositions. Nor should we abandon the attempts of ethology to counteract the ignorance of the ancients of sexual differences in animal behavior. We must by all means continue to investigate hormonal differences and the relations between social events and hormone level.[43] Investigations into differences in brain structure or organization, along with research on how such differences affect learning ability, must continue. The feminists who condemn such studies are shortsighted indeed.[44] If, in fact, as the classicist Thomas Gould insists, there are forces in a democracy which prevent unpopular research into the inferiority of women (an inferiority which he posits on faith) these forces must be combated.[45]

Even militant feminists might find some sociobiological

research useful. They could, for example, exploit the conclusions reached by Hrdy on the competitiveness of female primates. But many feminists are satisfied with "first order" explanations of sex differences, convinced that social and cultural explanations are sufficient to explain differences we observe. The adequacy of cultural explanations, however, should not lead us to foreclose the attainment of power through new biological knowledge. Such power may well help us to accomplish our egalitarian aims more effectively.

Nevertheless, it is true that attempts to base our vision of desirable human behavior largely on biological norms are mistaken. Nor can the sociobiologists' attempts to explain past norms succeed. For it is not only efforts like those which try to show that variations in women's skirt lengths can be explained and assigned numerical significance on the basis of biological predispositions that are fallacious.[46] All biological explanations of culture suffer from the impossibility of reducing an independently valid domain with valid explanatory principles of its own to what are considered more basic principles. But just as it does not make much sense to "explain" that the table represented in Cézanne's painting "The Card Players," is "really" only a system of electrically charged particles in motion, it does not make sense to assert that women do not paint great pictures for biological reasons.

Richard Lewontin, who opposes the sociobiologists' tendency to explain away discrimination against women on the basis of new scientific research, states the objections to such reductionism forcefully. Although earlier "quaint justifications for sexism have lost their force," he warns us against the view that "genes make hormones and hormones influence neural development and neural development makes professors." These new views that chemistry, rather than anatomy, are destiny he finds "equally baseless."[47]

In a sense, Plato himself shared some of the crucial assumptions of sociobiology. And it is partly perhaps for this reason that Lewontin, as we have seen, finds Plato an enemy of current affirmative action programs. For Plato does base his proposals for women on selective biological arguments. Nature, rather than convention, makes women weaker at all pursuits, and ethology helps convince us that women can guide the flock along with men. In Socrates' dialectical process it becomes clear that *if* biological divergence relevant to guardianship, that is, differences other than the reproductive, could be shown to exist, then, no matter what might seem fair, the society must be organized without equality of role. This sociobiological strain underlies his entire concept of justice. For establishing justice involves each one doing what he or she is biologically best suited to do.

All those commentators of the last hundred years who have rejected Plato's proposals did so not because Plato ignored the constraints of biology, for only one with little acquaintance with Plato could believe that. Their objections over and over again were rather that the philosopher was ignorant of or mistaken about the true biological nature of women.

Another frequent objection has been that Plato's society is totalitarian. Women, they insist, must always have the choice of pursuing a career or devoting themselves to their husbands and children. Even among committed feminists, few are willing to declare themselves as "anti-choice." But the crux of the problem lies in the fact that human choices are never made in a vacuum. An infant can perhaps "decide" whether to sleep on her stomach or her side, but even a four-year-old cannot decide which toys to play with in any given society without her choices being shaped, though not entirely determined, by the expectations of the culture. Plato realized that if one refuses to rule, one is doomed to being ruled by "inferiors." So, too, if we refuse to guide choices rationally, our options will be controlled by hidden factors. And these will reflect the desires of the current power structure. Women's choices will, in fact, represent the interests of the Thrasymachuses among us—that is, the interests of the physically dominant group.

But am I really suggesting that women who wish to stay home and bear, nurture, and raise children, cook and clean their houses, as Plato would say "sew and spin," should really be prevented or at the very least discouraged from doing so? Isn't there as much satisfaction in facilitating the development of others, in "ruling one's own roost" in the words of Wilamowitz, as in being a doctor, lawyer, merchant chief ? Or if we discard Plato's three-tier society in favor of a democratic ideal, isn't it all the more likely that the satisfactions of homemaking will often be even greater than those of the non-creative, menial jobs that most men have always done and will inevitably continue to have to do? Surely many would say there can be a division of labor which provides equal status for men and women without thrusting them into identical roles. Even if one takes the extreme Platonic position that sexual differences are in fact as minor as the differences between the bald and the curly-headed, shouldn't women be allowed to maximize or increase those differences if they so choose?

Heretical as it may seem, the answer to these questions must be that in the long run, both society as a whole and women in particular will benefit from the conscious abandonment of the idea of separate but equal roles. If the rewards of nest-building and child-rearing are great—as I believe they can be—then, in the interests of fairness, men must be allowed to participate in these satisfactions. If there is no way to eliminate dull, potentially alienating jobs in modern industrial societies, then women must do their share. In short, we must devise a mode of life and job sharing which satisfies the needs of all, and we must keep these needs from being artificially or "naturally" divided on the basis of sex.

One can always play the "animal game" to support one's own opinions. Instead of looking to sheep dogs or chimpanzees, we could as well find the natural in the arrangements of most birds. We can choose a species in which there is heavy male investment in the incubating and rearing of offspring. Our model might well be male and female birds in which there is lifelong pairing and also polyandry. The point is that present family arrangements are neither desirable nor inevitable. To continue to tell women that they can "choose" to be housewives when their lifespan will soon be more than eighty years, of which only twenty or so can possibly be taken up with childbirth and rearing, is cruel to women and wasteful to society.

The *Republic* proposes a society which succeeds in fulfilling the natures of all. But it is a class society based on a very dubious idea that some people's biological nature fits them *only* to serve others through manual labor. Plato firmly believed that very early we could decide what each citizen could do best, and that by each one pursuing his natural bent, the welfare of all would automatically be fostered. His *polis* would be led by those who are genetically bred for all-round superiority and who have gained true knowledge and great love for the best and the most beautiful. Among the best he proposes absolute equality with the lighter tasks assigned to the females. He assumes that males *as a class* do everything better, an assumption which belies an undeniable unconscious prejudice against women. Nevertheless, he also assumes that this slight class superiority of men will not affect the process of finding women to make up their share of the guardian group. Given the cultural context, his assurance of complete equality in kind, no matter what its motivation, stands out as a unique declaration. It adds to the importance of the *Republic*, contributes to its continued vitality, and explains some of the renewed interest in it today.

For Plato, the only innate differences are the reproductive ones. We still do not have a clear picture of what the precise biological differences between the sexes are. In general, we are far from discovering the genetic encoding, neurochemical processes, or brain structures that produce specific abilities or make it easier for us to acquire specific psychological traits. The Athenian clearly believed that there were no inborn barriers to women's participation in the highest positions. Plato thought mastery of mathematical principles necessary for his philosopher-rulers. And recently, there have been controversial studies showing that mathematical giftedness appears less often in adolescent females than in males.[48] But no reputable scientist has yet come forward with evidence that women cannot excel in the characteristics Plato considered essential to ruling his city-state. Although some classicists still believe that women are not capable of the greatest achievements, not even the most extreme of the biologists would claim to have any evidence to support such a prejudice.

In arguing for equality of role, Plato looked not only to biology, but also to the myths about and the actual practices in Sparta to show that societal arrangements varied and were therefore to some extent as we should put it, the products of culture. The choice of whether to use biological or environmental arguments to support his point depended for Plato, as it does for the commentators we have discussed, on the preconceived opinion he wished to buttress!

Plato proposed that private property and the family could both be abolished. We do not know any better today than he did then whether the cost of eliminating these is inevitably greater than the benefit sought. Surely we now have an anthropological record of more *kinds* of families than he might have imagined. If Spiro is right that the family is in some sense universal, new issues of what constitute a family—surrogate mothers, known and unknown sperm donor, Anna Freud's concept of "psychological parenting" taking the place of biological units—all challenge not only the conventional Greek family Plato wanted eliminated, but our own norms of the nuclear family. Clearly, no one form of human communal life is instinctive, that is, biologically necessary.[49] But we do know that the institution of family as practiced, in which women have almost always been considered as property, has caused great suffering.[50]

On the other hand, we have, as Plato did not, examples of the actual costs that have resulted from twentieth century totalitarian efforts to abolish private property. Contemporary examples of such abolition, whatever benefits they have produced, have not succeeded in establishing societies consistent with Plato's vision of the well-being of all. This hardly proves, as interpreters have claimed, that Plato himself knew very well what the effects of equalization would produce and therefore knew his *Republic* to be an "impossible dream." Nor can we be sure that collective ownership and new forms of families are doomed to failure.

Plato considered his proposals for equal education for female and male guardians would be sufficient to guarantee the development of a superior group composed of both sexes. He wanted their training to begin in earliest childhood. So far as we can establish, he wanted gifted children socialized by officers of both sexes who would guide them to assume identical positions in society. Such a city would point the way to true justice. And there is no convincing textual evidence that he considered the equality he proposed laughable or unattainable.

Regardless of recent feminist objections to the word and the concept, the androgyny Plato advocated remains an achievable and desirable goal. The old cry of "*vive la différence*" has a hollow ring when one considers the devastating effects such assumptions have had on the potentialities of women. Modern science cannot show any inevitable relation between anatomical differences and the expression of personality traits. Plato's goal of guardians that are both spirited and gentle remains a worthy aim. If Freud and Plato were right that death can only be outwitted by the production of new life or great works, both of these possibilities ought to be available to both sexes. If child care and the nurturing and teaching of the young is a valuable activity, then it is valuable for both sexes. If mechanical labor is alienating, then it is alienating for all. If many of the jobs that must be performed in an industrialized society are better performed by machines, then men and women should benefit equally from the freedom technological progress ought to provide.

There is no value in seeking to label standards of excellence as "masculine" and therefore to be abandoned. If the ability to compete is necessary in modern society, then it must be encouraged for both sexes. If a measure of altruism and cooperation is crucial for human survival, then we must facilitate the development of these traits in men and women. If gentleness and compassion are useful, then they are useful to male and female surgeons as well as to male and female grandparents. If creating a comfortable and aesthetically pleasing setting for human pursuits is valuable, then the ability to choose and decorate a human "nest" should be fostered in both men and women. Excellence in needlepoint is excellence whether performed by a football player or by Homer's Penelope. In their eagerness to upgrade traditionally feminine jobs, some feminists fall into the trap of assigning different scales of evaluation. But this is doomed to failure. The fastest marathon racer can be judged in only one way. And if the strength of the male and the percentage of muscle to body fat will always make it the case that the best male will beat the best female, then it is gross self-deception to act as if the race is not really, not actually, not, when all is said and done, to the swiftest. In today's world, there are few activities where brute strength is important. With the exception of athletic contests, none of the activities Plato valued, including excellence in warfare, depend today on muscle power. To refuse to recognize that women in fact *did not* contribute to such great cultural achievements as the Italian Renaissance and suggest that they did make an important contribution so long as we desert the "masculine definition" of importance is ultimately self-defeating. One ought to assume only that sociological reasons can adequately account for why there has not thus far been a female Michelangelo. We have every reason to believe that there will be great women sculptors. Nor must one change the standards of excellence to say that Sappho and George Eliot and Emily Dickinson made outstanding literary contributions. The call of some feminists for different standards of excellence is indeed misguided.

In fact, what we need today, are clear standards of excellence, and perhaps more than ever, leaders who possess a *combination* of the traits that have in the past been identified as exclusively either masculine or feminine. And above all, we must be passionately committed to the uses of reason. We must cultivate the ability to think clearly not only in a superior elite, but in all citizens. Any scientific research that will help us achieve these goals must be fostered. It is important not to discourage biological investigations into sex differences, but we must be ever vigilant to reveal hidden agendas and unconscious assumptions.

We must now undertake measures that Plato did not know would be necessary to counteract the damage done through centuries of exaggerating gender differences. We know far better than he the enormous cost of clinging to the view that there is a separate male and female human nature. We know both the intrapsychic costs, and the cost to society in general. We have seen the damage done to women raised to think of themselves as second class and second-rate, to men forced to suppress their feelings and conform to a pattern of self-serving aggressiveness.

Before this species goes the way of the other 85 percent now extinct, we must change the current relations between the sexes. We can no longer afford to waste the abilities of more than half of our population. This is even more true now than when Plato proclaimed it in the *Laws*. Just as in Plato's day, proposals for a better society must include radical changes in economic relations. Economic life must be organized so that men and their offspring are not denied the benefits and satisfactions of involvement in child-rearing. All the commentators we have discussed, chauvinists and feminists alike, have asserted that Plato was overzealous in eliminating families entirely. If in fact he was mistaken, and pair bonds are necessary for rearing of the young, ideas of what constitute a family nevertheless require thorough restructuring.

Certainly, if marriages are to involve more permanence than Plato desired they must become, as they have never yet been, partnerships between equals.

Our review of the recent history of Plato's egalitarian proposals leads us to a final paradoxical conclusion. Just as the world will know no surcease from ills until philosophers become kings, so, too, philosophy will know no end to prejudice until women become philosophers. But doesn't this contradict my entire thesis? If men and women have the same capacities, and reason with identical skill, then surely there can be no special reason why female philosophers are needed. Men can point out inequities and suggest reforms as effectively as women. But the truth is that for generations to come women will have a unique connection with all females before them who were condemned because of their physiology. Women philosophers will have a "special relation" to those who were once thought, in Aristotle's words, to provide only the "matter" for the offspring for whom men provide the *psyche*. For there is no philosophy performed by disembodied souls, and all thought arises out of a particular situation. As we have attempted to show, philosophy is not only abstract reasoning, but also social expression. Women are needed to recite as the Jews do each year at the Passover, "We were slaves unto Pharoah in Egypt." It is we who were confined to household chores, whose sex life was regulated and whose mental capacities were denigrated. This was done to us, to us throughout the centuries. We who reason, think, imagine alternatives, weigh the just with the unjust, must keep alive the memory of those inequities. We must see that full equality is reached and maintained, not only in the ideal city, in the city of speech, but here in the real world where philosophers, though not kings, are a small voice for sanity and the life of the mind.

Notes

INTRODUCTION

1. Leonardo Bruni, *Epistolae,* lx, 4. "Multa sunt in iis libris abhorrentia a moribus nostris, quae pro honore Platonis tacere satius est, quam proferre." Quoted in G. Holmes, *The Florentine Enlightenment: 1400–1450* (New York: Pegasus, 1969), p. 114. Three centuries later, H. Spens in the first translation of the *Republic* into English in 1763 exhibits the same attitude. R. Gannett remarks in his preface to the reissued edition that in Spen's analysis, "the delicate question of the community of women is evaded." H. Spens, *Republic of Plato* (London: Dent, 1906), p. xi.

2. For an account of Greek misogyny see, e.g., Sarah Pomeroy, *Goddesses, Whores, Wives, and Slaves: Women in Classical Antiquity* (New York: Schocken, 1975). M. R. Lefkowitz and M. B. Fant present excellent documentary evidence of Greek attitudes. They provide numerous examples including an excerpt from Aristotle's will (taken from Diogenes Laertius) to show that "restrictions of women's rights to own property and to determine the course of their own lives" illustrate the Athenian male's low estimation of females' capabilities and general value. *Women in Greece and Rome* (Toronto: Samuel Stephens, 1977), p. 19. See also K. J. Dover's section on "the unusual extent to which the Athenians had come to regard women as objects," in *Greek Popular Morality in the Time of Plato and Aristotle* (Berkeley: University of California Press, 1974), pp. 95–102.

3. Leonardo Da Vinci describes experiment (guided by reason) as "the one true mistress." *The Literary Works of Leonardo Da Vinci* (London: 1880), #12, quoted in Anthony Blunt, *Artistic Theory in Italy 1450–1600* (New York: Oxford University Press, 1956), p. 26. And Peirce writes in "The Fixation of Belief," that man's logical method should be loved and reverenced as his bride whom he has rightly chosen; he will work and fight for her and will "strive to be the worthy knight and champion of her from the blaze of whose splendors he draws his inspiration and courage," 5.387 p. 247, in *Collected Papers of Charles S. Peirce,* vols. V & VI, ed. C. Hartshorne and Paul Weiss (Cambridge, Mass.: Harvard University Press, 1965). Such figures of speech cannot easily be translated for the use of female readers and tend to add to women's sense of exclusion.

4. *The Collected Dialogues of Plato,* ed. Edith Hamilton and Huntington Cairns (Princeton: Princeton University Press, 1963), p. vi.

5. A. E. Taylor, *Plato: The Man and His Work* (New York: Meridian, 1956), p. viii.

6. This was a pervasive theme in George Boas' work. He wrote that when the "so-called immortal masterpieces" are admired it has been for shifting reasons; "men can read with the mind of an Athenian only by a definite act of will and even then one forgets that a real Athenian did not have to make the effort." From "A Sermon for Humanists," in *The Johns Hopkins Magazine,* October 1984, p. 16.

7. Joachim Bannes, *Hitlers Kampf und Platons Staat* (Berlin: W. de Gruyter, 1933). See below, p. 53.

8. Information about women in Plato's Academy comes from Diogenes Laertius. He mentions two women disciples, Lastheneia of Mantinea and Axiothea of Phlius, and says of the latter that she "is reported by Dicaearchus to have worn men's clothes." Diogenes Laertius, *Lives of Eminent Philosophers,* Book III. 46 with English trans. R. D. Hicks (Cambridge, Mass: Harvard University Press, 1966), vol. 1, p. 317. Although Diogenes is not always reliable, G. C. Field accepts the information and says that Dicaearchus, a pupil of Aristotle, "was probably well informed." *Plato and his Contemporaries* (London: Methuen, 1967), p. 118.

As for women's participation in modern academies, studies done in the 1980s show that inequality of treatment persists. C. G. Krupnick found that when men are in the majority in a classroom and the instructor is also male, women are called on and speak up less often. B. R. Sandler and R. M. Hall reported that instructors inadvertently practice discrimination by such behavior as coaching men more when they do not know an answer and asking men "higher order" questions, involving more theory and analysis. For a summary of these studies, see A. M. Heim, "Harvard Study Reveals Gender Inequality in the Classroom," *Second Century: Radcliffe News,* April 1986, p. 2. I would not claim that such studies are decisive. Nor can statistical information or even personal reports conclusively prove my claim of women's continued exclusion. Nevertheless, one measure of the degree of their acceptance would undoubtedly be the number of females in the top ranks of university faculties today. In the United States the statistics remain discouraging. Of slightly more than 115,000 full professors, 103,380 are male, 11,830 female. That is, there are about nine times as many males as females at the highest levels. For the latest available figures see W. V. Grant and Thomas D. Snyder, *Digest of Education Statistics: 1985–1986* (Washington, D.C.: U.S. Government Printing Office, 1986), p. 113.

9. Thomas Gould, *Platonic Love* (New York: Free Press, 1963), p. 54.

10. Jean B. Elshtain, *Public Man, Private Woman* (Princeton: Princeton University Press, 1981), p. xv.

11. The assessment is Karl Popper's and is particularly striking because

Popper devoted a lengthy work to demonstrating Plato's "reactionary" and totalitarian tendencies. *The Open Society and Its Enemies* (London: Routledge & Kegan Paul, 1945).

12. I have attempted to paraphrase at this point only as literally and straightforwardly as possible to prepare for the discussion of varying interpretations that follow. All quotations are from the translation of Allan Bloom, *The Republic of Plato, with Interpretive Essay* (New York: Basic Books, 1968), except where indicated otherwise.

13. Plato, *Republic*, 454e.

14. Ibid., 455e.

15. Ibid., 473d.

16. Gilbert Ryle, "Plato: Moral and Political Theory," in *Encyclopedia of Philosophy*, ed. Paul Edwards (New York: Macmillan, 1967), Vol. VI, p. 331.

17. Plato, *Timaeus*, 90e. In *The Dialogues of Plato,* trans. Benjamin Jowett (New York: Random House, 1937), vol. II.

18. For a summary of attitudes of the early church and a bibliography on the subject, see Marie Augusta Neal, "Women in Religious Symbolism and Organization" in *Religious Change and Continuity*, ed. H. M. Johnson (San Francisco: Jossey-Bass, 1979).

19. See al-Fārābī, *De Platonis Philosophia,* ed. F. Rosenthal and R. Walzer (London: Warburg Institute, 1943).

20. It would take us too far afield to enter the controversy over whether Islam is essentially anti-feminist. However, even the political leader Benazir Bhutto who sees the Qur'an itself as basically egalitarian admits that "a reactionary interpretation" by men has resulted in women's inferior status in Muslim countries. Thus, although she sees Islam as less sexist than Christianity, she admits that a discriminatory patriarchal society reemerged after the death of the Prophet Muhammed. See the account of her Rama Mehta Lecture at Radcliffe College, in *Second Century: Radcliffe News*, June 1985, pp. 1, 3.

21. William James, *Some Problems of Philosophy* (New York: Longmans, Green & Co., 1948), p. 7.

22. *Averroës' Commentary on Plato's Republic*, ed. E. I. J. Rosenthal (Cambridge: Cambridge University Press, 1966). Rosenthal here stresses Averroës' regret that no proper use is made of women in the service of the community. See also his "The Place of Politics in the Philosophy of Ibn Rushd," in *Bulletin of the London School of African Studies*, xv, 2, p. 252. In my view the fact that Averroës in his explication of Plato introduces such ideas as "melodies are perfect if men invent them and women perform them" (454) suggests that his egalitarianism, though remarkable, is not as total as Rosenthal maintains. For no matter how important and necessary performance is, invention—the male activity—is surely superior.

23. Rosenthal, *Averroës*, 456, 9, p. 166.

24. Ibid., 454, 3, p. 164.
25. Martha Nussbaum,"Women's Lot," *The New York Review of Books,* January 30, 1986, p. 7.

1: THE PREVALENCE OF ANTI-FEMALE BIAS IN PLATO SCHOLARSHIP, 1870–1970. SEVEN TYPES OF HOSTILITY.

1. I have concentrated in this section mainly on those books which have had an influence on students and fellow scholars, which have been frequently reprinted, quoted, and cited. When I have deviated from this policy—e.g., used a work addressed to students in China, and a little known commentary by a woman—I have explained my reasons for doing so in the text. Although I have aimed at including as many major works as possible, my survey is by no means exhaustive.

2. This is B. Bosanquet's view. In *The Education of the Young in The Republic of Plato* (Cambridge: Cambridge Press, 1900), p. 11, he speaks of "the violence of the revolution" which Plato advocated.

3. V. F. Asmus, ed., *Platon: Sochinenia v Trekh Tomakh,* vol. 3, no. 1, (Moscow, 1971), p. 606.

4. Z. Diesendruck, *The Republic: Translated into Hebrew with Introduction and Notes* (Tel Aviv: Newman, 1953), p. 3 (Gimel).

5. K. Popper, *The Open Society and Its Enemies* (London: Routledge & Kegan Paul, 1945), p. 307.

6. Nicholas White, A *Companion to Plato's Republic* (Oxford: Blackwell, 1979).

7. Ernest Barker, *Greek Political Theory: Plato and His Predecessors* (London: Methuen, 1947), p. vi. He refers to the 1914–1917 world war which was taking place as he wrote.

8. Ibid., p. 261. In the same vein he wrote that the fact of a woman's sex colors her whole being; "it makes her able indeed to inspire noble enthusiasms, but not to direct a policy or drill a regiment as Plato would require his woman-ruler or woman soldier to do." Ernest Barker, *The Political Thought of Plato and Aristotle* (New York: Dover, 1959), p. 148. Werner Jaeger has a similar view and notes that Plato "does not expect as we should do" that women "will make their creative contribution to the community through family life." *Paideia* (London: Oxford University Press, 1943), Vol. II, p. 244.

9. Barker, *Political Thought of Plato and Aristotle,* p. 244. This is an earlier, longer version of *Greek Political Theory.*

10. See, e.g., Aristotle, trans. Benjamin Jowett, in *The Basic Works of Aristotle* (New York: Random House, 1941). *Politics,* 1254b. "The male is by nature superior, and the female inferior, and the one rules, and the other is ruled. This principle, of necessity, extends to all mankind." See also 1259b, 1260a.

11. The explanatory comment on *Republic,* 452c appears in the anno-

tated edition begun in the 1860s that Jowett did not live to complete. It was published after his death as B. Jowett and L. Campbell, *Plato's Republic: The Greek Text,* ed., with notes and essays (Oxford: Clarendon Press, 1894).

12. Ibid., vol. III, pp. 215–16.

13. Ibid., p. 216. His wording here is ambiguous and I am not certain I have correctly interpreted his statement that Plato did not consider "the other differences to which the difference of sex gives rise in mind and feeling." He may be referring only to the fact that biological differences cause men to *think* and *feel* differently about each sex. On this alternative interpretation women's differences would not be innate but rather universally acquired.

14. Ibid., p. 216. Jowett identifies Plato's view with the line "woman is the lesser man" which he quotes merely from "the poet." The unidentified line is no doubt from Tennyson's "Locksley Hall"; but, considering the context, the British poet's view is actually more reminiscent of the misogyny of Socrates' audience. For in the lines immediately preceding Jowett's quote, Tennyson describes women thus: "Nature made them blinder motions/bounded in a shallower brain." *The Poetical Works of Alfred Lord Tennyson* (Boston: Houghton Mifflin, n.d.), p. 60.

15. *Republic*, Introduction and Analysis, in *The Dialogues of Plato,* trans. by Benjamin Jowett, 3rd ed. (Oxford: Clarendon Press, 1892), p. lxxxix. He does comment in *Greek Text,* p. 234, on the singular nature of "the infrequency of the opportunity for nuptial intercourse."

16. F. J. Dover, *Greek Homosexuality* (New York: Random House, 1978), p. 154.

17. Walter Pater, *Plato and Platonism* (London: Macmillan, 1910), pp. 257, 258.

18. Ibid. He does not deny that the proposals are consistent with animal "nature"; in fact, he sees the family arrangements as "a movement backwards, to a barbarous or merely animal grade of existence" (p. 257). And he says of women guardians that if we see them as a reinstatement of the Amazon we must condemn them as "a survival from a half-animal world," which adult reason has long since overcome (p. 259).

19. Bosanquet, *Education in the Republic,* p. 11.

20. Bernard Bosanquet, *A Companion to Plato's Republic* (London: Rivingtons, 1925), p. 182.

21. Taylor, *Plato: The Man and His Work* (New York: Meridian, 1956), p. 278.

22. Demosthenes, lix122. Dover insists we cannot consider this *the* decisive fourth-century view. See *Greek Popular Morality in the Time of Plato and Aristotle* (Berkeley: University of California Press, 1974), p. 14.

23. Taylor, *Plato: Man and Work,* p. 278.

24. Dover, *Greek Homosexuality,* p. vii.

25. This was the view of John Stuart Mill writing in the 1860s. He denied that "anyone knows, or can know, the nature of the two sexes, as

long as they have only been seen in their present relation to one another." We cannot possibly know the capabilities of women, he says, because "most of them have never been called out." His discussion at this point is still stirring and applicable today. See "The Subjection of Women," in *The Feminist Papers,* ed. Alice S. Rossi (New York: Bantam, 1974), pp. 203, 204. Richard Jenkyns thinks Plato's "striking feminism" must have encouraged Mill and perhaps guided him, but provides no evidence for this speculation. *The Victorians and Ancient Greece* (Cambridge, Mass.: Harvard University Press, 1980), p. 230.

26. Since my aim in this study is to focus on the statements of complete identity of nature and education (and the interpreters' rejection of these), I have restricted my analysis as far as possible to *Republic,* Book V. Although the *Laws* contains many interesting and provocative points, I have in general avoided any extended treatment of the altered provisions for women in that work.

27. In R. C. Lodge, *Plato's Theory of Education,* with an appendix on the education of women according to Plato, by Rabbi Solomon Frank (London: K. Paul, Trench, Trubner, 1947).

28. Ibid., p. 307.

29. Plato, *Republic,* Bloom trans., 466d, p. 146.

30. R. C. Crossman, *Plato Today* (New York: Oxford University Press, 1939), p. 202.

31. Leo Strauss, *The City and the Man* (Chicago: Rand McNally, 1964), p. 127.

32. Bloom, *Republic, Interpretive Essay,* p. 382.

33. Ibid., p. 385.

34. See below, p. 191.

35. N. E. Fehl, *A Guide to the Study of Plato's Republic* (Hong Kong: Chung Chi College, 1961), p. 1.

36. Ibid., p. 50.

37. Ibid., p. 53.

38. Plato, *The Republic,* trans. with introduction by Desmond Lee (London: Penguin, 1974), p. 47.

39. Richard Nettleship, *Lectures on The Republic of Plato* (New York: Macmillan, 1967), p. 173.

40. This is the view of W. K. Lacey, *The Family in Classical Greece* (Ithaca: Cornell University Press, 1968), p. 174. He stresses that Greek women had greater economic security than married women today, including protection from the "wayward husband" of the modern divorce courts who could support his family but refuses to do so. He considers Plato's state not so vast an intellectual jump from the society in which he lived "as it is sometimes thought to have been" (p. 176). On the other hand he defends the fact that women didn't go out to eat with their husbands or dine with them at home when there were other nonrelated males present. Giving the same reason offered for asking women to

leave when the port was served at modern British upper-class dinner parties, Lacey suggests that women are thus protected from quarreling and drunkenness. Susan G. Bell, editor of *Women from the Greeks to the French Revolution* (Stanford: Stanford University Press, 1980), objects that "it is debatable whether women wanted to be protected from raucous male society" (p. 122). Lacey seems to have no awareness at all of what a missed opportunity it was for women to be excluded from banquets like that described in the *Symposium.*

41. Nettleship, *Lectures,* p. 173.

42. Ibid., p. 174.

43. U. v. Wilamowitz-Moellendorff, *Platon: Beilagen und Textkritik* (Berlin: Weidmannsche Buchhandlung, 1919), Vol. II. In another work in which he worries that Plato is trying to turn women into incomplete men, he says that we are setting the cause of equality back by making a political issue out of it. Plato, he says, is not in the spirit of modern female emancipationists whose attempts when healthy are based on the *differences* between the sexes. *Die Griechische und der Platonische Staatsgedanke* (Berlin: Weidmannsche Buchhandlung, 1919), pp. 18, 19.

44. George Grote, *Plato and the Other Companions of Socrates,* Vol. IV (London: John Murray, 1888), p. 171, says there is no point on which he speaks in terms of more decided conviction than that women are fit for the same duties as men.

45. Constantin Ritter, *The Essence of Plato's Philosophy* (New York: Russell & Russell, 1933), p. 332.

46. Karl Nohle, *Die Statslehre Platos* (Leipsig, 1880), pp. 136, 137.

47. Adela M. Adam, *Plato: Moral and Political Ideals* (Cambridge, 1913), p. 131.

48. Wilamowitz, *Platon,* p. 199.

49. Ibid.

50. Ibid., p. 200.

51. I. M. Crombie, *An Examination of Plato's Doctrine,* Vol. 1 (London: Routledge & Kegan Paul, 1962), pp. 100–101.

52. Paul Friedlander, *Plato: The Dialogues,* 2nd and 3rd Periods (Princeton: Princeton University Press, 1969), p. 103.

53. He writes, "let us not take away his [that is, Friedlander's] joy in this discovery" that Plato's purpose was to shock the bourgeois. I have assumed from his tone that he does not agree with Friedlander's assessment. See H. Gauss, *Philosophischer Handkommentar zu den Dialogen Platos* (Bern, 1958), p. 159.

54. Jean Ithurriague, *Les idées de Platon sur la condition de la femme* (Paris: Librairie Universitaire, 1931), p. 136. This self-proclaimed egalitarian believes that the, as he puts it, "near nudity" is the *cause* of the *perversions de l'amour* in ancient Greece.

55. W. K. Lacey, *Family in Greece,* p. 25.

56. For a reproduction of a detail of the Roman mosaic at Piazza

Armerina of Roman women in scanty bathing suits and modern hair-dos, see the photo of "La sportive romaine" in Guy Fau, *L'émancipation féminin dans la Rome antique* (Paris, 1978).

57. Strauss, *The City and the Man,* (Chicago, 1964) p. 61.

58. Bloom, *Republic, Interpretive Essay,* p. 381; my emphasis. See below, pp. 205ff, for all those learned scholars who disagree. This would mean that not only Wilamowitz but most of the commentators from Aristotle on have failed in their understanding.

59. See Praxagora's speech before the assembly in Aristophanes, *Ecclesiazusae,* trans. B. B. Rogers, Vol. III (Cambridge, Mass.: Harvard University Press, 1924). For a lively modern version, see Douglass Parker's *Aristophanes, The Congresswomen* (Ann Arbor: University of Michigan Press, 1967), pp. 2, 21f.

60. See Sarah B. Hrdy, *The Woman That Never Evolved* (Cambridge, Mass.: Harvard University Press, 1981), pp. 10, 11.

61. Bloom, *Republic, Interpretive Essay,* p. 382. All references in the following section are taken from Bloom's discussion, pp. 383–89.

62. Ibid., p. 383. This becomes a major issue in later feminist commentary.

63. Bennett Simon, *Mind and Madness in Ancient Greece* (Ithaca: Cornell University Press, 1978), pp. 176, 177, 179.

64. See, e.g., Sigmund Freud, *Analysis Terminable and Interminable,* Standard Edition (London: Hogarth Press, 1964), Section VIII, pp. 250–53.

65. Plato, *Republic,* 465.

66. Simon, *Mind and Madness,* p. 241.

67. Dover, *Greek Popular Morality, in the Time of Plato and Aristotle* (Berkeley: University of California Press, 1977), p. 101.

68. Taylor, *Plato: The Man and Work,* p. 278.

69. For a view contrary to Taylor's, see Winspear and Silverberg, *Who Was Socrates?* (New York: Russell & Russell, 1960). In questioning the veracity of Plato's account of Socrates' death they nevertheless claim that the dramatic picture is accurate in showing Socrates' anti-female, pro-homosexual "disregard for ordinary human ties" (p. 40).

70. Maurice Croiset, *La République de Platon* (Paris, Editions Mellottée, 1946), p. 191.

71. Joachim Bannes, *Hitlers Kampf und Platons Staat* (Berlin: W. de Gruyter, 1933).

72. Adolf Hitler, *Mein Kampf* (Berlin: F. Eher, 1932), pp. 459–60.

73. Xenophon, *Memorabilia,* 2.7.1–12.

74. For an interesting, if highly speculative, account of Hitler's pathological attitudes toward women, see W. C. Langer, *The Mind of Adolf Hitler* (London: Secker & Warburg, 1973). In this study prepared for the U.S. government in 1944, Langer writes that many had commented on Hitler's "feminine characteristics," including what Langer enigmatically calls "his ways of thinking" (p. 172). Langer interprets much of Hitler's

neurosis as a reaction against hatred and fears of his own "femininity" (p. 194).

75. C. H. Hoole, *An Analytical Paraphrase of the Republic of Plato* (Oxford: J. Vincent, 1875), p. 27.

76. Jowett, *Greek Text,* p. 218.

77. Jowett, *Dialogues,* 1875 Edition, Vol. III, p. 62.

78. See Jenkyns, *The Victorians,* on Jowett's other attempts to "give the reader license to discount whatever he finds uncongenial" (p. 245).

79. W. Fite, *The Platonic Legend* (New York: Charles Scribner's Sons, 1934), pp. 157–58.

80. This is the phrase of R. Garnett, commenting on H. Spens' "long disquisition on Plato" in which the "delicate question" is evaded. (Spens published the first translation of the *Republic* into English in 1763.) R. Garnett in H. Spens, *Republic of Plato* (London: Dent, 1906), p. xi.

81. Jowett, *Dialogues,* 1875, p. 61.

82. James Adam, *The Republic, ed. with Critical Notes, Commentary, and Appendix* (Cambridge, 1905). Note to V, 457, p. 291.

83. T. H. Warren, *The Republic* (London: Macmillan, 1888). Note to V, 457; also discussed in ibid., p. 291.

84. Some feminists would deny this since rewards of more frequent intercourse are mentioned only for male guardians.

85. *The Republic of Plato,* trans. F. M. Cornford (London: Oxford University Press, 1941), p. 154.

86. Ibid., p. 160. Compare Grote, *Plato and Other Companions,* who forthrightly speaks of "a larger license of copulation with different women" (p. 43).

87. Alexandre Koyre, *Discovering Plato,* trans. L. C. Rosenfield (New York: Columbia University Press, 1945), p. 85, n. 24.

88. *Republic,* Cornford, p. 160.

89. Charles M. Bakewell, *Plato, The Republic with Introduction* (New York: Charles Scribners, 1928), p. 53.

90. Ibid. The consequences of such usage are with us still. In the 1980s in searching for a new member of the philosophy department at a major institution, a tenured female was struck by the continued use of the phrase "the man we need" at meetings, despite the fact that the gender of the candidate was ostensibly irrelevant. The use of such language, betraying unconscious assumptions, even when females participate in the deliberations, no doubt contributes to the continued disparity in the numbers of women faculty. Gerda Lerner reports that as late as 1972 even in women's colleges the majority of teaching and administrative jobs were held by men, while in the administration of coeducational colleges women remain a minority. *The Female Experience* (Indianapolis: Bobbs-Merrill, 1977). For information about tenured women in the 1980s, see above, note 8 to the introduction.

91. Bernard Bosanquet, *The Education of the Young in The Republic of Plato* (Cambridge: Cambridge University Press, 1900), p. 15.

92. Jean Ithurriage, *Les idées de Platon sur la condition de la femme,* pp. 124, 145, 150.
93. Ibid., pp. 151ff.
94. Ibid., p. 142.
95. Ibid., p. 154.
96. Ibid.
97. F. A. Wright, *Feminism in Greek Literature: From Homer to Aristotle* (Port Washington: Kennikat Press, 1969), p. 169.
98. Ibid., p. 176.
99. Ibid., p. 177.
100. Ibid., p. 182.
101. Ibid.
102. Grote (1794–1871) was seventy-one when the first edition appeared. Karl Popper describes him as "that great democrat"; his wife was active with Harriet Taylor in the nineteenth-century British feminist movement.
103. Grote, *Plato and Other Companions*, Vol. IV, p. 204.
104. Ibid., p. 189.
105. These singularly non-sexist usages appear respectively in ibid., pp. 170, 171, 195, 206.
106. Ibid., p. 172.
107. Ibid., p. 196.
108. Ibid., p. 197. It is interesting to note that although women remain less adept than men at many sports they still excel in archery.
109. We know that representations in sculpture of mythical and biblical women who exhibited great physical prowess and performed aggressive acts have historically been seen as dangerous examples of female power. Donatello's statue of "Judith and Holofernes" was banished from the Piazza Signoria (City Hall) in the early sixteenth century partly because the rulers thought it was a bad example "to have a woman kill a man." Previously it had been a symbol of Florentine liberty, and of pride vanquished by humility, "of incontinence crushed by chastity." Eva Borsook, *The Companion Guide to Florence* (London: Collins, 1973), p. 47.
110. Grote, *Plato and Other Companions,* p. 177.
111. Ibid., pp. 189–90.
112. Thus, although I find Martha Nussbaum's analysis of Plato's egalitarian views exemplary, I disagree with her about the means through which change will come. She holds out hope that women will get the jobs they deserve through "consideration one by one on an equal basis." She says that "a willingness on the part of each member of the educational community to look searchingly into his or her own heart" is preferable to affirmative action. The latter, she writes, will have a disastrous effect on women's self-esteem. If more women do not publicly describe or legally protest sexism in hiring it is sometimes because they have "made the difficult choice to get on with their work." "Letters:

Plato and Affirmative Action: Nussbaum-Lewontin Exchange," *New York Review of Books*, January 31, 1985. Here I agree with Grote that the problem is the impetus for reforms. Richard Lewontin answers her appropriately; the problem he says for women in academia and in society at large "is not a lack of merit, but a lack of power." Ibid. I believe that in the best of all possible worlds a small component of women's self-respect might come from the method of selection for a particular job. In the present climate, however, self-esteem can, and does, come from their own and others' judgment of the quality of their teaching and scholarship, once they are given a chance. Before organized pressure the very possibility of getting on with scholarly work was foreclosed for most women. See discussion of Nussbaum and Lewontin's disagreement about Plato below, pp. 91ff.

113. Theodor Gomperz, *Greek Thinkers* (London, 1905), Vol. III, p. 110.

114. Gomperz refers to an experimental community founded by Noyes in 1811 on the Platonic model called "Perfectionists," ibid., p. 123.

115. Ibid., p. 109.

116. Ibid., p. 115.

117. J. Adam uses this phrase and speaks of Plato's "customary disregard of the limitations of ordinary human nature." *The Republic, ed. with Critical Notes*, pp. 291–92.

118. Gomperz, *Greek Thinkers*, p. 124.

119. Ibid. Given the strength of Gomperz's statements it is difficult to see why Adela Adam considers that Gomperz is "not willing to go so far as Plato in admitting women to political life." *Plato: Moral and Political Ideals*, p. 131.

120. In the 1960s, Thomas Gould is still maintaining that women have not produced *any* works of the first order. *Platonic Love*, pp. 53ff. Clearly, he would not accept Gomperz's assessment of the contribution of nineteenth-century women to literature. See below, pp. 144–45.

121. Gomperz, *Greek Thinkers*, p. 124.

122. Ibid., p. 126.

123. Ibid.

124. Mill defends the sexual division of duties within the family, assuming that the husband will earn the family income while the wife does the housework, terming this "the most suitable division of labour between the two persons." Susan Moller Okin astutely points this out, referring to Mill's *On the Subjection of Women*, pp. 473, 474, 483. See *Women in Western Political Thought* (Princeton: Princeton University Press, 1979), p. 334, n. 92.

125. Adela M. Adam, *Plato: Moral and Political Ideals* (Cambridge: Cambridge University Press, 1913). See chap. XIII.

126. Ibid., p. 124.

127. Ibid., pp. 126, 129.

128. Ibid., p. 126. For my disagreement with this criticism of Plato, see the discussion of the views of J. Martin, who also interprets *Republic*, 540c, in this way, below, pp. 119ff.
129. A woman can easily see herself as a ruler, guardian, or guard, but never as a king!
130. Even Grote and Gomperz in my view are more genuine feminists. A. Adam seems to see herself as going further in admitting women to political life than Gomperz, but I think she is mistaken. See above, n. 119.
131. Adam, *Plato: Moral and Political Ideals*, pp. 132, 131.

2: THE RESURGENCE OF INTEREST IN PHILOSOPHER-QUEENS

1. See Rosamond Sprague, *Plato's Philosopher-King: A Study of the Theoretical Background* (Columbia, S.C., 1976). Another example is Louise Loomis, who, in her introduction to the *Republic*, has little to say about gender equality in Book V.

2. Such aspirations are now shared by women in other developed countries, too, although significant differences remain in women's expectations from country to country. In some countries there are still servants to support the work of the middle-class scholar, as subordinates were intended to perform the manual labor for Plato's guardians. In the United States, United Kingdom, and some European countries, day care facilities have to a certain extent replaced the extended family and servant class. Thus in an outstanding book to which I refer in my final chapter the young scientist specifically expresses gratitude to her child's day care provider for making her work possible. She is well aware that "such centers are . . . gardens of privilege for a privileged species in a privileged portion of the globe. . . . " Sarah B. Hrdy, *Woman That Never Evolved*, p. ix.

3. In introducing his chapter on women and the state in the ancient world, H. M. Currie describes the current situation well. Although I reject his implication that feminists have confused equality and similarity, I agree with his assessment that "the modern emancipation of women has meant that whilst they have gained many new functions they have lost few of the old ones." *The Individual and the State* (London: Dent, 1973), p. 122.

4. Christine Pierce, "Equality: *Republic* V," *The Monist*, 57, 1 (Jan. 1973), p. 3.

5. Ibid., p. 10.

6. Ibid., pp. 10–11.

7. As Grote correctly suggests, for Plato the first best city, better than that of the society proposed in the *Republic*, would require "a communion that should pervade all persons and all acts and sentiments, effacing alto-

gether the separate self." *Laws* V, 739D. See Grote, *Plato and Other Companions*, p. 179.

8. H. D. Rankin, *Plato and the Individual* (London: Methuen, 1964), p. 98.

9. Ibid., p. 100.

10. This professor says that one way of dealing with the disparities between the athletic promise and achievement of men and women is to view the latter as truncated males. Unlike Plato, he would therefore permit them to engage in men's sports, but in "foreshortened versions." In his chapter on women athletes Weiss also writes: "A woman is less abstract than a man because her mind is persistently ordered toward bodily problems." Paul Weiss, *Sport: A Philosophical Inquiry* (Carbondale: Southern Illinois University Press, 1969), pp. 215, 217.

11. Abigail Rosenthal, "Feminism Without Contradictions", *The Monist*, 57, 1 (Jan. 1973), p. 29.

12. Martha Lee Osborne, "Plato's Unchanging View of Woman: A Denial That Anatomy Spells Destiny," *The Philosophical Forum*, Summer 1975, p. 447.

13. See Anne Dickason, "Anatomy and Destiny: The Role of Biology in Plato's Views of Women," *The Philosophical Forum*, V (Fall-Winter 1973–1974), pp. 45–53.

14. Christine G. Allen, "Plato on Women," *Feminist Studies*, 2, 2–3 (1975), p. 132. Allen herself is aware that the actual role women play in the dialogues complicates the issue of equality. She quotes from the historian Mary Beard that Diotima, the wise priestess of the *Symposium*, may have been based on an actual living woman philosopher. But there is in fact no evidence for this, and Beard is not a reliable source of information on philosophers in the ancient world. Beard cites a discussion by A. W. Benn where the influence of ancient women philosophers is "made important." Mary Beard, *Women as a Force in History* (New York: Colliers, 1971), p. 349. But in *Greek Philosophers* (New York: Dutton, 1974), Benn makes only two brief references to women and philosophy and does not claim any importance at all for the few who may have existed. Beard's enthusiasm provides us with an added example of how eager women writers have been to show that females did make a public contribution even when the evidence is to the contrary. Most of the information we have about the existence of women philosophers comes from Diogenes Laertius, who is himself a not entirely reliable source. Besides Plato's two women disciples that I have previously mentioned, Diogenes describes Hipparchia of Maroneia, a fourth to third century B.C. female philosopher who married the philosopher Crates and chose education "instead of wasting further time upon the loom." *Lives of Eminent Philosophers*, VI, 96–98, vol. 2, p. 101. It is important to remember, however, that we do not have a single word written by a female philosopher in the ancient world.

Allen makes another error in accepting a quote from Simone de Beauvoir to show Plato's mysogyny. De Beauvoir wrote: "The first among the blessings for which Plato thanked the gods was that he had been created free, not enslaved, the second, a man, not a woman." *The Second Sex* (New York: Bantam Books, 1968), p. xxi. But in fact there is no source for this in Plato. Even the oft-expressed claim that it was Socrates who thanked God (as Orthodox Jews actually have for centuries) that he was not made a woman cannot be substantiated.

15. C. G. Allen, "Plato on Women," pp. 133, 134. This is not the place to consider the general role of Plato's myth in his total philosophy. For an excellent discussion, see Ludwig Edelstein, "The Function of the Myth in Plato's Philosophy," *Journal of the History of Ideas,* vol. 10, October 1949, pp. 463–481. For our purposes, there is an important question of whether ideas put forth by characters in a dialogue (even by a Platonic adversary) in some sense nevertheless represent unconscious attitudes of Plato. An extreme psychoanalytic position taken by Hans Kelson is that since they arose from Plato's imagination they have great relevance. Kelson assumes that the myths reveal, "although Plato does not expressly say this . . . that he recognizes in the masculine principle the good, and in the feminine the evil." Hans Kelson, "Platonic Love," *American Imago,* 3(1–2) (April 1942), p. 14.

16. Dorothea Wender, "Plato: Misogynist, Paeodophile and Feminist," *Arethusa,* VI(1) (Spring 1973), p. 76.

17. James E. White summarizes Jaggar's five types from her "Political Philosophies of Women's Liberation" in *Feminism and Philosophy* (Totowa, N.J.: Littlefield, Adams 1977) ed. M. Vettling-Braggin, F. A. Elliston, and J. English. "Liberal feminists believe that changing discriminatory laws and practices can be accomplished without changing either capitalism or the technology of reproduction. They emphasize equal opportunity for individuals within the existing system. Radical feminists think that the source of women's oppression is fundamentally biological. In order to achieve equality . . . women must be relieved of the burden of childbearing; this could be done by technological means. They also endorse the end of exclusively heterosexual relationships. Classical-Marxist feminists see capitalism as the primary cause of women's oppression, and hold that women's liberation requires the dissolution of the capitalist society. Lesbian separatists believe that women should refrain from heterosexual relationships. Some see this as a temporary necessity, while others want permanent lesbianism. Socialist feminism . . . agrees with the Marxist contention that socialism is the main precondition for women's liberation. But. . . . other changes in the production of goods, reproduction, sexuality, and socialization are required, too." I agree with White's statement of the necessary condition for calling a person a feminist. He/she must believe, he writes, "that sexism is unacceptable, . . . that women should no longer accept unjust treatment . . . that justice requires equality

for women." *Contemporary Moral Problems* (St. Paul: West, 1985), pp. 211–12.

18. Wender, "Plato: Misogynist . . . ," p. 75.
19. Ibid., p. 76.
20. W. W. Fortenbaugh, "On Plato's Feminism in *Republic* V," *Apeiron,* IX, 2 (1975), p. 1.
21. Brian Calvert, "Plato and the Equality of Women," *Phoenix,* 29, 3 (1975), pp. 242, 243.
22. Joseph Ghougassian, *Toward Women* (San Diego: Lukas, 1977), p. 41.
23. Other inaccuracies include a confusion between the *Laws* and the *Republic,* p. 41, and a misleading reference to Aristophanes, suggesting communism before Plato, p. 43. Clearly female advocates of gender equality have no monopoly on excesses.
24. Mary Cohart, ed., *Unsung Champions of Women* (Albuquerque: University of New Mexico Press, 1975), pt. 4.
25. Elizabeth G. Davis even makes the patently false statement that "in Plato's time and for long before in enlightened Greece, boys and girls received identical educations and prepared for identical lives of the mind." *The First Sex* (New York: Putnam, 1971), p. 331.
26. Richard C. Lewontin, "A Simple Problem Science Can't Solve," *New York Review of Books,* April 12, 1984, p. 21.
27. Richard C. Lewontin, "Plato's Women," Letters to the Editors, *New York Review of Books,* Oct. 25, 1984. This is part of his answer to R. J. Nelson's rebuttal of his original review. Nelson maintains that "contrary to Lewontin and his wayward exegesis, Plato might well be set as a standard for women's rightful status in all intellectual and cultural pursuits including business, the professions, and science." This places the philosopher Nelson squarely among those who consider Plato unequivocally a great champion of women's rights.
28. Ibid.
29. Martha Nussbaum, "Plato and Affirmative Action: Nussbaum-Lewontin Exchange," *New York Review of Books,* Jan. 30, 1985.
30. Ibid.
31. Elizabeth Janeway, *Powers of the Weak* (New York: Knopf, 1980), p. 82.
32. Sarah Pomeroy, "Feminism in Book V of Plato's *Republic,*" *Apeiron,* VIII, 1 (1974), p. 33.
33. E.g., he clearly had mixed feelings about the arts. While writing powerful literary pieces himself, he banned poets from the state. The aesthetic philosopher-psychologist Rudolf Arnheim discusses another Platonic ambivalence, the "ambiguous attitude" Plato takes toward knowing objective existence. Arnheim sees a contradiction difficult to eliminate in Plato's belief on the one hand that we know through logical operations and on the other that we grasp reality through "direct vision."

See "Plato of Two Minds," in *Visual Thinking* (Berkeley: University of California Press, 1971), pp. 6–8.

34. Pomeroy, "Feminism in Book V," p. 33.

35. That is, "shared by all." Dover discusses this dual sense of *ktema.* He notes "the use of the verb *ktasthai,* 'obtain,' 'acquire' in a very wide sense," in discussing the fact that the "acquisition" of a sympathetic wife recommended by Euripides does not support the idea of women solely as property. *Greek Popular Morality,* p. 96, n.2.

36. Fortenbaugh, "On Plato's Feminism," p. 1.

37. For an excellent summary of Aristotle's use of *koinōnia, see* Martin Ostwald's glossary in his translation of the *Nichomachean Ethics* (New York: Bobbs-Merril, 1962), pp. 309–10. Ostwald translates "community, society, human relations, social organism," and also "partnership" depending on the context. He points out that the term refers to any kind of group whose members are held together by something they have "in common" with each other; a club, a village, a family are spoken of as different kinds of *koinōnia.*

38. Marylin B. Arthur in *Becoming Visible: Women in European History* ed. R. Bridenthal and C. Koonz (Boston: Houghton Mifflin, 1977), pp. 72, 73.

39. M. I. Finley, *The World of Odysseus,* rev. ed. (New York: Viking Press, 1978), pp. 127–28.

40. Julia Annas, "Plato's *Republic* and Feminism," *Philosophy,* 51 (1976), p. 309.

41. Ibid.

42. Ibid., p. 311.

43. Annas points to the irony that even the utilitarian Mill starts his essay on the subjection of women with the idea that the subordination of women is wrong *in itself,* though she admits that he also offers utilitarian reasons. The question is how Mill would define "in itself" in this context; and I think we have reason to believe that just as he offers his own interpretation of "good" he might well offer a reinterpretation of "wrong in itself" which referred to consequences.

44. Annas, "*Republic* and Feminism," p. 314.

45. Ibid., p. 315.

46. Lynda Lange, "The Function of Equal Education" in Lorenne M. G. Clark and L. Lange, *The Sexism of Social and Political Theory* (Toronto, 1979), pp. 3, 4.

47. Ibid., p. 9.

48. Arlene Saxenhouse, "The Philosopher and the Female in the Political Thought of Plato," *Political Theory,* 4 (May 1976), p. 203.

49. Ibid., p. 199. Two Italian feminist classicists make a similar point. They object to the fact that because "complete uniformity within the body politic" is required "the natural role of the mother" is cancelled. Silvia Campese and Silvia Gastaldi, *La donna e i filosofi: archeologia di un'immagine culturale* (Bologna: Zanichelli, 1977), p. 16.

50. Saxenhouse, "The Philosopher and the Female," p. 211.

51. Susan Moller Okin, "Philosopher Queens and Private Wives: Plato on Women and the Family," *Philosophy and Public Affairs,* 6 (Summer 1977), p. 365. Okin first discussed the relation between female guardians and private wives in this article, and then in a slightly revised version in her *Women and Western Political Thought* (Princeton: Princeton University Press, 1979), in which the first three chapters are devoted to Plato.

52. See above, pp. 33ff.

53. Okin, "Philosopher Queens," pp. 346, 347.

54. Ibid., p. 361.

55. Okin, *Women and Western Thought,* p. 69.

56. Okin, "Philosopher Queens," p. 368.

57. Rousseau, *Emile,* 4: 699–700, quoted in ibid., p. 356.

58. Ibid.

59. In her earlier article she states only that Taylor does not give "any reasons" (ibid., p. 356), but in the later book she makes the accusation even stronger, referring to his dogmatism.

60. Taylor, *Plato: Man and Work,* p. 278.

61. Nohle, *Die Statslehre,* pp. 137–38.

62. Okin, "Philosopher Queens," p. 359

63. William Jacobs, "Plato on Female Emancipation and the Traditional Family," *Apeiron,* XII, 1 (1978), p. 29.

64. Okin, *Women and Western Thought,* p. 38 and n.38. She nevertheless retains the expression "entails as a corollary," p. 41. See also p. 69.

65. Dover, *Greek Popular Morality,* p. 98.

66. Okin, *Women and Western Thought.*

67. Okin, "Philosopher Queens," p. 357.

68. See also Jacobs, *Plato on Female Emancipation,* p. 30 and p. 31, n. 3.

69. Okin, *Women and Western Thought,* p. 38.

70. Ibid., p. 29.

71. Although the usage is very common, I agree with A. E. Taylor's objection that the practices recommended have little to do with our modern understanding of the word. *Plato: Man and Work,* pp. 277–78.

72. Okin, *Women and Western Thought,* p. 29.

73. Ibid., p. 51.

74. Ibid., p. 52.

75. At one point she attempts a qualification of this nature-nurture bifurcation, but in general she argues for Plato's stress on nurture. Ibid., p. 57.

76. Ibid.

77. See *Phaedrus* and Okin, *Women and Western Thought,* p. 57.

78. For example, J. P. Sartre's existentialist ontology with its formulation "existence precedes essence" is designed to counter the Platonic stress on the fixity of human nature and the consequent devaluation of change and choice.

79. John Wild, *Plato's Modern Enemies and the Theory of Natural Law* (Chicago: University of Chicago Press, 1953), p. 150. Wild shows that for Plato the goal for any entity whatsoever is to realize its "essential tendencies and capacities," p. 73.
80. Cornford, *From Religion to Philosophy,* quoted in Okin, *Women and Western Thought,* p. 52.
81. Okin, *Women and Western Thought,* p. 53.
82. Cornford, *Republic,* 485.
83. Jowett, *Republic,* 485.
84. Okin, *Women and Western Thought,* p. 59.
85. Plato, *Laws,* 795.
86. Okin, *Women and Western Thought,* p. 64.
87. Ibid., pp. 64, 65.
88. Glen Morrow, *Plato's Cretan City,* p. 331, quoted in ibid., p. 316, n.48.
89. Taylor, *Laws,* 802e. In Hamilton and Cairns, *Collected Dialogues,* p. 1374.
90. Okin, *Women and Western Thought,* p. 71, and n.44.
91. Jowett, *Laws,* 781.
92. See discussion of F. A. Wright above, pp. 62-63.
93. Bloom translates "produce"; Rouse, "engender"; Shorey, "create"; and Jowett, "implant." Jowett assumes that Plato believed that good education has a cumulative force and "affects the breed." Jowett, *Greek Text,* III, p. 151.
94. *Laws,* 834d. The Greek text states that a woman may participate if her nature is not averse, *mē dyscherainē;* the reason a woman's nature might make her vexed or uncomfortable with horsemanship is not here specified.
95. Jowett, *Laws,* 834d, 781.
96. Okin, *Women and Western Thought,* p. 59.
97. Ibid., p. 68.
98. Plato, *Laws,* 805c–d.
99. The wording is *hoti malista,* which Jowett translates "to the greatest possible extent." Jowett, *Laws,* 805.
100. Okin, *Women and Western Thought,* pp. 40–41.
101. Jane R. Martin, "Equality and Education in Plato," in *Feminism and Philosophy,* ed. M. Vetterling-Braggin, F. A. Elliston, J. English, (Totoma, N.J.: Littlefield, 1977), pp. 280, 282.
102. Ibid., p. 1.
103. Ibid., pp. 286, 287.
104. Ibid. p. 289.
105. I have preferred to extend the terminology in English to "Philosopher-Kings" and "Philosopher-Queens" only because the former has become standard usage, and demands some equivalent. Of course "female philosopher-ruler" would be more accurate but also more awkward and less suggestive of the intended parallelism. Plato, of course, does not use

basileia. Jowett translates *archontas* as "governers" and *archousas* as "governesses." This choice may be well intentioned (since the Oxford English Dictionary defines "governess" first as a woman who governs, e.g. a kingdom, province, community, or religious institution), but it hardly conveys equality to the contemporary reader. Nussbaum points out that the frequently anthologized translation of Paul Shorey renders *archontas* as "rulers" and *archousas* as "women" rather than "female rulers." She connects this misleading usage to Shorey's endowment of a bequest for "single young men studying Plato" and sees both facts as instances of bias, bias of the sort I have detailed above in other earlier Plato scholars. She reports holding a different fellowship in the same classics department, an award which allowed her "(unjustly) to be the first female in that guardian class." This was possible because the term "men" in the conditions of her award was henceforth to be construed to mean "members of the human species." Twenty-five hundred years after Plato's formulation the powers in the university have finally come around to his conclusion! Nussbaum, "Plato and Affirmative Action."

106. Martin, "Equality in Plato," p. 288.

107. Ibid. See p. 298, n.29.

108. This was the observation of Mrs. Ferraro, made in a public broadcast after her daughter Geraldine Ferraro was nominated at the Democratic Party Convention in August 1984.

109. Martin, "Equality in Plato."

110. Ibid., p. 288.

111. I use this concept in the sense popularized by the British psychiatrist Winnicott who concluded that although perfect parents cannot exist, children's mental health can be adequately assured by "good enough" parenting.

112. E. O. Wilson points out that "the best women athletes are better than most male athletes," *On Human Nature* (Cambridge, Mass.: Harvard University Press, 1978) p. 127.

113. Martin, "Equality in Plato," p. 293.

114. Plato, Republic. 541a.

115. G. Mitchell agrees we should focus our research on power and leadership, on getting things done, rather than on gender-related variables. It is interesting, however, that she describes the masculine or "agentic" pattern in power situations as one that promotes the individual, glorifies individual achievement, and separates the individual from the group. Whereas the female or "communal pattern promotes the welfare of the group and stresses relations with others." By these criteria Plato's rulers follow the female pattern! See *Human Sex Differences: A Primatologist's Perspective* (New York: Van Nostrand, Reinhold, 1981), p. 18.

116. Jean B. Elshtain, *Public Man, Private Woman* (Princeton: Princeton University Press, 1981), pp. 20–41.

117. In her preface Elshtain writes "*Public Man, Private Woman* is a nasty book. It is intended to be" (p. xi). She justifies her tone by refer-

ring to a letter by Ludwig Wittgenstein. He wrote that thinking really honestly about our own and other people's lives is not really thrilling, but often downright nasty, and when nasty then it's most important. Quoted from Norman Malcolm, *Ludwig Wittgenstein, A Memoir,* p. 39. However, it should be noted that Wittgenstein was describing the process of thinking; and his own work, as published by his disciples, is *not* nasty. My disagreement with Elshtain here is pronounced. Nastiness generally provokes only more nastiness and does not in fact illuminate important questions. The temptation to respond in kind is strong and may result in the exaggeration of differences and the obscuring of crucial agreement. I am not sure I have succeeded in avoiding this trap.

118. She writes, "The key problem is not so much Plato's personal antipathy toward women but his conceptual adequacy to the task at hand. Here Plato's somewhat muddled treatment of the category "nature" becomes critical." *Public Man, Private Woman,* p. 37.

119. Jane R. Martin makes a similar point in her book *Reclaiming a Conversation: The Ideal of the Educated Woman* (New Haven: Yale University Press, 1985). According to Martha Nussbaum in her review essay, Martin makes the important point that contemporary theorists on women's education seldom consult the philosophical discussions that have taken place for centuries. The result is that public debate is impoverished and important public figures repeatedly make assumptions that have been successfully challenged. Nussbaum points out that the U.S. White House Chief of Staff Donald Regan made just such an erroneous assumption about women when he stated that they did not have the ability to comprehend arms negotiations. See Nussbaum, "Women's Lot," p. 7. Feminist thinkers who neglect previous scholarship may also make false assumptions.

120. Elshtain, *Public Man, Private Woman,* p. 21, n.4.

121. See Hans Kelson, "Platonic Love," *American Imago,* 3, 1–2 (April 1942). p. 3.

122. Elshtain, *Public Man, Private Woman,* p. xiii.

123. Russell wrote that Plato possessed the art to dress up illiberal suggestions in such a way that they deceived future ages who admired the *Republic* without ever becoming aware of what was actually involved in its proposals. "It has always been correct to praise Plato but not to understand him. . . . My object is the opposite. I wish to understand him, but to treat him with as little reverence as if he were a contemporary English or American advocate of totalitarianism." B. Russell, *History of Western Philosophy,* (New York: Simon and Schuster, 1945), p. 85. Elshtain's account, though more filled with that spirit of *ressentiment* that she elsewhere derides, would seem in intention at least to be similar.

124. E.g., Bertrand Russell complains that in spite of all the fine talk, skill in war and enough to eat is all that will be achieved by Plato's ideal society. The philosopher had lived through famine and defeat in Athens, and as Russell puts it, "perhaps *subconsciously* he thought the avoidance

of these evils the best that statesmanship could accomplish." (My emphasis.) *History of Western Philosophy*, p. 85.
125. Elshtain, *Public Man, Private Woman*, pp. 31–32.
126. Jean B. Elshtain, "Against Androgyny," *Telos*, 47, Spring 1981, p. 19.
127. Elshtain, *Public Man, Private Woman*, pp. 15, 16, 27. One cannot be sure of the extent to which Elshtain would be prepared to defend this idea. She writes in her introduction that "the question to be put, then, is not just what politics is for but what politics has served to defend against." Ibid., p. 16. But then in her chapter immediately following she describes her calling "normative ideals of collective life" a defense as "a playful and provocative note." Ibid., p. 19.

Hans Kelson, in his psychoanalytic analysis of Platonic love, takes a similar view of Plato's deficiencies. He, too, speculates on Plato's unconquered incest wish and accuses the philosopher of ignoring "the woman as such" and denying her any sexual peculiarity (*Platonic Love*, p. 17). Ultimately it is Plato's perverse sexual orientation that is responsible for his stance toward women in the *Republic.* Plato's mistaken view of the relations between the sexes stems from the fact that "nature has denied him all knowledge of motherhood." Ibid., p. 19.
128. Ibid., p. 335.
129. While Elshtain's attempt at a lively and personal style is admirable, her lack of precision places a burden on the reader. For example, in *Public Man, Private Woman,* she uses the word "imperative" repeatedly without clarifying its meaning. She speaks of "political and philosophic imperatives," p. 20; "psycho-social imperatives," p. 25; "feminist imperatives," p. 298; "public imperative," p. 299; "universal, bureaucratic, and socioeconomic imperatives," p. 305; "moral and theoretical imperative," p. 310; "inborn imperative," p. 318; "human imperative" and "familial imperative," p. 332; "humanizing imperative," p. 333; "Nazi imperative," p. 335; and "bedrock imperatives," p. 339, as well as numerous other vague uses of the term. Many of her metaphors are equally confusing, such as her assertion that those who undervalue the importance of the body "need to hold the body at arm's length."
130. She quotes with enthusiasm this view of what women's political urgency must be from Hélène Cîxous, "Poetry is/and (the) Political," in *The Second Sex—Thirty Years Later* (Mimeographed, New York Institute for the Humanities, 1979), p. 37. Quoted, *Public Man, Private Woman*, p. 335.
131. Elshtain, *Public Man, Private Woman*, p. 311.
132. Elshtain, "Against Androgyny," p. 14. Elshtain insists that such feminist theory automatically involves us in a belief in Lockean atomistic individuals as well as in the post-industrial capitalist use of people as interchangeable units. Ibid., p. 11.
133. Elshtain, *Public Man, Private Woman*, p. 318.
134. Ibid., p. 35. See also "Against Androgyny," pp. 7, 10, 16, 17,

where the assumption is that androgyny automatically means "blandness," p. 21.

135. See e.g., Elshtain, *Public Man, Private Woman,* p. 38. In "Against Androgyny" she speaks of the "iron cage of . . . liberal dualism," p. 11.

136. Elshtain, *Public Man, Private Woman,* pp. 326, 327.

137. Ibid., p. 39.

138. Ibid., p. 248.

139. Carol Gilligan, *In a Different Voice* (Cambridge, Mass.: Harvard University Press, 1982), pp. 335–36.

140. Elshtain, *Public Man, Private Woman,* pp. 335, 336.

141. Gilligan, *In a Different Voice,* pp. 2, 8ff.

142. Ibid., pp. 11–12, 19ff. She also argues very convincingly against the psychiatrist-researcher George Vaillant's minimizing of the value of attachment and using as models for mental health men distant in their relationships. I would claim that Gilligan's view of morality is not only different, but that her values, as the Greeks would say, are better. See p. 153.

143. Ibid., p. 37.

144. Elshtain, *Public Man, Private Woman,* p. 19.

145. She writes, "Whatever nightmares rocked his sleep and terrors filled his days, Plato's solution is an overreaction." Ibid., p. 35.

146. Ibid., p. 16 and n.12.

147. For Elshtain's objections to other interpretations of Freud see e.g., ibid., pp. 249, 273–74. Freud's view of the consequences of a lack of castration anxiety on women's mental life and the resulting different sense of justice appears in "Some Psychical Consequences of the Anatomical Distinctions Between the Sexes," *The Complete Psychological Works of Sigmund Freud,* ed. J. Strachey (London: Hogarth Press, 1961), vol. 19, p. 243.

148. Elshtain, *Public Man, Private Woman,* p. 310.

149. Ibid., p. 317.

150. Georges M. A. Grube, *Plato's Thought* (Boston: Beacon Press, 1935), p. 136.

151. Ibid. Adela N. Adam writes: "There is an element of passion and ardour in Plato's 'reason' which is very remote from our usual understanding of the term. Reason is afire with love of beauty and of goodness as well as love of truth, and so is capable of inspiring life and action. . . ." *Plato: Moral and Political Ideals,* p. 116.

152. Elshtain, *Public Man, Private Woman,* p. 27.

153. Ibid., p. 27.

154. Ibid.

155. Dover, *Greek Homosexuality,* p. 164.

156. Ibid.

157. Ibid., p. 157.

158. Erich Segal, "Platonic Love," review of Dover's *Greek Homosexuality* in the *New York Times Book Review,* April 8, 1979, p. 9.

159. Elshtain, *Public Man, Private Woman,* p. 27, n.22.
160. T. Gould maintains that the earlier speeches in the *Symposium* though representing false views most probably show Plato extracting the best from popular notions. *Platonic Love,* p. 21.
161. Anton-Hermann Chroust, *Socrates, Man and Myth* (South Bend: Notre Dame Press, 1957).
162. T. Gould, *Platonic Love,* pp. 54, 55.
163. Ibid., p. 54.
164. Ibid., p. 55.
165. Ludwig Wittgenstein, *Philosophical Investigations* (Oxford: Blackwell, 1972) I, 67, p. 32e.
166. Elshtain, *Public Man, Private Woman.*
167. Mary Midgley, *Beast and Man: The Roots of Human Nature* (Ithaca: Cornell University Press, 1978), p. 75.
168. Ibid., p. 353.
169. Ibid.
170. Ibid., pp. 75, 76.
171. Ibid., p. 331.
172. Ibid., p. 76, n.27.
173. Ibid.
174. Ibid., p. 327.
175. Elshtain, *Public Man, Private Woman,* p. 30.
176. Ibid.
177. *The Undergraduate Woman: Issues in Educational Equity,* ed. P. J. Perun (Lexington, Mass.: D.C. Heath, 1982), p. 406.
178. Lili S. Hornig makes this point about the reluctant support of women's sports, and offers this quote from Judge J. J. Fitzgerald of Connecticut. In ibid., p. 418.
179. Elshtain, *Public Man, Private Woman,* p. 37.
180. Opposition to androgyny has already "rallied" many in the United States. The leaders of the so-called Moral Majority have called vociferously for the elimination of text books in which women appear in nontraditional roles, and the question has become a political issue in the South and Midwest. See Elshtain, "Against Androgyny," p. 19.
181. For an excellent examination of the logical implications of Plato's argument, including a critique of Bloom's (and others') interpretation, see Brian Calvert, *Plato and Equality,* pp. 234ff. He points out that there is no inconsistency between saying that the class of men is superior to the class of women, and that "the best women are equal to the best men."
182. Katherine Ralls, "Mammals in which Females are Larger than Males," *Quarterly Review of Biology,* June 1976.
183. See above, pp. 45–47.
184. Dale Hall, "The Republic and the 'Limits of Politics,' " *Political Theory,* 5, 3 (August 1977), p. 296.
185. Ibid.

186. Bloom, *Republic, Interpretive Essay.*
187. Bloom, "Response to Hall," *Political Theory,* 5, 3 (August 1977), p. 315.
188. Ibid., p. 324.
189. Ibid.
190. It is interesting to note that even a scholar as open-minded as K. J. Dover seems to assume in his *Greek Homosexuality,* p. 156, that his readers will be either heterosexual or homosexual males. In quoting this passage from Kharmides to illustrate Plato's philosophical exploitation of homosexuality, Dover tries to make the fact that Socrates is "on fire" at the sight of Kharmides' torso or genitals more understandable to his readers. He writes: "If we translate this scene into heterosexual terms, so that Socrates' glimpse inside Kharmides' cloak becomes a glimpse of a young woman of extraordinary beauty, as she leans forward to ask an unaffected question, we come as close to seeing through ancient Greek eyes as we are likely to come." He also explains that those with a mainly or entirely homosexual orientation may see clearly enough through Greek eyes already. What he does not concern himself with at all is whether the appeal of Kharmides' anatomy would already sufficiently clarify the intended exploitation of erotic appeal for his female readers; or whether perhaps some other male type would be necessary. This oversight is particularly ironic since Dover cites the female classicist Wender in this very paragraph (though she is using the passage for other purposes). It may seem a trivial point, but after centuries of androcentric explications, it is surely time to address explanations to female as well as male audiences.
191. In the vaudeville review "Oh! Calcutta," where nightly nude dancing of men and women was a theatrical spectacle, just such control was exercised for hundreds of performances. I cannot vouch for the rehearsals, of course.
192. Bloom, "Response to Hall," p. 324.
193. See above, p. 43.
194. In an appendix to his edition of the *Republic,* James Adam reviews over 100 scholars who have discussed the subject, considering the nature of the connection far from self-evident, pp. 352–55. Adam himself argues that the idea of female guardians was part of a well-reasoned and deliberate attempt by the Socratic school to improve the position of women in Greece, p. 280, and asserts that Plato "touches with serious purpose on nearly all the proposals which Aristophanes had tried to make ridiculous" p. 355.
195. Aristophanes, *Ecclesiazusae,* ed. R. G. Ussher (London: Oxford University Press, 1973), p. xx.
196. A. Bloom, "Response to Hall," p. 324. It is simply not conceivable to Bloom that intelligent, imaginative thinkers living with a woman and priding themselves on speculation, exposed to females' intelligence despite their lack of education, might well have seriously considered

alternatives before Plato. The great classicist Schleiermacher, whose translation of the *Republic* Bloom admires, takes that view, though he states it without any of Bloom's dogmatism. About the subject of egalitarianism in Book V he writes: "It does not appear to me that the way in which it is introduced, Socrates' reluctance to enter upon it, and his wish to avoid the subject, refers to the circumstance that he was here about to introduce into the language of the people a thing contrary to all current opinion, and as yet unheard-of. I rather discover in this the clearest traces of the fact the *this doctrine was already known,* as it naturally might be from the oral lectures and the communications of his pupils, and had experienced some satirical treatment" (*my emphasis*). Bloom's arrogance contrasts sharply with the hesitance of Schleiermacher who adds: "But this is so completely a matter of critical feeling lying without the limits of argument, that I can do nothing but invite those readers who are interested in such questions . . . to an attentive consideration of the passage." F. Schleiermacher, *Introductions to the Dialogues of Plato* (New York: Arno Press, 1973), see pp. 377–81.
197. Bloom, "Response to Hall," p. 326.
198. Ibid., p. 318.

3: THE CONTINUING IMPORTANCE OF PLATO'S QUESTIONS

1. This frequently quoted dictum is from Whitehead's major work, *Process and Reality* (New York: Macmillan, 1929), p. 63. Okin (who evidently had difficulty locating it and speculated that he must have said it in some unpublished lecture) disagrees. This is because she believes Aristotle's functionalism and outright subordination of women have been ascendent in the history of philosophy. But of course Aristotle's discussion is in part an answer to his teacher Plato; and what Whitehead intends is precisely that Plato initiated the discussion of all the significant issues (not, of course, that all of his solutions have prevailed). See Okin, *Women in Western Thought,* p. 335 and chapter 10, n.1.
2. Wilson, *On Human Nature.*
3. Ibid., p. 135.
4. Donald Symons, *Evolution of Human Sexuality* (New York: Oxford University Press, 1979).
5. Clifford Geertz, in "Sociosexology," his review of Symons' book in the *New York Review of Books,* Jan. 24, 1980, p. 4. Geertz refutes Symons' "sociosexology," saying, "to write a book that says men and women are radically mismatched in their basic sexual natures, that sex is a basic disruptive force in marriage and a primary obstacle to human happiness, that copulation is a female service provided to men for an appropriate return, that men want sexual novelty and women sexual constancy, that male sexuality is rigidly channeled and female highly

malleable, . . . and expect it all to be taken, at this time and in this place, as 'just the facts' is so wildly unrealistic as to suggest a highly uncertain grasp on the ways of the world."

6. David Barash, *The Whisperings Within* (New York: Harper and Row, 1979), p. 6.

7. Stephen Jay Gould, "Genes on the Brain," *New York Review of Books*, June 30, 1983, p. 6.

8. E. O. Wilson, *Sociobiology* (Cambridge, Mass.: Harvard University Press, 1975), p. 562. See also his *On Human Nature*, p. 5.

9. Wilson, *On Human Nature*, p. 132.

10. Hrdy, *Woman that Never Evolved*, pp. 200–201.

11. Wilson, *On Human Nature*, p. 135.

12. Ibid., pp. 133–34.

13. Ibid., p. 133.

14. Ibid.

15. Ibid., p. 134.

16. Melford Spiro, *Gender and Culture: Kibbutz Women Revisited* (Durham, N. C.: Duke University Press, 1979), p. 99.

17. Ibid., p. 86.

18. Ibid., p. 85.

19. See, e.g., the discussion of R. L. Blumberg, "The Erosion of Sexual Equality: A Structural Interpretation," in *Beyond Intellectual Sexism: A New Woman, a New Reality*, ed. J. I. Roberts (New York: David McKay, 1976). Blumberg rejects the "unilateral and deterministic view that, due to the intrinsic nature of human females, 'Laundry is Destiny,' " p. 331.

20. I am indebted to Barbara Tizard, Head of the Thomas Coram Research Unit of the University of London and an authority on early childhood development, for this suggestion.

21. Wilson, *Sociobiology*, p. 575.

22. Melvin Konner, *The Tangled Wing: Biological Constraints on the Human Spirit* (New York: Holt, Rinehart and Winston, 1982), p. 121, and n.

23. Ibid., pp. 106–07.

24. Ibid., p. 106.

25. R. Barnett, G. Baruch, and C. Rivers, *Life Prints: New Patterns of Love and Work for Today's Women* (New York: New American Library, 1983) pp. 38, 143–49.

26. Aristotle, on *The Generation of Animals*, 728a 18, quoted in Caroline Whitbeck, "Theories of Sex Difference," *The Philosophical Forum*, 5 (Fall 1973–74), p. 56.

27. Konner, *The Tangled Wing*, p. 126.

28. Ibid. The philosopher Mary Midgley, who would agree that considerations of our innate biological nature are crucial to planning a just society, also maintains that women are "rather less competitive by nature." But she sees that to arrive at the place where they could do something to bring about a saner climate, "they would have to compete

without catching the competitive spirit." She is less sanguine about this possibility than Konner, and admits that "this is a lot to expect." *Beast and Man,* p. 330. My own view is that there is no reason at all to believe that it would occur.

29. Hrdy, *Woman that Never Evolved,* pp. 42–43.

30. Symons, *Evolution of Human Sexuality.* More than 100 years before sociobiologists like Symons claimed that the existing sex roles were biologically prescribed, Herbert Spencer assumed before he even started investigating that there was an "unlikeness of mental facilities" which went along with the unlikeness of "parental activities" between the sexes. See J. Sayers, *Biological Politics,* pp. 34–35. Such "scientific" thought no doubt indirectly influenced nineteenth-century British Plato commentators.

31. Mitchell, *Human Sex Differences,* p. 205. Also see n.115 above.

32. Midgley, *Beast and Man,* p. 125, n.7.

33. David Barash, *Sociobiology and Behavior* (New York: Elsevier, 1977), p. 293.

34. See, for example, Barash, *The Whisperings Within,* p. 49.

35. Dover, *Greek Popular Morality,* p. 101. He writes that the Greeks tended to think that women desired and enjoyed sexual intercourse *more* than men. He quotes from Hesiod (fr. 275), who "relates a myth in which Teiresias (since he had been both man and woman) was asked by Zeus and Hera to say which sex got more pleasure from intercourse, and his answer was that the woman got nine-tenths, the man one-tenth." See also Aristotle, "Females are naturally libidinous, incite the males to copulation, and cry out during the act of coition." *De Historia Animalium* 5.2.540 11–13.

36. Barash, *The Whisperings Within,* p. 87.

37. Barash, *Sociobiology and Behavior,* p. 301.

38. Barash, *The Whisperings Within,* pp. 233–34. His fellow sociobiologist, Daniel Freedman, also makes an attempt to allow for free will saying it is "universal" and "species-specific" but adding "therefore within the realm of biology." He reveals his prejudices when he writes that "[d]espite . . . shifting patterns, certain male-female differences can be expected to remain the same," in his section on "Male Bragging and the Double Standard." *Human Sociobiology* (New York: Macmillan, 1979), p. 18.

39. "His and Hers Brains," *Science,* 3, 7 (September 1982), p. 14.

40. David Gelman and John Carey, "Sex Research—On the Bias," *Newsweek,* May 18, 1981, p. 81.

41. Erik Erikson in *Childhood and Society,* and discussed in the excellent popular summary of recent scientific research, "Just How the Sexes Differ," *Newsweek,* May 18, 1981, p. 81.

42. Research of Paula Caplan, Toronto psychologist, reported in "Sex Research—On the Bias," p. 81.

43. It is well known that a drop in social status in monkeys can result in

a lower level of testosterone. See, e.g., Konner, *The Tangled Wing,* p. 119 and n. We have much to learn about the way women's destiny affects her anatomy.

44. University of Chicago psychologist Jerre Levy, a pioneer in studies of brain lateralization, withdrew from public discussion of her work after being harassed by hostile letters and phone calls. And S. B. Hrdy relates that when she participated in a panel discussing possible differences in male and female math ability, a feminist suggested to her that it was evil to do such studies. Reported in *Newsweek,* May 18, 1981.

45. Gould, *Platonic Love,* p. 84.

46. C. Lumsden and E. O. Wilson, *Genes, Mind and Culture* (Cambridge, Mass.: Harvard University Press, 1981), p. 172.

47. Lewontin, "A Simple Problem Science Can't Solve," p. 21.

48. The anthropologist Peter Wilson writes in *Man, the Promising Primate* (New Haven: Yale University, 1980), that "it is a distinguishing feature of the human species that although individuals are naturally impelled toward living in company and it is necessary for them to do so, there is no universal instinctive *form* that this company will take," pp. 160, 161.

49. See, e.g., C. Benbow and J. Stanley, "Sex Differences in Mathematical Ability: Fact or Artifact?" *Science,* December 12, 1980.

50. W. D. Wandersee points out in *Women's Work and Family Values 1920–1940* (Cambridge, Mass.: Harvard University Press, 1981), that the family was as often a source of power as a tool of oppression. She says if family life is to be revolutionized to allow for women's full equality, because of women's historical commitment to the family, "the revolution will have to be gentle" if it is to have a broad base of support, pp. 121–22. But, of course, a gentle revolution is a contradiction in terms. Wandersee herself finds this a feminist dilemma, and "one that is not much closer to being resolved today than it was half a century ago." In the light of *Republic* V and Aristotle's pro-family rejoinder to it, one might say the dilemma is as unsolved as it was twenty-three centuries ago! The important point as Plato saw was that changes of some kind are essential.

References

Adam, Adela M. *Plato: Moral and Political Ideals.* Cambridge: Cambridge University Press; New York: G. P. Putnam's, 1913.

Adam, James. *The Republic, ed. with Critical Notes, Commentary, and Appendix.* Cambridge, 1905.

Allen, Christine G. "Plato on Women." *Feminist Studies,* 2, 2–3 (1975), p. 132.

Annas, Julia. "Plato's *Republic* and Feminism." *Philosophy,* 51 (1976), p. 309.

Aristophanes. *Ecclesiazusae.* Ed. R. G. Ussher. London: Oxford University Press, 1973.

———. *Ecclesiazusae.* Trans. B. B. Rogers. Vol. III. Cambridge, Mass.: Harvard University Press, 1924.

Aristotle. *Politics.* Trans. Benjamin Jowett, in *The Basic Works of Aristotle.* New York: Random House, 1941.

Arnheim, Rudolf. "Plato of Two Minds." In *Visual Thinking.* Berkeley: University of California Press, 1971.

Arthur, Marylin B. " 'Liberated' Women: The Classical Era." In *Becoming Visible: Women in European History.* Ed. R. Bridenthal and C. Koonz. Boston: Houghton Mifflin, 1977.

Asmus, V. F., ed. Platon: *Sochinenia v Trekh Tomakh Tom* 3. Moscow, 1971.

Bakewell, Charles M. *Plato: The Republic with Introduction.* New York: Charles Scribner's, 1928.

Bannes, Joachim. *Hitlers Kampf und Platons Staat.* Berlin: W. de Gruyter, 1933.

Barash, David. *The Whisperings Within.* New York: Harper and Row, 1979.

———. *Sociobiology and Behavior.* New York: Elsevier, 1977.

Barker, Ernest. *Greek Political Theory: Plato and His Predecessors.* London: Methuen, 1947.

———. *The Political Thought of Plato and Aristotle.* New York: Dover, 1959.

Barnett, R., G. Baruch, and C. Rivers. *Life Prints: New Patterns of Love and Work for Today's Women.* New York: New American Library, 1983.

Beard, Mary. *Women as a Force in History.* New York: Colliers, 1971.

de Beauvoir, Simone, *The Second Sex*. New York: Bantam Books, 1968.

Bell, Susan G., ed. *Women from the Greeks to the French Revolution.* Stanford: Stanford University Press, 1980.

Benbow, C., and J. Stanley. "Sex Differences in Mathematical Ability: Fact or Artifact?" *Science*, December 12, 1980.

Benn, A. W. *Greek Philosophers*. New York: Dutton, 1974.

Bloom, Allan. "Response to Hall." *Political Theory*, 5, 3 (August 1977).

———, trans. *The Republic of Plato, with Interpretive Essay*. New York: Basic Books, 1968.

Blumberg, R. L. "The Erosion of Sexual Equality: A Structural Interpretation." In *Beyond Intellectual Sexism: A New Woman, a New Reality*, ed. J. I. Roberts. New York: David McKay, 1976.

Blunt, Anthony. *Artistic Theory in Italy, 1450–1600*. New York: Oxford University Press, 1956.

Boas, George. "A Sermon for Humanists." *The Johns Hopkins Magazine*, October 1984, 16.

Borsook, Eva. *The Companion Guide to Florence*. London: Collins, 1973.

Bosanquet, Bernard. *A Companion to Plato's Republic*. London: Rivingtons, 1925.

———. *The Education of the Young in The Republic of Plato*. Cambridge: Cambridge Press, 1900.

Calvert, Brian. "Plato and the Equality of Women." *Phoenix*, 29, 3 (1975).

Campese, Silvia, and Silvia Gastaldi. *La donna e i filosofi: archeologia di un' immagine culturale*. Bologna: Zanichelli, 1977.

Chroust, Anton-Hermann. *Socrates, Man and Myth*. South Bend: Notre Dame Press, 1957.

Cohart, Mary, ed. *Unsung Champions of Women*. Alburquerque: University of New Mexico Press, 1915.

Cornford, F. M., trans. *The Republic of Plato*. London: Oxford University Press, 1941.

Croiset, Maurice, *La République de Platon: étude et analyse*. Paris: Edition Mellottée, 1946.

Crombie, I. M. *An Examination of Plato's Doctrine*. Vol. I. London: Routledge & Kegan Paul, 1962.

Crossman, Richard C. *Plato Today*. New York: Oxford University Press, 1939.

Currie, H. M. *The Individual and the State*. London: Dent, 1973.

Davis, Elizabeth G. *The First Sex*. New York: Putnam, 1971.

Dickason, Anne. "Anatomy and Destiny: The Role of Biology in Plato's Views of Women." *The Philosophical Forum*, V (Fall-Winter 1973–1974).

Diesendruck, Z. *The Republic: Translated into Hebrew with Introduction and Notes*. Tel Aviv: Newman, 1953.

Diogenes Laertius. *Lives of Eminent Philosophers*, with English translation by R. D. Hicks. Cambridge, Mass.: Harvard University Press, 1966.

Dover, K. J. *Greek Homosexuality.* New York: Random House, 1978.

———. *Greek Popular Morality in the Time of Plato and Aristotle.* Berkeley: University of California Press, 1974.

Edelstein, Ludwig. "The Function of the Myth in Plato's Philosophy." *Journal of the History of Ideas,* 10 (October 1949).

Elshtain, Jean B. *Public Man, Private Woman.* Princeton: Princeton University Press, 1981.

———. "Against Androgyny." *Telos,* 47 (Spring 1981).

Erikson, Erik. *Childhood and Society.* New York: Norton, 1950.

al-Fārābī. *De Platonis philosophia,* ed. F. Rosenthal and R. Walzer. London: Warburg Institute, 1943.

Fau, Guy. *L'Émancipation féminin dans la Rome antique.* Paris, 1978.

Fehl, N. E. *A Guide to the Study of Plato's Republic.* Hong Kong: Chung Chi College, 1961.

Field, G. C. *Plato and His Contemporaries A Study in Fourth-Century Life and Thought.* London, 1930.

Finley, M. I. *The World of Odysseus.* Revised Edition. New York: Viking Press, 1978.

Fite, W. *The Platonic Legend.* New York: Charles Scribner's Sons, 1934.

Fortenbaugh, W. W. "On Plato's Feminism in *Republic* V." *Apeiron,* IX, 2, (1975).

Freedman, D. *Human Sociobiology.* New York: Macmillan, 1979.

Freud, Sigmund. *Analysis Terminable and Interminable.* Standard Edition. London: Hogarth Press, 1964.

Friedlander, Paul. *Plato: The Dialogues.* 2nd and 3rd Periods. Princeton: Princeton Unversity Press, 1969.

Gauss, H. *Philosophischer Handkommentar zu den Dialogen Platos.* Bern, 1958.

Geertz, Clifford. "Sociosexology" *New York Review of Books,* January 24, 1980.

Gelman, David, and John Carey. "Sex Research—On the Bias." *Newsweek,* May 18, 1981, p. 81

Ghougassian, Joseph. *Toward Women.* San Diego: Lukas, 1977.

Gilligan, Carol. *In a Different Voice.* Cambridge, Mass.: Harvard University Press, 1982.

Gomperz, Theodor. *Greek Thinkers.* Vols. I–V. London, 1905.

Gould, Stephen Jay. "Genes on the Brain." *New York Review of Books,* June 30, 1983.

Gould, Thomas. *Platonic Love.* New York: Free Press, 1963.

Grant, W. V., and Thomas D. Snyder. *Digest of Education Statistics: 1985–1986.* Washington, D.C.: U.S. Government Printing Office, 1986.

Grote, George. *Plato and the Other Companions of Socrates.* Vol. IV. London: John Murray, 1888.

Grube, Georges M. A. *Plato's Thought.* Boston: Beacon Press, 1935

Hall, Dale. "The *Republic* and the 'Limits of Politics.' " *Political Theory*, 5(3) (August 1977).

Hamilton, Edith, and Huntington Cairns, eds. *The Collected Dialogues of Plato.* Princeton: Princeton University Press, 1963.

Heim, A. M. "Harvard Study Reveals Gender Inequality in the Classroom." *Second Century: Radcliffe News*, April 1986.

"His and Hers Brains." *Science*, 3, 7 (September 1982).

Holmes, G. *The Florentine Enlightenment: 1400–1450.* New York: Pegasus, 1969.

Hoole, C. H. *An Analytical Paraphrase of the Republic of Plato.* Oxford: J. Vincent, 1875.

Hrdy, Sarah B. *The Woman That Never Evolved.* Cambridge, Mass.: Harvard University Press, 1981.

Ithurriague, Jean. *Les idées de Platon sur la condition de la femme.* Paris: Librarie Universitaire, 1931.

Jacobs, William. "Plato on Female Emancipation and the Traditional Family." *Apeiron*, XII, 1 (1978).

Jaeger, Werner. *Paideia.* Vol. II. London: Oxford University Press, 1943.

Jaggar, Alison. "Political Philosophies of Women's Liberation." In *Feminism and Philosophy.* Ed. M. Vetterling-Braggin, F. A. Elliston, J. English. Totowa, N.J.: Littlefield, 1977.

James, William. *Some Problems of Philosophy.* New York: Longmans, Green, 1948.

Janeway, Elizabeth. *Powers of the Weak.* New York: Knopf, 1980.

Jenkyns, Richard. *The Victorians and Ancient Greece.* Cambridge, Mass.: Harvard University Press, 1980.

Jowett, Benjamin, trans. *The Dialogues of Plato.* 3rd Edition. Oxford: Clarendon Press, 1892.

Jowett, B., and L. Campbell, eds. *Plato's Republic: The Greek Text, Edited, with Notes and Essays.* Oxford: Clarendon Press, 1894.

"Just How the Sexes Differ." *Newsweek*, May 18, 1981.

Kelson, Hans. "Platonic Love." *American Imago*, 3, 1–2 (April 1942).

Konner, Melvin. *The Tangled Wing: Biological Constraints on the Human Spirit.* New York: Holt, Rinehart and Winston, 1982.

Koyre, A. *Discovering Plato.* Trans. L. C. Rosenfield. New York: Columbia University Press, 1945.

Lacey, W. K. *The Family in Classical Greece.* Ithaca: Cornell University Press, 1968.

Lange, Lynda. "The Function of Equal Education." In *The Sexism of Social and Political Theory*, ed. Lorenne M. G. Clark and L. Lange. Toronto, 1979.

Langer, W. C. *The Mind of Adolf Hitler.* London: Secker & Warburg, 1973.

Lee, Desmond. *The Republic*, translated, with Introduction. London: Penguin, 1974.

Lefkowitz, M. R., and M. B. Fant. *Women in Greece and Rome*. Toronto: Samuel Stephens, 1977.
Lerner, Gerda. *The Female Experience*. Indianapolis: Bobbs-Merrill, 1977.
Lewontin, Richard C. "Plato's Women." Letters to the Editors. *New York Review of Books*, Oct. 25, 1984.
———. "A Simple Problem Science Can't Solve." *New York Review of Books*, April 12, 1984.
Lodge, R. C. *Plato's Theory of Education*. With an appendix on the education of women according to Plato, by Rabbi Solomon Frank. London: K. Paul, Trench, Trubner, 1947.
Lumsden, C., and E. O. Wilson. *Genes, Mind and Culture*. Cambridge, Mass.: Harvard University Press, 1981.
Martin, Jane R. "Equality and Education in Plato." In *Feminism and Philosophy*, ed. M. Vetterling-Braggin, F. A. Elliston, and J. English. Totowa, N. J.: Littlefield, 1977.
———. *Reclaiming a Conversation: The Ideal of the Educated Woman*. New Haven: Yale University Press, 1985.
Midgley, Mary. *Beast and Man: The Roots of Human Nature*. Ithaca: Cornell University Press, 1978.
Mill, John Stuart. "The Subjection of Women." In *The Feminist Papers*, ed. Alice S. Rossi. New York: Bantam, 1974.
Mitchell, G. *Human Sex Differences: A Primatologist's Perspective*. New York: Van Nostrand, Reinhold, 1981.
Neal, Marie Augusta. "Women in Religious Symbolism and Organization." In *Religious Change and Continuity*, ed. H. M. Johnson. San Francisco: Jossey-Bass, 1979.
Nettleship, Richard. *Lectures on The Republic of Plato*. New York: Macmillan, 1967.
Nohle, Karl. *Die Statslehre Platos*. Leipzig, 1880.
Nussbaum, Martha, "Plato and Affirmative Action: Nussbaum-Lewontin Exchange." *New York Review of Books*, January 31, 1985.
———. "Women's Lot." *New York Review of Books*, January 30, 1986.
Okin, Susan Moller. "Philosopher Queens and Private Wives: Plato on Women and the Family." *Philosophy and Public Affairs*, 6 (Summer 1977).
———. *Women and Western Political Thought*. Princeton: Princeton University Press, 1979.
Osborne, Martha Lee. "Plato's Unchanging View of Woman: A Denial That Anatomy Spells Destiny." *The Philosophical Forum*, Summer 1975.
Ostwald, Martin, ed. *Aristotle, Nichomachean Ethics*. New York: Bobbs-Merrill, 1962.
Parker, Douglass, trans. *Aristophanes, The Congresswomen*. Ann Arbor: University of Michigan Press, 1967.
Pater, Walter. *Plato and Platonism*. London: Macmillan, 1910.
Peirce, C. S. "The Fixation of Belief." In *Collected Papers of Charles S.*

Peirce, vols. V & VI, ed. C. Hartshorne and P. Weiss. (Cambridge, Mass.: Harvard University Press, 1965).

Pierce, Christine. "Equality: *Republic* V." *The Monist*, 57, 1 (Jan. 1973).

Perun, P. J., ed. *The Undergraduate Woman: Issues in Educational Equity*. Lexington, Mass.: D.C. Heath, 1982.

Pomeroy, Sarah. *Goddesses, Whores, Wives, and Slaves: Women in Classical Antiquity*. New York: Schocken, 1975.

———. "Feminism in Book V of Plato's *Republic*." *Apeiron*, VIII, 1 (1974).

Plato. *Republic*.

———. *Timaeus*.

———. *Laws*.

———. *Symposium*.

Popper, Karl. *The Open Society and Its Enemies*. (London: Routledge & Kegan Paul, 1945).

Ralls, Katherine. "Mammals in which Females are Larger than Males." *Quarterly Review of Biology*, June 1976.

Rankin, H. D. *Plato and the Individual*. London: Methuen, 1964.

Ritter, Constantin. *The Essence of Plato's Philosophy*. New York: Russell & Russell, 1933.

Rosenthal, Abigail. "Feminism Without Contradictions." *The Monist*, 57, 1 (January 1973).

Rosenthal, E. I. J. "The Place of Politics in the Philosophy of Ibn Rushd." *Bulletin of the London School of African Studies*, XV:2.

———, ed. *Averroës Commentary on Plato's Republic*. Cambridge: Cambridge University Press, 1966.

Russell, Bertrand. *History of Western Philosophy*. New York: Simon and Schuster, 1945.

Ryle, Gilbert. *The Concept of Mind*. New York: Barnes and Noble, 1971.

———. "Plato: Moral and Political Theory." In *Encyclopedia of Philosophy*, ed. Paul Edwards. New York: Macmillan, 1967, Vol. VI.

Saxenhouse, Arlene. "The Philosopher and the Female in the Political Thought of Plato." *Political Theory*, 4(May 1976).

Sayers, J. *Biological Politics: Feminist and Anti-Feminist Perspectives*. London: Tavistock, 1982.

Schleiermacher, F. *Introductions to the Dialogues of Plato*. New York: Arno Press, 1973.

Segal, Erich. "Platonic Love." *New York Times Book Review*, April 8, 1979.

Simon, Bennett. *Mind and Madness in Ancient Greece*. Ithaca: Cornell University Press, 1978.

Spens, H., trans. *Republic of Plato*. London: Dent, 1906.

Spiro, Melford. *Gender and Culture: Kibbutz Women Revisited*. Durham, N. C.: Duke University Press, 1979.

Sprague, Rosamond. *Plato's Philosopher-King: A Study of the Theoretical Background*. Columbia, S.C., 1976.

Strauss, Leo. *The City and the Man.* Chicago: Rand McNally, 1964.

Symons, Donald. *Evolution of Human Sexuality.* New York: Oxford University Press, 1979.

Taylor, A. E. *Plato: The Man and His Work.* New York: Meridian, 1956.

Tennyson, A. *The Poetical Works of Alfred Lord Tennyson.* Boston: Houghton-Mifflin, n.d.

Wandersee, W. D. *Women's Work and Family Values 1920–1940.* Cambridge, Mass.: Harvard University Press, 1981.

Warren, T. H., trans. *The Republic.* London: Macmillan & Co., 1888.

Weiss, Paul. *Sport: A Philosophical Inquiry.* Carbondale: Southern Illinois University Press, 1969.

Wender, Dorothea. "Plato: Misogynist, Paeodophile and Feminist." *Arethusa,* VI, 1 (Spring 1973).

Whitbeck, Caroline. "Theories of Sex Difference." *The Philosophical Forum,* 5 (Fall 1973–74).

White, James E. *Contemporary Moral Problems.* St. Paul: West, 1985.

White, Nicholas. *A Companion to Plato's Republic.* Oxford: Blackwell, 1979.

Whitehead, A. N. *Process and Reality.* New York: Macmillan, 1929.

Wilamowitz-Moellendorff, U. V. *Die Griechische und der Platonische Staatsgedanke.* Berlin: Weidmannsche Buchhandlung, 1919.

———. *Platon: Beilagen und Textkritik.* Vol. II. Berlin: Weidmannsche Buchhandlung, 1919.

Wild, John. *Plato's Modern Enemies and the Theory of Natural Law.* Chicago: University of Chicago Press, 1953.

Wilson, E. O. *On Human Nature.* Cambridge, Mass.: Harvard University Press, 1978.

———. *Sociobiology.* Cambridge, Mass.: Harvard University Press, 1975.

Wilson, Peter. *Man, the Promising Primate.* New Haven: Yale University Press, 1980.

Winspear, Alban Dewes and Tom Silverberg. *Who Was Socrates?* New York: Russell & Russell, 1960.

Wittgenstein, Ludwig. *Philosophical Investigations.* Oxford: Blackwell, 1972.

Wright, F. A. *Feminism in Greek Literature: From Homer to Aristotle.* Port Washington: Kennikat Press, 1969.

Xenophon. *Memorabilia.* With English translation by E. C. Marchant, Cambridge, Mass.: Harvard University Press, 1965.

Index

*Only those references to the *Republic* that are not clearly indicated in the Contents have been included.

Twayne's United States Authors Series

EDITOR OF THIS VOLUME

Sylvia E. Bowman

Indiana University

Thomas Jefferson

TUSAS 327

Courtesy of the New-York Historical Society

Thomas Jefferson

THOMAS JEFFERSON

By WILLIAM K. BOTTORFF
The University of Toledo

TWAYNE PUBLISHERS
A DIVISION OF G. K. HALL & CO., BOSTON

Published in 1979 by Twayne Publishers,
A Division of G. K. Hall & Co.

Printed on permanent/durable acid-free paper and bound
in the United States of America

First Printing

Library of Congress Cataloging in Publication Data

Bottorff, William K 1931-
Thomas Jefferson.

(Twayne's United States authors series ; TUSAS 327)
Bibliography: p. 141-59
Includes index.
1. Jefferson, Thomas, Pres. U.S., 1743-1826.
2. Presidents — United States — Biography.
E332.2.B58 973.4'6092'4 [B] 78-12112
ISBN 0-8057-7260-X

for
a young woman named
Amy
and a young man named
Adam

Contents

About the Author

William K. Bottorff was born in 1931, in Toledo, Ohio. He received a standard public school education, and edited his high school newspaper in Perrysburg, Ohio, in 1949. In 1951, he enlisted in the United States Navy; during his four years in uniform he served on the aircraft carrier Intrepid and played interservice football. In 1955 he entered Bowling Green State University, and was graduated *summa cum laude* in 1958, the first recipient of a B.A. degree in American Studies from that institution. In the same year he married Marjorie King. They have two children. In 1959 he completed the M.A. degree in American Culture at Western Reserve University where he was a Woodrow Wilson Fellow. He then went to Brown University as a Fellow in American Civilization, and was awarded a Ph.D. in American Civilization in 1964.

Mr. Bottorff is author of *James Lane Allen* (TUSAS 56). He has edited seven other books, mostly of early American poetry. His scholarly and critical articles on Edward Taylor, Emerson, Thoreau, T. S. Eliot, Jefferson, and other subjects have appeared in several books and journals. He taught at Boston University, the State University College at Geneseo, New York, and Ohio University. He is currently Professor of English and Director of American Studies at the University of Toledo.

Preface

Since the lifetime of Thomas Jefferson, hundreds of books, articles, poems, plays, and stories have been written about him. Many of them represent only his idealism, and try to raise him above the level of everyday matters and human weaknesses. He is pictured as a demigod, worthy of unqualified homage. This pattern began at least as far back as 1809. In that year, as Jefferson left the presidency, Philip Freneau sang his hero's ascendancy into the national mythos:

> At length the year, which marks his course, expires,
> And JEFFERSON from public life retires....
> Each bosom, faithful to its country's claim,
> Hail'd JEFFERSON, that long applauded name....
> That INDEPENDENCE we had sworn to gain,
> By you asserted (nor DECLARED in vain)....
> May peace and soft repose, attend you, still,
> In the lone vale, or on the cloud-capp'd hill....

The author of the *Declaration of Independence,* and the third President of the United States, makes his way to the serenity of Monticello, his American apotheosis already complete even then.

There was another side to Jefferson's reputation, of course, and the poet knew it:

> We saw you libell'd by the *worst of men,*
> While hell's red lamp hung quivering o'er his pen,
> And friends congenial every effort try
> To blast that merit which shall never die —

No one is perfect, and no public figure is immune to vilification and hatred. Jefferson, certainly flawed, was at times attacked justifiably. Still, his character contained much merit, and many of the charges brought against him were unfair or were based on distortions. There was, then, as much wisdom as wit in President John F. Kennedy's remark in 1962, when a number of Nobel Prize winners were seated around him, that "This is the most extraordinary collection of talent . . . that has ever been gathered together at the White House — with the possible exception of when Thomas Jefferson dined alone.'' But there is also reason to regard with tolerance those assaults on Jefferson in recent years that point to his slave keeping as hypocrisy of the most serious kind.

Where, then, do thoughtful Americans go to find Jefferson's true spirit? Few people will read hundreds of pages, let alone hundreds of works, to satisfy their curiosity. To peruse his own letters and papers is a labor of years. To visit the site of his home, and his other architectural achievements, is possible for only a comparatively few. Clearly, though, if the truth is ever to be approached, it will be found in the words and works of their author.

This book is therefore based on the writings and the architecture by Jefferson himself. The aim here is to employ representative quotations and faithful descriptions of numerous, objectively existing items created from the mind of Jefferson. His letters and public documents (aside from dry and lifeless state papers), and his architectural accomplishments, are offered here copiously, so that he may, as it were, represent himself. This biography, if it be one, is of ideas and works of art subjected to analysis and interpretation. The author has tried to tell the truth about the subject, or else to help the reader discover the truth.

Furthermore, this is an ''American Study,'' an attempt to approach a single subject — Jefferson — from a number of angles. He had many surfaces, contours, depths, and nuances of character, as any person of genius does, and only an interdisciplinary approach might hope to locate ''him.''

The book begins with a biographical sketch. Chapter One, ''Introduction: Thomas Jefferson Still Lives,'' traces the subject's rise through a gentleman's education; through his emergence as a writer (especially as the author of the *Declaration of Independence*); through his ambassadorship to France; through his rise to the Presidency of the United States; and to his retirement at his beloved Monticello. Jefferson's associations with John Adams, Alexander Hamilton, his wife Martha, and the slave woman Sally Hemings, are explored. The various interests and pursuits of Jefferson — in the sciences, the arts, politics, and other areas — are all introduced. Subsequent chapters expand upon these topics.

Chapter Two, ''The Public Pulse,'' for example, investigates Jefferson's revolutionary spirit. His original version, or ''Rough Draft,'' of the *Declaration* is analyzed. His belief in the concept of natural rights is stressed, and his status as an idealist is established.

"Varieties in the Race of Man," Chapter Three, is an exposition of Jefferson's thoughts on slavery and the capabilities of Blacks; on Indians; and on the status of women. Questions about his prejudices are raised, especially in regard to opinions he expressed in his book, *Notes on the State of Virginia.* Here the American idealist confronts American realities, in regard to such figures as Benjamin Banneker (the Black surveyor and mathematician), and Jefferson's common law wife, Sally Hemings.

Then Chapter Four, "An American Education," explores Jefferson's theories for a system of education, from early childhood to the university level. His plan is seen to be open to all, but highly competitive, and with advanced learning available only to males. His educational ideal, to promote better citizenship, including respected democratic leaders within the American culture, is clarified.

The subject emphasized in Chapter Five, "Beyond the Constitution," is politics. Jefferson's theories (or political principles), and his practices (or party politics), are both highlighted. That he believed in a higher law than the United States Constitution — natural rights — is made clear. Also remarked upon are his insistence on majority rule and his goal of further extending democracy.

"Cooperating with Nature," Chapter Six, discusses Jefferson's activities in the areas of science and invention. That he was generally a careful, empirical investigator of natural phenomena is demonstrated. The basis for calling Jefferson an "agrarian" is explored, along with his invention of the moldboard plow.

At times, Jefferson felt a need to retreat from politics and "practical" affairs, and to pursue philosophic interests. His Common Sense philosophy is the subject of Chapter Seven, "Fix Reason Firmly." Jefferson's so-called "epicureanism" is investigated, as is his religious "unitarianism." Stress is placed on his compendium known as the "Jefferson Bible." Once again, his idealism, here regarding such matters as religious and intellectual freedom, is discussed.

Then, in Chapter Eight, "What We Call Beautiful," Jefferson's relationships to the fine arts are revealed at length. His status as a collector of paintings and sculptures (and his theories on these arts); his opinions on literature; his love of music, and of gardens and landscaping — all are shown to have been important parts of his daily life. Finally, the art in which he manifested genius, architecture, is approached. Emphasis here naturally falls upon his designs for Monticello and the University of Virginia. His thoughts on the concept of the "sublime" are clarified.

"What Is Called Style," Chapter Nine, is a treatment of Jefferson's writing style and of his "lifestyle." Based largely on an examination of his letters, the discussion reveals Jefferson's equanimity, balance, and careful diction. He emerges as a witty, occasionally poetic writer, who ranges from the abstract phrase to the homely metaphor, and always with clarity. His lifestyle is shown to have featured a pride in America and a dedication to the welfare of his people, as well as a gentlemanly sophistication in his personal relationships.

In conclusion, Chapter Ten is entitled "Their Good Old Faith." Once again, American idealism, as distinct from harsh reality, is seen to have been manifested in Thomas Jefferson. His legacy as his people's finest spokesman is established.

Jefferson was a fallible, finite human being; he was idealist and realist. He had a great understanding of potentially tragic events, especially in regard to the peculiarly American dilemma, the tension between the races. But he was a great spokesman for the democratic faith, and a force for good in the American nation. Jefferson may be seen, in short, as the very personification of the paradox that is the United States of America: the ideal and the real, the vision and the actuality unresolved. We should not expect simple resolutions of our problems from Thomas Jefferson, for he had none. He could but declare the ideal, live the reality, and himself pass into history.

Finally, this study is dedicated to the advance of American ideals in confrontation with American realities. If it is, in a modest way, Jeffersonian, its author could ask no more. Hopefully, the true Jefferson emerges from a haze of folklore and misconception, to be introduced to anyone who has time for a little book on a large subject.

WILLIAM K. BOTTORFF

Toledo, Ohio

Chronology

1743 Thomas Jefferson born April 13 in the Colony of Virginia.
1757 His father, Peter Jefferson died.
1760 Entered the College of William and Mary at Williamsburg, Virginia.
1762 Graduated from the College of William and Mary; entered the law office of George Wythe.
1767 Admitted to the Virginia Bar.
1769 Elected to the Virginia House of Burgesses.
1772 Married Martha Wayles Skelton; first dauthter, Martha born.
1773 Became Surveyor of Albemarle County.
1774 Second daughter, Jane Randolph born; *A Summary View of the Rights of British America.*
1775 Elected to and attended the Continental Congress at Philadelphia.
1776 Jefferson's mother died; wrote the *Declaration of Independence;* appointed to the Committee to Revise the Laws of Virginia.
1777 A son born, but soon died.
1778 Third daughter, Mary born.
1779 Elected Governor of the State of Virginia.
1780 Reelected Governor of Virginia; fourth daughter born.
1781 Resigned governorship; appointed a peace commissioner, by the Continental Congress, but declined; daughter Lucy Elizabeth born.
1782 Mrs. Jefferson died.
1783 Elected delegate to Congress; awarded honorary Doctor of Civil Law degree by the College of William and Mary.
1784 Sailed for France as United States Minister.
1785 Youngest daughter, Lucy died; *Notes on the State of Virginia.*
1786 Awarded honorary Doctor of Laws degree by Yale College; An Act for Religious Freedom passed in Virginia.
1788 Awarded honorary Doctor of Laws degree by Harvard College.

1789 Sailed for America.
1790 Became first Secretary of State in Washington's cabinet; daughter Martha married to Thomas Mann Randolph.
1793 Resigned as Secretary of State.
1796 Elected Vice President of the United States.
1797 Elected president of the American Philosophical Society; daughter Mary married to John Wayles Eppes.
1798 *Essay on Anglo-Saxon;* drafted Kentucky Resolutions; revised James Madison's Virginia Resolutions.
1800 Began plans for the University of Virginia.
1801 Elected third President of the United States.
1803 The Louisiana Purchase.
1804 Reelected President of the United States.
1807 Signed bill ending slave trade; signed Embargo Act.
1809 Embargo repealed; retired to Monticello.
1814 Resigned presidency of the Philosophical Society.
1815 Congress bought Jefferson's private library.
1825 The University of Virginia opened.
1826 Thomas Jefferson died on the Fourth of July, the fiftieth anniversary of the *Declaration of Independence.*

CHAPTER 1

Introduction: Thomas Jefferson Still Lives

I *Becoming a Gentleman*

THOMAS Jefferson was born April 13, 1743, on an estate called Shadwell, County of Albemarle, in the English Colony of Virginia. Shadwell lay near the frontier of colonial settlement, close to Charlottesville, and to the future site of Monticello. Its proprietor was Peter Jefferson, Thomas' father, and a prominent citizen of some means. Peter was a farmer and a surveyor who, though possessing little formal education, managed to teach his son a good deal about such things as Indian lore, mapmaking, and how successfully to aspire to the status of gentleman.

To the latter end, Thomas was sent, in 1748, to the English school at Tuckahoe, some fifty miles distant from Shadwell. Four years later, he began to attend a Latin school, acquiring the seeds of a Classical education. Then Peter Jefferson died in 1757, leaving his son deeply bereaved. Thomas had two additional years of basic learning, however, and showed a strong, youthful determination to pursue further studies.

In the spring of 1760, then, young Jefferson entered the College of William and Mary, at Williamsburg, near the Atlantic coast. "It was great good fortune," he wrote many years later, "and what probably fixed the destinies of my life, that Dr. William Small of Scotland, was then Professor of Mathematics, a man profound in most of the useful branches of science, with a happy talent of communication, correct and gentlemanly manners, and an enlarged and liberal mind."[1] With such a brilliant example to follow, Jefferson graduated from the College in 1762. His formal education, as good as could be found in the Colonies, had come to an end.

Still not quite the well rounded gentleman, and still not decided on a career, Jefferson (with the help of Dr. Small) entered upon the reading of the law. Again an outstanding older man came forth to encourage him, and to teach him his new profession. This was George Wythe, one of the leading attorneys there in the Colonial capital. "Mr. Wythe continued to be my faithful and beloved mentor in youth, and my most affectionate friend through life," Jefferson said. With Wythe's aid, he was admitted to the bar in 1767, and he practiced law to the time of the Revolution.

In these same years, Jefferson pursued other interests too, including music. He took violin lessons, and he played in string quartets, sometimes in no less company than that of the Colonial Governor, Francis Fauquier. Heady, mature conversations, fine dinners, theatergoing, and other gentlemanly activities formed a milieu the young Jefferson loved. Throughout his long life he continued to cultivate such relationships as he had with Fauquier, Small, and Wythe, to play his violin, and to live in general a life of high culture.

Small and Wythe also influenced Jefferson in other ways, however. They impelled him not only toward a gentleman's life, but in a direction seemingly quite the opposite. In religion and in politics, they freed his mind of orthodoxy and conservatism. Falling away from his Anglican background, Jefferson inclined toward Deism and secularism. And from his quasi aristocratic political position he moved profoundly into the ranks of democracy. Of course, his own reading and observations also helped effect these changes; yet his two mentors urged him on more rapidly and more surely toward liberalism than would have been the case without them.

There remained only three more steps to take in order that Jefferson become the complete Colonial gentleman. One of these was to enter into public service. In 1769 he was elected a Burgess. As a member of Virginia's legislative body — the House of Burgesses, sitting at Williamsburg — he was very active. He drew much favorable attention to himself in Virginian political circles. Little could he have dreamed that, for some forty years to follow, he would serve the people in various stations of government, even ascending to leadership in a new nation that he himself would help to create.

Next, the rising gentleman had to establish an estate, including a fine residence, all his own. And so, also in 1769, he began the construction of Monticello, his little mountain retreat near his birthplace. Levelling of the mountaintop began; the building of a mansion of his own design, commenced. It was the darling project — to draw plans, to build, to alter, to refine and expand — of, again, forty years. It was not until his retirement from the Presidency, in 1809, that Monticello would take on its final, beautiful shape. During those years, it was his sanctuary from politics and public affairs.[2] At Monticello he was a creative artist, an agrarian patriarch, and a private citizen. One final step remained to complete his growth into the dignity of high social status that he desired.

In 1772 the gentleman, Thomas Jefferson, married Martha Wayles Skelton, a widow of some prestige, and of great charm. She brought a dowry of property — including slaves — that added significantly to the considerable holdings he had inherited. It must not be assumed, however, that love was wanting in their relationship. If not at first, then soon, Thomas became deeply bound to Martha, and theirs was a warm union throughout her lifetime.

A family legend illustrates their affinity. A couple on horseback are seen gliding through the January snow, climbing the little mountain, and arriving at Monticello as bride and groom. They are greeted by smiling servants and a fireplace to warm them. They take up residence, not in the main house, which is as yet in no state for occupancy, but in a little brick structure across the white covered lawn. The gentleman and his lady are snug in their picturesque honeymoon retreat. This version of the start of their domestic life, whether it be fact or fiction, properly conveys the spirit of their marriage.

Within the year, the Jeffersons' first child, their daughter Martha, was born. (They were to have other children, but only Martha and another daughter, Mary, would live to adulthood.) Meanwhile, work at Monticello and public service went on for Thomas. In 1773 he attended his first meeting of the Virginia Committee of correspondence, that revolutionary group — manifested throughout the Colonies — which through exchanges of letters among politicians opposed the pinch of arbitrary rule from England up and down the coast. Jefferson began his move to the forefront of the American cause.

Then, in 1774, he used his pen to bring to himself recognition in the newly formed Continental Congress at Philadelphia. He wrote what many felt was the best remonstrance against the King, and defense of Colonial rights, that had yet been seen. It was Jefferson's first major public document, a pamphlet he called *A Sum-*

mary View of the Rights of British America. His tone was moderate, his style clear, and his cause just, as he called for Colonial equality under British law. Jefferson was on his way to Philadelphia, an elected delegate to Congress in less than a year. The gentleman had certainly arrived.

II *Delegate and Governor*

Seventeen-seventy-six was a busy and fateful year for both Jefferson and his country. He drew up several bills to be submitted to the Virginia Assembly. In them, he sought to effect sweeping changes from Colonial law to a more democratic system. His draft of a new constitution for Virginia was intended to broaden the franchise, for example. Another measure was meant to change the inheritance laws so that property might be more equally distributed. As a member of a committee to revise completely the body of laws in Virginia, as the latter became a state in the new nation, Jefferson tried to halt cruel punishments for minor crimes, and to otherwise make more humane the legal processes. Most of the liberal measures he outlined in 1776 became, over the years to come, law in Virginia.

The outstanding event of that year, of course, was the break the American Colonies made with their mother country. Thomas Jefferson, the person who articulated the reasons for the separation, stated the principles upon which a new nation could be founded. The Revolution was already in progress, then, when he was appointed to the committee — two of whose members were the beloved Benjamin Franklin, and a leader of the New England rebels named John Adams — organized to prepare a document announcing the break. Within the committee, apparently at Adams' insistence, Jefferson was selected to write the paper declaring American independence. "I turned to neither book nor pamphlet while writing it," he later claimed. "I did not consider it as any part of my charge to invent new ideas," he said, "but to place before mankind the common sense of the subject." To Jefferson, and to many others ever since, the *Declaration of Independence* was, and is, "an expression of the American mind."

July 4, 1776 saw the dawn of a new era in human history, Jefferson believed. He was forever proud of the part he played in the great drama. It was he who asserted human equality, and who insisted that governments should serve the people in their "pursuit of happiness.'' And it was Jefferson who sought to stop slavery, in a clause in the *Declaration* deleted by Congress. Finally, just three years later, it was Thomas Jefferson who introduced in Virginia a Bill for Establishing Religious Freedom. This measure (which was not passed until 1786) ended all forms of governmental support, or support by public taxes, of religious sects. It served as a model for the other states, and it influenced the separation-of-church-and-state concept in the United States Constitution. Jefferson was so proud of having been the writer of the *Declaration* and of the Act for Religious Freedom that he asked, near the end of his life, that on his tombstone he be commemorated as their author.

In the same year that the Act was written, 1779, Jefferson was elected Governor of the State of Virginia (he was reelected in 1780). The Revolution was all but foundering in Virginia when he took office. He called out the militia to repel the invasion of the state by British forces, led by Benedict Arnold and other high-ranking officers. After great damage was done through Arnold's pillaging and burning, the state was saved from collapse by a detachment sent at George Washington's orders, and commanded by the Marquis de Lafayette. One object of the British onslaught was the capture of Thomas Jefferson, Governor, and author of the *Declaration of Independence.* The legend of his escape is another example of folk history which, whether entirely factual or not, evokes the spirit of the time and the man.

A tall, dignified, red-haired gentleman calmly takes his breakfast after being warned that British dragoons under Colonel Banastre Tarleton, known as a vicious antagonist, are racing to take him. He casually burns a few papers, to keep them from enemy eyes, and packs other documents as he prepares to leave Monticello. He walks from the house and, from a vantage point there on the mountain, scans the area of Charlottesville with his telescope. The British are swarming through the town. With utter tranquility, he issues a few last instructions to his servants (to hide the silverware), then mounts his horse, cantering off into the trees and down the slope opposite the roadway to the house. Within minutes British troops gallop to the doorway, push into the mansion, and then curse their luck at having missed a chance to capture the man who personifies the American passion for independence. Thomas Jefferson has escaped.

His term as Governor ended in June of 1781. But, for reasons that are still not clear (probably petty political intrigue), the Virginia Legislature undertook an investigation to establish whether or not Jefferson had been guilty of malfeasance of office. Not only was he cleared, but before the year was out he was voted the Legislature's thanks for valuable public service. Nevertheless, Jefferson was hurt by the affair, and for years believed that his reputation had been irreparably damaged. A far greater hurt lay just ahead, however.

In September of 1782, life at Monticello — which was so pleasant between crises and duties away from home — was shattered. Jefferson's beloved wife, Martha, died. The story of her passing, and of its effect on Jefferson, was recorded by their daughter, who was also named Martha, after her mother:

> He nursed my poor mother . . . sitting up with her and administering her medicines and drink to the last. For four months that she lingered he was never out of calling; when not at her bedside, he was writing in a small room which opened immediately at the head of her bed. A moment before the closing scene, he was led from the room in a state of insensibility by his sister, Mrs. Carr, who, with great difficulty, got him into the library, where he fainted, and remained so long insensible that they feared he would never revive. . . . He kept his room three weeks. . . . He walked almost incessantly night and day, only lying down occasionally, when nature was completely exhausted. . . . When at last he left his room, he rode out, and from that time he was incessantly on horseback, rambling about the mountain, in the least frequented roads, and just as often through the woods. In those melancholy rambles I was his constant companion — a solitary witness to many a burst of grief. . . .

Years later, his grief subdued, but his memory of their life together yet keen, Jefferson composed her epitaph, which read, in part, "To the Memory of Martha Jefferson . . . Intermarried with Thomas Jefferson . . . Torn from him by Death . . . This Monument of his Love is inscribed."[3]

Thus, while Monticello was still being built, as was also the new nation, the domestic life of Thomas Jefferson was forever altered. The gentleman was strong, however, and he slowly emerged from his seclusion to engage once again in the service of his country, and in his own pursuit of happiness.

III *Gentleman Abroad*

In 1783 Jefferson was elected once more a delegate to Congress.

He accepted, and in the following year became Chairman of that body. Then, still in 1784, he was made Minister to France, a post which he also accepted, perhaps to effect a total change of scene from Virginia and America, where sadness continued to haunt him.

Jefferson's errand in Europe was to secure trade agreements between the new United States and the countries of the Old World. (Once again he was to serve with John Adams, who would work in England, and Franklin, in France.) To acquire a more solid knowledge of the American economy, he decided to embark from Boston, only after a tour of the New England states, where he assiduously gathered "such information as to their commerce and other circumstances as might in some degree enable me to answer the purposes of my mission." If he was only moderately successful in gaining commercial advantages for his country, it was not from a failure to make every effort to do so.[4]

After celebrating the eighth anniversary of the *Declaration of Independence* in Boston, Jefferson sailed for France on the fifth of July, 1784. He embarked in the ship *Ceres,* aptly named after the goddess of agriculture, for its gentlemanly passenger was a true agrarian, and the country he represented was still largely a nation of farmers. He arrived at Paris in August, to spend the next five years in Europe.

Among Jefferson's earliest activities in France was to arrange for the printing of his only book-length publication, *Notes on the State of Virginia* (published in French in 1785 and in English two years later). "Before I had left America," he wrote later, "I had received a letter from M. de Marbois, of the French legation in Philadelphia, informing me, he had been instructed by his government to obtain such statistical accounts of the different States of our Union, as might be useful for their information; and addressing to me a number of queries relative to Virginia. I had always made it a practice, whenever an opportunity occurred of obtaining any information of our country, which might be of use to me in any station, public or private, to commit it to writing." Jefferson kept statistics indeed — on the weather, crops, the changing seasons, and sundry other phenomena — virtually all his life. He catalogued information useful to him as a farmer, but he compiled "impractical" data to satisfy his curiosity as a scientist, too.

"These memoranda," he went on, "were on loose papers, bundled up without order, and difficult of recurrence, when I had occasion for a particular one. I thought this a good occasion to embody their substance, which I did in the order of Mr. Marbois' queries, so as to answer his wish, and to arrange them for my own use." Marbois had inquired into such subjects as geography, raw materials, manufacturing, climate, crops, "aborigines," political structure, religious beliefs, and "manners." Jefferson answered each in turn, and at length. Here was an opportunity to systematize his own philosophy, and to clarify in his own mind the condition of his people. Just at mid-life, then, Jefferson summed up his beliefs, most of which remained quite consistent through the last decades of his lifetime. Those beliefs, as set forth in the *Notes* and elsewhere, will be discussed in chapters to follow. It may merely be remarked, at this point, that in his *Notes* Jefferson made public his opinions on many subjects other than politics (his political position was already widely understood), opinions that still define or identify him for succeeding generations of Americans.

Along with the publication of the *Notes on the State of Virginia,* 1785 brought Jefferson other important experiences. First, he learned of the death of the youngest of his children, Lucy Elizabeth. His eldest daughter, Martha (called Patsy, aged thirteen), had come to France with him. Now, he felt he must arrange for the transit to France of his only remaining child, Mary (nicknamed Polly), who was seven. "Kiss my dear, dear Polly for me," he wrote to her guardian in America. "Oh! could I do it myself!" And so he ordered her passage, with suitable chaperonage, to Paris.

Second, Jefferson was appointed by Congress to assume the duties of Minister Plenipotentiary to the Court of France. Benjamin Franklin, the incumbent Minister, was anxious to retire, and to spend the rest of his long life in the United States. Franklin left in triumph, the darling of the French people. Jefferson's taking the office — a much younger man, as yet untried in international intrigue — originated another legendary scene, in which factual history gives way to fiction, yet where the truth also is told. The celebrated and crafty Minister of Foreign Affairs in the French government, the Count de Vergennes, remarked to Jefferson, "You replace Monsieur Franklin, I understand." Jefferson, emulating the wit of Franklin himself, replied. "Sir, I only succeed Dr. Franklin. No one can replace him."

Finally, it was also in 1785 that Jefferson designed the Capitol at Richmond, one of his finest architectural contributions. Invited to submit a plan by the Virginia authorities, he considered the invitation "a favorable opportunity of introducing into the State an example of architecture, in the classic style of antiquity." He chose "antique" or "Cubic" style because he considered it monumental, permanent, and tasteful. He would have to make it functional as well: "To adapt the exterior," resembling a Roman temple, "to our use, I drew a plan for the interior, with the apartments necessary for legislative, executive, and judiciary purposes; and accomodated in their size and distribution to the form and dimensions of the building." In all this, he succeeded marvelously, and the Virginia Capitol remains not only functional, but an important part of the esthetic heritage of its architect's people.

Jefferson's second full year in Europe, 1786, provided him with a chance to visit his least favorite nation on earth, England. During the Revolution, Jefferson had advocated the burning of English coastal towns in retaliation for the British practice of destroying American villages. Even earlier, he had railed against English architecture as an awkward, brick-kiln-like mode of design. Always certain that English newspapers deliberately distorted the American scene, he was equally sure that British politics were quite corrupt. Now, Jefferson the Anglophobe was admitted to the Court of King George III, the same eminence he had so caustically attacked in the *Declaration of Independence.* Jefferson the gentleman emerged unscathed and unembarrassed by his audience with the King, who was surprisingly civil; and he enjoyed his English tour immensely.

For the first of many times in his life, Jefferson sat for his portrait while in England. The painter was Mather Brown, an American artist living in London. The portrait shows a youthful-looking gentleman, bewigged and fashionably attired in a tasteful suit and a lace trimmed shirt. This was a Jefferson little known to Americans, but it was the Jefferson much admired by the Europeans of his time.

The most pleasant part of Jefferson's English sojourn concerned another of the fine arts (as it was then thought of), gardening. Here was one aspect of English culture, along with some of its literature, which he often read, which the American tourist could admire. The English garden, with its serenity, rationality, sense of texture in the play of light and shadow as well as in forms and voids, satisfied his esthetic standards. But it was with some reservations that he admired the English garden, for he felt it was often too well made, too rigid, too far removed from nature. His own grounds at Monticello would transcend the English model to strike a balance between the wild and the cultivated.

Jefferson returned to Paris in late spring, intending to apply himself once again to his official duties. He did resume his work, of course; yet the next several months in France brought with them a great change for the American widower. The gentleman met a lady, and a love affair flowered for which he was quite unprepared. The woman was Maria Cosway, an artist, the very beautiful and charming wife of a foppish man who was himself a fashionable painter. Jefferson and Maria saw each other often, at musicales, during dinners, and at the theater. They were frequently alone together. When apart, they exchanged letters, some of which expressed considerable affection. But the Cosway romance could not go on forever and, at any rate, neither party seemed to have considered their taking up residency together, or marriage. Their affair was broken off, sadly but without recrimination. The lady was to be one of the gentleman's fondest memories. Their relationship, though more than a flirtation, was not a fated union.

Subsequently, in June of 1787, Jefferson's little girl, Polly, arrived. Her chaperone was not an adult, as her father had desired, but a female slave of fourteen, named Sally Hemings. They had been met at London, where they went prior to their final passage across the Channel, by Abigail Adams, whose husband John was Minister to England. The appearance of Sally surprised Mrs. Adams, not only because of the girl's age, but because she was physically mature, a strikingly beautiful young woman. She must have impressed Jefferson similarly, for she quickly became a privileged servant — well dressed, with light duties. Such, in fact, would be her official status for the rest of Jefferson's life. In whatever way their relationship began, there in Paris, it became a most touching and tender association. The forty-four year old gentleman, and the lovely girl in her mid-teens, fell in love sometime during the years remaining to them in France. When they left for America in October of 1789, Sally Hemings was pregnant by Thomas Jefferson. She was to bear him several children in the years to come. They lived together, in the face of all social prohibitions in their time and place, for nearly four decades, in common law marriage. The difficulties of such a life, though great, were endured with each other's support, even in slavery-ridden Virginia.[5] It was, after all, their secret pursuit of happiness.

It was to his home state, and to Monticello, that Jefferson and his family returned on Christmas Eve of 1789. He had been appointed Secretary of State by George Washington, first President under the new United States Constitution. Now began Jefferson's long service in the Federal government, in which he would rise to the highest office in the land.

IV *Third President*

By March of 1790, Thomas Jefferson was in New York, then the seat of the national government. He was one of the two outstanding members of Washington's cabinet. The other was Alexander Hamilton, who gradually became Jefferson's bitter enemy. The Constitution had met with Jefferson's approval while he was still in France, especially when James Madison — Father of the Constitution — had assured him that a Bill of Rights would soon be added to the basic document. Jefferson approved because he felt that the new American political structure would further the purposes of the Revolution, the purposes of which he had stated in the *Declaration.* He detested Hamilton because he felt that the Secretary of the Treasury sought to plunge his country back into the morass of monarchy.

Years afterward, in his *Anas,* an autobiographical manuscript, Jefferson fully recorded his opinion of the leader of the Federalists: "Hamilton was not only a monarchist, but for a monarchy bottomed on corruption. . . . Hamilton was, indeed, a singular character. Of acute understanding, disinterested, honest and honorable in all private transactions, amiable in society, and duly valuing virtue in private life, yet so bewitched and perverted by the British example, as to be under thorough conviction that corruption was essential to the government of a nation." Jefferson felt that as long as George Washington was president, the republican form of government would prevail. But the Secretary of State also felt that the Secretary of the Treasury had made the Vice President — John Adams — his dupe. Inevitably, then, when Adams assumed the highest office, the nation's first principles would, Jefferson believed, be threatened; and, perhaps, after Adams left the presidency, Hamilton might then become in fact a king-maker who could obstruct democratic progress.

Meanwhile, Jefferson decided not to remain in the cabinet. The job was too frustrating, too full of conflict with Hamilton. He resigned his post at the end of 1793 and left for Monticello, where he could supervise construction and remodelling, could see to his crops, and could work on his plan for an improved plow. For nearly three years Jefferson maintained the home life that he had imagined while yet in France.

This stay at Monticello, however, proved not to be the permanent retirement Jefferson sometimes said he wanted. Others who opposed Hamilton too (Madison, for example), saw to it that Thomas Jefferson was elected vice president, under Adams. The two comrades of former times — in Congress, on the *Declaration* committee, in Europe — took office in March of 1797, for just one term together, as it turned out. Because Jefferson had recently been elected head of the American Philosophical Society, going north again involved scientific and cultural activities as well as political duties. This suited him fine, for only through a variety of interests could someone of his temperament pursue happiness. Thus, the next three years saw him draft his "Kentucky Resolution" against the excesses of government, write his linguistic treatise, *Essay on Anglo-Saxon,* plan the University of Virginia, compile a parliamentary manual for the Senate, search for fossils with the artist-scientist Charles Willson Peale and, finally, bow to the will of his party (then called Republicans, but subsequently called Democrats) that he be nominated for the presidency.

It was not until February of 1801 that Congress broke the presidential vote-tie, in the electoral college, between Jefferson and Aaron Burr of New York. Ironically, Hamilton swayed the vote toward the Virginian, for he considered Jefferson the lesser of two evils. (Burr, who became vice president, came to hate Hamilton, and killed him in their infamous duel of 1804.) And so, Thomas Jefferson was the third President of the United States. The cultivated, highly sophisticated, enlightened gentleman had ascended to power. It remained for him to govern on behalf of his people as his principles impelled him to do, and also to heal political wounds as best he could. Alienated now from John Adams (the loser in the election), with Hamilton in eclipse, and with Burr already falling from his favor, Jefferson turned for support to Madison and to the rising generation, personified by James Monroe (his successors as president). The new President was to have great success over the next four years.[6]

Jefferson began his campaign to set the ship of state back on its proper course ("to steer with safety the vessel in which we are all embarked," he said) in his Inaugural Address of March 4, 1801. The presidential campaign had been a bitter one. The Federalists had called Jefferson an atheist (which he was not), a slave holder (which he was), and a dreamer (which, in the best sense, he also was). For their part, the Republican-Democrats abused Adams severely. They pictured him as a harsh, narrow puritan, with no real leadership ability. While Jefferson had remained aloof from the rhetoric of both sides, he knew that it fell upon him as President of the United States to reassure everyone that the "vessel" would not founder. And so, he addressed the people in this fashion:

> During the contest of opinion through which we have passed, the animation of discussion and of exertions has sometimes worn an aspect which might impose on strangers unused to think freely and to speak and to write what they think; but this being now decided by the voice of the nation, announced according to the rules of the constitution, all will, of course, arrange themselves under the will of the law, and unite in common efforts for the common good. All, too, will bear in mind this sacred principle, that though the will of the majority is in all cases to prevail, that will, to be rightful, must be reasonable; that the minority possess their equal rights, which equal laws must protect, and to violate which would be oppression. Let us, then, fellow citizens, unite with one heart and one mind. . . . We are all republicans — we are federalists.

Here were the words of a gentleman of high principle, for all the people to see. Here was an enlightened paternalism, as it were, wherein the new President echoed Washington, the nation's Father, who had been, after all, a Virginian too. With such a figure at its helm, the "vessel" was safe. The voters would, in 1804, give Jefferson a landslide victory, for a second term in office.

Beyond the image of President Jefferson held in people's minds, however, lay the man's deeds. Certainly, chiefest among his accomplishments was the Louisiana Purchase, of 1803. Though he worried about the constitutionality of purchasing land for the country's enlargement, he went through with it, and his fellow Americans enthusiastically approved.

Early in the year of the Purchase, Jefferson had persuaded Congress to send Meriwether Lewis and William Clark on their famous expedition into the western areas of what is now the United States, areas which were then considered largely open territory. The people and their representatives in Congress were quite prepared to lay claim to the West. In May, then, Robert Livingston and Monroe, United States Ministers to France, seized upon Napoleon's offer to sell the French possession called Louisiana. It was an area that stretched from the Gulf of Mexico to Canada, and from the Mississippi River (already the western American border) to the Rocky Mountains. The Louisiana Treaty, which was ratified by the Senate in October, doubled the size of the United States. The Purchase was a great triumph for the people and for the President. It seemed that nothing could go wrong for the gentleman from Virginia.

Then, once more and without warning, death came to Monticello. Jefferson's younger surviving daughter, Polly, died in April of 1804. He was terribly bereaved; this left him only Patsy as a legacy from his wife Martha. Patsy (properly, Martha) served as hostess at Monticello, and generally oversaw household operations, for many years. (Sally Hemings, of course, could not serve publicly in any such capacities.) Her father leaned upon Martha a great deal all the rest of his life. In 1806, death again deeply touched Jefferson, when his beloved mentor of many years before, George Wythe, was murdered. These events might appear to have foreshadowed the political troubles that arrived during his second term as president.

Aaron Burr, the scandal of his having killed Hamilton still fresh in people's memories, emerged early in 1806 as an apparently treasonous character. Jefferson, at least, always thought that the so-called Burr Conspiracy was aimed at breaking up the Union. The President issued a proclamation in November, which warned all citizens to refrain from cooperating with Burr and his small force of men, who were descending the Mississippi Valley. Jefferson was convinced that a plot was afoot to take the western territories out of the Union. In 1807, Burr was brought to trial for treason. The full force of President Jefferson was behind the government's indictment of his former vice president. But Burr was acquitted, and the President suffered considerable embarrassment.

One event during Jefferson's second term in office was something of which he might have been very proud. The President recommended, and Congress passed, a bill ending the importation of slaves into the United States. Jefferson signed the bill in December of 1807. Although slavery itself was to continue until the Civil War, a giant step had been taken to hold slave keeping in check. As leader of the nation, Jefferson shared in the accomplishment. But since he had sought such a goal as far back as 1776 (in his original draft of the *Declaration*), his satisfaction in ending the slave trade decades later must have been rather small.

The central controversy for Jefferson as president came in 1807, and lasted until his retirement. The Napoleonic Wars raged in

Europe, and American ships of commerce were often threatened by both English and French naval forces. Both nations seemed ready to fight the United States. President Jefferson, however, ardently desired to preserve the peace; there would be no war for his country while he was in office. In December, therefore, Jefferson sent to Congress a message urging passage of a bill that would end commerce between the United States and the belligerents of Europe. As he signed the Embargo Act, the President hoped that economic pressures would restore free trade in the Atlantic. But the strategy, to which he clung tenaciously, failed.

One result of the Embargo was that many Americans turned to smuggling. Such behavior by his fellow citizens shocked Jefferson, who never dreamed that his policies would cause criminal acts. Another was that New Englanders, who suffered severe economic losses because their shipping industry was all but paralyzed, threatened to secede from the Union. They took a position such as Jefferson himself had taken in his "Kentucky Resolution," objecting to excessive and "unconstitutional" government power. There was much bitter feeling against the President, even within his own party. He too was bitter that the American people failed to support their leader, whose intentions were entirely honorable. Jefferson signed the repeal of the Embargo just before he left office, and made it clear that he was very glad to retire indeed. He did not leave public office in disgrace, but neither was he the extremely popular figure he had been earlier. March of 1809 saw him back at Monticello, quite happy to be home to stay.

V *Home at Last*

Thomas Jefferson never returned to political office — or wanted to. He advised Madison and Monroe from time to time, during their presidencies, and his high reputation as a statesman was in his remaining years restored to him. But he was finally free to pursue his personal happiness as it suited him, with his loved ones — he was surrounded by grandchildren — on top of his little mountain. In 1810, he wrote:

> I am retired to Monticello, where, in the bosom of my family, and surrounded by my books, I enjoy a repose to which I have been long a stranger. My mornings are devoted to correspondence. From breakfast to dinner [lunch], I am in my shops, my garden, or on horseback among my

farms; from dinner to dark, I give to society and recreation with my neighbors and friends; and from candle light to early bed-time, I read. My health is perfect; and my strength considerably reinforced by the activity of the course I pursue; perhaps it is as great as usually falls to the lot of near sixty-seven years of age. I talk of ploughs and harrows, of seeding and harvesting, with my neighbors, and of politics too, if they choose, with as little reserve as the rest of my fellow citizens, and feel, at length, the blessing of being free to say and do what I please....

Here was the retired gentleman, beset by constant visitors, frequently entertaining dignitaries, devoted to music and to meteorology, serene in his now finished mansion and in his young nation. Yet he had a fraternal fence to mend, further domestic embarrassment yet to endure, and one more creative act to perform.

Thomas Jefferson and John Adams had been alienated from one another for some eleven years when, in 1812, their old friendship was renewed. Through the agency of a mutual friend, they began an exchange of letters that lasted for the rest of their lives.[7] The Adams-Jefferson correspondence became justly famous. It revealed the classic, conservative-liberal division in American politics. Jefferson, of course, took the liberal path toward a more democratic society. Adams held back, less fearful of the people than formerly, but still conservative, and a believer in political privilege. But their debate was perfectly amiable. They never saw each other again — Adams in Massachusetts, and Jefferson in Virginia, both too old for long journeys — but their mutual respect was firm. Friendship was indeed like wine, as Jefferson once put it, mellowing over the years.

Meanwhile, Jefferson experienced considerable economic strife. His farms had not prospered as they might have had he been present to direct their progress, instead of having been constantly caught up in public duties. His estate was burdened with debts. And so, upon learning of the destruction by the British of the Congressional library (in the War of 1812), Jefferson offered to sell his own large collection of books to the government. He was proud of his library, saying: "I have been fifty years making it, and have spared no pains, opportunity or expense, to make it what it is." But he needed to raise funds, and assured Congress that "eighteen or twenty wagons would place it in Washington in a single trip of a fortnight." Thus, in 1815, Jefferson sold his books to his nation. They became the basis of the Library of Congress, a sound beginning for one of the great collections of the world. The $23,950 he received helped Jefferson survive his economic embarrassment, and he then turned his attention to a more pleasant matter.

Jefferson had long entertained the idea of creating a public university to serve the people of his native state. Now, in the last years of his life, that dream was to come true. He planned the entire curriculum of the university; he saw to the hiring of its professors; he sold the concept to the politicians who voted to fund it; he became its Rector. Most importantly, however, Jefferson designed the buildings themselves, as well as their physical locations within a brilliant landscape scene. That is to say, Thomas Jefferson was the architect of the University of Virginia in every sense that can be given to the term "architect," including the literal one. His meticulous drawings of every detail of the structures and ground plan still exist, themselves a monument to his creative genius. The buildings also, at once functional and beautiful, reveal the artistry of a master.

For some years, Jefferson oversaw construction of the university. When not at the site itself, in Charlottesville, he stood upon a terrace at Monticello and watched the builders' progress through his telescope. He was justifiably proud, and filled with a sense of achievement, when the university opened in March of 1825. "We studiously avoid too much government," he wrote in August, less than a year before his death. "We treat [the students] as men and gentleman, under the guidance mainly of their own discretion. They so consider themselves, and make it their pride to acquire that character for their institution." The Father of the University of Virginia could ask no more.

As the year of 1826 began, the tall, erect, sandy-haired figure of Thomas Jefferson was seen less and less frequently in Charlottesville and in the woods and fields around Monticello. At the age of eighty-three, he was infirm of body, though still clear of mind. He continued the letter writing that was his habit of many decades, and he saw a few visitors. But his work was finished. He approached his death, which he seemed to know was imminent, with equanimity. He looked forward only to the Fourth of July, which would mark the fiftieth anniversary of the *Declaration of Independence.*

Jefferson was invited to celebrate the occasion at a gathering, in the nation's capital, of those signers of the *Declaration* who yet lived. He could not make the journey, but he replied by letter:

> The kind invitation ... on the part of the citizens of the city of Washington, to be present with them at their celebration on the fiftieth anniversary of American Independence, as one of the surviving signers of an instrument pregnant with our own, and the fate of the world, is most flattering.... I should, indeed, with peculiar delight, have met and exchanged there congratulations personally with the small band, the remnant of that host of worthies, who joined with us on that day ... and to have enjoyed with them the consolatory fact, that our fellow citizens, after half a century of experience and prosperity, continue to approve the choice we made.... With my regret that ill health forbids me the gratification of an acceptance, be pleased to receive ... the assurance of my highest respect and friendly attachments.

This letter, written at Monticello on June 24, 1826, is the last from Jefferson's hand.

In a remarkable coincidence — which many said was providential when they learned of it — Jefferson died on that July Fourth of 1826, just half a century from the day on which his *Declaration* had been signed. John Adams, who had also been invited to attend the Washington celebration and who, like Jefferson, was incapable of travelling so far, shared in the coincidence. With his fellow member of the *Declaration* committee, Adams too died that day. Jefferson preceded him in death by a few hours but, at such a distance, Adams did not know it. As his own eyes closed for the last time, legend has it, Adams said, "Thomas Jefferson still lives." If Adams was factually wrong, he was correct in spirit. Jefferson was the spokesman for his country at the time of the Revolution. In many respects, he has remained the spokesman, through two centuries, of both its ideals and its realities. Thomas Jefferson indeed still lives.

CHAPTER 2

The Public Pulse

I *In Congress Assembled*

IN 1774, in his little book entitled *A Summary View of the Rights of British America,* Thomas Jefferson first essayed to speak for "the American public." He called attention, more effectively than anyone yet had, to the growing American struggle for justice — and he also called a good deal of attention to himself as the brilliant expositor of American ideals. "Every individual" in America, he wrote, "is equal to every individual" in Great Britain "in virtue, in understanding, and in bodily strength."[1] He advised his readers to "Let those flatter, who fear: it is not an American art."[2] Writing clear, forceful prose was an American art, he felt, an art that must not corrupt itself in attempts to appeal to an elite or to flatter. He wrote with an historic sense, knowing full well that the present is the future's legacy. But he carefully controlled his style, so that any literate reader might follow his argument. His appeal was to be broad and essentially democratic. Ideology and style were to be one, as he expressed his thoughts on behalf of all free-born Americans, in words they could understand. His reputation as a writer and as an idealist led to his being chosen as the author of the *Declaration of Independence.*

"My country will have my political creed in the form of a 'Declaration &c,' "[3] he said on the eve of the great occasion. And he deeply felt that his creed was his country's creed as well. He always believed that he had grasped public sentiment and expressed it in his great treatise on American independence. Twenty years later when he looked back, in a letter to James Monroe, he commented that "the public pulse beat . . . full and in . . . universal union on . . . the declaration of Independence."[4]

Jefferson's public career began, then, in Congress, in *A Summary View,* and in the *Declaration,* because he could speak the

American mind, in American terms.[5] It was his intention and his life-long hope that the *Declaration of Independence,* from July 4, 1776, onward, would forever remain the essential expression of the people's philosophy, as it was of his own philosophy.

II *Equality and Happiness*

The heart of the *Declaration of Independence,* in Jefferson's original words, reads as follows:

> We hold these truths to be sacred & undeniable; that all men are created equal & independant, that from that equal creation they derive rights inherent & inalienable, among which are the preservation of life, & liberty, & the pursuit of happiness; that to secure these ends, governments are instituted among men, deriving their just powers from the consent of the governed; that whenever any form of government shall become destructive of these ends, it is the right of the people to alter or to abolish it, & to institute new government, laying it's foundation on such principles & organising it's powers in such form, as to them shall seem most likely to effect their safety & happiness. prudence indeed will dictate that governments long established should not be changed for light & transient causes: and accordingly all experience hath shewn that mankind are more disposed to suffer while evils are sufferable, than to right themselves by abolishing the forms to which they are accustomed. but when a long train of abuses & usurpations, begun at a distinguished period, & pursuing invariably the same object, evinces a design to subject them to arbitrary power, it is their right, it is their duty, to throw off such government & to provide new guards for their future security.[6]

The differences between this "Rough Draft," as it is now called, and the final Congressional form so familiar to all Americans are quickly sensed, and have often been analyzed. Fortunately, his colleagues in Congress did little violence to Jefferson's philosophy, and several phrases even became more memorable at their hands.[7] Yet *these* words represent the author of the *Declaration of Independence* most truly, and "The Rough Draft is the most extraordinarily interesting document in American history."[8] It should be read closely, analytically, and without preconceptions; for this declaration is relevant even after two centuries of American independence.

"*We* hold these truths" rhetorically fuses self and public, the Congress and the people (the phrase would become, with more directness, "We the people" in the Preamble to the United States Constitution). Truth to Jefferson was usually plural, as here, not an abstract, monolithic Truth. Some truths were to him absolute, however, or "sacred," in common terms. These were "undeniable" truths, "inherent & inalienable." Philosophers call them *a priori* truths. Common sense or intuition announces such truths to all persons. These are the "natural rights," rights with which every human being is born, "independant" (that is, no one is dependent upon anyone, or upon any other power, for a claim to these rights). It is in this respect that "all men are created equal."

Much has been said of this phrase these two hundred years, of course. The great American philosopher John Dewey held that Jefferson meant a "moral" equality,[9] and that is quite close to the truth. Others have denied this interpretation,[10] but less convincingly. Middle aged Americans will recall how, during the Great Depression, the New Deal understood Jefferson to mean equality of economic opportunity. Conservatives have rejected such an interpretation, just as racial bigots have long denied any application of the phrase to ethnic minorities. Others have asserted that the concept did not include women. At any rate, no one has ever doubted that Jefferson subscribed to the popular notion of natural rights, as did all thinking persons of his time. Natural rights were as objectively true as natural laws (or, the laws of God, as many phrased it),[11] and only on such a base could persons assert any kind of equality.

Jefferson occasionally returned through the years to the subject of equality. During the Revolution, he drafted legislation for Virginia to ensure equality before the law. Judges, he said, will "do equal right to all manner of people, great and small, high and low, rich and poor."[12] This "legalism" is still, perhaps, the most widely held interpretation of Jefferson's phrase. It is fundamental to American law (which was derived in large part from the tradition of British common law), and the Constitution was to elaborate on the idea in Article Six of the Bill of Rights:

> In all criminal prosecutions, the accused shall enjoy the right to a speedy and public trial, by an impartial jury of the State and district wherein the crime shall have been committed, which district shall have been previously ascertained by law, and to be informed of the nature and cause of the accusation; to be confronted with the witnesses against him; to have compulsory process for obtaining witnesses in his favor, and to have the Assistance of Counsel for his defence.

In 1816, Jefferson expressed a more conservative view relative to equality (as political conservatives have always done, in emphasizing property among human rights): "The true foundation of republican government is the equal right of every citizen, in his person and property, and in their management."[13] These notions became manifest in Articles Four and Five of the Bill of Rights: "The right of the people to be secure in their persons, houses, papers, and effects, against unreasonable searches and seizures, shall not be violated," nor shall the citizen "be deprived of life, liberty, or property, without due process of law." (Notice that the conservative concept of "property" replaced Jefferson's "pursuit of happiness.") But then, in 1824, he reaffirmed the "equal political rights" of every "freeman,"[14] though he had also indicated in 1816 that people have political duties as well as rights: "[government should] declare and enforce only our natural rights and duties, and . . . take none of them from us. No man has a natural right to commit aggression on the equal rights of another; and this is all from which the laws ought to restrain him; every man is under the natural duty of contributing to the necessities of the society; and this is all the laws should enforce on him. . . . the idea is quite unfounded, that on entering into society we give up any natural right."[15] Clearly, Jefferson and his countrymen in Congress at the time of the Revolution had felt that the English had violated these principles of government, and that it had become an American "duty, to throw off" the yoke.

Yet, a genuine American pragmatism — a conservative radicalism, as it were — prevailed in Jefferson's thinking about political revolution. Only "a long train of abuses" and abridgments of natural rights should prompt a people to assert its natural right to pull down a government. He advised people to suffer long, and patiently to seek redress; but, when their duty became clearly evident, they were to insist on government by the consent of the people, as opposed to "arbitrary power." The end to which the declaration of national independence was to lead, then, was the recovery of certain natural rights and, ultimately, to the creation of a new government set up to protect them ("to provide new guards for their future security"). There was to be a re-assertion of the inviolability of the natural rights of "life, & liberty, & the pursuit of happiness" — the "safety" of "life," the "security" of "liberty," the equal chance at "happiness."

Conflicting opinions over a government's relationship to individual happiness, or to the happiness of a society, existed then as they do now. Even whether it was an ancient or a radically modern idea that Jefferson expressed has been debated.[16] Whether Jefferson used "pursuit" to mean "to seek after" or "to maintain" (as in following a profession, say the pursuit of medicine) has been disputed.[17] Certainly, the "happiness principle" was of great importance in his mind and in the minds of the Americans of his time.[18] It is, in common sense terms, only human nature to seek or to preserve happiness; and, at the very least, the government should not interfere with its pursuit.

Furthermore, since governments are instituted to protect life, a natural possession, these institutions must recognize that human beings are naturally at liberty, and insure that at law they are safe in their liberty ("civil liberties"). And so it is imperative that the government allow each citizen to define personal happiness independently, provided there is no attempt to interfere with another's natural rights. There could be — there well nigh was — a nation in which all this was true; but one terrible flaw remained in the fabric of the new society.

III *Against Human Nature*

Jefferson and Congress blamed the English government for slavery during Colonial times. With independence, slavery would be an *American* abridgment of natural rights; and Jefferson knew that slavery had to be abolished. He wrote an antislavery clause into the Rough Draft, a clause which Congress, in its only great change, tore from its author's grasp:

> he has waged cruel war against human nature itself, violating it's most sacred rights of life & liberty in the persons of a distant people who never offended him, captivating & carrying them into slavery in another hemisphere, or to incur miserable death in their transportation thither. this piratical warfare, the opprobrium of *infidel* powers, is the warfare of the CHRISTIAN king of Great Britain. determined to keep open a market where MEN should be bought & sold, he has prostituted his negative for suppressing every legislative attempt to prohibit or to restrain this execrable commerce: and that this assemblage of horrors might want no fact of distinguished die, he is now exciting those very people to rise in arms among us, and to purchase that liberty of which *he* has deprived them, by murdering the people upon whom *he* also obtruded them; thus paying off former crimes committed against the *liberties* of one people, with crimes which he urges them to commit against the *lives* of another.[19]

This clause may have deserved deletion due to its bald rationalization that blamed George III for slavery, an accusation at the very least an oversimplification of the facts. Furthermore, Americans were so heavily involved in the slave trade themselves that to point the finger of guilt elsewhere was simply hypocritical. The United States, after all, was also a Christian country, and it was violating its own morality through slave keeping and through mass kidnapping of Africans. Still, one of the terrible negative moments in history occurred when Jefferson's antislavery statement was entirely dropped from the *Declaration of Independence.* The deletion defeated Jefferson's intention, and thrust his nation into decades of darkness which only the Civil War would begin to end.

Thomas Jefferson, then, as a major slave holder himself, knew that under early American law slaves were denied their natural rights because as "property," they were considered subhuman.[20] But he also recognized that they were perfectly human in their natural desire to pursue happiness and to have liberty. These were, as he believed, their natural life rights, their human heritage. Ambivalent about the intellectual abilities of Blacks — as will be seen — Jefferson never equivocated about their equal claim to the "sacred rights" specified in both passages, from the Rough Draft, quoted above. His only real failure in life was not resolving this peculiarly American dilemma; but in agonizing over it he was typically American.

IV *The Flames Kindled*

Nevertheless, Jefferson's *Declaration of Independence* very much changed the world for the better, and Thomas Jefferson knew it. "The equal rights of man," he wrote in 1823, "and the happiness of every individual, are now acknowledged to be the only legitimate objects of government."[21] There is a profound sense of history in his words, "the flames kindled on the 4th of July, 1776, have spread over too much of the globe to be extinguished by the feeble engines of despotism; on the contrary, they will consume these engines and all who work them." The *Declaration,* he said, "was intended to be an expression of the American mind."[22] As such, it is truly a masterpiece. "I did not consider it as any part of my charge to invent new ideas altogether," or to include sentiments that "had never been expressed before"; his objective was to state plainly the common sense of the matter. But he also wrote, "I pray God that these principles may be eternal."[23]

The conclusion of the Rough Draft still rings with the desire for freedom from England and for independence of action:

> We therefore the representatives of the United States of America in General Congress assembled do, in the name & by authority of the good people of these states, reject and renounce all allegiance & subjection to the kings of Great Britain & all others who may hereafter claim by, through, or under them; we utterly dissolve & break off all political connection which may have heretofore subsisted between us & the people or parliament of Great Britain; and finally we do assert and declare these colonies to be free and independant states, and that as free & independant states they shall hereafter have power to levy war, conclude peace, contract alliances, establish commerce, & to do all other acts and things which independant states may of right do. And for the support of this declaration we mutually pledge to each other our lives, our fortunes, & our sacred honour.[24]

Abraham Lincoln's encomium on the eve of another long and bloody American war also remains genuine: "All honor to Jefferson — to the man who, in the concrete pressure of a struggle for national independence by a single people, had the coolness, forecast, and capacity to introduce into a merely revolutionary document, an abstract truth, applicable to all men and all times, and so to embalm it there, that to-day, and in all coming days, it shall be a rebuke and a stumbling-block to the very harbingers of reappearing tyrany and oppression."[25] In America in 1776, the human race took a new direction, and Thomas Jefferson pointed the way.

CHAPTER 3

Varieties in the Race of Man

I *Between Master and Slave*

"OLD Master very kind to servants," said Jefferson's slave Isaac in 1847.[1] Jefferson had inherited a number of slaves, as had his wife, and by the time of the Revolution he was keeper in an involuntary servitude of nearly two hundred Blacks. Although he seldom bought or sold slaves most of his life, his economic stability depended entirely upon the slave labor that did the "farming, gardening, manufacturing of nails, coopering, carpentry, masonry, shoemaking, spinning and weaving, housework." "Children till 10. years old to serve as nurses," he directed; "from 10. to 16. the boys make nails, the girls spin. at 16. go into the ground [farming] or learn trades."[2] Clearly, every Black at Monticello, or at any of Jefferson's other land holdings, was to labor from childhood to death for their "master" and his family.

Jefferson's "Farm Book" — the plantation accounts that he kept over the decades — shows that the Blacks at Monticello were vaccinated against smallpox in 1801 and in later years and that they were otherwise cared for humanely.[3] Those who were errant, however, were punished according to custom (not specifically according to law). Occasionally there were runaways and, like all slave keepers, Jefferson placed newspaper advertisements for their recovery. One slave was such a great troublemaker that he drew this comment from his master: "if he could be sold in any other quarter so distant as never more to be heard of among us, it would to the others be as if he were put out of the way by death." Of another, Jefferson recorded: "I had him severely flogged in the presence of his old companions." Slaves in the nailery, Jefferson's darling experiment in commerce, were not to be whipped "but in extremities."[4] At times he matter-of-factly wrote such messages as, "Be so good as to inform Davy that his child died of the whooping cough."[5] In regard to Jefferson the slave owner, he was no more than the typical one of his time and place. The number of slaves he kept was larger than average, but his attitudes and practices towards Blacks in bondage would have surprised no one.

In spite of, or perhaps because of, his personal situation, Jefferson made frequent attempts at stopping slave importation, and he continually spoke and wrote against the practice of slave keeping, as in the Rough Draft clause, and in his draft of a new Virginia constitution in 1776.[6] As he grew older, though, he suspended such activities because he sensed that no effort of his could end slavery in his lifetime. In a letter of 1814 when he again denounced slavery he likened the Blacks' desire for freedom to the Revolutionary quest for independence. Emancipation was inevitable, he said, whether bloody or benign; all slaves would be freed; and then they would have to be aided in expatriating themselves to another country,

> for, man, probably of any colour, but of this color we know, brought up from their infancy without necessity for thought or forecast, are by their habits rendered as incapable as children of taking care of themselves, and are extinguished promptly wherever industry is necessary for raising the young. in the meantime they are pests in society by their idleness, and the depredations to which this leads them. their amalgamation with the other colour produces a degradation to which no lover of his country, no lover of excellence in the human character can innocently consent.[7]

Jefferson believed, therefore, that the integration of the freed Blacks into American society would be impossible. Whites were too prejudiced to accept them — as his own words amply illustrate — and the Blacks would never forgive so many long-standing, humiliating abuses.[8]

Following emancipation (whatever form it took), freed Blacks would have to relocate in South America or in Africa;[9] such a relocation would be a proper "getting rid of them." If such a scheme split up families, "The separation of infants from their mothers . . . would produce some scruples of humanity. But this would be straining at a gnat, and swallowing a camel." After all, he blandly remarked, freed Blacks could take civilization with them to the benefit of primitive regions![10] There is no evidence that Jefferson ever consulted with Blacks about their own destiny in or out of the United States. Slave or free, they were to be shunted about at the will of the whites. It is small wonder, in light of such evidence, that the scholars engaged in editing the *Papers of Thomas Jefferson* concluded that he "adhered with undeviating conviction throughout life" to the belief that Blacks were inferior to whites.[11]

Perhaps it is proper to present here a series of statements from Jefferson concerning Blacks and whites as he saw them, drawn chiefly from the only full-length book he published during his lifetime (written 1781–1785), *Notes on the State of Virginia.* To Jefferson, the "Negroes ... [were] more ardent" than whites; but the whites were more beautiful in color, hair, and "symmetry of form" (Blacks sexually prefer Whites on these grounds). He saw the Blacks' "own judgment [was] in favour of the Whites, declared by their preference of them as uniformly as is the preference of the Oran ootan for the black woman over those of his own species." Physically, the Blacks "secrete less by the kidnies, and more by the glands of the skin, which gives them a very strong and disagreeable odor." As for their characters, Jefferson thought that the Blacks were "at least as brave, and more adventuresome." Compared to the Whites, he believed, the Blacks were "more ardent after their female." But beyond lust, he said, "Love" was scarcely within the Blacks' capacity, their regard for one another being "more an eager desire, than a tender delicate mixture of sentiment and sensation," as it was among white people. "Their griefs are transient," he asserted, once again recognizing their humanity but finding them shallow: "Those numberless afflictions, which render it doubtful whether heaven has given life to us in mercy or in wrath, are less felt, and sooner forgotten with them."

Jefferson also expressed his views relative to the intellectual and artistic capabilities of the Blacks:

> In general their existence appears to participate more of sensation than reflection; it appears to me that in memory they are equal to the whites; in reason much inferior, as I think one could scarcely be found capable of tracing and comprehending the investigations of Euclid: and that in imagination they are dull, tasteless, and anomolous. Never yet could I find that a black had uttered a thought above the level of plain narration; never seen even an elementary trait of painting or sculpture. In music they are more generally gifted than the whites, with accurate ears for tune and time, and they have been found capable of imagining a small catch. Whether they will be equal to the composition of a more extensive run of melody, or of complicated harmony, is yet to be proved. Among blacks is misery enough, God knows, but no poetry. Love is the peculiar oestrum of the

poet. Their love is ardent, but it kindles the senses only, not the imagination.

Then Jefferson commented with casual smugness about miscegenation; about Black character in terms of loyalty; and, finally, about Blacks in regard to slavery as an economic system:

> The improvement of the blacks in body and mind, in the first instance of their mixture with the whites, has been observed by every one, and proves that their inferiority is not the effect merely of their condition of life; Whether further observation will or will not verify the conjecture, that nature has been less bountiful to them in the endowments of the head, I believe that in those of the heart she will be found to have done them justice; we find among them numerous instances of the most rigid integrity, and as many as among their better instructed masters, of benevolence, gratitude, and unshaken fidelity.[12] I believe the negro does not perform quite as much work, nor with as much intelligence; I have observed that our families of negroes double in about 25. years, which is an increase of the capital, invested in them, of 4. per cent over & above keeping up the original number.[13]

In this astonishing flow of remarks, Jefferson echoed and recorded most of the persistent, prejudiced stereotyping of Blacks so noticeably American. He originated none of these beliefs, of course, yet did little in his lifetime to erase them from the American mind. (He wrote his *Notes on the State of Virginia* for a French correspondent, but he soon released the book for American readers as well.) Now, two hundred years later, a review of his opinions is still relevant.

Jefferson alleged, with no supporting testimony or other evidence, an unusual sensuousness in Blacks. If he based this opinion on hearsay, he might more wisely have omitted it. If he based it on personal experience or observation, he might have been prudent enough to have omitted it for the sake of his own reputation in a prejudiced society — one that was so narrow in its point of view that it doubtlessly nodded in agreement upon reading about the Blacks' sensuousness and about the greater beauty of white skin and features. While fair minded people in Jefferson's Virginia, or anywhere in the new United States, might have felt that he went too far with his absurd simian comparison, they again might well have smugly approved of his observation on the "disagreeable odor" of Blacks. His shabby, pseudoscientific analysis of Black kidneys and skin glands has been repeated endlessly by bigots everywhere, and no person with scientific knowledge can be excused for it.

Jefferson's next allegation — that Blacks were emotionally shallow — was also presented without supporting testimony or other evidence. It is scarcely to be believed that, even by the 1780s (the time of his *Notes,* a book he never repudiated), let alone in later life, that he had never observed tenderness and love among the Black families around him. It seems impossible that he never had the kind of experience given to Huckleberry Finn by Samuel L. Clemens, of coming to know firsthand of a Black's being deeply moved by either remorse or compassion. In this regard, Jefferson was caught in the same web of superstition as were his unenlightened fellow citizens.

The same is true in regard to his beliefs about Blacks' intellectual capacities and about their failure to produce objects of art. Utterly ignoring their lack of opportunity in a society which denied them learning and any occasion for artistic expression, he pompously declared their incapacity. Deprived as they were of literacy and economic means, the slaves could scarcely write, paint, or sculpt. Any artifacts they did create, any oral poetic or narrative tradition in which they shared, any music through which they expressed themselves — all were regarded as trivially primitive. Jeffersonian blindness could only assert the old saw about the Blacks' special sense of rhythm.

Finally, Jefferson fell back on the typical bigot's belief that white "blood" improved Black heredity. Without using this strange, persistent "blood" metaphor directly (a figure of speech perhaps excusable in an era untaught genetics), the author of *Notes* alleged one more unsupportable concept precious to every theory of white supremacy. "Everyone," he wrote, knew these things. Observation *proved* them, he said.[14] And so, Blacks existed to be exploited, to be computed as economic entities, and to be bred by whites to increase their fortunes. Therein lay the seed and root of prejudice.

Jefferson did allow Blacks the attributes of bravery and integrity, two very precious virtues. And he commiserated over their plight in the United States when, during his presidency, he refused to pardon a slave importer (by 1803 slave running was illegal), and observed that not only are slaves victims, but in Africa their "wives, children & parents are now suffering for want of their aid & comfort." The slave runner had to be punished "to operate as a terror to others meditating the same crime"; slavery had to be contained.[15]

Ultimately, Jefferson contradicted himself in his *Notes* in an effort to temper his remarks and to appear as the objective, open-minded person that he frequently could be:

> It will be right to make great allowances for the [Blacks'] difference of condition, of education, of conversation, of the sphere in which they move. . . . The opinion that they are inferior in the faculties of reason and imagination, must be hazarded with great diffidence. To justify a general conclusion, requires many observations, even where the subject may be submitted to the Anatomical knife, to Optical glasses, to analysis by fire or by solvents. How much more then where it is a faculty, not a substance, we are examining; where it eludes the research of all the senses; where the conditions of its existence are various and variously combined; where the effects of those which are present or absent bid defiance to calculation.

Given that Jefferson was practically substituting a cold anthropology for blind prejudice, he had hardly made any real advance in these statements, however.

Yet Jefferson recovered, for a moment, the spirit of the *Declaration:* "let me add too, as a circumstance of great tenderness, where our conclusion would degrade a whole race of men from the rank in the scale of beings which their Creator may perhaps have given them. . . . I advance it, therefore, as a suspicion only, that the blacks, whether originally a distinct race, or made distinct by time and circumstances, are inferior to the whites in the endowments both of body and mind."[16]

While he was Secretary of State Thomas Jefferson met with a chance to assess the talents of a free Black, Benjamin Banneker. The Secretary had helped secure for Banneker a position as a surveyor of the District of Columbia, and he knew of Banneker's mathematical capabilities. The surveyor was grateful, but he challenged the Jefferson of the *Notes* to rise to the Jefferson of the *Declaration:*

> Here, Sir, was a time in which your tender feelings for your [white] selves engaged you thus to declare, you were then impressed with proper ideas of the great valuation of liberty, and the free possession of those blessings to which you were entitled by nature; but Sir how pitiable is it to reflect, that altho you were so fully convinced of the benevolence of the Father of mankind, and of his equal and impartial distribution of those rights and privileges which he had conferred upon them, that you should at the Same time counteract his mercies, in detaining by fraud and violence so numerous a part of my brethren under groaning captivity and cruel oppression, that

you should at the Same time be found guilty of that most criminal act, which you professedly detested in others, with respect to yourselves.

Essentially dodging the question, Jefferson replied in 1791:

No body wishes more than I do to see such proofs as you exhibit, that nature has given to our black brethren, talents equal to those of other colors of men, and that the appearance of a want of them is owing merely to the degraded condition of their existence, both in Africa & America. I can add with truth, that no body wishes more ardently to see a good system commenced for raising the condition both of their body & mind to what it ought to be, as fast as the imbecility of their present existence . . . will admit.

Yet, as late as 1809, Jefferson was still skeptical about Blacks and about Banneker in particular: "We know he had spherical trigonometry enough to make almanacs, but not without suspicion of aid from Ellicot [a white], who was his neighbor and friend, and never missed an opportunity of puffing him. I have a long letter from Banneker, which shows him to have had a mind of very common stature indeed."[17] While there is no reason to doubt the sincerity of Jefferson's good wishes, neither can it be doubted that, on this issue, he was no more than a pathetic creature of his time and place, as this last letter shows.

"There are," after all, he tried to explain, "varieties in the race of man, distinguished by their powers of body and mind."[18] It seemed likely to him that there might not only be outstanding individuals in the human race — identified by their accomplishments — but also superior and inferior ethnic strains that could perhaps be identified by their colors as well as by their accomplishments. Then, again in 1809, the spirit of the *Declaration of Independence* more fully reasserted itself when Jefferson wrote that

no person living wishes more sincerely than I do, to see a complete refutation of the doubts I have myself entertained and expressed on the grade of understanding allotted to them by nature, and to find that in this respect they are on a par with ourselves. My doubts were the result of personal observation on the limited sphere of my own State, where the opportunities for the development of their genius were not favorable, and those of exercising it still less so. I expressed them therefore with great hesitation; but whatever be their degree of talent it is no measure of their rights.[19]

Although the concept of natural rights was fully applied to Blacks, they could scarcely assert in Jefferson's lifetime their claim to them, let alone publicly realize possession of them. One reason was that their claim, though he affirmed it in principle, was given too little support, in practice, by Thomas Jefferson.

II *My Friends and Children*

In his consideration of the Indian, who was not the victim so much of American slavery as of American slaughter, Jefferson was extremely paternalistic. He certainly wished to avoid violence with them if at all possible, but he felt that they had to be led into the ways of white civilization, even if this proved to be against their will. For some thirty years, Jefferson collected and systematized the vocabularies of about fifty distinct Indian languages, all of which were stolen and destroyed before he could publish or otherwise utilize them.[20] He had learned respect for native Americans literally at his father's knee, and he admired them all his life. As late as 1813, he hoped they "would have mixed their blood with ours, and been amalgamated and identified with us."[21] He often said that the Mingo chief, James Logan *(Tah-gah-jute),* was as great an orator as Demosthenes or Cicero.[22] In his *Notes on the State of Virginia* (in which he printed Logan's great discourse on white injustice and Indian dignity), Jefferson argued that the American Indian "is neither more defective in ardor, nor more impotent with his female than the white reduced to the same diet and exercise;... he is brave"; "he is affectionate to his children ... his friendships are strong and faithful"; "his sensibility is keen." Indians possess the arts, primitively, "such as prove their reason and sentiment strong, their imagination glowing and elevated."[23]

Thus Indians were seen by Jefferson as decidedly superior to Blacks in feeling and in creativity. "The proofs of genius given by the Indians of N. America, place them on a level with Whites in the same uncultivated state"; "I believe the Indian then to be in body and mind equal to the whiteman."[24] Even with its tone of condescension, Jefferson's view was a liberal one. But, when Indians made themselves the enemy, and when the government policy had then to be devised toward them, Jefferson had another voice.

In 1776, he regretted the intrusion of some Indians into the Revolution on the British side (a clause in the *Delcaration* shows this) and called them "wretches." He added, "I would never cease pursuing them while one of them remained on this side the Misisippi."[25] In 1791, as Indian fighting persisted, he wrote, as Secretary of State, "I hope we shall drub the Indians well this summer & then change our plan from war to bribery. We must . . . keep them in peace by liberal & constant presents. . . . In this way hostilities being suspended for some length of time, a real affection may succeed on our frontiers to that hatred now existing." He had no illusions about the hard-fighting Indians: "They waged [war] in their usual cruel manner, murdering and scalping men, women, and children, indiscriminately, burning their houses, and desolating the country."[26] Jefferson, who knew well of the cost of total war, wished to avoid it with a policy that would "civilize" the "savage."

It has been asserted that Jefferson's Indian policy was cynical and lowly motivated,[27] but this assertion may be an overstatement of the case. Actually, in spite of his close knowledge of Indian languages, he simply had no real appreciation of their cultures: he wanted them to become white-like Americans. He began his public statements on the Indians in his draft of a Virginia constitution: "no lands shall be appropriated until purchased of the Indian natives."[28] This edict sounds like a fair policy, though undoubtedly the Indians would have been forced to sell. In *A Summary View,* he had already revealed his notion that migration into other lands, even those occupied by other peoples, was as legitimate as it was inevitable. When the colonists came to the New World, they had exercised "a right, which nature has given to all men, of departing from the country in which chance, not choice has placed them, of going in quest of new habitations."[29] This supposed natural right of expatriation became Jefferson's justification for the westward movement in America. He was thus instrumental in the American compulsion which came to be called the United States' "Manifest Destiny." Indians would have to pay the price of white advancement.

Yet Jefferson meant not so much to dislodge the Indians as to absorb them — to destroy their folkways and beliefs but to preserve their lives. As President of the United States, he wrote, "In truth, the ultimate point of rest & happiness for them is to let our settlements and theirs meet and blend together, to intermix, and become one people. Incorporating themselves with us as citizens of the U.S., this is what the natural progress of things will of course bring on, and it will be better to promote than to retard it."[30] This solution was not truly to be a blend, of course, but a domination through a kind of benevolent despotism.

In a message to Congress in 1803, President Jefferson exhibited a pronounced Great-White-Father paternalism:

The Indian tribes residing within the limits of the United States, have, for a considerable time, been growing more and more uneasy at the constant diminution of the territory they occupy. . . . In order peaceably to counteract this . . . and to provide an extension of territory which the rapid increase of our numbers will call for, two measures are deemed expedient. First: to encourage them to abandon hunting, to apply to the raising stock, to agriculture and domestic manufacture, and thereby prove to themselves that less land and labor will maintain them. . . . The extensive forests necessary in the hunting life, will then become useless, and they will see advantage in exchanging them for the means of improving their farms, and of increasing their domestic comforts. Secondly: to multiply trading houses among them, and place within their reach those things which will contribute more to their domestic comfort, than the possession of extensive, but uncultivated wilds.

He then explained what he thought "the greatest good" would be for the Indians: "In leading them to agriculture, to manufactures, and civilization; in bringing together their and our settlements, and in preparing them ultimately to participate in the benefits of our governments, I trust and believe we are acting for their greatest good."[31] No Indian voices are heard in Jefferson's policy, for they were scarcely consulted on the subject of their future. Jefferson simply but almost unctuously assumed that white ways would be a boon to the primitive inhabitants of the American wilderness. His focus was upon "our" (white) interests, upon expediency and condescension.

When some Indians did raise their voices among their various nations to impede white progress, the Prseident, in his Second Inaugural Address, denounced them harshly. The civilizing of the savages which was proceeding, he said, was being retarded "by the habits of their bodies, prejudice of their minds, ignorance, pride, and the influence of interested and crafty individuals among them . . . [who] inculcate a sanctimonious reverence for the customs of their ancestors; that whatsoever they did, must be done through all time; that reason is a false guide."[32] Jefferson was deaf to the notion that "pride" in "the customs of their ancestors" was healthy and desirable, for white "reason" had to overcome such "prejudice."

Jefferson's words read like a declaration of Indian dependence, as indeed they were meant to be. "My Friends and Children," he addressed the Cherokee Nation in 1804, "give up your old ways and join us in the march of civilization. Is it not apparent to you that to be like us is your destiny?"[33] "To be like us or die," he might have said. Official United States policy was yet to become fixed; the sad drama of the death of the fighting Indian was yet to be acted out; but Thomas Jefferson was already helping set the stage by failing to see that his benign intentions were a form of subtle attack that could lead only to tragedy.

III *Domestic Economy*

In his racial prejudices, Jefferson was quite representative of the America of his time.He agonized over his personal failure to manifest in practical accomplishment his idealism toward the human race. (This is still the American dilemma as opposed to the American dream, of course, this inability to create in reality the full justice and equality the Republic believes in ideally.) Another of his prejudices, however, gave Jefferson no disturbance of self-doubt. It was his consistent male point of view toward society, a point of view probably shared by all men of that era. Always humanity was "mankind" or "man" to Jefferson and his contemporaries. Men directed human affairs in nearly every realm. Only "domestic economy" — household management — was reserved for women.[34] Though the "female" should pursue "dancing, drawing, and music" while young, "no lady dances after marriage."[35] Properly, women were to be hostesses, wives, and mothers; and their education was to be limited. In theory, women shared fully in the natural rights identified in the *Declaration of Independence;* but, in practice, they were to keep their places as protected and beloved helpmates, and as young ladies who were to look forward to the same destiny.

"A plan of female education has never been a subject of systematic contemplation with me," he wrote in 1818. "It has occupied my attention so far only as the education of my own daughters occaisionally [*sic*] required. . . . I thought it essential to give them a solid education, which might enable them, when become mothers, to educate their own daughters, and even to direct the course for sons, should their fathers be lost, or incapable, or inattentive."[36] His daughters were well educated compared to other young women of the time, as his biographers have shown; and he never doubted their intelligence and capabilities. He was simply paternalistic in the fullest sense, very loving and protective; for he never dreamed that women might penetrate life in the way of men.

Women were not — and were not to be — a part of American political life. American women were "Women, who, to prevent depravation of morals and ambiguity of issue, could not mix promiscuously in the public meetings of men."[37] Female legislators were unthinkable; a crop of illegitimate children would presumably result as women inevitably succumbed to, or elicited the advances of, male legislators.

In the realm of organized religion (a realm Jefferson usually avoided personally), women were at times downright contemptible: "In our Richmond there is much [religious] fanaticism, but chiefly among the women. They have their night meetings and praying parties, where, attended by their priests, and sometimes by a hen-pecked husband, they pour forth the effusions of their love to Jesus, in terms amatory and carnal, as ... to a mere earthly lover."[38]

Jefferson, who had great trepidations about female sexuality, mistrusted any public display of passions. Yet, like many men of his time, he allowed his male point of view to lead him occasionally to look upon women as mere sex objects. Before his own marriage, for example, he repeatedly attempted an affair with the wife of a friend.[39] He is said to have had an affair with a lovely young married woman while in France (he was by then a widower). If these were great compromises in the gentlemanly standards he set for himself, however, he never was the profligate that his handsomeness and his social position might have allowed him to become.

Expectedly, his views of slave women were often most exploitive in the economic sense: "It is usual to estimate a woman at half the [market] value of a man." Yet, paradoxically, he said, "I consider the labor of a breeding woman [a slave woman who begets children by Black male slaves] as no object [in regard to lightening her work load], and that a child raised every 2. years is of more profit than the crop of the best laboring man. . . . it is not their labor, but their increase which is the first consideration."[40] Nevertheless, he perhaps came to regard one Black woman with lasting and genuine affection.

Jefferson's first great love had been his wife, Martha, according to all testimony and every biographer. She was lovely, talented, gracious; and he was apparently perfectly true to her while she lived. Then came his French affair with the painter Maria Cosway, whose art he thought proper, though not "domestic." (Years before, he had denigrated the poetry of Phillis Wheatley, the first Black American poet, saying "Religion, indeed, has produced a Phyllis Whately [*sic*] but it could not produce a poet."[41] There is more antireligious bias, racial prejudice, and male chauvinism here than literary judgment.) Finally, there was his relationship with Sally Hemings, a Monticello slave.

In Jefferson's time political foes often addressed themselves, as did others later, to the allegedly sordid liaison between Jefferson the "master" and Sally Hemings the slave girl. And recent Black writers have pointed to such allegations in attempts to prove Jefferson's hypocrisy on all subjects.[42] Certainly, biographical attempts to whitewash Jefferson on this subject — which is to insinuate that any such affair must be improper, the *sin* of miscegenation — ring as hollow as the old political attacks did.[43] White biographers have tended, then, to deny any such relationship, usually on the grounds that Jefferson possessed toc much dignity to exploit a slave woman sexually. Black writers, in turn, have tended to insist on such an exploitation as an inevitable outcome of the slavery system, and have assumed its truth in Jefferson's case. But the most judicious interpretation of known facts and testimony establishes the probability that Sally Hemings and Thomas Jefferson were deeply in love and that they had to love clandestinely because of just the kind of prejudice that Jefferson himself often expressed.

Professor Fawn M. Brodie has suggested that neither party was at fault in a loving relationship that endured for thirty-eight years, and which produced seven children. Rather, society, then as now, has been at fault in its inability to sympathize with two people who, far from engaging in debauchery, remained steadfast in the face of great adversity. Theirs was a common law marriage, and they were loyal to one another. "We were the only children of his by a slave woman," their son Madison Hemings insisted. That Sally Hemings was "mighty near white," as Isaac testified, may help explain how Jefferson overcame his usual aversion to intimacy with Blacks (Sally Hemings, a quadroon, was the half-sister of Jefferson's wife, Martha).[44] But by whatever steps they became intimate, the most plausible explanation of the relationship is that they fell in love. As Professor Brodie has asserted, love — however intangible and difficult to document completely such a conclusion may be — is the answer. This interpretation helps make Jefferson once again human — to be the warm, sensitive, intelligent person he was capable of being — and it acknowledges Sally Hemings' humanity far more fully than any other theory ever advanced. It removes the question from the level of recrimination and acrimony, and from the slough of racial prejudice, Black or white, as well.

In matters of sex and race in which Jefferson set only a negative example, then, great lessons exist for the American people. Their prejudices and their imperfect sense of a common humanity with those not yet having equal access to American rights and privileges can be overcome. The base of natural rights still exists, as Jefferson's generation of Americans asserted; and the *Declaration of Independence* still expresses some of the nation's greatest principles. "Varieties in the race of man" there may be, but *e pluribus unum* remains as a rallying cry for those who would make manifest the old ideals.

Perhaps Jefferson, through private letters to influential people, through his presidential policies, and through his *Notes on the State of Virginia* (which these two centuries has seldom been out of print) did considerable harm regarding those ideals. Yet he did voice those very ideals, voice them as clearly and effectively as anyone ever has. He was a learned man, one who saw the chasm between ideal and real, and one who helped each subsequent generation of Americans to share in that same vision. But, in his life, he also shared and suffered intellectual and emotional conflicts still common today.

CHAPTER 4

An American Education

I *Crusade Against Ignorance*

THOMAS Jefferson had as fine a formal education as Virginia could provide its young gentlemen. Preparatory tutoring and the College of William and Mary grounded him in the liberal arts. Both the private teaching and the college experience were his as a birthright of the privileged few in his colony. Although his was a truly Classical, traditional schooling,[1] of the sort that is now virtually unknown, Jefferson's education did not cease upon his leaving the classroom. He studied the law with an established attorney, as was then everywhere the custom, and he then followed the lifelong process of self-education that was the mark of the Enlightenment man.

Few subjects of human inquiry eluded him, and that he was a great collector of books alone illustrates this. He amassed huge personal libraries over the years (one of which became the foundation of the Library of Congress),[2] and he frequently advised others on book purchases and on measures for their personal improvement. In 1771, he sent "a List of Books for a Private Library" in a letter to a friend; and, in 1783, he wrote his daughter Patsy to encourage her pursuit of music, dancing, drawing, writing, her learning of French, and her reading of "the best poets and prose writers" in English. In 1785, he wrote a now famous letter to his nephew Peter Carr in which he inculcated honesty, integrity, and the study of "antient history," "Modern history," poetry, and philosophy.[3]

"He who receives an idea from me," Jefferson said in 1813, "receives instruction himself without lessening mine; as he who lights his taper at mine, receives light without darkening me. That ideas should freely spread from one to another over the globe, for the moral and mutual instruction of man, and improvement of his condition, seems to have been peculiarly and benevolently designed by nature."[4] One of the leading intellectuals of his time, he used his learning well.

His democratic idealism led him far beyond tradition in his educational theories, for he considered education to be necessary for gaining and safeguarding the people's "freedom and happiness." It "may teach them how to work out their own greatest happiness, by shewing them that it does not depend on the condition of life in which chance has placed them, but is always the result of a good conscience, good health, occupation, and freedom in all just pursuits." "No other sure foundation can be devised for the preservation of freedom, and happiness." There had to be "a crusade against ignorance" in America[5] to preserve American freedoms. Here the spirit of the *Declaration of Independence* clearly surges forth again, raising the right to a free education virtually to the level of the natural rights, and certainly identifying education as the chief tool required for the maintenance of those rights.

That Jefferson became the earliest advocate for a thoroughgoing, free, public educational system paid for by the state[6] is best seen in his "A Bill for the More General Diffusion of Knowledge" which he introduced in Virginia in 1779 but which was "never . . . put into practice by any people."[7] From common schools, modeled after the New England village school, through a state university (he tried to convert the College of William and Mary into a state institution), a number of young people were to rise, without cost to themselves, as far as their abilities would take them.

Years later Jefferson stated that the purpose of the "primary education," as he conceived it, was

> To give every citizen the information he needs for the transaction of his own business; To enable him to calculate for himself, and to express and preserve his ideas, his contracts and accounts, in writing; To improve, by reading, his morals and faculties; To understand his duties to his neighbors and country, and to discharge with competence the functions confided to him by either; To know his rights; to exercise with order and justice those he retains; to choose with discretion the fiduciary of those he delegates; and to notice their conduct with diligence, with candor, and judgment; And, in general, to observe with intelligence and faithfulness all the social relations under which he shall be placed.[8]

This objective was very different from the elitist education Jefferson himself had received. A practicality dominated Jefferson's objectives, for he wished citizens to keep their houses, their budgets, and their persons in good order. His idealism was also apparent, however, in the notion that a person's morals were sounder under the influence of learning and that concepts of duty and of social regard were made clearer by education. Furthermore, good citizenship included voting intelligently and critically observing those in public office. An ignorant populace could do neither. The rudiments he outlined in "A Bill for the More General Diffusion of Knowledge" were the irreducible foundation of a sound society.

"All the free children, male and female," would acquire learning that was to be based on instruction in "reading, writing, and common arithmetick," with some Greek, Roman, English, and American history.[9] The primary schools would be close to the students' homes, for "To render a child independant of it's parents is to ruin it's education, it's morals, it's reputation and it's fortune."[10] This observation about being close to home must have been meant by Jefferson to apply to girls, for only boys would advance farther up his ladder of education in the public schools by leaving their homes.

Only one qualified boy from each primary school would advance to the "grammar" school level. Then, as the years went by, one boy from these secondary schools would be sent to college to be "educated, boarded, and clothed three years" at state expense.[11] Today, this suggested method of selection may seem rather narrow or restrictive, and needlessly competitive. But, in eighteenth-century America, such a plan was bold, democratic, and forward-looking.[12] At once pragmatic and idealistic, it was at least as workable as any later scheme.[13]

II *The University*

Failing to turn William and Mary into a state college, Jefferson eventually devised a new plan for the creation of a state institution of higher learning: very late in his life he gave to his state and to the nation the University of Virginia. Here he was even more radical than he was in his scheme for lower education, for he promoted a very untraditional university structure.[14] He inaugurated the elective system (as opposed to a completely prescribed curriculum); he began a kind of honors plan (based on the integrity of the students); and he instituted the first professorship of modern foreign languages in America.[15] The first two of these innovations which idealistically assumed the good judgment of students have remained imperfectly workable at the great number of colleges and universities that have since attempted them. The third, also much copied, has helped make legitimate the study of other tongues and cultures in a too often self-centered society.

Looking backward as well as forward, Jefferson was also the first to make Old English a subject for study at an American college. He had pursued it himself for years and had written a treatise he called *Essay on Anglo-Saxon.* Such learning would promote a fuller understanding of current usage, he felt, and would also liberalize the students' minds toward a freer use of language.[16] He was an excellent language scientist (philologist, or linguist); and, as a liberal thinker in the linguistic realm, advocated freedom in regard to new word coinages. Neologisms were welcome, he said, because "Where brevity, perspecuity, and even euphony can be promoted by the introduction of a new word, it is an improvement to the language."[17]

To understand why Jefferson had such interests in creating a freer educational structure is also to understand why he wrote the *Declaration of Independence.* He did these things not for personal gain or glory but on behalf of humanity. And he did them consciously, deliberately in a new — an American — way. The practice of sending young men to England to get their college education, for example (a common pattern in preRevolutionary Virginia), was to him quite pernicious: "Of all the errors which can possibly be committed in the education of youth, that of sending them to Europe is the most fatal." In England, they would only learn of frivolous, aristocratic pursuits; and they would observe examples of sexual debauchery. It was better that they acquire "an useful American education" on the Jeffersonian model.[18] Since understanding other civilizations had to begin with a thorough comprehension of one's own culture, perception of America had to develop from within America, as surely as a perception of self grew from within each person. Jefferson tried to set an example for the realization of both of these ideals in his *Notes on the State of Virginia.* He also seems to have hoped that the University of Virginia might serve as an exemplary institution for his nation.

The University, then, Jefferson's dream realized, remains his chief educational legacy. He designed its campus, including all of its buildings; he oversaw its construction; he hired its professors; and he planned its curriculum. Here is his listing of the main aims of the University:

To form the statesmen, legislators and judges, on whom public prosperity and individual happiness are so much to depend; To expound the principles and structure of government, the laws which regulate the intercourse of nations, those formed municipally for our own government, and a sound spirit of legislation, which, banishing all arbitrary and unnecessary restraint on individual action, shall leave us free to do whatever does not violate the equal rights of another [note that, as late as 1818, Jefferson restates the principles of the *Declaration*]; To harmonize and promote the interests of agriculture, manufactures and commerce, and by well informed views of political economy to give a free scope to the public industry; To develop the reasoning faculties of our youth, enlarge their minds, cultivate their morals, and instill into them the precepts of virtue and order; To enlighten them with mathematical and physical sciences, which advance the arts, and administer to the health, the subsistence, and comforts of human life; And, generally, to form them to habits of reflection and correct action, rendering them examples of virtue to others, and of happiness within themselves."[19]

As with Jefferson's scheme for the earlier years of education, the university was meant to promote good citizenship among the electorate and the elected. It was meant to furnish the American society with leaders — not mere politicians, but persons of sound morality and of sound reason. In addition, it was meant to promote the pursuit of happiness. It would maintain "the combined spirit of order and self-respect, so congenial with our political institutions, and so important to be woven into the American character."[20]

Jefferson was well acquainted with most of the areas of study he chose for the university curriculum; for, remarkable as this fact may seem, he had mastered many of them. The course of study is still as impressive as any yet devised for an American education:

I. Languages, ancient:
Latin
Greek
Hebrew
II. Languages, modern:
French
Spanish
Italian
German
Anglo-Saxon
III. Mathematics, pure:
Algebra

Fluxions
Geometry, Elementary
Transcendental
Architecture, Military
Naval
IV. Physico-Mathematics:
Mechanics
Statics
Dynamics
Pneumatics
Acoustics
Optics
Astronomy
Geography
V. Physics, or Natural Philosophy:
Chemistry
Mineralogy
VI. Botany
Zoology
VII. Anatomy
Medicine
VIII. Government
Political Economy
Law of Nature and Nations
History, being interwoven with Politics and Law
IX. Law, Municipal
X. Idealogy
General Grammar
Ethics
Rhetoric
Belles Lettres and the fine arts.[21]

This thorough education in the liberal arts, Jefferson style, is a formidable curriculum; and those who mastered it would truly constitute the "natural aristocracy" of which Jefferson sometimes spoke: persons who would on merit alone rise to positions of leadership. Even casting about in such a curriculum, under the right of election of courses, no student would emerge as a narrow specialist; no humanist would fail to grasp the processes of the hard sciences; no scientist would miss the humanizing experience of exposure to esthetic values. There would be no overwhelming of the student's mind by mere utilitarian training, no ignorance of the past in deference to an overpowering, present-day search for useful skills. Jefferson's was at once a modern scheme and an ancient one:

his plan fostered progressive change, but it conservatively transmitted, in the old manner, such traditional standards as intellectual integrity and freedom of inquiry.

III *Our Liberty*

As the pursuit of such a curriculum freed the mind, allowing open investigation into so many realms of thought, it militated against that very darkness which the Enlightenment sought to destroy. "Bigotry is the disease of ignorance. . . . Education and free discussion are the antidotes,"[22] Jefferson wrote to John Adams in 1816. The "free discussion" he had in mind included a free press: "Our liberty depends on the freedom of the press, and that cannot be limited without being lost." Envisioning an electorate with at least a basic literacy, he felt that citizens would receive constant education through the press. "Were it left to me to decide whether we should have a government without newspapers, or newspapers without a government, I should not hesitate a moment to prefer the latter," Jefferson hyperbolized.[23]

Again on the subject of self-education, he cautioned his young nephew that, since "A Strong body makes the mind strong," he should walk daily into nature, being keenly observant. "Habituate yourself to walk very far," he said, but avoid useless exercise: "Games played with the ball and others of that nature, are too violent for the body and stamp no character on the mind."[24] In a just society, the kind Jefferson sought for his America, the pursuit of knowledge and of health would approximate the pursuit of happiness. The society was to provide the means, but each separate person was to envision and practice the common end.

As with the individual, then, so with the nation. If each person were not free, neither would the society be. Should any individual be denied free access to education, the country would suffer. If the spirit of the *Declaration of Independence* was not manifest in all the people, the society would decay. Finally, "If a nation expects to be ignorant and free, in a state of civilization, it expects what never was and never will be."[25] The body politic would have to be sound in body and in mind if the American experiment was to continue.

CHAPTER 5

Beyond the Constitution

I *The Sovereign Powers*

"HISTORY, in general, only informs us what bad government is," Jefferson wrote late in his presidency.[1] Certainly his administration was no example of bad government, for his involvement with politics was something he did, as he knew all civil servants should do, on behalf of the educated citizenry. The people, the sole repository of political power, delegated the wielding of power to elected representatives; and presidents were not to govern people, they were to govern *for* people. Any government not so arranged was bad government.

Naturally such a system was based on the belief that, generally, an informed electorate was fair and capable, a sound base for power.[2] And, certainly, power should not rest with any privileged minority such as, for instance, a wealthy few. Although a person of any station might manifest integrity, Jefferson wrote in 1776 that "my observations do not enable me to say I think integrity the characteristic of wealth."[3] He admired his good friend Joel Barlow's poem *The Conspiracy of Kings,* and his essay *Advice to the Privileged Orders. . . . Resulting from the Necessity and Propriety of a General Revolution in the Principle of Government.*[4] These radical, democratic tracts manifested the spirit of the *Declaration of Independence,* for "Kings" and "Privileged Orders" meant not only a hereditary aristocracy — not an American problem — but any class, group, or individual whose power did not derive from merit. As Barlow put it, " 'Tis dark deception . . . Man sunk in titles . . . 'Tis Rank, Distinction, all the hell that springs / From those prolific monsters, Courts and Kings. / These are the vampires. . . ." A democratic revolution — and the government that resulted — Barlow said, "was an operation designed for the benefit of the people; it originated in the people, and was conducted by the people."

"The President of the United States," Barlow continued, "who has more power while in office than some of the kings of Europe, is chosen with as little commotion as a churchwarden. There is a public service to be performed, and the people say who shall do it. The servant feels honored with the confidence reposed in him, and generally expresses his gratitude by a faithful performance.... Only admit the original, unalterable truth, *that all men are equal in their rights,* and the foundation of every thing is laid ... [then] the people will form an equal representative government; in which it will be impossible for *orders* or *privileges* to exist...." Barlow was representative of the people's democratic liberalism in the age of Jefferson.

From government's point of view, the citizen was to be left alone, especially in the realms of belief; for coercion of opinion by the government was intolerable. For example, Jefferson wrote, "our civil rights have no dependance on our religious opinions, any more than our opinions in physics or geometry"; "the opinions of men are not the object of civil government, nor under its jurisdiction."[5] As Barlow expressed it, "In the United States of America there is no [established, government-sanctioned] church; and this is one of the principal circumstances which distinguish that government from all others.... it ensures the un-embarrassed exercise of religion, the continuation of public instruction in the science of liberty and happiness, and promises a long duration to a representative government." Freedom of belief was a natural right unabridgable by government; for, as Jefferson indicated in *A Summary View,* Americans were not simply seeking their rights as Englishmen; they were seeking their natural rights as human beings.[6]

The fundamental natural political right, then, was government by the consent of the governed: "From the nature of things, every society must at all times possess within itself the sovereign powers of legislation."[7] In 1776, certain acts of the British Parliament were null and void not simply because they were unjust (they were), but because Parliament ruled without the consent of the governed in America.[8] "The holy cause of freedom," in political terms, was "the blessings of self-government." "The will of the majority, the Natural law of every society, is the only sure guardian of the rights of man.... Let us ... for ever bow down to the general reason of the society" "The republican [representative] is the only form of government which is not eternally at open or secret war with the rights of mankind."[9]

There were, however, severe restrictions on citizenship in Jefferson's America; and its laws excluded many from the full realization of their rights. Some of those laws were written by Thomas Jefferson. "Let mercy be the character of the law-giver," he said, "but let the judge be a mere machine."[10] Despite this view, he advanced such legal tenets as these: "Rape, buggery &c. punish by castration"; traitors should be hanged; capital punishment, though "the last melancholy resource," was appropriate for murderers; in some cases, poisoning, maiming, or disfiguring were allowable.[11] No "Negroe, Mulattoe or Indian" should testify in trials regarding whites, but only "against or between" their own kind (they were not citizens). Citizens of Virginia were to be "white persons," "free and adult male citizens."[12] Jefferson again exemplified — and still exemplifies — the American disharmony between ideals and actualities.

Nevertheless, he was the most liberal lawmaker and political theorizer of his time. To reform criminals, not to "exterminate instead of reforming," was his ideal. "Cruel and sanguinary laws defeat their own purpose." He sought to give court-appointed, free legal counsel to the poor. He worked for "a general suffrage" that would not base the vote on property ownership.[13] And always he worked to promote what he felt was "the present democratical spirit of America."[14]

II *Whigs and Tories*

"When at home I took great pains to enquire into the sentiments of the people," wrote Jefferson, the practical politician, in 1776.[15] Then a delegate to the Congress, he little dreamed that politics in America would become a party affair and that the Revolution would be a continual experiment and process, not merely a military struggle. This consultation with the people, and his subsequent belief in confiding in them, made him the liberal party politician as opposed to the conservative, who did neither, except among the privileged few. Parties did evolve in the new United States — in the 1790s — and Jefferson was tapped as the Republican (Democrat) leader[16] who opposed the Federalists, led by Alexander Hamilton.

As early as 1793, in a letter to a friend, Jefferson railed against "Hamilton himself & the monocrats of his cabal." ("Monocrats," a Jefferson coinage, was a neologism.) But he knew, as stated in a letter to the Marquis de Lafayette in 1823, that "the parties of Whig and Tory, are those of nature.... The sickly, weakly, timid man, fears the people, and is a tory by nature. The healthy, strong and bold, cherishes them, and is formed a whig by nature." "Call them ... liberals and serviles, Jacobins and Ultras, whigs and tories, republicans and federalists, aristocrats and democrats" (these latter two reverse his parallelism), all persons were one or the other politically.[17] But only the liberals truly exhibited the spirit of the *Declaration of Independence.*

At times, because of partisan strife, Jefferson lamented the free press; he noticed that one newspaper "is a paper of pure Toryism, disseminating the doctrines of monarchy, aristocracy, & the exclusion of the influence of the people. We have been trying to get another *weekly* or *half weekly* paper set up ... so that it might go through the states, & furnish a whig vehicle of intelligence."[18] He was able to establish one under the editorship of the poet Philip Freneau who, he said, "saved our constitution which was galloping fast into monarchy."[19]

As the American party system developed, while he was Secretary of State and while Hamilton was Secretary of the Treasury under President George Washington, Jefferson wrote many letters to boost republicanism and to fight privilege, "the monster aristocracy." There were numerous "stock jobbers" (monied interests) and "king jobbers" (privileged classes) in America, but he believed that "our people are firm & constant in their republican purity." "It is but too true," he wrote to Thomas Paine in 1792, "that we have a sect preaching up & pouting after an English constitution of king, lords, & commons, & whose heads are itching for crowns, coronets & mitres."[20] Whether this statement was literally so, or whether it was simply more Jeffersonian hyperbole, is still debated by historians. The republic might actually have been in danger from within, but Jefferson believed that it would not fall because "The people through all the states are for republican forms, republican principles, simplicity, economy, religious & civil freedom." And he added to the assessment of 1800 that "A majority [is] firm in all those principles which we have espoused and the federalists have opposed."[21] Jefferson, who knew how to fight in the context of party politics, ultimately triumphed by rising to the presidency and by democratizing the government of the United States as much as in his era he could. In doing so, however, he felt at times aided, at other times hampered by, the United States Constitution.

III *All Laws Present and Future*

Jefferson's first brush with constitutionalism — providing for the people a permanent, written statement of laws and rights — was in his drafting of a new constitution for Virginia in 1776. In it, he outlined the classical separation-of-powers and the checks-and-balances system of Legislative, Executive, and Judicial branches of government which were to "be for ever separate." House members would be chosen annually; senators would be appointed by the house for life; the governor, who would be chosen anew each year, would have no veto power, and would not be able to succeed himself in office. Supreme Court members would be appointed by the House, and they would serve during good behavior.[22] This frequent turn-over in office, and the vesting of the greatest power in the House, illustrated his ideal of getting government as close as possible to the control of the electorate.

At the same time, Jefferson thought that he would democratize inheritance laws and thereby rid his people of the ancient, aristocratic tradition of primogeniture. "Descents, instead of being to the eldest son, brother or male cousin of the ancestor, as directed by the laws heretofore shall be to all the brothers & sisters of the sd. heir at law who shall be of the whole blood of the ancestor, each of whom shall have an equal portion with the heir at law." Jefferson later spelled out that "females shall have equal rights with males" in matters of inheritance. He succeeded in this scheme when his bill for abolishing primogeniture was passed in 1785.[23] This law was a devastating blow to the vestiges of "aristocracy" in America. No longer would huge land holdings be perpetuated; they would instead be distributed evenly — democratically it might be said — among immediate heirs.

In both this and his later state constitution-draft of 1783, which was never adopted, Jefferson insisted that, as was to be the case with the United States Constitution, "all laws present and future shall be subordinate" to the proposed charter of laws.[24] Although Jefferson was in France during the framing of the national Constitution in the summer of 1787, he had written in 1783 that he felt a stronger central government was needed; and he even advocated the national assumption of state debts to strengthen the central government. He also favored a version of assumption in 1790, but later bitterly opposed Hamilton's plan for it. Jefferson's final "acquiescence in assumption was primarily to forestall a dissolution of the union threatened by those who were not bound to it, as he was, by ligaments of liberty."[25]

When Jefferson first learned about the new Constitution from James Madison in the latter's famous letter giving an account of the Constitutional Convention, Jefferson expressed suspicion, even hostility to the new document.[26] First of all, he thought the presidency would evolve into a monarchy. He viewed the politician figure rather cynically, saying that a man who *is* president will seek to *be* president for life, even illegally. Yet that defect would easily pass public judgment because of the man everyone knew would first hold the office: "the perpetual re-eligibility of the same president, will probably not be cured during the life of General Washington. His merit has blinded our countrymen to the dangers of making so important an officer re-eligible."[27] Jefferson did not oppose, however, the elevation of Washington to the presidency, for he was always glad of the example his fellow Virginian had set.

The main flaw in the Constitution, according to Jefferson, was "the omission of a bill of rights."[28] Assured by Madison that it would follow, Jefferson warmed to the new foundation for American government; and he knew that "it would gain on the public mind, as I confess it has on my own." "After all, it is my principle that the will of the Majority should always prevail," and he could support the Constitution if the people would.[29] "I sincerely rejoice," he said finally, "at the acceptance of our new constitution. . . . It is a good canvas, on which some strokes only want retouching." He also felt that *The Federalist,* the series of papers which achieved its acceptance, had formed "the best commentary on the principles of government which was ever written." The change from the post-Revolutionary Articles of Confederation, to the Constitution, Jefferson called a welcome "philosophic revolution, phylosophically effected."[30] A triumph for and of the American people, it amounted to a second, bloodless, benign revolution.

As to how the Constitution should be construed — what "construction" was to be put on it — Jefferson has been known historically as a strict constructionist, for he allowed little leeway in interpreting it. In 1791, for example, he opposed the formation of a national bank on the grounds that no such power was specifically given to the federal government by the Constitution. But Jefferson lost that fight, and others like it, which may have been a blessing for his country.[31] The problem, as he came to see, was not whether to interpret the Constitution — to construe it other than literally — but how and when to interpret it, for interpretation was inevitable.

In one special case Jefferson, however reluctantly, laid aside his theory of Constitutional construction in order to take pragmatic action. This change occurred for the purchase of the Louisiana Territory which doubled the size of the United States and stretched it into the far west. When theory and necessity clashed — when the people could gain so magnificently — he did not feel strictly bound by the Constitution.[32] He explained his purchase this way in 1803: "The Executive in seizing the fugitive occurence which so much advances the good of their country, have done an act beyond the Constitution. The Legislative in casting behind them metaphysical subtleties, and risking themselves like faithful servants, must ratify & pay for it, and throw themselves on their country for doing for them unauthorized what we know they would have done for themselves had they been in a situation to do it."[33] Another triumph for the American people had been achieved by Jefferson, and another expansive revolution had been fostered by him.

IV *A Little Rebellion Now and Then*

Paradoxically, Jefferson appreciated the written guarantees of the United States Constitution while remaining skeptical about the sanctity of the document itself. "No society," he wrote to Madison in 1789, "can make a perpetual constitution, or even a perpetual law. The earth belongs always to the living generation." "The spirit of resistance to government is so valuable on certain oaccasions, that I wish it to be always kept alive," he told John Adams. "I hold it that a little rebellion now and then is a good thing."[34] Such statements identify the radical strain in Jefferson; they reflect his distrust of power arbitrarily used or of government badly administered. They need not, of course, be taken literally, for "rebellion" comes in many forms aside from a shooting revolution. Jefferson simply did not want succeeding generations chained to the patterns of their predecessors; he did not want government to become a monolith perpetuated blindly.

Nonetheless, he had great faith in the Union, or so he said many times; but his was really a faith in the people who composed the Union: "I have no fear that the result of our experiment will be that men may be trusted to govern themselves without a master." Under the Articles of Confederation he saw the states as subordinate to the central government, for he wrote that, "when any one state in the American Union refuses obedience to the Confederation by which they have bound themselves, the rest have a natural right to compel them to obedience," even by force. With the coming of the Constitution, however, Jefferson sought to identify spheres of power, national and state: "with respect to every thing external we [must] be one nation only, firmly hooped together. Interior government is what each state should keep to itself."[35] This position was essentially his lifelong one under the Constitution. Foreign affairs (Jefferson, it will be remembered, was the first Secretary of State) were the province of the central government, but the states, the counties, and the municipalities were to be responsible for the people's interests in all those respects in which governments normally function. This gross oversimplification concerning the levels of government not only haunted Jefferson the rest of his life, but also became part of a bequest he left to the American people that troubled them as much as it did him.

By 1798, with the Constitution firmly established, Jefferson once again worried about an irresponsible use of federal power by President John Adams. Jefferson now perceived not a hypothetical but a real problem; yet he had to proceed with caution, since he himself was Vice President. (Adams had, Jefferson felt, fostered severe curtailments of certain natural rights, as will be seen.) In private letters, though, he was quite frank, as usual. "I sincerely wish," he said, "that the whole Union may accomodate their interests to each other . . . mutually as members of the same family, that the wealth & strength of any one part should be viewed as the wealth & strength of the whole." Then a worry intruded itself, a worry he tried to rationalize away:

> I do not think it for the interest of the general government itself, & still less of the Union at large, that the State governments should be so little respected as they have been. However, I dare say that in time all these as well as their central government, like the planets revolving round their common sun, acting & acted upon according to their respective weights & distances, will produce that beautiful equilibrium on which our Constitution is founded, and which I believe it will exhibit to the world in a degree of perfection, unexampled but in the planetary system itself.[36]

Changing his metaphor to a scientific one was unfortunate, for his new analogy depicted a sun-nucleus upon which the "planets" depended for their existence as satellites. Moreover, his metaphor of the family had been a powerful one that revealed Jefferson at his most serious. Within the family, the parent expects that the offspring will establish separate domiciles and in them will naturally oversee their own affairs. While it was clear, in the second or solar-system figure, that he meant each level of government to have its own sphere, the further implications of perpetual dependence belied his intention. The two metaphors were symptomatic of his dilemma concerning government, a sign of the constitutional paradox in which he ever found himself, and which formed part of his legacy to his nation.

Basically, all levels of government, each in its own capacity, existed to serve the people. But the question arose about who was to protect the rights of the people from any one government which infringed upon them. The answer, short of rebellion, had to be — another level of government. When Jefferson saw the federal government abridging or denying the people's rights, those guaranteed in the Constitution or their own natural rights, he called upon the states to make a corrective adjustment. The chief instance in which all this occurred concerned the Alien and Sedition Acts of the Adams administration. As one of Jefferson's editors has put it, "As early as April 26, 1798 ... Jefferson was predicting and disapproving of possible Alien and Sedition bills.... Thoroughly opposed to disunion ... yet believing these Federalist measures [abridging free speech and rights to citizenship] only initial steps towards a dictatorship or monarchy, Jefferson ... hit upon the now famous doctrine of nullification of Federal statutes by means of resolutions of state legislatures."[37] This situation developed prior to the practice of judicial review, where the Supreme Court decides on the constitutionality of federal laws — a concept Jefferson also opposed.

"Where powers are assumed" by the national government, Jefferson wrote in his Kentucky Resolution of 1798 (the Resolution was sponsored by the Kentucky legislature), "which have not been delegated [to it], a nullification of the act is the rightful remedy." In other words, the states, in compacting under the Constitution, never agreed to the assumed powers; they had the sole check on their assumption. "Every State has a natural right in cases not within the compact ... to nullify of their own authority" such assumptions of power.[38] Late in life, in his *Autobiography,* Jefferson showed that he realized that the Articles of Confederation had failed because any state could neglect requisitions from the central government. "This allowed, in fact, a negative to every [state] Legislature, on every message proposed by Congress . . . so . . . as to benumb the action of the Federal government."[39] Still, he never applied this conclusion to state nullification under the Constitution. In his late years, in fact, he wrote many "states' rights" letters; and he even foresaw the possibility of the "dissolution of our Union" as an extreme measure "after long abuse."[40]

Nevertheless, modern consensus is that Jefferson was opposed to secession and that his "states' rights" position was actually a defense of the civil rights and the natural rights of all citizens since these had to be protected by the states in case of federal abuse.[41] Going beyond the Constitution was no easy task for Jefferson, who did not advocate it lightly. "Let the national government be entrusted with the defense of the nation, and its foreign and federal relations; the State governments with the civil rights, laws, police," he said many times.[42] But what of instances in which a state government itself became abusive of the people's rights? Could not the federal government, operating under the Constitutional guarantees of civil rights, correct the state's behavior? Jefferson, who never adequately confronted this possibility, omitted from his legacy to his people his thoughts on perhaps the most persistent of difficult constitutional questions. "The constitution of the United States is a compact of independent nations," he said, incredibly, in the year of his death; but to save "the Republic . . . is the first and supreme law" of American political life.[43] Once again, the paradoxical Jefferson through his own words surfaces.

To Jefferson, natural rights were above and beyond the United States Constitution, which rested on them, not the reverse. Therefore the Constitution was not sacred, and neither was the Union itself. The *Declaration of Independence,* with its right of rebellion, took precedence. Jefferson never resolved his political paradox, never eluded the horns of his dilemma. To him, natural rights were absolute, "inalienable," "sacred." Man-made laws were relative, even when based on the higher laws. The question of what agency could, or should, resolve conflicts between them remained moot. The *Declaration* began a political experiment which, under the Constitution, tried its own author severely.

CHAPTER 6

Cooperating with Nature

I *On the Basis of Experiment*

ALL his political life — of some forty years — Jefferson sought relief from the trials of what he called "the dry & dreary waste of politics." Perhaps every man owed a "tour of political duty" to his country, but neither law nor reason required him to serve indefinitely. Therefore, he was very happy to retire from the presidency to settle in at Monticello in 1809. He had often made trips there, for it was to him a wonderfully refreshing retreat and his favorite place on earth. While at Monticello, he could indulge his fondest interests, gardening, farming, building, and various scientific and mechanical pursuits. He wrote to the American inventor-scientist David Rittenhouse that politics and science scarcely mix: "No body can conceive that nature ever intended to throw away a Newton upon the occupations of a crown." "Men of an ordinary stature," he added, can administer government; but a person such as Rittenhouse is called to higher occupations.[1]

Jefferson also felt strongly called to things "above" practical politics. He was, when he could be, a generally careful scientist and an ingenious technician. As such, he was by turns openminded, skeptical, dogmatic, practical, and impractical. His interests were as diverse as any American's of his time, his *Notes* and other writings indicate. The freedom of the scientific mind appealed to him most, along with the constant potential for self-education. This interest in science and in invention was one of the ways in which he pursued his own happiness, through which he sought to make a contribution to the happiness of others.[2]

In principle, Jefferson had a "cautious philosophy" regarding science. He advocated suspended judgment where evidence was short, for "he is less remote from the truth who believes nothing, than he who believes what is wrong." Scientific assertions should be "built on the basis of experiment" and on "facts." If these were lacking, then "In the mean time doubt is wisdom."[3] Jefferson made mistakes as a scientist, but he held in principle the most enlightened of scientific attitudes.

As a basis for scientific inquiry, Jefferson schooled himself in mathematics; later he also made certain that a more prominent place in the curriculum of the University of Virginia was reserved for mathematics than at any other American college.[4] He once utilized his mathematical skills in devising a cryptographic device (for decoding secret messages) called a wheel cypher, which was a century in advance of similar inventions used by diplomatic agencies everywhere. As a scientist, he was, as has been noted earlier, also ahead of most Americans in advocating general innoculation as early as 1766.[5] These two areas alone mark him as a revolutionary experimenter in eighteenth-century science.

One of his favorite scientific interests was paleontology. In 1781, as Governor of Virginia, he asked George Rogers Clark (who was in the midst of war) to gather fossil samples with great care "on the Ohio." Jefferson was in pursuit of the mammoth. In 1801, when he offered, as President, federal aid to Charles Willson Peale in excavating mammoth bones, he established government interest in paleontology.[6] His curiosity at times led him to some charming conclusions. He once contended, for example, that shells found in mountainous formations must have *grown* there; but he later revised his opinion: they were carried there, he said, by "some great convulsion of nature." He also once contended that — very probably — no species ever became extinct: "Such is the economy of nature, that no instance can be produced, of her having permitted any one race of animals to become extinct; of her having formed any link in her great work so weak as to be broken."[7] Jefferson, in being so certain that mammoths still had to be alive somewhere, provided a classic example of eighteenth-century logic overcoming eighteenth-century reason.

The most interesting case in which Jefferson suffered from illusion concerned the *Megalonyx jeffersoni,* as the creature was ultimately named.[8] He had come by some strange bones from a Virginia dig, which in 1797 he carried with him to Philadelphia when he became Vice President. There he published his only paleontological tract, "A Memoir on the Discovery of Certain Bones of a Quadruped of the Clawed Kind in the Western Parts of Virginia," in the journal of the American Philosophical Society.

He described the bones thus:

> 1 st. A small fragment of the femur or thigh bone; being in fact only its lower extremity, separated from the main bone at its epiphysis, so as to give us only the two condyles, but these are nearly entire.
> 2 d. A radius, perfect.
> 3 d. An ulna, or fore-arm, perfect, except that it is broken in two.
> 4 th. Three claws, and half a dozen other bones of the foot; but whether of a fore or hinder foot, is not evident.
> These bones only enable us to class the animal with the unguiculated quadrupeds; and of these the lion being nearest him in size, we will compare him with that animal . . . I will venture to refer to him by the name of the Great-Claw or Megalonyx to which he seems sufficiently entitled by the distinguished size of that member . . .

Jefferson then compared the bones to those of the large cat and advanced the theory that a huge American cat must still exist. He later realized that he had forgotten about a description and sketch seen earlier, which had described a *Megatherium,* not a cat. That animal had in some ways resembled his *Megalonyx,* but his memory had betrayed him.[9] The *jeffersoni* was a large ground sloth, closely related to the *Megatherium;* Jefferson proved scientist enough to correct himself. He was equally scrupulous, and at least as careful, in other scientific pursuits.

As a geologist, however, he advanced one more curious thesis regarding strata in rocks: "It is now generally agreed that rock grows, and it seems that it grows in layers in every direction, as the branches of trees grow in all directions. Why seek further the solution of his phaenomenon? Every thing in nature decays. If it were not reproduced then by growth, there would be a chasm."[10] It is not demonstrable that this idea was "generally agreed" upon — and whether anyone else believed it seems remarkable. Once again Jefferson's inference was, at best, overly hasty. As an archeologist, he was more correct, and excavations he directed near Monticello exhibited sound method.

Meteorology so fascinated Jefferson that he was virtually a one-man weather bureau for decades,[11] for he habitually recorded weather data every day. His *Notes on the State of Virginia* revealed this interest and habit, but the fullest source of that sort of information he compiled was what scholars now refer to as his *Garden Book.* Although Jefferson sent Meriwether Lewis across the continent in 1803 seeking, among other ends, meteorological data, he also kept his own incredibly detailed figures that are beyond what any explorer might accomplish. A sample, for instance, from his *Garden Book* reads: "Of the three thousand nine hundred and five observations made in the course of seven years, two thousand seven hundred and seventy six were fair; by which I mean that the quarter part of the sky was unclouded. This shows our proportion of fair weather to be as two thousand seven hundred and seventy six to one thousand one hundred and twenty nine, or as five to two, equivalent to five fair days to the week."[12] This statement was a condensation of his figures and tables from only 1810–1816. He maintained the *Garden Book,* though irregularly at times, for almost sixty years. These data were not experimental only but also practical, for they supplied useful knowledge to Jefferson the farmer.

He was also enthusiastic about all sorts of technological advances, or inventions, which appeared during his lifetime. While in France, he described and sketched the new "science" of ballooning (he apparently never went up himself). He also heralded the new screw, or water propeller, he saw in France: "There is lately a simple invention in mechanics here which may be of some use. It is nothing more than the application of the screw to the air, water or any other fluid." When he saw it work on boats, he thought that it might be applied to balloons, submarines, and other vessels; and he suspected that the French had struck upon a device that had been employed earlier on David Bushnell's "Connecticut turtle" (it had indeed been used in that prototype submarine).[13]

He complimented Eli Whitney upon his patenting the cotton gin. Jefferson little realized, of course, how this invention would reinvigorate the then decaying institution of slavery (nor did Whitney). As Secretary of State, an office which at the time included the duties of what is now the Secretary of Interior, he wrote to Whitney in 1793, "I feel a considerable interest in the success of your invention, for family use."[14] The new machine would be a boon, he felt, to every farmer who attempted self-sufficiency, for any family could then easily produce its own clothing. The gin was, in Jefferson's mind, a democratic invention, a kind of equalizer that would actually help prevent large scale manufacturing. Moreover, he always looked upon science and technology as benign influences in human life — as evidences of progress in the pursuit of happiness. His own plantation experience might have caused him to realize, however, how such a device would inevitably lead to cotton farming on a huge scale and how slave labor would increasingly be needed, to feed the maw of the machine.

One more technological breakthrough Jefferson greatly admired was the application of the concept of interchangeable parts for manufactured guns (and clocks as well; Whitney and Seth Thomas were also among those who exploited this idea in America). Although Jefferson celebrated such discoveries that would lead to the betterment, or happiness, of humanity,[15] ironically, he may also have helped erect the false god, Technology, for Americans to worship.[16]

II *Labor in the Earth*

Jefferson's most precious object in the field of "mechanics" was an invention, or development, all his own, his moldboard plow, which was applicable to his real love, farming. He was a pioneer in soil conservation, in contour plowing, in crop rotation, in animal husbandry, and in other agricultural areas.[17] He loved to philosophize about the cultivation of the earth, the pursuit or calling of the farmer: "Those who labour in the earth are the chosen people of God, if ever he had a chosen people, whose breasts he has made his peculiar deposit for substantial and genuine virtue. It is the focus in which he keeps alive that sacred fire, which otherwise might escape from the face of the earth. Corruption of morals in the mass of cultivators is a phaenomenon of which no age nor nation has furnished an example." And again: "Cultivators of the earth are the most valuable citizens. They are the most vigorous, the most independant, the most virtuous." "The earth is given as a common stock for man to labour and live on. . . . The small landholders are the most precious part of a state."[18]

These statements became the foundation of Jefferson's continuing reputation as an "agrarian." He clearly felt that the closer people were to nature, the freer they were. They could lead more "natural" lives (without factory made, artificial goods; without having modes of behavior, such as etiquette, forced upon them). They could, perhaps, experience more directly what the full possession of natural rights feels like. Apparently, they might also feel closer to their God, the source of those rights. Even moral problems would be fewer and simpler on small farms because of a lifestyle in which considerable labor would occupy much of their time. Work would become something of an end in itself, more redemptive, actually, than simply a means to material ends.

These views, it must be remembered, originated in the mind of a person himself not a small farmer, but very sophisticated, practiced in all the ways of courts and cities, and who, rather than himself laboring in the earth, allowed captive Blacks, working out their fates on his vast land holdings, to do so. Jefferson spoke in this mode for his countrymen, not for himself (though he liked to think that, at Monticello, he had grasped the essence of his theory through his personal experience). He helped to create an American mythos. By singing of the American farmer in his *Notes on the State of Virginia,* and elsewhere, he became instrumental in establishing a mystique of the independent, industrious tiller of the soil which would survive well into the twentieth century.

This philosophy — or poetry —[19] about farming, however, never carried Jefferson away from the practical concerns of cultivation. And in no way did he contribute more to the American farmer than in his creation of the moldboard plow, or *"mould board of least resistance,"*[20] as he styled it. "An experience of five years," he wrote in 1798, "has enabled me to say, it answers in practice to what it promises in theory. The Mouldboard should be a continuation of the wing of the ploughshare, beginning at it's hinder edge, & in the same plane. it's first office is to receive the sod horizontally from the wing, to raise it to a proper height for being turned over, & to make, in it's progress, the *least resistance possible;* & consequently to require a minimum in the moving power."

Since Jefferson's plow went deeper into the ground and turned the sod over better than any previous device, it set a new standard and worked a little revolution in tilling the land.[21] His first important biographer, Henry S. Randall, writing in 1858, was much closer to the impact of the plow than twentieth-century readers who know farming only in terms of advanced mechanization. The plow, Randall said, "ranks its author among those practical benefactors of their species . . . who have lightened the labors, and added to the enjoyments of the toiling masses of mankind."[22] For Jefferson, cooperating with nature was a matter of philosophical principle and of practical necessity. Certainly, for him, the pursuit of scientific and agricultural experimentation naturally paralleled the American political experiment. To Jefferson, farming was also the pursuit of happiness.

CHAPTER 7

Fix Reason Firmly

I *The Things which Are*

FARMING did not always bring Thomas Jefferson serenity, for he experienced, after all, such things as crop failures and market recessions. Monticello was lovely, but it was no Eden. Another retreat, an intellectual one, was required to complement the sense of intermittent beauty presented by nature. This need made Jefferson a philosopher, a contemplative person who cultivated the life of the mind. As in most other areas of thought and action, in philosophy Jefferson, who manifested a basic pragmatism, generally avoided abstract speculation. He relied on common sense, the only dependable foundation of all philosophy.[1]

Noah Webster's earliest dictionary (1806) gave a meaning to "common sense" that Jefferson would have found quite satisfactory: "Common, ... equal.... Sense, ... a faculty of perceiving." The attribute of common sense was possessed by all persons. Everyone shared in the ability to perceive, through the five senses, the phenomena that composed the knowable world. Naturally, the data available — what there *was* to be perceived or learned — were equally there for all persons to perceive. Therefore, a truth not potentially available to all was no truth. All of this was another meaning behind Jefferson's phrase, "all men are created equal."

This was not to say, however, that all humans would reason alike from the same data, or that all were equal intellectually. The inferences drawn by the rational process, from the data, would differ; but the *given* was always the same. Reason to Jefferson and his time was the darling human attribute. Individual judgment which remained true to the peculiarly human characteristic of reason, affirming only experiential knowledge, was the key to wisdom. Only certain *a priori* truths seemed exceptions to the empirical foundation, but even these were a matter of experience, of individually perceived, inborn knowledge.

"Fix reason firmly in her seat," Jefferson admonished a young correspondent, "and call to her tribunal every fact, every opinion. Question with boldness even the existence of a god.... Your own reason is the only oracle given you by heaven."[2] He was never more sincere than in this great passage, one which has been often quoted by both his defenders and his attackers. Not without pride he added, "I never submitted the whole system of my opinions to the creed of any party of men whatever in religion, in philosophy, in politics, or in any thing else where I was capable of thinking for myself. Such an addiction is the last degradation of a free moral agent."[3] In this respect, Jefferson succinctly anticipated what Ralph Waldo Emerson, in 1841, would call "Self-Reliance." Although Jefferson's reference to the individual human as "a free moral agent" further revealed his philosophic seriousness, he considered pursuit of truth, as well as that of happiness, a high moral obligation.
asserted. This victory would come about through "her natural weapons, free argument and debate"; "Reason and free inquiry are the only effectual agents against error"; "the sufficiency of human reason for the care of human affairs" was scarcely to be doubted.[4] Furthermore, there was an inborn, natural moral sense common to all persons; for Jefferson considered knowledge of right and wrong to be a birthright. "He who made us would have been a pitiful bungler if he had made the rules of our moral conduct a matter of science." To Jefferson, morality was not merely a matter of empirical observation, and it was certainly not a realm suitable for experimentation. The moral sense "is as much a part of [humanity's] nature as the sense of hearing, seeing, feeling.... It is given to all human beings in a stronger or weaker degree. It may be strengthened by exercise." Even "Questions of natural right are triable by their conformity with the moral sense & reason of man." Such was the "common sense" of philosophy; these were "the common feelings of human nature."[5] In letters and other written or spoken communications during his mature years, Jefferson philosophized thusly. These statements, and over the decades many like them, formed a perennial, personal declaration of ethical independence.

The highest ethical quest for Jefferson was, of course, happiness. In this ideal, he was profoundly influenced by the ancient thinkers,

Epicurus and Lucretius; and he felt that Epicurus was the greatest of the ancient philosophers. "I . . . am an Epicurean," he said; and he formulated his own "Syllabus of the doctrines of Epicurus," the culmination of which was "Happiness the aim of life." He owned seven copies of Lucretius' *De rerum natura,* the great Roman poetic exposition of Epicureanism,[6] and it was not his habit to collect books which he left unread. The realism or materialism of these philosophers greatly appealed to Jefferson, for their position was a far cry from the dominant Platonic influence in western philosophy, which he hated. Jefferson once called Plato's *Republic* "the heaviest task-work I ever went through." It was, he told John Adams, full of "whimsies . . . puerilities, and unintelligible jargon . . . nonsense . . . sophisms, futilities and incomprehensibilities." He was disgusted with Plato's "foggy mind."[7]

When again writing to Adams as late as 1820, Jefferson gave this long exposition of his version of Epicurean realism:

> 'I feel, therefore I exist.' I feel bodies which are not myself: there are other existences then. I call them *matter.* I feel them changing place. This gives me *motion.* Where there is an absence of matter, I call it *void,* or *nothing,* or *immaterial* space. On the basis of sensation, of matter and motion, we may erect the fabric of all the certainties we can have or need. I can conceive *thought* to be an action of a particular organization of matter, formed for that purpose by its Creator, as well as that *attraction* is an action of matter. . . . When once we quit the basis of sensation, all is in the wind. To talk of *immaterial* existences, is to talk of *nothings,*

and even God and soul would become "nothings." This equality-of-perception faculty was a common sense view of the reality which surrounds humanity. Jefferson's straightforward reasoning and exposition of ideas was unflinching and serene in its radical simplicity.

Jefferson also explained the benefit of his common sense philosophy:

> Rejecting all organs of information, therefore, but my senses, I rid myself of the pyrrhonisms with which an indulgence in speculations hyperphysical and antiphysical, so uselessly occupy and disquiet the mind. A single sense may indeed be sometimes deceived, but rarely; and never all our senses together, with their faculty of reasoning. They evidence realities, and there are enough of these for all the purposes of life, without plunging into the fathomless abyss of dreams and phantasms. I am satisfied, and

sufficiently occupied with the things which are, without tormenting or troubling myself about those which may indeed be, but of which I have no evidence.[8]

No more cogent or concise philosophic statement from the Age of Reason, from the voice of common sense, from those who believed in an innate moral sense, or from a "modernized" Epicurean philosophy may exist than the grouping of statements in these few passages from the pen of Thomas Jefferson. Through this simple philosophy he pursued happiness all his adult life — and achieved a larger share of it than most.

II *One Only God*

There has been considerable disagreement concerning the religious beliefs of Thomas Jefferson. Early in his political life — up to the time of his first presidency — he was attacked from paper and pulpit as either an atheist or an infidel.[9] His early biographers, who were usually defensive, tried to present their subject as the orthodox Christian he had been reared. In 1839, William Linn wrote:

A few words respecting the religious opinions of Mr. Jefferson, and we close the volume. He has been represented as it suited party rancour: at one time, as the athcistical desparado, warring against the God of heaven; at another, as the ribald scoffer, throwing malignant sneers upon the declarations of His word. But he was far, very far, from being either of these. However opposed Mr. Jefferson may have been to what he considered the corruptions or abuses of Christianity, yet to the spirit and precepts of the gospel he was strongly attached; and of the character of our Saviour he was a warm and professed admirer.

Henry S. Randall, in the first major biography (1858, three volumes), established Jefferson's early religious education as Episcopalian, or Anglican. He then painted his subject as a fairly regular churchgoer and as a quite faithful Episcopalian.[10] Later commentators insisted, however, that although Jefferson early sloughed off his Episcopal heritage, he did not thereby become an atheist. Other writers merely hedged their bets, as did Charles A. Goodrich in 1833: "Of his peculiar opinions on religious subjects, we are designedly silent. In respect to these, the best and wisest of his countrymen have entertained very different sentiments. At a future day, it will be easier to decide in respect to their true character and tendency."[11]

One thing has become clear about Jefferson and religion: freedom of religion was among "the natural rights of mankind." Furthermore, religious toleration was for him a fundamental principle of a democratic society.[12] These beliefs led Jefferson to what he considered to be one of the finest accomplishments of his life, "A Bill for Establishing Religious Freedom" that he presented in Virginia in 1779, and that was adopted in 1786.[13] He had begun thinking and agitating about religious freedom even earlier, and independence made it obvious to him that freedom of conscience had to be made manifest in America. Such freedom was essential to the happiness of the people, and such liberty was a capstone of the new political structure.

In his first draft of a new Virginia constitution, Jefferson had written that "All persons shall have full & free liberty of religious opinion, nor shall any be compelled to frequent or maintain any religious service or institution."[14] This statement was intended to separate the established (Episcopal) church from the state government. If colonial status permitted an established church after the pattern of England's, statehood certainly did not. To require people to contribute money to maintain any church was to penalize dissenters needlessly, thereby depriving them of a natural right. Such a requirement was a form of intolerance amounting to tyranny, and "Rebellion to tyrants is obedience to God," as Jefferson worded his personal motto in 1776.[15]

When Jefferson introduced a resolution in the Virginia House of Delegates for the disestablishment of the Church of England, he asserted that "no pre-eminence may be allowed to any one Religious sect over another."[16] In the "Bill for Establishing Religious Freedom," he presented these ringing phrases: "Almighty God hath created the mind free.... our civil rights have no dependance on our religious opinions.... all men shall be free to profess, and by argument to maintain their opinions in matters of religion." This in effect was a bill of liberation, for it freed opinion and practice and went beyond simply ending the state-church connection. It also permitted refusal, on grounds of conscience, to take prescribed oaths; and it permitted a citizen to substitute a personal pledge upon entering public office or upon giving testimony.[17] In these respects, Jefferson was once more the radical, opting for a measure far ahead of its time.

Jefferson believed, then, in an *a priori* truth which he spoke of as "the Moral law to which Man has been subjected by his creator, & of which his feelings, or Conscience as it is sometimes called, are the evidence with which his creator has furnished him."[18] When any force attempting to control the individual conscience arose, he was ready to fight. His favorite adversary was organized Christianity, which he felt in one form or another throughout colonial America had long attempted such unnatural control. In the new United States, freedom of religion was realized, because Jefferson had led the way.

In 1808 President Jefferson refused to declare a national day of fasting and prayer, saying that the Constitution gave him no such power.[19] It was also the kind of pseudoreligious trapping for which he had little tolerance. In 1789 he spoke of a "demonism" within Christianity, "in the being worshipped by many who think themselves Christians." In the same year he wrote to Deist Thomas Paine — a very sympathetic correspondent — of "the rags in which religion robes the true god."[20] His favorite topic for radical assessment was Jesus Christ, with whom he sympathized as a most abused figure.

"According to the ordinary fate of those who attempt to enlighten and reform mankind, [Jesus] fell," thought Jefferson, "an early victim to the jealousy & combination of the altar and the throne." His teachings had been "disfigured by the corruptions of schismatising followers, who . . . found an interest in sophisticating & perverting the simple doctrines he taught by engrafting on them the mysticisms of a Grecian sophist [Plato], frittering them into subtleties, & obscuring them with jargon." To Jefferson, Jesus' great contribution was teaching a brotherhood that "the philosophers" of old and "the Jews" had not.[21]

Ever the anticleric, Jefferson also said, "The clergy, by getting themselves established by law, & ingrafted into the machine of government, have been a very formidable engine against the civil and religious rights of man." "History, I believe, furnishes no example of a priest-ridden [here he meant "clergy-ridden"] people maintaining a free civil government." In 1814, when he complained to Adams of an "artificial Christianity," he observed that this religion was one perpetually infested with Platonism: "The Christian priesthood, finding the doctrines of Christ levelled to every understanding, and too plain to need explanation, saw in the mysticism of Plato [he later added Aristotle] materials with which they might build up an artificial system" and keep themselves in power.[22] To Jefferson, the clergy were an unfairly privileged and artificially powerful class, and this station was undemocratic.

He also wrote to Adams in 1813:

> It is too late in the day for men of sincerity to pretend they believe in the Platonic mysticisms that three are one, and one is three; and yet that the one is not three, and the three are not one.... But this constitutes the craft, the power and the profit of the priests. Sweep away their gossamer fabrics of factitious religion, and they would catch no more flies. We should all then, like the Quakers, live without an order of priests, moralize for ourselves, follow the oracle of conscience, and say nothing about what no man can understand, nor therefore believe.[23]

This sharp attack on the doctrine of the Trinity is quite typical of Jefferson, who found no way to resolve such a theological paradox in his own mind.

A number of other aspects of Christian theology he likewise found unbelievable. Among them, he listed "The immaculate conception of Jesus, his deification, the creation of the world by him, his miraculous powers, his resurrection and visible ascension, his corporeal presence in the Eucharist, the Trinity; original sin, atonement, regeneration, election, orders of Hierarchy, &c." He seems particularly rough in this passage on Roman Catholic theology (up to the semi-colon in the quotation) and then also Calvinist theology (he once referred to "the maniac ravings of Calvin").[24] Such concepts defied common sense, according to Jefferson; and he felt that acceptance of them could only rest on the rejection of human reason. They were merely superstitions.

His faith in the empirical method — science — rendered it as impossible, for example, to believe in transubstantiation as to believe in an alchemical changing of lead into gold. Since no amount of experimentation could establish the validity of such a belief, Roman Catholicism fell short of favor with Jefferson. As to Calvinism, he was sure that no admirer of democracy, which was based on the trustworthiness of the common citizen, could believe that all persons were born evil, possessed of an inborn ("original") sinfulness. Finally, his own personal experience offered no indication to him that any one of these concepts was reasonable.

In 1803, Jefferson shared such ideas with the illustrious Dr. Benjamin Rush: "They are," he wrote, "the result of a life of inquiry & reflection, and very different from that antiChristian system imputed to me by those who know nothing of my opinions. To the corruptions of Christianity I am indeed opposed; but not to the genuine precepts of Jesus himself. I am a Christian, in the only sense he wished any one to be; sincerely attached to his doctrines, in preference to all others; ascribing to himself every *human* excellence; & believing he never claimed any other."[25]

Of course, in Jefferson's lifetime, his opinions like the ones expressed to Dr. Rush were scarcely known to the public. Aside from a few "leaks" to newspapers, they were contained only in letters to friends. He firmly believed that his religious views were private, and that the general public had no right to know them, or to test him by them. He never pried into others' religious beliefs, and he carefully protected his own. All this was for him a precious part of the freedom of religion. Since his time, however, there has come to light a remarkable document which has helped to show how Jefferson could say of himself, "I am a *real Christian*." It has become known as *The Jefferson Bible.*[26]

The *Bible,* dated 1804–1819, was titled "The Life and Morals of Jesus of Nazareth, extracted textually from the Gospels in Greek, Latin, French & English." What Jefferson did was to cut up a number of actual copies of the New Testament — the four Gospels — paste them into his own arrangement, and then have them bound into a book which he carefully preserved. Why he pasted the parallel texts on facing pages in four languages is not clear, but a reading of the English selections does clarify Jefferson's notion of a Christian morality he insisted he subscribed to so fondly. In 1771, he had listed, among other books, the traditional Bible under a category of knowledge he called "History. Antient." Later, in 1824, he asserted that The Sermon on the Mount was all that was needed for brotherhood.[27] But he sought in his *Bible* to rid scripture of the additions of other men, and prune it down to the sayings of Jesus alone. Naturally, Jefferson relied on his own judgment in determining which passages were authentically Christ's.

> I have made a wee-little book, [he said] which I call the Philosophy of Jesus. It is a paradigma of his doctrines, made by cutting the texts out of the book and arranging them on the pages of a blank book, in a certain order of time or subject. A more beautiful or precious morsel of ethics I have never seen; it is a document in proof that I am a real Christian, that is to say, a disciple of the doctrines of Jesus, very different from the Pla-

tonists, who call me infidel and themselves Christians and preachers of the gospel, while they draw all their characteristic dogmas from what its author never said or saw.

He had been engaged, he maintained in "extracting the pure principles which [Jesus] taught," discovering "the matter which is evidently his, and which is as easily distinguishable as diamonds in a dunghill."[28] It is interesting to note, then, that Jefferson's method was the opposite of the standard mode of theological exegesis, which expands upon the text. Paring and gleaning, Jefferson applied "Occam's razor" to save only the kernels of Christian thought.

In further explanation Jefferson later noted,

We find in the writings of his [Christ's] biographers [those who indited the Gospels] matter of two distinct descriptions. First, a ground-work of vulgar ignorance, of things impossible, of superstitions, fanaticisms and fabrications. Intermixed with these, again, are sublime ideas of the Supreme Being, aphorisms, and precepts of the purest morality and benevolence, sanctioned by a life of humility, innocence and simplicity of manners, neglect of riches, absence of worldly ambition and honors, with an eloquence and persuasiveness which have not been surpassed. These could not be inventions of the grovelling authors who relate them. They are far beyond the powers of their feeble minds. They show that there was a character, the subject of their history, whose splendid conceptions were above all suspicion of being interpolations from their hands. Can we be at a loss in separating such materials and ascribing each to its genuine author? The difference is obvious to the eye and to the understanding.[29]

Although many other such statements appeared in the letters of Thomas Jefferson,[30] he was never more succinct than in this brief condensation of the Gospels from the 160-odd pages of his *Bible.* "The doctrines of Jesus are simple and tend all to the happiness of man: 1. That there is one only God and he all perfect. 2. That there is a future state of rewards and punishments. 3. That to love God with all thy heart and thy neighbor as thyself, is the sum of religion."[31]

In his *Bible,* Jefferson mixed Matthew, Mark, Luke, and John as it suited him; for he followed no traditional sequence. He began with Luke 2.1, "And it came to pass in those days." But nowhere was the Christmas story represented — no immaculate conception, no star in the East or wisemen, no virgin birth. There were to be no angelic voices or appearances, no temptations of Jesus, and certainly no miraculous healings by the Lord. Finally, he omitted the injunction to perpetuate the Last Supper, and of course the Resurrection was left out. He diligently tried to establish the chronology of Jesus' life, to retain only biographical "facts" (those elements he found credible, natural), and to clarify the development of Christ's teachings.

Jefferson obviously liked certain of Jesus' maxims or phrases: "The sabbath was made for man, and not man for the sabbath" (Mark 2.27); "Neither do men light a candle, and put it under a bushel, but on a candlestick; and it giveth light unto all that are in the house" (Matthew 5.15 was the probable source of Jefferson's own candle imagery); "Lay not up for yourselves treasures upon earth" (Matthew 6.19); "For by thy words thou shalt be justified and by thy words thou shalt be condemned" (Matthew 12.37).

The builder of Monticello must have especially appreciated, "Therefore whosoever heareth these sayings of mine, and doeth them, I will liken him unto a wise man, which built his house upon a rock: And the rain descended, and the floods came, and the winds blew, and beat upon that house; and it fell not; for it was founded upon a rock" (Matthew 7.24–25). Another favorite of the longtime, gifted public servant was, "For unto whomsoever much is given, of him shall be much required: and to whom men have committed much, of him they will ask the more" (Luke 12.48).

The democratic Jefferson may also have been particularly fond of, "But when he saw the multitudes, he was moved with compassion on them" (Matthew 9.36); "He that is without sin among you, let him first cast a stone at her" (John 8.7); and "God is not the God of the dead, but of the living" (Matthew 22.32). Most certainly he would have appreciated the sentiment, "The Lord our God is one Lord" (Mark 12.29), for Jefferson was a great admirer of the Unitarian movement.[32] His *Bible* project had led him finally to a complete repudiation of the doctrine of the Trinity. Jesus was to him, then, a great person and a profound teacher, but not god. To Jefferson, deity was unity.

Even the term "Deism" had long meant to Jefferson simply "the belief of one only God."[33] In a letter of 1788 he declined to become a godfather for an acquaintance's child, saying that, as for "faith" in the articles of the Church, "I had never sense enough to comprehend" them. "The difficulty of reconciling the ideas of Unity and Trinity, have, from a very early part of my life, excluded me from the office of sponsorship."[34] To Joseph Priestley, the great Unitarian leader, he wrote in 1801 of "the Christian philosophy, — the most sublime & benevolent, but most perverted system that ever shone on man."[35] The chief "perversion" was, for Jefferson, the doctrine of the Trinity.

Late in his life, a number of Unitarian sentiments appeared in his letters (at times, he meant the Unitarian sect; at times, he simply meant a theistic belief in one God, not a god of three persons). "I confidently expect that the present generation will see Unitarianism become the general religion of the United States." In the same year, 1822, he believed that "the genuine doctrine of one only God is reviving, and I trust," he concluded, "that there is not a *young man* now living in the United States who will not die an Unitarian."[36] He was wrong, of course; he was an old man clinging to a personal version of an ethical Christianity based on common sense and reason. Perhaps at times he felt that neither quality abounded in humankind to the extent that he had hoped. Yet any disappointments he had over human nature could not have been bitter. He had many consolations, and enough esthetic pursuits, along with those which were agricultural and philosophic, to bring him a certain beautiful vision of happiness.

CHAPTER 8

What We Call Beautiful

I *The Favorite Passion of a Soul*

IN 1783, when the College of William and Mary awarded Thomas Jefferson an honorary doctorate "in the civil law," "all the fine arts seem to foregather in one man."[1] The award honored him as the author of the *Declaration of Independence* and for his political work in Virginia; but the part of the charge concerning the fine arts was entirely true. The college was early in its recognition of Jefferson's esthetic dimension, for his full blossoming in the arts was still to occur. All his life, though, his sense of beauty was keen. It was a sense he believed to be inborn, a part — in one degree or another — within all members of the common human heritage. As he expressed it, "We have indeed an innate sense of what we call beautiful . . . exercised chiefly on subjects addressed to the fancy, whether through the eye in visible forms, as landscape, animal figure, dress, drapery, architecture, the composition of colors, etc., or to the imagination directly, as imagery, style, or measure in prose or poetry."[2]

Jefferson considered art to be a liberating influence, one leading to increased happiness. He began to bridge the great shift in the arts during his lifetime from neoClassical to Romantic,[3] and in this way was a "modern." He made art a daily part of his life, as he hoped all Americans would; for he carefully ordered a stock of books in the fine arts for the library of the university.[4] He loved to talk in terms of the eighteenth-century notion of the "sublime," by which he sometimes simply meant the "beautiful." A typical, contemporaneous characterization by Hugh Blair, a philosopher of the Scottish Common Sense School, of the sublime was:

It is not easy to describe, in words, the precise impression which great and sublime objects make upon us when we behold them, but every one has a conception of it. It produces a sort of internal elevation and expansion; it raises the mind much above its ordinary state; and fills it with a degree of wonder and astonishment, which it cannot well express. The emotion is certainly delightful; but it is altogether of the serious kind; a degree of awfulness [awesomeness] and solemnity, even approaching to severity, commonly attends it when at its height. . . ."[5]

A sense of the sublime could come from storms, mountains, great waterfalls; from architecture; from painting; from poetry; and, of course, from music. Among the arts other than architecture, music was Jefferson's favorite; it was, he said in 1778, "the favorite passion of my soul, and fortune has cast my lot in a country [Virginia] where it is in a state of deplorable barbarism." He then speculated as to whether workers emigrating to America would bring musical skills with them. If they did, he could employ them, at the same time, not only as gardeners and otherwise as artisans but as musicians. He wanted to form a band of players on the "French horn, clarionet, or hautboy and bassoon,"[6] but this scheme was never fulfilled. Although some of the slaves at Monticello frequently performed musically, their talent was for Jefferson not sufficient, for "The instrument proper to them is the Banjar, which they brought hither from Africa, and which is the original of the guitar, its chords being precisely the four lower chords of the guitar."[7]

The musical interests of the Master of Monticello were wide ranging, but his tastes in serious music centered on the European heritage. He knew, though, that musical appreciation was experiential — music was a *personal* passion with him. Music could create a "delerium both of the player and hearer" he said, quite Romantically.[8] In 1789, he wrote from Paris to the American composer Francis Hopkinson to thank him for "the book of songs," *Seven Songs for Harpsichord or Forte Piano,* the latter had sent, which was dedicated to Washington: "I will not tell you how much they have pleased us, nor how well the last of them merits praise for its pathos, but relate a fact only, which is, that while my elder daughter was playing it on the harpsichord, I happened to look towards the fire, and saw the younger one all in tears. I asked her if she was sick? She said 'no; but the tune was so mournful.' "[9] Jefferson always made sure his family was provided with musical instruments and scores so that he could frequently share with them such precious experiences.

While overseas and at Monticello, Jefferson owned several musical instruments during his lifetime; and he frequently attended musical performances of all kinds.[10] He was also a performer himself; he owned harpsichords, pianos, and violins; and he knew how to tune and maintain them.[11] As a musician, he was a violinist of some talent, at least during the first half of his life when he took professional lessons.[12] He was often heard singing in "a fine clear voice"[13] as he walked or rode on horseback around the grounds at Monticello. He experimented with and improved upon the new metronome he found in France, and he designed a convenient music stand for as many as five musicians to gather around.[14]

In addition to these accomplishments, Jefferson collected a large musical library consisting of books on music and many dozens of scores. Most of it was secular music, ranging from symphonies to ballad operas, written by a variety of composers.[15] Jefferson did not speculate on the theory or nature of music. As usual he avoided abstractions, fastening his attention on performance and attendance, or on the immediate experience. He summed up his position in 1818: "Music is invaluable where a person has an ear. Where they have not, it should not be attempted. It furnishes a delightful recreation for the hours of respite from the cares of the day, and lasts us through life."[16] He himself certainly had "an ear," and in an age and place that provided him little access to the concert hall, he yet managed to make music an important part of his milieu.

II *Canons of Criticism*

On the subject of literature, Jefferson had a bit more to say, both in the role of reader and as a theorizer, or moralist. "No republic is more real than that of letters," he told Noah Webster in 1790. But such a metaphor by 1816 gave way to a statement that based his esthetic position entirely upon personal experience: "I have always very much dispised the artificial canons of criticism. When I have read a work in prose or poetry, or seen a painting, a statue, etc., I have only asked myself whether it gives me pleasure, whether it is animating, interesting, attaching? If it is, it is good for these reasons."[17] His early list of readings recommended for a gentleman's education had as its largest category, by far, books about the "Fine Arts." These included works in gardening and painting and many volumes of fiction, poetry, plays, and essays. "Criticism on the Fine Arts," that area of thought which drew his skepticism, listed the common sense writers chiefly, with a few others.[18] Literature and life were to be constantly intermixed in the life-long process of self-education.

In the same letter of 1771, he described a real life scene much like the fictional one that later appeared in Charles Brockden Brown's early American novel *Wieland* (1798). People of sensibility should have a retreat for "the scene of every evening's joy. . . . There we should talk over the lessons of the day, or lose them in Musick, Chess, or the merriments of our family companions."[19] In fact, Jefferson would have delighted in fiction that resembled life, for he felt it could have no other justification. To him, the fiction that lacked verisimilitude was socially and morally dangerous.[20]

He liked such stories as "Gil Blas" and "Don Quichotte," he said, and also the works of Laurence Sterne.[21] His early opinions gave fiction a high position in his reading, along with the "learned lumber" of the Classics. "The entertainments of fiction," he wrote, "are useful as well as pleasant," for "every thing is useful which contributes to fix us in the principles and practice of virtue." People tended to imitate, Jefferson felt, the fictional good deeds they read about or witnessed on the stage; and they also conceived "an abhorrence of vice" that was presented to them in novels or dramas. This moralistic pragmatism was the standard line of defense for fiction, one often employed by its writers themselves, in the eighteenth century. But Jefferson would have been naive to have used it without qualification.

Upon the publication of *Wieland,* Charles Brockden Brown proudly sent Jefferson a copy of the novel, and said to him that he hoped "an artful display of incidents, the powerful delineation of characters and the train of eloquent and judicious reasoning which may be combined in a fictitious work, will be regarded by Thomas Jefferson with as much respect as they are regarded by me." In reply, Jefferson promised to read the book, and he added: "Some of the most agreeable moments of my life have been spent in reading works of imagination, which have this advantage over history, that the incidents of the former may be dressed in the most interesting form, while those of the latter must be confined to fact. They cannot therefore possess virtue in the best and vice in the worst forms possible, as the former may." "We never reflect," he said at another time, "whether the story we read be truth or fiction. If the painting be lively [lifelike], and a tolerable picture of nature, we are thrown into a reverie, from which if we awaken it is the fault of the writer." For the "reader of feeling and sentiment" — the sensitive person — great deeds are sublime: they "elevate his sentiments."[22] This statement, his key point, qualified his moralistic stance with an esthetic measure — good deeds, in their sublimity, raised and inspired; bad deeds did no such thing. Instead, such bad deeds caused aversion from imitation of those deeds. Literature and life were neatly linked in his mind.

Nevertheless, with maturity and after long reflection, Jefferson modified his thinking about fiction. He wrote in 1818:

> A great obstacle to good education is the inordinate passion prevalent for novels, and the time lost in that reading which should be instructively employed. When this poison infects the mind, it destroys its tone and revolts it against wholesome reading. Reason and fact, plain and unadorned, are rejected. . . . The result is a bloated imagination, sickly judgment, and disgust towards all the real businesses of life. This mass of trash, however, is not without some distinction...

for a novel modeled "on the incidents of real life" could promote "a sound morality."[23] To Jefferson, a "true" novel could still advance true morality; the fantastic novel — he probably had in mind the Gothic novel — corrupted, for it lied about life. This view was the common sense of the matter to Jefferson, and the backward pull of the Age of Reason was very strong on him regarding fiction.

When Jefferson considered poetry, he was more progressive; he enjoyed verse with Romantic elements, as well as older modes. The neoClassical poetry of Phillis Wheatley, in fact, he rudely rejected: "The compositions published under her name are below the dignity of criticism."[24] Yet he eagerly received the works of her contemporaries, David Humphreys (he was a subscriber to *The Miscellaneous Works of David Humphreys,* 1804), John Trumbull, and Joel Barlow. He admired their poetry even though, as "Connecticut Wits," Humphreys and Trumbull were members of his political opposition. Barlow, of course, an apostate from the Federalist Wits, eventually became a true Jeffersonian and close friend of the third President.

Jefferson knew well the works of the transitional poet Philip Freneau. He called Freneau, who led the way in America from eighteenth-century traditionalism into Romanticism, "a man of genius."[25] If Jefferson never appreciated the major British Romantics such as Byron and Wordsworth, as Randall maintains, he nonetheless "was fond of . . . nearly all the Scotch song writers, and of both the lyrical and pastoral ballads of every land. This showed that he loved *poetry.*"[26] It may well have been that, as was the case with English architecture, he was less than enthusiastic about "modern" English verse partly *because* it was English. Conversely, he may have collected a certain amount of American poetry simply on nationalistic grounds.

Unfortunately, the poetry Jefferson was most taken with — or taken in by — was the work of the great bard "Ossian." "These peices," he wrote too hastily in 1773, "have been, and will I think during my life continue to be to me, the source of daily and exalted pleasure. The tender, and the sublime emotions of the mind were never before so finely wrought.... I am not ashamed to own that I think this rude bard of the North the greatest Poet that has ever existed." He even wanted to learn the language of "Ossian" to be able to read such verse in the original, rather than in Macpherson's "translation."[27] Jefferson, like many others in his day, was completely fooled by the "false sublime" (faked emotion or elevation) of Charles Macpherson's literary hoax. "Ossian" was a figment of the "translator's" imagination, a famous fraud. The poetry, a delight to read, was scarcely great literature. Jefferson's personal-experience standard betrayed him where a more objective set of criteria of literary judgment might have served him better. One aspect, however, of his standard was perfectly sound: he unflinchingly accepted a contemporary poet's works on what he thought was its own merit rather than waiting conservatively for the test of time to "reveal" them. His comparatively liberated critical mind led him at times into error, just as his experimental mind in the sciences did; but he was admirably independent.

Jefferson's critical judgment was sounder when, upon receipt of her *Poems, Dramatic and Miscellaneous,* in 1790 he applauded the work of Mercy Warren: "it will soothe some of my moments of rest from drudgery, and will add another illustrious name to the roll of female worthies, made for the ornament as well as vindication of their sex." In 1823 he was pleased to say that "Miss [Fanny] Wright had before favored me with the first edition of her American work; but her 'Few days in Athens,' was entirely new, and has been a treat to me of the highest order.... and may we not hope more from the same pen?"[28] Her Romantic liberalism, her feminism, and her anti-slavery position all intrigued Jefferson. She must have appeared to him as the representative of a new, hopeful generation that was coming upon the scene.

Even after considering all these reactions relative to poetry, Jefferson's truest opinion was best expressed in a letter of 1801: "of all men living I am the last who should undertake to decide as to the merits of poetry. In earlier life I was fond of it, and easily pleased. But as age and cares advanced the powers of fancy have declined. Every year seems to have plucked a feather from her wings till she can no longer waft one to those sublime heights to which it is necessary to accompany the poet."[29] This is a most poetic and humble disclaimer from an essentially unpoetic but not unfeeling person.

III *A Most Lovely Mixture*

As music ornaments the emotions, and literature, at its best, adorns the mind and morals, so painting, sculpture, and gardens decorated everyday life at Monticello. In regard to the gardens, Jefferson was a doer, or at least a director of activity; but, relative to sculpture and paintings, he was a collector and an occasional commentator. His sojourn in France heightened his appreciation of all the arts: "Were I to proceed to tell you how much I enjoy their architecture, sculpture, painting, music, I should want words."[30] It was especially during the years in France that he became a collector of paintings and sculptures, as well as of many books on those subjects. That most of the paintings were copies, not the original masterworks, was not evidence of poor taste on Jefferson's part, but merely reflected the way collecting was done then, especially by those who were not wealthy.[31]

Jefferson acquired paintings of various Christian scenes, presumably for their esthetic appeal, not for their religious associations. He had portraits of Americus Vespucius, Columbus, and other explorers. There were a few landscapes and still life paintings.[32] But he primarily liked to collect portraits of American heroes, and this collection included likenesses of the Marquis de Lafayette, John Adams, Thomas Paine, Benjamin Franklin, James Madison and, of course, George Washington. "I have two pictures of Genl. Washington," he proudly wrote in 1785, "the one a whole length by Peale taken at the beginning of the war; the other a half length taken by [Joseph] Wright the last year. The first is better coloured, more softly painted, more flattering, but less like. The last is dryer, however, but more like. The painter has seised the gravest lineaments from the General's face. . . . it shews him as he was in the moments of his gravest difficulties."[33]

This criticism was a rather good one, for Jefferson appreciated Peale's ability as a colorist, and he seemed to like the picture's texture. But his primary criterion — as with the novel, that art be "lively" or lifelike — compelled him to choose a favorite. And yet, portraiture should have feeling, should go beyond mere documentation. Wright's painting better showed its subject's character and evoked an emotional response from the viewer; as for Peale's, it was too nearly only pleasant. So Jefferson repeated his notion that the appreciator of the arts should set personal standards of enjoyment, based on experience. The viewer's judgment was free; art had presented a liberating experience. In 1788 he wrote, "I am but a son of nature, loving what I see and feel, without being able to give a reason, nor caring much whether there be one."[34] This view was perhaps the most Romantic of all of Jefferson's sentiments about any subject.

He remained doubtful about America's future in collecting and appreciating the arts. Making notes for Americans traveling in Europe, he said: "Painting, statuary. Too expensive for the state of wealth among us. It would be useless therefore and preposterous for us to endeavor to make ourselves connoisseurs in those arts. They are worth seeing, but not studying [musing over, considering attentively]."[35] He collected what sculpture he could but he special ized in portrait busts of himself, Voltaire, Turgot, Czar Alexander of Russia, Napoleon, Lafayette, Franklin, John Paul Jones, Alexander Hamilton, and Washington. Some of these were by Giuseppe Ceracchi, still others by the greatest of living sculptors, Jean-Antoine Houdon (both of whom corresponded with Jefferson). It was Jefferson who introduced Houdon to America, ensuring the portraiture in plaster and stone of the "Founding Fathers."[36] The great statue of Washington in Jefferson's Capitol at Richmond was a significant breakthrough in monumental sculpture in America and in governmental patronage of the arts.[37] Jefferson must be ranked as a great pioneer in bringing the art of sculpture — at its best — to the new nation.

To Washington in 1787 Jefferson wrote a letter echoing his criterion of the "lively" in art: "I was happy to find . . . that the modern dress for your statue would meet your approbation. I found it strongly the sentiment of [Benjamin] West, [John Singleton] Copeley, [John] Trumbul and [Mather] Brown in London, after which it would be ridiculous to add that it was my own. I think a modern in an antique dress as *just* an object of ridicule as an Hercules or

Marius with a periwig and chapeau bras."[38] Jefferson agreed, therefore, with the "moderns" in the eighteenth-century quarrel over whether a Classical or a realistic — contemporary — costume should adorn a portrait sculpture (a debate not settled for some estheticians as late as 1833–1841 when Horatio Greenough sculpted Washington in a toga). Jefferson had the good sense in this case to buttress his own opinion with the judgment of certain prominent artists of the time.

Jefferson's summary view of sculpture came early, in 1785, when he wrote in opposition to "monster" statues: "A statue is not made, like a mountain, to be seen at a great distance. To perceive those minuter circumstances which constitute it's beauty you must be near it, and, in that case, it should be so little above the size of the life, as to appear actually of that size from your point of view."[39] In sculpture, at least, Jefferson would have nothing to do with the "false sublime," where size alone was meant artificially to promote soaring emotions. He had a good sense of the three-dimensional nature of sculpture and, as usual, of the immediacy of the esthetic experience. It is small wonder, then, that he had perhaps the best collection of art in the America of his day.[40]

He may also have had the finest gardens and the most carefully landscaped homesite in the new nation. All his life he directed the many activities that enhanced the beauty of Monticello. In this the use of the curve greatly appealed to him, as opposed to exclusively squared off, geometric designs. This was a Romantic tendency, but one he never pushed to excess,[41] for restraint and balance within an asymmetry were his measures. He liked the English gardens he toured in 1786 — virtually the only thing English he ever approved of — but even on that subject he had his reservations. Too many of the gardens were blatantly artificial: "shews still too much of art"; "Art appears too much." He liked a changing texture, the rhythms of curves and of high and low places. Of one garden he said, "A most lovely mixture of concave and convex"[42]; this "lovely mixture" he strove to attain at Monticello.

There were (and are) flower gardens, in ovoid forms, a "roundabout" walk encircling the large west lawn (with gentle curves), a small fish and reflecting pool, orchards, a mulberry row, and sloped or terraced vegetable garden areas. All this was arranged in a general oval plan atop the little mountain.[43] There were wonderful vistas toward the mansion and, obversely, toward the surrounding hills and valleys. Landscaping at Monticello subserved the house, existing in a marvellously organic relationship with it. A lovelier mixture could scarcely have been conceived.

As a collector of art, then, Thomas Jefferson knew the beautiful in the daily life within his home. At the same time, he promoted the patriotic urge to do homage to the American heroes of his era.[44] As a landscapist, he used that art to enhance what he considered the greater art of architecture. It was, after all, as an architect that Jefferson chiefly, and brilliantly, expressed himself in the fine arts.

IV *Superior in Beauty*

Wherever Jefferson travelled he collected sociological data, botanical specimens, gadgets and inventions, art of course, and construction and architectural ideas. Through these ideas, he said, "a taste for a chaste and good style of building" might be "formed in our countrymen." He found architecture in his native land inadequate to the task of creating a new nation. The old capitol of Virginia, for example, had "a pediment, which [was] too high for its span." The College of William and Mary was to him a "mis-shapen" pile of bricks very nearly like "brick-kilns." Because the Governor's Palace at Williamsburg was "not handsome,"[45] he made sketches to remodel the building; and he also designed his own homesite, as well as many other structures.

Over the years, he became one of America's leading architects, if only a gifted amateur. It is widely believed, in fact, that his architectural contributions to American culture are outweighed only by his political ones.[46] In 1958, some five hundred American architects, when polled to name the chief American architectural masterpieces, put Jefferson's University of Virginia eleventh and Monticello twelfth; and master architect Frank Lloyd Wright once complimented Jefferson as a great practitioner of the art.[47] Furthermore, Jefferson was not chained to foreign or antique models, as some have claimed; for he was an architect who freely adapted influential designs to the American environment.[48] In that way his architecture achieved an organic relationship to its cultural and physical surroundings. In the use of native materials, and because his designs were integral to his own personality, his creations took on the qualities of an organic, American architecture.

Sometimes he approached his art on the scale of town planning. In 1791 he devised a design for the Federal City (Washington, D.C.) that included walks, tree plantings, and avenues. He also entered the competition — anonymously — to design the President's house. The White House would look far different today had his plan won: comparatively squat, and surmounted by a dome. He also did a freehand sketch for a United States Capitol building, but did not enter that competition. Later, as President, Jefferson continued the development of the District under secure federal financing. James Hoban's White House design and Pierre Charles L'Enfant's city plan prevailed for the District, but Jefferson's guiding hand dominated and insured the success of both.[49]

He also mapped out Jeffersonville, Indiana, for Governor William Henry Harrison in 1802. The plan originally featured alternating improved and open squares; every other block would forever remain green. "Take, for instance," he wrote, "the chequer board for a plan. Let the black squares only be building squares, and the white ones be left open, in turf and trees. Every square of houses will be surrounded by four open squares, and every house will front an open square. The atmosphere of such a town would be like that of the country, insusceptible of the miasmata which produce yellow fever."[50] (He had firsthand knowledge of the dreaded yellow fever from the days of the great epidemic in Philadelphia, in 1793, when he was Secretary of State.) When the "agrarian" confronted the city, in Jefferson's scheme the city would be made to yield. Esthetic and social concerns — beauty and health — would accordingly blend. Any American might have a kind of Monticello.

Jefferson usually worked at architecture on a smaller scale than town planning; however, one of his cherished projects began while he was still in France. Becoming aware that Virginia was about to build a new capitol, he supplied plans of his own because of his fear that the project would be bungled. Through his design he introduced Roman Classicism into government architecture in America — where it has long remained.[51] In 1785, he wrote Madison from Paris concerning his capitol plan: "I shall send . . . one taken from the best morsel of antient architecture now remaining. It has obtained the approbation of fifteen or sixteen centuries, and is therefore preferable to any design which might be newly contrived. It will give more room, be more convenient and cost less than the plan" proposed in Virginia. "It will be superior in beauty to any thing in America, and not inferior to any thing in the world. It is very simple."[52] This is a clear statement of several of Jefferson's architectural standards: tradition; functionalism; economy; beauty; simplicity. America would have an architecture in which it could take true pride, an architecture of dignity and grace.

Years later he reminisced about the project in his *Autobiography:* "Thinking it a favorable opportunity of introducing into the State an example of architecture, in the classic style of antiquity, and the Maison Quarrée of Nismes, an ancient Roman temple, being considered as the most perfect model existing of what may be called Cubic architecture. . . . only changing the order from Corinthian to Ionic. . . . To adapt the exterior to our use, I drew a plan for the interior, with the apartments necessary for" the three branches of government.[53]

Jefferson certainly did simplify the building compared to the Maison Carrée, the Roman ruin he found during his travels through France. This simplification was made partly because of the scarcity of craftsmen in Virginia, and partly to restrict expenditures. All statuary was eliminated from the exterior; the highly elaborate entablature was smoothed; the three-and-a-half column depth of the portico was cut to two-and-a-half; the fluted columns were made plain; and the ornate capitals were changed to simple volutes at the column tops. Windows were added as a functional feature[54] (to accommodate offices, meeting rooms, and the like).

Any allegation that Jefferson merely copied from the Roman example would be false, as would be any charge that the French architect Clérisseau dominated the drawing of the plan.[55] Jefferson, not a copier in any area of life, *was* a great pragmatic borrower who worked as an artist with independence and integrity. The Maison Carrée inspired him — as did other works and drawings from previous centuries — but it did not intimidate him.

Unfortunately, the builders who executed the Virginia capitol did not adhere to the integrity of the architect's design and its flaws were not his. They added pilasters along the sides (perhaps enhancing the building, but losing some of the original plainness), and altered proportions throughout. Insofar as the structure succeeded esthetically, the credit must be given chiefly to Jefferson. The setting for Houdon's Washington was a wonderfully arranged monumental hall two stories high, the cella, or central room. Jefferson conceived the building from the start with this arrangement in mind.[56] As for the office and meeting spaces, the capitol must have been at least as light and airy as any building with such a function in America. It was executed in common native materials, wood and brick, and stuccoed over. It expressed, in Jefferson's mind, a simple republican dignity: the beginning of the "classical revival" in

America was to him a contemporary or "modern" statement, not a conservative, looking backward one.

V *The Independence of Monticello*

If the capitol was a public, monumental expression, Jefferson's smaller designs were comparatively personal and lyrical. Before Monticello, there had been the President's house, of course, and a design for a new governor's house for Virginia, too. The latter, also unexecuted, featured a large octagonal room, a departure from purely cubic motifs as surely as the dome of the President's house design was. He also drew plans for residences called Edgemont (one story), in Albemarle County with Monticello; Farmington, built in Lexington, Kentucky (with several round and semicircular windows; again there were octagons); Poplar Forest (his retreat, entirely octagonal); Ampthill in Cumberland County; and Barboursville in Orange County (cross plan, with octagonal room and low dome).[57] None of these plans was as grand as the one for his own permanent homesite.

As if to show again his virtuosity, he designed late in his life Christ Church at Charlottesville. But he had very early sketched an octagonal chapel for the same location.[58] One source of inspiration for that chapel had been Andrea Palladio's *The Four Books of Architecture.* The sixteenth-century Italian architect — whose works had as a base those of the Roman architect Vitruvius — was Jefferson's ancient exemplar. But Palladio's Temple of Vesta was round, whereas Jefferson's chapel was octagonal.[59] This design was a perfect example of how Jefferson learned from others' works, how they spurred him on, but also of how he transcended every model in achieving his own free esthetic.

Such was the case, then, with Monticello, which was his freest, most personal and lyrical artistic expression. Yet, paradoxically, it too was Palladian in spirit and execution. This could have been Jefferson writing rather than Palladio: "that house only ought to be called convenient, which is suitable to the quality of him that is to dwell in it, and whose parts correspond to the whole and to each other." Here is expressed an organicism among structural elements and between dweller-architect and homesite that is truly Jeffersonian. Palladio went on about the occupant of "the country house": "the time will be passed in seeing and adorning his own possessions, and by industry, and the art of agriculture, improving his estate; where also by the exercise which in a villa is commonly taken, on foot and on horseback, the body will the more easily preserve its strength and health; and, finally, where the mind, fatigued by the agitations of the city, will be greatly restor'd and comforted, and be able quietly to attend the studies of letters, and contemplation."[60]

These remarks can be compared with what has already been learned about Jefferson's lifestyle at Monticello and from letters that Jefferson wrote: "I am savage enough to prefer the woods, the wilds, and the independence of Monticello, to all the brilliant pleasures of this gay Capital" (Paris, 1785); "I am retired to Monticello, where, in the bosom of my family, and surrounded by my books, I enjoy a repose to which I have been long a stranger. My mornings are devoted to correspondence. From breakfast to dinner, I am in my shops, my garden, or on horseback among my farms; from dinner to dark, I give to society and recreation with my neighbors and friends; and from candle light to early bed-time, I read" (1810).[61]

Palladio had added: "build upon elevated and chearful places, where the air is, by the continual blowing of the winds, moved; and the earth, by its declivity, purged of all ill vapours and moisture: and where the inhabitants are healthy and chearful, and preserve a good colour." Then Jefferson wrote in 1786: "And our own dear Monticello, where has nature spread so rich a mantle under the eye? mountains, forests, rocks, rivers. With what majesty do we there ride above the storms! how sublime to look down into the workhouse of nature, to see her clouds, hail, snow, rain, thunder, all fabricated at our feet! And the glorious Sun, when rising as if out of a distant water, just gilding the tops of the mountains, and giving life to all nature!"[62]

The site for Monticello, then, was adopted not only because of the Palladian influence but because it struck Jefferson as sublime. As early as 1767 the name was chosen, though how he selected or derived it is unknown (it means, in Italian, "little mountain").[63] His major achievement, of course, was the architectural design of the mansion itself. Yet, ideally, all exterior and interior elements were organically related to the house to reflect his personality. So, off and on over the years, he oversaw its construction, modifications, and completion (the drastic remodelling, which put Monticello in approximately the state to which it is now restored, began in 1796; by about 1809, upon his retirement from the presidency, the project was completed).[64] He supervised the levelling of the hilltop, and he designed, as has been observed, the landscaping. He not only formed a collection of paintings, sculptures, musical instruments, and scores, but so carefully did he select the furnishings, room by room, as scarcely to have neglected any detail. Many of Jefferson's "sketches of tables, chairs, and other furniture, and with minute calculations for their construction," still exist. The sketches also included his own designs for a number of curtains, some "of crimson damask silk, lined with green and a yellow fringe."[65]

There were (and are) some thirty-five rooms in the finished three-story mansion. The visitors' entrance was from the east. On the east portico roof was a weather vane; on the ceiling of the portico, a large compass was placed, so that the wind direction could be read from the floor of the portico without exposure to the elements (the vane was connected to the compass arrow by a long rod through the roof). Coming through the east portico door, a visitor passed under the seven-day clock designed by Jefferson. As the clock struck, Revolutionary War cannonball weights descended into the basement, to operate the mechanisms. Jefferson's ingenious folding ladder was used to climb to the timepiece for winding. Antlers from the Lewis and Clark Expedition flanked the clock. In the hall were various busts on pediments and numerous fossils, paintings, chairs, and other paraphernalia. On three sides of the two-story hall was a balustraded second-story balcony, with angled corners, a marvelous variation from the box-room design. The ceiling of this east entrance hall was ornamented with Jefferson's delicate design of an American eagle, in relief, with eighteen stars (Jefferson's guess at what would be the ultimate number of states in the Union, perhaps; also, there were, by the time the mansion was essentially finished, seventeen states and the Louisiana Territory).

Into the drawing room, a large chamber which reached out, with angled corners, under the west portico, glass doors were levered so that when one was pushed, both opened (a chain mechanism in the floor, Jefferson's invention, effected this invisibly). The drawing room was light and airy, with large windows and a portico door. Delicate modillions and other designs, with a door pediment, topped the windows and walls. There were large mirrors and a music corner with a piano. Paintings and busts abounded, as did comfortable furniture. Evenings by the fireplace could have only been serene in such a setting.

The dining room, also two stories in height, connected at the north wall of the drawing room. It was elegant though simple. There was a service area alcove under a large, low arch, and a fireplace with dumbwaiters built into its ends, concealed by doors, for easy access to the wines that Jefferson in great abundance stored in his cellar. (Jefferson once designed a delicate coffee urn that was executed by a French silversmith. Its shape was a graceful oval, with finely curved handles. He also designed two half-oval silver goblets.)[66]

Opposite the fireplace was another low arch, with a wide, glass doored entrance into the tea room (also two stories). This was one of the most pleasant retreats in the house, with large windows in its semioctagonal sides, busts above eye level, and pleasant vistas to the north and west. Completing the north wing were an open porch and two guest bedrooms, one square, one octagonal.

The south wing was largely devoted to Jefferson's bedroom, study, library, and conservatory. The bedroom, which rose two stories, and had a skylight, contained his alcove bed (opening on one side to the bedroom, on the other to the study), his comfortable swivel chair, various scientific instruments such as his telescope, and also several busts and other objects of art. The study, very well lighted by large windows, opened through an arch, such as those in the dining room, to the library. Among thousands of books, Jefferson could in complete privacy retreat to total immersion in philosophy, architecture, or other subjects.

Also on the first floor were found privies (with connections to small tunnels for the carrying away of waste; privies on all floors, in fact, led to shafts and tunnels, with little carts, for this purpose), air shafts to the upper floors, and the interesting, narrow staircases for access to the higher levels. These staircases were very delicately designed, conveniently located, and specifically functional, for no such thing as a grand staircase had any place in Jefferson's mature thinking. To Jefferson it would have been a waste of space and blatantly ostentatious.

The second story, where first-floor rooms did not rise into it, was composed chiefly of guest bedrooms. Windows in these rooms were arranged near the floor; from outside, they appeared to be the tops of the tall, first-floor windows, and made the house look one story high from the lawns. The third story also had a number of guest bedrooms, airshafts, skylights, and attic areas. The interior of the west portico dome was a high, octagonal room, the only indication from outside that a third floor even existed. A grand room, with circular and semicircular windows and a panelled ceiling, its function during Jefferson's residency was never recorded.[67]

Under the house was located a transverse tunnel that led to cellars for storage and to servant areas. Airshafts, dumbwaiters, and stairways penetrated to this underground level. It was, of course, from above ground and from the outside that Monticello was familiarly described and pictured by travellers. A very grand house, it was large enough to approach the sublime, stately while not pretentious, and utterly charming in its setting.

Jefferson's general design derived in part from Palladio — in its hilltop location (and therefore its name) — and in its arrangement of a central living section with projecting arms.[68] These arms were arranged to run east and west, perpendicular to the house, flanking the large west lawn, and were thrust out from the house by north-south terraces, which turned west at right angles and continued the length of the arms. Under the arms (on the basement level) were the "dependencies" — kitchen, dairy, smoke house, servants' quarters, ice house, horse stalls, carriage garage, and laundry room. These areas, accessible from under cover of a collonade, were entirely invisible from either entrance or from the lawns because of the slope of the hilltop. Visitors to Monticello in the early nineteenth century would scarcely have seen its slaves or other servants, and they would never have seen its workspaces, or smelled either the cooking or the horses.

In spite of a debt to Palladio, Jefferson showed a great lyricism and independence in designing Monticello.[69] He derived some of his sense of "just proportions" from Palladio[70] (it was also partly instinctive), but he turned to native materials and his own sense of propriety to produce the essence of the place. Indeed, the use of native materials was important to the achievement of his organic effect. These materials produced blended textures of smooth, white-painted wood and moderately rough, soft-red brick entirely Jeffersonian. Intricate plays of light and shadow, from shallow overhangs as well as in the porticoes, from receding angles and shapes, from the interplay of voids and solids, and even from balustrades, were all his effects. The asymmetrical floor plan and the window arrangement were also Jefferson's.[71]

The foundations were made of local gneiss, and the mortar was compounded from local limestone. Clay from the region was baked into bricks on the premises, and stone for walls and chimneys was collected or dug there. All timber was cut nearby for floors, joists, or any other purpose.[72] In this respect, Jefferson built for permanency; for the oak floor joists were surrounded by crushed brick and stone, and the planking in the floors finely fitted and secured with iron pins.[73] A few items, however, not available in America, or in Virginia at least, were imported, such as some molded work, window sashes, and glass.[74]

To walk around the exterior of the house was perhaps as great a pleasure as to tour its interior. The east front was dominated by four large columns, a fairly high entablature with a fluted triglyph, metope pattern from Palladio,[75] and a simple pediment with a semicircular window within it. All this was white-painted wood, as was the window-door group of three, beneath the portico. These glass areas were given semicircular tops, and all but filled the porch wall. Two story-and-a-half windows (also many paned) were located on each facade side — white against mellow brick, with dark shutters. There was a string of fluted triglyphs and of metopes in white just under the roof level (this course was strung completely around the house). A white balustrade, purely decorative, coursed above the roof on all sides. The proportions were so carefully wrought as to produce an impression of complete repose.

Above the slope of the roof, around the flat top portion, another balustrade was placed (this time of criss-crossed, angled slats rather than the lower turned posts) that was barely visible. The brick chimneys protruded skyward — to take sparks well into the air — but without disturbing the silhouette. At ground level, the criss-crossed balustrade was then echoed in the railing around the terraces and dependent arms. These arms, which were wide-topped and could be walked upon, provided delightful vistas of both house and region (from the north terrace, Jefferson, with a telescope, could see the University of Virginia being built in nearby Charlottesville). Everywhere the semirough brick and smooth wood presented a superb contrast of texture and color, punctuated judiciously by rectangular and round-topped windows.

There were small porches and steps half hidden at the corners, between the north and south ends. These corners were not squared off, but made to recede and project by right- and bevel-angled wall surfaces. Each end was surmounted by its own small pediment, within which was placed a semicircular window. Outward from these ends, then, projected the terraces, which then right-angled into the dependent arms. At the end of the north arm (its west end, of course) was the simple brick structure known as Jefferson's law office. It had low, pedimented ends and a central chimney. Across the lawn, at the corresponding southwest corner (or end of the south dependent arm), was a twin building, the first to be built at Monticello, which once served as Jefferson's honeymoon house.

To stand between these two little buildings, and to look east across the lawn, was to view the grand west front with its portico and dome. (This facade is most familiar to Americans, for it is everywhere pictured to represent Monticello — even on nickel coins.) This portico was made almost identical to the east one with its entablature, pediment, semicircular window, and four-column front. But it was rendered two columns deep in the porch, instead of one, and underneath was positioned a porch-facade of semi-octagonal shape (instead of flat), with two large, rectangular windows and a rectangular, pedimented doorway. Jefferson wanted a grander passageway between the drawing room and the huge, landscaped green space to the west, than between the short east approach and the entrance hall. Also, the bevel-angle and right-angle corners, north and south, were made bolder on the west front. The windows, too, were somewhat taller (seemingly the height of one full story of the house), though still trimmed in white, with dark shutters. Amazingly, the proportions were fully as just and balanced here as on the other side, and equally serene.

The dominant feature of this view of the mansion, however, became the octagonal-based dome surmounting the west side — projecting, in fact, well out from it. The circular windows noticed from within the dome room became very evident outside — quite large — as did the semicircular one "interrupted" by the west portico pediment. The stepped octagonal shoulders of the dome led subtly up to its low roundness, all in white, and wonderfully light above the solidity of the brick. As everywhere, the blend of textures, shapes, lights, shadows, and colors was most pleasant.

To "walk" this way around Monticello (the south end being the inverse duplicate of the north), and to describe it so, is almost equivalent to *quoting* Thomas Jefferson. For here, beyond his drawings, he expressed himself, not in such words as already frequently quoted, but in masses, voids, colors, and textures — in tangible, material forms. His homesite was and is one of the very great examples of American architecture. It was fortunate that most of the decorative structures he drew — small "temples," towers, and other outbuildings — were never constructed on the little mountain.[76]

For, since the masterpiece was finished in the form described, it is small wonder that a cultivated French traveller wrote even as early as the 1780s, when the house and grounds were in humbler form, that "Mr. Jefferson is the first American who has consulted the fine arts to know how he should shelter himself from the weather."[77] It was "one of the architectural harmonies of the world," and yet, at the same time, "No other house in America so well reflects the personality of its owner."[78] Like all great art, Monticello is in its personal expression — of, in this case, lyricism — at the same time also a universal statement. The rich "public" esthetic gesture achieved in Monticello still evokes a feeling of independence and self-mastery that is inspirational.

VI *An Academical Village*

Another brilliant blend of the personal and the public in Jefferson's architecture was the cherished project of his old age, the University of Virginia, which was meant to be a monument to all he believed and a personal bequest to his people. Yet it was to be a public institution, and an American landmark for all to see. As at Monticello, there was the balance of white-painted wood and mellow, red brick; and the use of native materials was stressed. Once more there were a main building, terraces reaching out from it, and dependent arms that angled from the terraces with a large green space between them.[79]

"The general idea of an Academical village rather than one large building" came to Jefferson early in the nineteenth century,[80] though most construction awaited the 1820s. There would be, he wrote, "a small and separate lodge for each professorship, with only a hall below for his class, and two chambers above for himself; joining these lodges [would be] barracks for a certain portion of the students," with "The whole of the pavilions and dormitories to be united by a colonnade in front, of the height of the lower story of the pavilions," "a covered way to give a dry communication between all the schools." There came to be ten pavilion lodges, or houses, all "models of taste and correct architecture — and of a variety of appearance, no two alike, so as to serve as specimens of orders for the architectural lectures."[81] The pavilions, then, were to have multiple functions as dwellings, classrooms, and esthetic examples of various Classic forms. They all featured columned fronts, and were pedimented. From north to south, the houses were separated by increasing numbers of student dwelling units, so that from a northward vista, standing between the two end lodges, looking up the graduated green lawn, they presented the illusion of being equally distant from one another. All entrances were situated under the colonnades. Behind these housing dependencies there were separate gardens, divided by roads, and lined by serpentine brick walls of sufficient height for privacy.[82] (These walls amounted to a charming *tour de force,* very graceful and symmetrical.) Farther back yet were low brick ranges for more housing, with dining halls.

From any vantage point, viewing the pavilions was pleasant. Campus dwellers or visitors saw the same textural, color, and other features found at Monticello, where they had been done on a smaller scale, in each unit. But standing there at the south end of the campus yard and looking north, a viewer could focus upon the distant Rotunda, at once the head and the heart of the "Academical village." Connected to the pavilion arms by high terraces, it was, in terms of brick and wood, almost Monticello writ large — large enough to appear sublime from its north entrance, where it was cleverly elevated above long, wide flights of stone stairs. Inspiration for the Rotunda form came to Jefferson from Palladio, from what he knew of the Pantheon at Rome, and from the American architect Benjamin Henry Latrobe.[83] Here Jefferson's architecture most notably employed spherical masses, and balanced them off successfully against the "cubic" (rectangular and triangular) masses of the pavilions.[84]

In 1825 Jefferson wrote: "The ROTUNDA, filling up the Northernmost end of the ground plan is 77 feet in diameter, and in height, crowned by a Dome 120 deg. of the sphere. The lower floor has large rooms for religious worship, for public examinations, and other associated purposes. The upper floor is a single room for a Library, canopied by the Dome and it's sky-light."[85] That is, the height and the width of the building were made the same — the sphere of the dome, if filled out, would touch the walls of the circular building at its equator and would rest on the floor. His drawing of a front (the two fronts were identical when seen straight-on, the north being one unfluted Corinthian column deep in its portico to three deep on the south) continued in fact the dome's arc, in dashes, to the full circle, and the design vividly outlined the symmetry that remained invisible at the actual site of the finished building.

There were elaborately modillioned and dentilled pediments over both simple entablatures, atop the six-column-wide porches. All these features were in white-painted wood. The circular walls of the building were rendered in Jefferson's favorite brick, punctuated by two tiers of windows, with pedimented doors on the porches (the lower windows were also pedimented). A heavy string course of wood surrounded the entire structure, above the windows, yet well below the roof line, which was dentilled. The string course was decorated with carved modillions and dentils. These features combined to create the same splendid contrasts of light, shadow, color, texture, and also of line, as seen in the different shapes at Monticello. The dome, which was left shallow enough not to be obtrusive or heavy, was indeed the building's crown.

Inside, the circular first floor was a superb arrangement of two large, oval shaped rooms (meant for a chemical laboratory and other uses); one small oval (meant to be a museum); a resulting irregularly shaped hall; and curving staircases. Here were three cornerless workspaces within a circle, a most curious and imaginative — yet functional — arrangement, especially for its time.

Upstairs, the main hall (colloquially, the rotunda) impressed the visitor with spaciousness and elegance. It was lined with forty polished, unfluted columns with Corinthian tops, surmounted by an elaborate, circular entablature. From floor level, these columns loomed wonderfully upward, solid yet graceful, polished and serene. Near the top of the columns, a balustraded balcony encircled the room. Above them, the space soared aloft to a large skylight. The floor arrangement — the number of levels — showed that the building was intended not only to serve purposes already mentioned — plus areas for "drawing, music," and other activities — but to have served also as the university library to which Jefferson bequeathed many of his own books. One other function also occurred to him: "The Concave cieling of the Rotunda is proposed to be painted skyblue and spangled with gilt stars in their position and magnitude copied exactly from any selected hemisphere of our latitude."[86]

This multipurpose structure certainly reflected the manysided man who designed it and who also oversaw its construction. It was intended to be a house for the sciences, the arts, the ideas and values of the human race. Thomas Jefferson's creative intelligence itself housed all these elements of civilization, and the university became a splendid monument to his genius, a vision thrusting into the future through education. Yet here in the era of independence of the Age of Jefferson was a vision also firmly anchored in the concept of the pursuit of happiness.

CHAPTER 9

What Is Called Style

I The Imagination Is Warm

UNQUESTIONABLY, the style of Thomas Jefferson was reflected in his architecture just as fully as it was in his *Declaration of Independence.* Even its vestiges of Roman Classicism harmonized wonderfully with the elements of Roman philosophy in his thinking. The pervading "American" quality of it was also strongly evident, as surely as his patriotism was a major personal character trait. In his use of native materials, his building on the past, and in his desire to set a new example for his fellow citizens in dignified design, his architecture was both blossom and seed to America's esthetic growth. Furthermore, the serenity and refinement of the house and grounds at Monticello were in wood and brick, in gardens and paths — his personation. Even the lights and shadows, the varying textures, the blend of the functional and the esthetic — all reflected his personality as a delicate balance between complexity and simplicity.

Naturally, his words also displayed his style, a style evident in his prose writing, in the literary sense, and in what has come to be called his lifestyle as well. His general reputation as a writer has been high ever since the appearance of *A Summary View* impelled him into the authorship of the *Declaration,* for his style has often been called balanced, classic, restrained, or controlled. One of his early biographers, George Tucker, established the dominant critical view of Jefferson's prose in 1837 when speaking of the *Declaration:* "It is sufficiently elevated without being declamatory, and familiar, without being low."[1] There is, then, a touch of the sublime in the style, but none of the melodramatic. There is plainness, so that all might comprehend, without a pandering to popular tastes. If Jefferson seldom rose to the level of expression found in the *Declaration* — for many of his thousands of letters and other writings were mundane — a fair number of his works truly were exceptional in turn of phrase and in wit and wisdom.

At times Jefferson subjected his writing to considerable revision, for he was a conscientious craftsman.[2] An excellent example of this can be seen in the words found on his personal letter or document seal (a small mold to be pressed into the wax first applied to the paper) which bore the motto "Rebellion to tyrants is obedience to God" (borrowed from Benjamin Franklin in 1776). As late as 1823, he asserted the "strength and beauty of the antithesis" in the phrase; but he also remarked, "Correct it's syntax, 'Rebellion *against* tyrants is obedience to God,' it has lost all the strength and beauty."[3] In *A Summary View,* he changed the phrase "farmers, not lawyers" to "laborers, not lawyers" apparently as much for the sake of alliteration as for expressing a more democratically inclusive grouping.

Sometimes he was inordinately fond of such sound effects, as when he said that a British act "seems addressed to our fears rather than to our freedom," or that the law would have to be "Borne on the point of a bayonet" (1775). He once claimed that he sought scientific data on all animals "from the mouse to the mammoth" (1783), that he wanted a government of "men who will not bend their politics to their purses, nor pursue measures by which they may profit, & then profit by their measures" (1796).[4]

Jefferson was always capable of the vague expression when it suited him, as "From the nature of things." Upon such a phrase, he would sometimes base an argument or a point as if it were an actual logical premise. When he was young, such vagueness was often vagary and vanity. His earliest letters were selfconsciously serious, falsely "mature," and he too often strove to be witty or allusive, to pun in Latin, or to show off in Greek. In due time, of course, he stopped these measures and employed a felicity appropriate to his subject (rather than pressing all subjects into one patterned style). In 1818, for example, he wrote a biographical sketch of Benjamin Franklin, describing him in witty anecdotes — in short, he was utilizing Franklin's own style. In Jefferson's *Autobiography,* he at times exemplified a pattern of rhythmical increment, with many clauses and phrases, set off by commas and semicolons, instead of a diffuse series of independent clauses; his style produced a surprising amount of compression.[5]

At the start of his *Autobiography,* Jefferson briefly traced a family tree, remarking as to ancestry, "let every one ascribe the faith and merit he chooses" to it. "At the age of 77," he wrote, "I begin to make some memoranda, and state some recollections of dates and facts concerning myself, for my own more ready reference, and for the information of my family." Less than half way through, with no trace of his early vanity, he said, "I am already tired of talking about myself."[6]

Jefferson's ability to turn a good phrase was sometimes remarkable, as this series of quotations might show: "For themselves they fought, for themselves they conquered, and for themselves alone they have a right to hold" (*A Summary View*); "As our enemies have found we can reason like men, so now let us show them we can fight like men also"; ". . . the tender plant of liberty" (1775); "The tree of liberty must be refreshed from time to time with the blood of patriots and tyrants. It is it's natural manure" (1787).[7]

In the same year, he used a particularly French figure of speech in a letter to a French friend: "Here I am, Madam, gazing whole hours at the Maison quarrée, like a lover at his mistress." The following wonderfully American observation is from his *Notes on the State of Virginia:* "But it does me no injury for my neighbor to say there are twenty gods, or no god. It neither picks my pocket nor breaks my leg."[8]

On occasion, he could become charmingly aphoristic: "... force cannot give right"; "The whole art of government consists in the art of being honest"; "The god who gave us life, gave us liberty at the same time: the hand of force may destroy, but cannot disjoin them" (*A Summary View*); "A mind always employed is always happy. This is the true secret, the grand recipe for felicity" (1787); ". . . unmerited abuse wounds, while unmerited praise has not the power to heal" (1796); ". . . in truth ignorance is always the parent of vanity" (1805).[9] A remarkable freshness appears in the coinage of these adages; and, since *A Summary View* contained many such phrases, it is small wonder that it drew for Jefferson a certain amount of notice as a prose stylist. The passage from 1787 in particular succinctly expressed for him Jefferson's key to the pursuit of happiness; the other sayings surely were examples of Enlightenment wit at its best.

Jefferson was not without humor, though he was always subdued in that regard: "By an act passed in the 5th. year of the reign of his late majesty king George the second an American subject is forbidden to make a hat for himself of the fur which he has taken perhaps on his own soil" (*A Summary View*). In 1779, he wrote to Patrick Henry: "If the troops could be fed upon long letters I believe the gentleman at the head of that department in this country would be the best commissary upon earth."[10] In 1783, he wrote from Philadelphia about "our countrywomen" and their styles:

> The high head is made as flat as a flounder. Instead of the burthen of lawn, ribbon, false hair &c. the head is covered with a plain chip hat with only a ribbon round the crown. The shoulders are where the chin used to be, and the hips have succeeded to the place of the shoulders. The circumference of the waste is the span of the lady's own hands in order to preserve due proportion. All the residue of the figure is resigned to the possession of a hoop which at each angle before projects like two bastions of a fort. I am impatient to see whether our [Virginian] married ladies will be able to reduce and keep themselves to this form.

Of his daughter, he wrote in the same year, "The chance that in marriage she will draw a blockhead I calculate at about fourteen to one."[11] As these quotations indicate, Jefferson cast his barbs at male and female alike; he expressed the attitude of a typical father, fearful about his daughter's future; and he was a sharp observer of the vanities of society.

From Paris in 1786 he told Abigail Adams (toward whom he often tried in his letters to direct wit and humor) that he had asked a friend who was to visit her "to carry me in her pocket . . . but on examining the treaty of commerce, she found I should be contraband; that there might be a search — and seizure — and that the case would admit very specially of embarras." In 1792, he offered to George Washington (for whom he seldom tried for such effects) an assessment of hereditary succession in heads of government. Their power, he said, is "transmitted through the loins of knaves & fools passing from the debauches of the table to those of the bed."[12]

Jefferson thought highly of Thomas Paine, both as a political thinker and as a writer; and the traits he admired in Paine's works were among those he strove to achieve in his own. "No writer has exceeded Paine in ease and familiarity of style, in perspicuity of expression, happiness of elucidation, and in simple and unassuming language. In this he may be compared with Dr. Franklin." Jefferson must also have liked the passion with which Paine wrote, for he loved a vigor in "what is called style in writing or speaking," as it is seen, for example, "early in life while the imagination is warm."[13]

As if to illustrate such sentiments, Jefferson became especially lyrical in his *Notes* on the subject of his native place:

The passage of the Patowmac through the Blue ridge is perhaps one of the most stupendous scenes in nature. You stand on a very high point of land. On your right comes up the Shenandoah, having ranged along the foot of the mountain an hundred miles to seek a vent. On your left approaches the Patowmac, in quest of a passage also. In the moment of their junction they rush together against the mountain, rend it asunder, and pass off to the sea.... The *Natural Bridge,* [is] the most sublime of Nature's works.... It is impossible for the emotions arising from the sublime to be felt beyond what they are here; so beautiful an arch, so elevated, so light, and springing as it were up to heaven, the rapture of the spectator is really indescribable![14]

Jefferson's rendering dramatic the scene where the two rivers met and his picturing a sudden collision of forces revealed the intensity of his feelings for the region. The long process of erosion which, common sense reminded him, had created the pass he described, was devoid of emotional content. Figurative language in such a case had to overshadow scientific explanation. The bridge, solid and stationary in actual fact, *had* to be said to transcend its anchorage, and to soar as his emotions did upon his reminiscing of it. Through language alone, he could express his sense of organically relating to the natural setting of his youth. It was a case of a native son's paying homage to his source.

Jefferson once owned the property of the Natural Bridge of Virginia, and he was very proud of it. He referred to himself as "an American" *and* "a citizen of Virginia"; and he as often used the term "country" to mean the state as the nation.[15] To later generations, his "American" self-definition has prevailed; for simply as an *American* personality does Jefferson loom important in the American mind.

II *An American*

While himself away from Monticello, Jefferson once admonished his daughter, "This is a scolding letter for you all. I have not received a scrip of a pen from home since I left it which is now eleven weeks.... there is not a sprig of grass [back home] that shoots uninteresting to me." Always homesick when removed from the little mountain, if he was as far away as France or England he compulsively contrasted the other culture to the American. He once met a British officer he found to be "intolerably insolent and haughty," for example. English newspapers, in speaking of

America, were "infamous fountains of falshood." "I heard," he wrote Abigail Adams, "the Nightingale in all it's perfection: and I do not hesitate to pronounce that in America it would be deemed a bird of the third rank only, our mockingbird, and fox-coloured thrush being unquestionably superior to it."[16] (It remained for Walt Whitman, in the 1850s and beyond, to seize upon Jefferson's implication, and to drop the "poetic" nightingale for the indigenous birds named here.)

Americans visiting Europe, Jefferson insisted, should make it a point to attend the royal courts. The courts were "to be seen as you would see the tower of London or Menagerie of Versailles with their Lions, tygers, hyaenas and other beasts of prey, standing in the same relation to their fellows." He sympathized deeply with the French peasants with whom he conversed, because they were so hopeless in their poverty. By ugly contrast, the French women of the aristocracy wasted their lives in trivia, "eternally in the pursuit of happiness which keeps eternally before.... In America, on the other hand, the society of your husband, the fond cares for the children, the arrangements of the house, the improvements of the grounds fill every moment with a healthy and an usefull activity."[17]

He feared the success of the Society of Cincinnati, an elitist veterans group formed after the Revolution, because "the curses of hereditary aristocracy . . . would have followed in America had this institution remained." "My god!" he addressed James Monroe, "How little do my countrymen know what precious blessings they are in possession of, and which no other people on earth enjoy. I confess I had no idea of it myself," before going to Europe. "While we shall see multiplied instances of Europeans going to live in America, I will venture to say no man now living will ever see an instance of an American removing to settle in Europe." After all he had learned in Europe — and it was much — he never once entertained a thought of expatriating himself, not even to his beloved France. His native land would do well for a lifetime, as would his fellow Americans whom he once described in this fashion: "It is a part of the American character to consider nothing as desperate; to surmount every difficulty by resolution and contrivance."[18]

This statement contains an indirect self-portrait, of course, for Jefferson was ever *the* American and *an* American. But he could also make intensely personal remarks, which were directly self-portraying. He could picture himself, for example, as the stern moralist or as the self-righteous perfectionist: "my zeal in this business [disbursement of public lands] is public and pure." He was, he said, "a day labourer" in "the path of right"; "...it can never be the interest of any party to do what is unjust, or to ask what is unequal"; "I am never happier than when I am performing good offices for good people"; "The interests of a nation, when well understood, will be found to coincide with their moral duties." "Be assured, my dear Jefferson," he lectured his grandson, "that these little returns into ourselves, this self-catechising habit, is not trifling nor useless, but leads to the prudent selection & steady pursuit of what is right."[19]

With his adult friends, Jefferson was neither preachy nor condescending. He said, most sincerely, "I find friendship to be like wine, raw when new, ripened with age, the true old man's milk and restorative cordial." To Abigail Adams, he as President frankly wrote, "The appointment of a woman to office is an innovation for which the public is not prepared, nor am I." But he told her, "I pray you to observe that [on another occasion] I have used the term *people* and that this is a noun of the masculine as well as feminine gender."[20] Toward John Adams, he was apt to be more political or philosophical: "...we were fellow-laborers in the same cause, struggling for what is most valuable to man, his right of self-government. Laboring always at the same oar, with some wave ever ahead, threatening to overwhelm us, and yet passing harmless under our bark, we knew not how we rode through the storm with heart and hand, and made a happy port."

Their warm mutual respect once interrupted by political dispute, Jefferson and Adams were reunited through a correspondence which furnished the world with a most remarkable exchange of letters. There obtained, after all, a consideration above politics — the fine wine of friendship. In the realm of the political, he once compared and contrasted himself to Napoleon, saying, "Having been, like him, intrusted with the happiness of my country, I feel the blessing of resembling him in no other point. I have not caused the death of five or ten millions of human beings.... On the contrary, I have the consolation to reflect that during the period of my administration not a drop of the blood of a single fellow citizen was shed by the sword of war or of the law."[21]

Then too, there were times when Jefferson the letter writer waxed quite Romantic, as in a long epistle to Maria Cosway, when their French flirtation was broken off. Employing, for perhaps the only time in his life, the dialogue mode, he pictured his

Head in a debate with his Heart — the man of reason at odds with the lover. "Well, friend, you seem to be in a pretty trim.... I knew you were getting into a scrape," said his Head. "Thou art the most incorrigible of all the beings that ever sinned!" Heart fancifully replied, "I see things wonderfully contrived sometimes to make us happy." No, retorted Head, "This is not a world to live at random in as you do." Then Head tried to clinch the argument with: "The art of life is the art of avoiding pain.... The most effectual means of being secure against pain is to retire within ourselves, and to suffice for our own happiness....

"Hence the inestimable value of intellectual pleasures.... [wherein] we ride, serene and sublime, above the concerns of this mortal world, contemplating truth and nature, matter and motion." This Epicurean expostulation was followed by Heart's end to the dialogue, as if Heart had been the winner of the debate. Friendship was sublime: "Hills, vallies, chateaux, gardens, rivers, every object wore it's lovliest hue!" when *she* was near. Heart's was the province of "morals"; Head's, that of "science." Happiness lay "in sentiment, not in science." Nevertheless, Head — reason — finally prevailed, as Jefferson leaving Maria and France returned to America to fulfill his destiny in public office and domestic life.[22]

His was a fine writing style. His was a touchingly human life-style. Interestingly enough, he died on the fiftieth anniversary of the *Declaration of Independence*. On that July Fourth, 1826, John Adams, himself to die that same day, reflected with satisfaction that Jefferson was still alive. But Jefferson, who was by then "gone," had left behind the epitaph carefully prepared long before. It listed the accomplishments he was most proud of, and for which he wished to be remembered. It reflected his style through and through:

HERE WAS BURIED
THOMAS JEFFERSON
AUTHOR
OF THE DECLARATION OF
AMERICAN INDEPENDENCE
OF
THE STATUTE OF VIRGINIA
FOR RELIGIOUS FREEDOM, AND
FATHER OF THE UNIVERSITY
OF VIRGINIA[23]

CHAPTER 10

Their Good Old Faith

I *Correctness in Writing History*

WHEN Thomas Jefferson said he was able to take the public pulse, he was very probably correct. In fact, he must have been the keenest observer of the America of his time. He was, in effect, an allegorical figure of the civilization. Through him, today's American may truly read the early American story, for — with his talk of equality and happiness — he personified the very highest American ideals. This personification was especially evident in his Rough Draft of the *Declaration of Independence* and in his faith in the doctrine of natural rights. But he also exemplified many of his people's major weaknesses, their human failings, in his acts *against* human nature, in his belief that, because there were varieties in the human race, some people were inferior to others. Here can be observed a peculiarly American pattern of bigotry, oppression, or paternalism. The American experiment — which he began, and for which he was the spokesman — found fruition in neither his time nor his person.

Since the American experiment has not yet truly borne full fruit, Jefferson may still function as an allegorical American figure. If *he* showed patterns of prejudice, so do his people today, still. If *he* portrayed, in his crusade against ignorance and talk of life and liberty, the smiling aspects of the American dream, so today do his people. To look backward to Jefferson is to study the present, and to study the two centuries of national existence thus far given to the United States. He may be studied through the numerous literary works which have been written about him.[1] Or his rise and fall in the estimation of historians and biographers can be traced through any number of books.[2] But these approaches are ultimately unsatisfactory. The surest way to see Jefferson, that Jefferson who is a mirror to his culture, is as a paradox. He must be seen by his people as composed of that same mesh of good and evil they themselves are made of. In this way he can remain relevant to a people accustomed to unresolved contraries. There is no Thomas Jefferson alive today, but there is an immortal Jefferson. Though a different America exists today, it is still his.[3] For today's Americans can, in the terminology of their time, *identify* with Thomas Jefferson.[4] The public pulse of modern America continues to echo Jefferson's beliefs concerning America. "The people," he believed, were "confirmed in their good old faith" — the democratic faith.[5] Yet great numbers of the people remain benighted and bigoted, a "paradox-people" unable to realize their ideals.[6] He knew of their faith, but deep within he also knew that the pulse often faltered.

Some of the stories, poems, plays, and biographies that have been written about Jefferson would have pleased him, of course, and some of them would have so angered him that he probably would have disdained to reply to most. He probably would have hoped for the presentation of facts, verifiable facts alone, such as springing from reading of his own words (or viewing of his own architecture) on the part of his future judges. A voluminous letter writer himself, he concluded that "the letters of a person, especially of one whose business has been chiefly transacted by letters, form the only full and genuine journal of his life." Such factual matter, he felt, is all that can provide "that correctness in writing history, without which it becomes romance."[7] So, just as his own words have revealed him, and just as his buildings have revealed him, his life provides a summary view of the archetypal or allegorical American.

II *A Natural Aristocracy*

Beyond the Constitution, Jefferson believed, lay fixed principles — natural rights — that were not to be abridged. He expressed these in the *Declaration,* for he thought the people to be sovereign in their power. It was almost as if he was jealous of the other document, having been denied by circumstance any direct hand in drafting the United States Constitution, the fundamental statement of American laws that begins, "We the people," so he insisted that the people had a right to a little rebellion now and then, when the failure of nerve known as conservatism weighed them down. But who were these "people"? Certainly they were not to be construed as what Hamilton called mob or beast; but they also were not to be idealized. They were not to be thought of as noble savages for example, for, if they were to be considered ignorant, they would then have to forfeit their power. If his democratic faith was an ideal, his concept of the people was realistic.

Such statements as those which follow reveal the typically Jeffersonian admixture of realism and idealism, of common sense and faith. "I do not believe with the Rochefoucaults & Montaignes," Jefferson wrote, "that fourteen out of fifteen men are rogues: I believe a great abatement from that proportion may be made in favor of general honesty. But I have always found that rogues would be uppermost" (1795). "In truth I do not recollect in all the animal kingdom a single species but man which is eternally & systematically engaged in the destruction of its own species" (1797). "There is a natural aristocracy among men. The grounds of this are virtue and talents.... There is also an artificial aristocracy, founded on wealth and birth, without either virtue or talents" (1813). "I hope we ... crush in it's birth the aristocracy of our monied corporations which dare already to challenge our government to a trial of strength and bid defiance to the laws of our country" (1817). "Laws are made for men of ordinary understanding, and should, therefore, be construed by the ordinary rules of common sense" (1822).[8] As these words indicate, Jefferson feared privilege; he celebrated ordinary people. Yet he wanted a "natural aristocracy" to rise to lead the people, to become the most educated, to be the greatest cooperators with nature (as scientists and experimental farmers and inventors), to be the political leaders.

This "aristocracy" would fix reason most firmly and, under God, direct selflessly the affairs of the people. In that way, the concept of the democratic faith could become workable. This view was the paradox of Jefferson the democrat-aristocrat. But his faith was real, in spite of the "irregular" beat of his "pulse"; and he sincerely worked toward the wellbeing of the people. To the citizens of his home county, his original political constituency and his friends, he spoke in 1790 of "the general tide of happiness": "That it may flow thro' all times, gathering strength as it goes, and spreading the happy influence of reason and liberty over the face of the earth, is my fervent prayer to heaven." Only five years later he added, "This ball of liberty, I believe most piously, is now so well in motion that it will roll round the globe.... It is our glory that we first put it into motion."[9] Imperfect as the people were, they had beheld the ideal, had striven to realize it, and could look forward to the possibilities for which Jefferson was spokesman.

III *Blessings and Security*

Among American possibilities Jefferson opened was the blessing of a new sense of beauty. The creation of a dignified public architecture was an ideal that was partly realized by Jefferson. Fostering all the arts and living graciously were other ideals that his life at Monticello partially manifested; but they were tarnished by the forced labor that in large measure formed their base. He himself set the example for both good and bad, blessing and blight.

Another American possibility was security, so long sought after by human kind. There could be the security of peace of mind in philosophic contemplation, or of esthetic pleasure in never changing works of art. There could be the physical security of political peace in a given time, as when he boasted of having shed no national blood while President. Yet the public pulse was irregular; the democratic faith ebbed and flowed. He best knew this irregularity within himself, though surely it was evident all around him as well. The greatest hope for security, then, even taking into account the occasional rebellion, lay in independence. For the individual, that meant self-reliance; for the people, it meant self-government. But these were ideals.

Jefferson left, indeed, a legacy of ideals that cannot be discounted. No harsh or ugly reality that might be associated with him can erase them. Those realities were truths, it may be said, but those ideals were Truth. And so he may be honestly, validly quoted at his finest: "I have sworn upon the altar of god, eternal hostility against every form of tyranny over the mind of man." He may even be quoted, without shame, in his pride: "We can no longer say there is nothing new under the sun. For this whole chapter in the history of man is new."[10] He was right, of course. And the story — the experiment — goes on.

At last, only days before he died, Jefferson expressed regret that he could not attend the fiftieth Fourth of July celebration. He was too enfeebled by age. Of the *Declaration of Independence* he prayed, "May it be to the world, what I believe it will be, (to some parts sooner, to others later, but finally to all,) the signal of arousing men to burst the chains under which monkish ignorance and superstition had persuaded them to bind themselves, and to assume the blessings and security of self-government. . . . the mass of mankind has not been born with saddles on their backs, nor a favored few booted and spurred, ready to ride them."[11] This message was his last caution to his people. In the *Declaration of Independence* lay their blessings. Its ideals were their security. Its author died thinking of these seeds he had planted for his people to cultivate. Every American is a harvester now of the heritage of Thomas Jefferson.

Notes and References

Chapter One

1. The biographical data appearing in this chapter were derived from Jefferson's own *Autobiography,* his *Anas,* various letters, and from the standard biographies that have been written down through the years. See the Bibliography which follows, especially under Boyd, Foner, Ford, and Koch and Peden (in Primary Sources); and Brodie, Bullock, Dumbauld, Malone, Peterson, Randall, and Schachner (in Secondary Sources, Books). Certain quotations and points made in this chapter are expanded upon in subsequent, topical, chapters, where they are cited in full.

2. The notion that Monticello served a psychotherapeutic purpose for Jefferson is advanced by Page Smith, in *Jefferson: A Revealing Biography* (New York, 1976), *passim.*

3. The quotation from daughter Martha, and of the epitaph, can be found in Sarah N. Randolph, *The Domestic Life of Thomas Jefferson, Compiled from Family Letters and Reminiscences by His Great-Granddaughter* (New York, 1958), pp. 63–64.

4. William K. Bottorff, "Mr. Jefferson Tours New England," *The New-England Galaxy,* XX (Winter 1979).

5. No one who writes now about the life of Thomas Jefferson can fail to take into account the biographical work of Fawn M. Brodie. And no one who agrees with her thesis about the relationship between Jefferson and Sally Hemings can fail to acknowledge to Professor Brodie a great debt when approaching this facet of his life. Hopefully, that debt is fully acknowledged here; it is further documented in Chapter Three, "Varieties in the Race of Man" (Section III, "Domestic Economy"), and in the notes to Chapter Three.

6. For a discussion of the successes of the first term, and of the comparative failure of the second term of Jefferson, see Forrest McDonald, *The Presidency of Thomas Jefferson* (Lawrence, Kans., 1976), *passim.*

7. For this story, and for a brief review of the Jefferson-Adams relationship through the years, see Merrill D. Peterson, *Adams and Jefferson: A Revolutionary Dialogue* (New York, 1976), pp. 100–04, *et passim.*

Chapter Two

1. *The Papers of Thomas Jefferson,* ed., Julian P. Boyd et al., I

(Princeton, 1950–1974), 126. Hereafter cited as *Papers.*

2. *Papers,* I, 134.

3. *Papers,* I, 412–13.

4. *Writings of Jefferson,* ed., Paul L. Ford, VII (New York, 1892–1899), 58–59. Hereafter cited as *Writings.*

5. Also see David Hawke, *Transaction of Free Men: The Birth and Course of the Declaration of Independence* (New York, 1964), p. 173; Dixon Wecter, "Thomas Jefferson, the Gentle Radical," in *Thomas Jefferson: A Profile,* ed., Merrill D. Peterson (New York, 1967), p. 5; Gilbert Chinard, *Thomas Jefferson, the Apostle of Americanism* (Ann Arbor, 1964), p. 62. That Jefferson felt the American people were as good as a separate nation, with a distinct culture, before the Revolution is only now becoming known. See for example A. T. Baker *et al.,* "Independence: The Birth of a New America," *Time,* ["4 July 1776"] (May, 1975), pp. 10–11.

6. *Papers,* I, 423–24.

7. See Carl L. Becker, *The Declaration of Independence* (New York, 1942), pp. xii, 209; Chinard, ed., *The Commonplace Book of Thomas Jefferson* (Baltimore, 1926); Boyd, *The Declaration of Independence: The Evolution of the Text* (Princeton, 1945); Robert Ginsberg, ed., *A Casebook on the Declaration of Independence* (New York, 1967); John H. Hazelton, *The Declaration of Independence* (New York, 1906); Charles M. Wiltse, *The Jeffersonian Tradition in American Democracy* (New York, 1960); Hawke; Jefferson's "Autobiography" in Adrienne Koch and William Peden, eds., *The Life and Selected Writings of Thomas Jefferson* (New York, 1944), hereafter cited as *Selected Writings.*

8. Boyd, *The Declaration of Independence,* p. 18.

9. "The Moral Faith of the Declaration," in Ginsberg, *Casebook,* p. 164. Also see R. M. Black, "The Ethics of the Declaration of Independence," in Ginsberg, p. 82.

10. See for example Daniel J. Boorstin, *The Lost World of Thomas Jefferson* (New York, 1948; Boston, 1964), pp. 61, 195.

11. See Becker, "What Is Still Living in the Political Philosophy of Thomas Jefferson?" in Peterson, *Profile,* p. 44.

12. *Papers,* II, 567.

13. *Writings,* X, 39.

14. *Writings,* X, 303.

15. *Writings,* X, 32 (1816).

16. Chinard, *Apostle,* p. 75, and Boorstin, p. 53, seriously disagree.

17. See Arthur M. Schlesinger, "The Lost Meaning of 'The Pursuit of Happiness,' " in Ginsberg, *Casebook,* pp. 216–18 for the latter view. Jefferson used the term in this way in the last year of his life, *Writings,* X, 363.

18. See Richard Beale Davis, *Intellectual Life in Jefferson's Virginia* (Chapel Hill, 1964), p. 398.

19. *Papers,* I, 426. A weighty opinion that Jefferson meant to include Blacks under the blanket of natural rights was expressed in 1858 by Abraham Lincoln. *The Collected Works of Abraham Lincoln,* ed., Roy P. Basler, III (New Brunswick, 1953), 220. Jefferson's leading biographer agrees: Dumas Malone, *Jefferson the Virginian* (Boston, 1948), p. 228. For the central role of the slavery clause in the *Declaration,* see Edwin Gittleman, "Jefferson's 'Slave Narrative': The Declaration of Independence as a Literary Text," *Early American Literature,* VIII (1974), 239–56.

20. See Baker, *Time,* p. 33.

21. *Selected Writings,* p. 711.

22. *Selected Writings,* p. 703 (1821); *Writings,* X, 343 (1825).

23. *Writings,* X, 268, 269.

24. *Papers,* I, 427.

25. *Collected Works of Abraham Lincoln,* III, 376.

Chapter Three

1. "Memoirs of a Monticello Slave," in *Jefferson at Monticello,* ed., James A. Bear, Jr. (Charlottesville, 1967), p. 13. Isaac was Jefferson's slave from 1781 to 1824.

2. For details of slavery at Monticello, see *Thomas Jefferson's Farm Book,* Edwin M. Betts, ed. (Princeton, 1953), pp. 5–6, *passim.*

3. *Farm Book,* pp. 18–19, *passim.*

4. *Farm Book,* pp. 19, 20–23, 35, 36, 442.

5. *Farm Book,* p. 27.

6. *Papers,* I, 353. But see Merrill D. Peterson, *Thomas Jefferson and the New Nation* (New York, 1970), pp. 999–1000 for the opinion that Jefferson never really hazarded any personal inconvenience to work for emancipation.

7. *Farm Book,* pp. 37–39.

8. *Writings,* III, p. 244.

9. Jefferson advocated this so often not all instances can be cited. See *Papers,* II, 71; *Writings,* VIII, 106, 153; IX, 303; and X, 289, 344; *Selected Writings,* p. 51.

10. *Writings,* X, 291, 293, 303.

11. *Papers,* II, 472–73. Also see Peterson, *Jefferson and the New Nation,* pp. 256, 262 for Jefferson's racism. For a denial of racism in Jefferson, see Leonard Levy, "Jefferson as a Civil Libertarian," in *Thomas Jefferson, the Man, His World, His Influence,* ed., Lally Weymouth (New York, 1973), p. 201.

12. *Notes on the State of Virginia,* in *Writings,* III, 155, 244–49. "Oran ootan" was defined in Webster's first dictionary (1806) as "the largest of the ape kind, and the brute most like the human species."

13. *Writings,* VI, 84, 86 (1792).

14. That not every one of Jefferson's Virginia contemporaries believed these things, but allowed observation to prove otherwise, can be seen in the case of a little girl who lived on a plantation south of Monticello: "Mama & my-self went over the river to see Phill who was very ill when we got over he died in about an hour, his pour wife was greatly distress'd I never was sorry'r for a negro in my life." *The Diary of Frances Baylor Hill of "Hillsborough," King and Queen County Virginia (1797),* ed., William K. Bottorff and Roy C. Flanagan, *Early American Literature Newsletter,* II (1967), 33.

15. *Writings,* VIII, 231–32.

16. *Writings,* III, 245–46, 249–50.

17. See Silvio A. Bedini, *The Life of Benjamin Banneker* (New York, 1972), pp. 151, 154–55, and *Writings,* V, 377–78; IX, 261.

18. *Writings,* III, 162.

19. *Writings,* IX, 246–47. The subjects of the present chapter are also pursued at length by Boorstin in *The Lost World* in his "Varieties of Mankind: the Indian and the Negro," pp. 81–98, where he investigates (p. 81) the use of the term "varieties."

20. *Selected Writings,* pp. 598–99. Also see Bernard W. Sheehan, "The Quest for Indian Origins in the Thought of the Jeffersonian Era," *Midcontinent American Studies Journal,* IX (1968), 34–51.

21. *Writings,* IX, 431–32.

22. *Writings,* III, 155–57.

23. *Writings,* III, 151–53, 246.

24. *Papers,* VIII, 185–86 (1785).

25. *Papers,* I, 485–86.

26. *Writings,* V, 319; VI, 331 (1793).

27. Nathan Schachner, *Thomas Jefferson: A Biography* (New York, 1964), p. 731.

28. *Papers,* I, 344.

29. *Papers,* I, 121–22.

30. *Writings,* VIII, 214 (1803).

31. *Writings,* VIII, 194–99, 200.

32. *Writings,* VIII, 345.

33. *Selected Writings,* pp. 578–79.

34. *Writings,* X, 106.

35. *Writings,* X, 105. For an authentic and charming account of feminine life in Jefferson's Virginia, see *The Diary of Frances Baylor Hill, passim.*

36. *Writings,* X, 104.

37. *Writings,* X, 46 (1816).

38. *Writings,* X, 242 (1822).

39. Malone, *Jefferson the Virginian,* pp. 153–55.

40. *Farm Book,* pp. 33, 43.

41. *Writings,* III, 246.

42. For a partial listing of these, see Malone, *Jefferson the President* (Boston, 1970), p. 495.

43. See Peterson, *Jefferson and the New Nation,* p. 707, and Malone, *Jefferson the President,* pp. 494–98, where the subject is relegated to an appendix after the text.

44. Fawn M. Brodie, "The Great Jefferson Taboo," *American Heritage,* XXIII (1972), 48-57, 97–100; and Brodie, *Thomas Jefferson, an Intimate History* (New York, 1974), especially pp. 32, 433, 474. Also see Brodie, "Thomas Jefferson's Unknown Grandchildren: A Study in Historical Silences," *American Heritage,* XXVII (1976), 29, 30. Each known descendant is discussed; a family tree is given, pp. 32–33. In addition, see Isaac, "Memoirs of a Monticello Slave," p. 4.

Chapter Four

1. Malone, *Jefferson the Virginian,* pp. 37–61; Schachner, *Jefferson,* pp. 20–31.

2. Davis, *Intellectual Life,* pp. 89, 91, 90–94; E. Millicent Sowerby, *Catalogue of the Library of Thomas Jefferson* (Washington, 1952–59).

3. *Papers,* I, 76–81; VI, 360, 374; VIII, 405–08. Also *Papers,* X, 306.

4. *Selected Writings,* p. 630.

5. *Writings,* III, 252, 253; *Papers,* X, 244, 245.

6. Peterson, *Jefferson and the New Nation,* pp. 145–65.

7. The Bill is in *Papers,* II, 526–33. The judgment that the plan has never been implemented is that of the editors of *Papers* (II, 534).

8. *Basic Writings of Thomas Jefferson,* ed., Philip S. Foner (Garden City, N.Y., 1950), pp. 400–01. ("Report on the University of Virginia," 1818). Hereafter cited as *Basic Writings.*

9. *Papers,* II, 528.

10. *Papers,* XIII, 235.

11. *Papers,* II, 529–33.

12. This is the opinion also of the leading assessors of Jefferson's educational plan: Charles F. Arrowood, *Thomas Jefferson and Education in a Republic* (New York, 1930), pp. 16, 58ff; James B. Conant, *Thomas Jefferson and the Development of American Public Education* (Berkeley, 1962), pp. 7, 13; Roy J. Honeywell, *The Educational Work of Thomas Jefferson* (New York, 1964), pp. 26–31.

13. Gordon C. Lee, ed., *Crusade against Ignorance: Thomas Jefferson on Education* (New York, 1961), pp. 14, 20.

14. Peterson, *Jefferson and the New Nation,* p. 972; Schachner, *Jefferson,* p. 165.

15. Conant, pp. 25, 28; Honeywell, pp. 56, 113.

16. *Selected Writings,* pp. 152–70 (*Essay*); Albert C. Baugh, "Thomas Jefferson: Linguistic Liberal," in *Studies for William A. Read* (Baton

Rouge, 1940), pp. 90, 104; Honeywell, p. 114; H. C. Montgomery, "Thomas Jefferson as a Philologist," *American Journal of Philology,* LXV (1944), 371.

17. *Selected Writings,* p. 666.
18. *Papers,* VIII, 409, 636.
19. *Basic Writings,* p. 401.
20. *Basic Writings,* p. 408.
21. *Basic Writings,* pp. 403–04.
22. *Selected Writings,* pp. 676–77.
23. *Papers,* IX, 239; XI, 49.
24. *Papers,* VIII, 407.
25. *Writings,* X, 4.

Chapter Five

1. *Writings,* IX, 72 (1807).
2. Wiltse, p. 84; Malone, *Jefferson the Virginian,* p. 238.
3. *Papers,* I, 504.
4. *Writings,* VI, 88; *The Works of Joel Barlow,* ed., William K. Bottorff and Arthur L. Ford (Gainesville, Fla., 1970), I, 91–311 (*Advice,* 1792–93); II, 65–84 (*Conspiracy,* 1792).
5. *Papers,* II, 545–46.
6. Davis, *Intellectual Life,* p. 19.
7. *Papers,* I, 117, 121, 132.
8. *Papers,* I, 125.
9. *Papers,* XVI, 179, 225.
10. *Papers,* I, 505.
11. *Papers,* I, 505; II, 493–95.
12. *Papers,* I, 633; II, 476; *Writings,* X, 303.
13. *Papers,* II, 493, 628; *Writings,* VII, 454; X, 303.
14. *Writings,* VII, 491.
15. *Papers,* I, 292.
16. Joseph Charles, *The Origins of the American Party System* (New York, 1961), p. 90.
17. *Writings,* VI, 207; X, 281; X, 318.
18. *Writings,* V, 336–37.
19. *Poems of Freneau,* ed., Harry Hayden Clark (New York, 1929), p. xiii.
20. *Writings,* VI, 78, 87.
21. *Writings,* VII, 443, 450.
22. *Papers,* I, 340–42.
23. *Papers,* I, 344, 353; II, 391–93.
24. *Papers,* I, 353; VI, 295, 298.
25. *Papers,* VI, 248, 266; XVI, 537; XVII, 172 (the last passage quoted is the judgment of the editors of *Papers*).

26. *Papers,* XII, 270–84.
27. *Papers,* XII, 351, 442; XIII, 502.
28. *Papers,* XII, 440.
29. *Papers,* XIII, 208; XII, 442.
30. *Papers,* XIII, 442; XIV, 188; XVI, 292.
31. *Papers,* XIX, 275–80. Schachner believes the Constitution would have fallen by now had strict construction prevailed, *Jefferson,* p. 422.
32. Peterson, *Jefferson and the New Nation,* p. 782; Davis, *Intellectual Life,* p. 399.
33. *Writings,* VIII, 244.
34. *Papers,* XV, 395–96; XI, 93, 174.
35. *Papers,* XI, 526; X, 19; IX, 264. For Jefferson's reverence for the Union, see Boyd, "Thomas Jefferson's 'Empire of Liberty,' " in Peterson, *Profile,* p. 186.
36. *Writings,* VII, 201, 210.
37. Paul L. Ford, *Writings,* VII, 289.
38. *Writings,* VIII, 301.
39. *Selected Writings,* pp. 80–81 (1821).
40. *Writings,* X, 354–57 (1825).
41. Caleb P. Patterson, *Constitutional Principles of Thomas Jefferson* (Austin, 1953), pp. 163ff; Davis, *Intellectual Life,* p. 409; Malone, "Jefferson, Hamilton, and the Constitution," in Peterson, *Profile,* pp. 174–75; Wiltse, p. 127.
42. *Selected Writings,* p. 660.
43. *Writings,* X, 385; *Selected Writings,* p. 85.

Chapter Six

1. *Writings,* IX, 85; *Papers,* VI, 185; *Papers,* II, 203.
2. Charles A. Browne, "Thomas Jefferson and the Scientific Trends of His Time," *Chronica Botanica,* VIII (1944), 368, 371, 380, 418; Malone, *Jefferson and the Rights of Man* (Boston, 1951), p. 84. The fullest account of Jefferson as a scientist is Edwin T. Martin, *Thomas Jefferson: Scientist* (New York, 1961); see especially pp. 23, 32, 36–37, 208. For a number of photographs of scientific apparatus, see Bedini, "Jefferson, Man of Science," in Weymouth, pp. 128–37.
3. *Writings,* III, 134, 119; *Papers,* VIII, 186.
4. David E. Smith, "Thomas Jefferson and Mathematics," in *The Poetry of Mathematics and Other Essays* (New York, 1934), p. 51.
5. *Papers,* I, viii, 20.
6. *Papers,* VI, 139; Davis, *Intellectual Life,* p. 191; Martin, pp. 96–114.
7. *Writings,* III, 118, 90–91, 144.
8. For an account of the *Megalonyx* affair, and parts of the text of Jefferson's article, see Roland W. Brown, "Jefferson's Contribution to

Paleontology," *Journal of the Washington Academy of Science,* XXXIII (1943), 257–59. For a photograph of a skeleton of the *Megatherium,* see *National Geographic,* CXXXVI (1969), 474.

9. Boyd, "The Megalonyx, the Megatherium, and Thomas Jefferson's Lapse of Memory," *Proceedings of the American Philosophical Society,* CXII (1958), 422–34.

10. *Papers,* XII, 160.

11. Davis, *Intellectual Life,* p. 203, 194. Also see Martin, pp. 115–28.

12. *Writings,* VIII, 193–99; *Thomas Jefferson's Garden Book,* ed., Edwin M. Betts (Philadelphia, 1944), p. 625.

13. *Papers,* VII, 134–37, 642–43.

14. *Writings,* VI, 448. See Martin, pp. 62–95, for a discussion and Jefferson's sketches of mechanical devices he admired.

15. *Papers,* VIII, 455; Austin H. Clark, "Thomas Jefferson and Science," in Francis C. Rosenberger, ed., *Jefferson Reader, A Treasury of Writings about Thomas Jefferson* (New York, 1953), p. 152.

16. Boorstin, *Lost World,* p. 214.

17. Hugh H. Bennett, "Thomas Jefferson, Soil Conservationist," in Rosenberger, *Reader,* p. 188; Davis, *Intellectual Life,* pp. 164–67.

18. *Writings,* III, 268–69; *Papers,* VIII, 426, 682. Cities, by contrast, were for Jefferson breeders of "mobs" which weaken a republic, "pestilential to the morals, the health and the liberties of man." *Writings,* III, 269, VII, 459.

19. Malone, *Jefferson the Virginian,* p. 383.

20. Jefferson's detailed explanation of how to construct and employ his plow, with sketches, is in *Garden Book,* pp. 649–54.

21. Davis, *Intellectual Life,* p. 166; M. L. Wilson, "Jefferson and His Moldboard Plow," *The Land,* III (1943), 62, and "Survey of Scientific Agriculture," *Proceedings of the American Philosophical Society,* LXXXVI (1942), 58.

22. *The Life of Thomas Jefferson,* II (New York, 1858), 310.

Chapter Seven

1. Adrienne Koch, *The Philosophy of Thomas Jefferson* (Chicago, 1964; orig. 1943), *passim,* tries to fit the mantle of the French *philosophes* on Jefferson. Chinard, *Thomas Jefferson, the Apostle of Americanism* (orig. 1929), *passim,* clearly shows that this is false. Both show insight into Jefferson's rationalism. Malone, *Jefferson and the Rights of Man,* p. 215, and Karl Lehmann, *Thomas Jefferson, American Humanist* (New York, 1947), p. 73, both describe elements of the Scottish Common Sense school of philosophy adopted by Jefferson. Also see Wiltse, pp. 49, 126. Herbert Morais, *Deism in Eighteenth Century America* (New York, 1934), pp. 17, 19, 116, makes Jefferson out to be a Deist; he was not a patterned or a

typical Deist. Davis, *Intellectual Life,* p. 125, remarks on Jefferson's individualistic "Deism."

2. *Papers,* XII, 15, 17.
3. *Papers,* XIV, 650.
4. *Papers,* II, 546; *Writings,* III, 263; *Papers,* XVI, 179. Not to be unrealistic, Jefferson wrote Abigail Adams in 1804, "I know too well the weakness & uncertainty of human reason to wonder at it's different results." *Writings,* VIII, 312.
5. *Papers,* XII, 14, 15; *Writings,* VI, 225; *Papers,* I, 125.
6. *Writings,* X, 6, 143, 146; Sowerby, p. 349. See Stuart Gerry Brown, in "Epicurus, or the Pursuit of Happiness" in *Thomas Jefferson* (New York, 1963), pp. 231–35, where Lucretius is discounted.
7. *Writings,* IX, 462–63.
8. *Selected Writings,* pp. 700–01.
9. All biographers explore this subject, but see Henry Wilder Foote, *The Religion of Thomas Jefferson* (Boston, 1960), pp. 41–51; and W. D. Gould, "The Religious Opinions of Thomas Jefferson," *Mississippi Valley Historical Review,* XX (1933), 191–208 for brief reviews. Gould goes on to say that Jefferson subjected religion to the "pragmatic test" of usefulness toward "a good life," p. 200.
10. William Linn, *The Life of Thomas Jefferson* (Ithaca, 1839), p. 264. Randall, I, 17; III, 555. Also see George Harmon Knoles, "The Religious Ideas of Thomas Jefferson," in Peterson, *Profile,* p. 244.
11. Charles A. Goodrich, "Thomas Jefferson," in *Lives of the Signers of the Declaration of Independence* (Boston, 1833), pp. 404–05. Peterson, *Jefferson and the New Nation,* p. 50; J. Lesslie Hall, "The Religious Opinions of Thomas Jefferson," *Sewanee Review,* XXI (1913), 164. Boorstin refers to "Jeffersonian Christianity," pp. 151-66.
12. *Papers,* II, 546–47; *Writings,* III, 264–65.
13. The Bill is in *Papers,* II, 545–47. Also see Malone, "The Religion of a Reasonable Man," in *Jefferson the President,* pp. 190–205.
14. *Papers,* I, 344.
15. *Papers,* I, 495.
16. *Papers,* I, 530.
17. *Papers,* II, 545, 546, 638.
18. *Writings,* VI, 120–21.
19. *Writings,* IX, 174–76.
20. *Papers,* XIV, 421; XV, 522.
21. *Writings,* VIII, 227–28 (1803).
22. *Writings,* VII, 445 (1800); IX, 430, 463, 533.
23. *Writings,* IX, 412–14.
24. *Writings,* X, 144, 288.
25. *Writings,* VIII, 223.
26. *Writings,* X, 5. O.I.A. Roche, ed., *The Jefferson Bible* (New York, 1964). This edition gives a full photographic facsimile of the actual docu-

ment, as well as a typeset transcript of it, with letters and other material.

27. *Papers,* I, 79–80; *Writings,* X, 288.

28. *Bible,* pp. 325–26 (letter of 1816).

29. *Bible,* pp. 339–40 (letter of 1820).

30. See *Bible,* pp. 325–79.

31. *Bible,* p. 342 (letter of 1822).

32. Foote, pp. 69–76 ("Jefferson Adopts Unitarian Views in Later Life"). Hall, p. 170, denies that "Unitarian" should be used in a sectarian sense with Jefferson.

33. *Writings,* VIII, 226.

34. *Papers,* XIII, 418.

35. *Writings,* VIII, 21–22.

36. *Selected Writings,* p. 704; *Writings,* X, 220, 221, 242.

Chapter Eight

1. *Papers,* VI, 221.

2. *Selected Writings,* p. 637.

3. Horace M. Kallen, "The Arts and Thomas Jefferson," in Peterson, *Profile,* pp. 223, 233. Eleanor Davidson Berman, *Thomas Jefferson Among the Arts* (New York, 1947), pp. 3, 11, 48.

4. William B. O'Neal, *Jefferson's Fine Arts Library for the University of Virginia* (Charlottesville, 1956), p. 38 and *passim.* Berman, p. 111.

5. Hugh Blair, *Lectures on Rhetoric and Belles Lettres* (New York, 1824; orig. 1783), p. 29. Other authorities of the Scottish Common Sense school of philosophy whose works Jefferson knew were Henry Home, Lord Kames, and Thomas Reid. Berman, pp. 34, 43, 44, 45.

6. *Papers,* II, 196; Berman, p. 172; Marie Kimball, "Jefferson, Patron of the Arts," *Antiques,* XLIII (1943), 164; Charles E. Gauss, "Thomas Jefferson's Musical Interests," *Etude,* LI (1933), 419.

7. *Selected Writings,* p. 258.

8. *Papers,* X, 118.

9. *Selected Writings,* p. 459. Jefferson often corresponded with Hopkinson on musical matters.

10. Helen Cripe, *Thomas Jefferson and Music* (Charlottesville, 1974), pp. 5, 20, 21.

11. *Papers,* I, 71–72; IX, 579; Cripe, pp. 41, 64; Arthur S. Garbett, "Thomas Jefferson's Life-Long Love of Music," *Etude,* LIX (1941), 568; Helen D. Bullock, "Mr. Jefferson — Musician," *Etude,* LXI (1943), 633.

12. Bullock, *My Head and My Heart* (New York, 1955), p. 7; Cripe, pp. 27, 88; Davis, *Intellectual Life,* pp. 230, 237; Gauss, p. 367; Garbett, p. 510.

13. Isaac, "Memoirs of a Monticello Slave," p. 13; Davis, *Intellectual Life,* p. 239.

14. Cripe, pp. 70, 75.
15. Bullock, *My Head and My Heart,* pp. viii, 7; Cripe, pp. 9, 75, 81, 97–128.
16. Cripe, p. 93; *Selected Writings,* p. 689.
17. *Papers,* XVIII, 132; *Writings,* X, 61. For the background of letters in Jefferson's time, see John S. Martin, "Rhetoric, Society and Literature in the Age of Jefferson," *Midcontinent American Studies Journal,* IX (1968), 77–90.
18. *Papers,* I, 78–79.
19. *Papers,* I, 78.
20. For background, see Howard Mumford Jones, *Jeffersonianism and the American Novel* (New York, 1966), *passim.*
21. *Papers,* VI, 196, 374.
22. Russel B. Nye, and Norman S. Grabo, eds., *American Thought and Writing,* II (Boston, 1965), 335; *Papers,* I, 76, 77.
23. *Writings,* X, 104–05. Jefferson's position anticipates that of William Dean Howells later in the century.
24. *Writings,* III, 246. Also see John W. Wayland, "The Poetical Tastes of Thomas Jefferson," *Sewanee Review,* XVIII (1910), 283–89. Paul L. Haworth, "Thomas Jefferson — Poet," *Bookman,* XXXI (1910), 647–50, prints verses he attributes to Jefferson.
25. *Miscellaneous Works* (New York, 1804), p. 395, under "Subscribers' Names": "Thomas Jefferson, President of the United States"; *Papers,* VII, 317, Trumbull presents Jefferson with *M'Fingal,* 1784; XI, 473, Barlow sends him *The Vision of Columbus,* 1787; *Writings,* VI, 107. Sowerby lists additional works by these and other American poets, well into the nineteenth century.
26. Randall, III, 119.
27. *Papers,* I, 96.
28. *Papers,* XVIII, 77–78; *Writings,* X, 282.
29. *Writings,* VIII, 65.
30. *Papers,* VIII, 569.
31. *Papers,* XII, 245; Sowerby, IV, *passim;* Davis, *Intellectual Life,* pp. 227–28; Randall, III, 336–37; Wilstach, pp. 108–10.
32. Berman, pp. 77–80; Marie Kimball, "Jefferson, Patron of the Arts," pp. 164–67. Also see Marie Kimball, *Jefferson: The Scene of Europe, 1784 to 1789* (New York, 1950), pp. 323–27.
33. *Papers,* VIII, 176–77.
34. *Papers,* XIII, 104.
35. *Papers,* XIII, 269 (1788).
36. Marie Kimball, "Jefferson, Patron of the Arts," pp. 165, 167; Wilstach, p. 108. Chinard, *Houdon in America* (Baltimore, 1930), *passim.*
37. Fiske Kimball, *Thomas Jefferson and the First Monument of the Clasical Revival* (n.p., n.d.), *passim;* Fiske Kimball, *Thomas Jefferson, Architect* (New York, 1968), pp. 84, 86.

38. *Papers,* XII, 36 (the reference is to Trumbull the painter, not to the poet of the same name).

39. *Papers,* VIII, 290.

40. Fiske Kimball, *Jefferson, Architect,* p. 86.

41. Berman, pp. 65–66; Fiske Kimball, *Jefferson, Architect,* pp. 27, 28, 135.

42. *Papers,* IX, 369–73.

43. Frederick D. Nichols and James A. Bear, Jr., *Monticello* (Charlottesville, 1967), pp. 52ff. Also see the excellent sketches inside the two covers and on p. 54.

44. Berman, p. 74; Fiske Kimball, "Jefferson and the Arts," in Rosenberger, *Jefferson Reader,* p. 203.

45. *Papers,* XIII, 8; VIII, 538; *Writings,* III, 257, 258.

46. Fiske Kimball, *Jefferson, Architect,* p. 30; Davis, *Intellectual Life,* p. 210; O'Neal, *Jefferson's Fine Arts Library,* p. 44.

47. *Time,* 29 Sept. 1958, p. 83; O'Neal, ed., *American Association of Architectural Bibliographers Papers,* VI (Charlottesville, 1969), pp. 60–61.

48. Fiske Kimball, *Jefferson, Architect,* pp. 81, 143; Davis, *Intellectual Life,* p. 63; Lehmann, p. 171. For a number of excellent photographs of his architecture and other Jeffersoniana, see Wendell D. Garrett and Joseph C. Farber, *Thomas Jefferson, Redivivus* (Barre, Mass., 1971), *passim.*

49. Saul K. Padover, *Thomas Jefferson and the National Capitol* (Washington, 1946), opp. p. 28, p. 300, opp. p. 348, p. 472. Fiske Kimball, *Jefferson, Architect,* pp. 53, 54, 62ff, drawings 125, 126, 131, 132. Frederick Doveton Nichols, *Thomas Jefferson's Architectural Drawings,* p. 7, drawing 16, p. 41. Talbot Hamlin, *Greek Revival Architecture in America* (New York, 1964), p. 17. For a more detailed account of Jefferson's District plan, see John W. Reps, *The Making of Urban America* (Princeton, 1965), pp. 245–48; and Reps, *Town Planning in Frontier America* (Princeton, 1971), pp. 312–16.

50. Reps, *Urban America,* pp. 314–24; *Frontier America,* pp. 279–82 (with drawing).

51. Fiske Kimball, *First Monument,* pp. 5, 48; Nichols, p. 4.

52. *Papers,* VIII, 462. He sent a plaster model of the building in 1786. *Papers,* IX, 639.

53. *Selected Writings,* p. 48.

54. It has been suggested that Jefferson employed the Ionic order because in Freemasonry it symbolizes wisdom, which is more fitting for a government structure than the Corinthian connotation of beauty. Yet Jefferson was not a Mason. Alan Gowans, "Freemasonry and the Neoclassic Style in America," *Antiques,* LXXVII (1960), 175. For Jefferson's drawings see Nichols, 11, 12, 13 and Fiske Kimball, *Jefferson, Architect,* 110, 111, 112–16. Number 117 is a photograph of the plaster model.

Jefferson also knew the Maison Carrée from Andrea Palladio's *The Four Books of Architecture,* through the Leoni edition of 1721 or a later edition. For comparison the easily accessible edition of Palladian drawings (with statuary) is by Dover Publications (New York, 1965), pp. 106, 107–08, plates LXXXI-LXXXVI, Book Four.

55. Fiske Kimball, *First Monument,* pp. 5, 7ff, 23, 27; *Jefferson, Architect,* pp. 40, 41.

56. Fiske Kimball, *First Monument,* pp. 40–42; *Jefferson, Architect,* pp. 41, 43, 145–46, 147. Chinard, *Houdon in America,* pp. xivff, iff (photograph opp. p. 14). The statue was originally to have been equestrian.

57. Fiske Kimball, *Jefferson, Architect,* p. 33, drawings 101, 104; Nichols, Introd. to *Jefferson, Architect,* p. viii; drawings 171–74, 189–92; Nichols, pp. 6, 7, drawings 7, 8, 9, 19, 20, 22, 29, 30; *Jefferson, Architect,* pp. 73, 185, 186, drawings 203, 204, 205, 206. Among these lesser houses, at least Edgemont and Farmington still stand; Barboursville is in ruin. See Joseph Judge, "Mr. Jefferson's Monticello," *National Geographic,* CXXX (1966), 432.

58. Nichols, Introd. to *Jefferson, Architect,* p. ix; Nichols, p. 4, drawing 9.

59. Palladio, pp. 94, 95, plates XXXIV, XXXV, XXXVI, Book Four.

60. Palladio, pp. 37, 46.

61. *Selected Writings,* pp. 379, 602.

62. Palladio, p. 46; *Papers,* X, 447. Also see James S. Ackerman, *Palladio* (Baltimore, 1967), p. 70.

63. Berman, p. 47. Betts, *Garden Book,* pp. 11, 17.

64. Fiske Kimball, *Jefferson, Architect,* p. 159; O'Neal *Bibliographers,* p. 6; Nichols and Bear, p. 9.

65. Marie Kimball, *The Furnishings of Monticello* [n.p., 1940], p. 24. Fiske Kimball and Marie Kimball, "Jefferson's Curtains at Monticello," rpt. from *Antiques* (1947), n.p.

66. *Papers,* XV, opposite pp. 280, 281; Judge, p. 435.

67. Nichols and Bear is the best source for a word and photograph tour of Monticello. Also see Judge, *passim.* Good pictures of the staircases are in Nichols and Bear, p. 43, and Judge, pp. 430–31. Scholars disagree as to whether the staircases are a bungling or a *tour de force.* See Walter Muir Whitehill, "Thomas Jefferson, Architect," in Weymouth, p. 167; Davis, *Intellectual Life,* p. 211; Wilstach, p. 104; John S. Patton, *Monticello and Its Master* (Charlottesville, 1930), pp. 53–55.

68. See, for example, Palladio, plates XXXII, XXXIX, Book Two.

69. For Jefferson's plans of the mansion and its dependencies, see Nichols, drawings 2, 3, 4; Fiske Kimball, *Jefferson, Architect,* drawings 4–7, 18, 24; 8, 10, 12, 30–32; 139, 140, 150–52, and others.

70. Ackerman, pp. 160ff; Lehmann, pp. 160–61.

71. This latter point is made also by Fiske Kimball, *Jefferson, Archi-*

tect, p. 22. Kimball finds no "literal" precedent for Monticello in Palladio or elsewhere, p. 24; also see pp. 82–83. Concurring is Wayne Andrews, *Architecture, Ambition and Americans* (New York, 1955), p. 62.

72. Malone, *Jefferson and the Ordeal of Liberty* (Boston, 1962), pp. 233–34; Betts, *Farm Book,* p. 337.

73. Wilstach, p. 106.

74. Fiske Kimball, *Jefferson, Architect,* p. 29; Betts, *Farm Book,* p. 337; Malone, *Ordeal,* p. 234.

75. For details of door plans, see Fiske Kimball, *Jefferson, Architect,* drawings 19, 20; details for entablatures and other elements, directly from Palladio, are drawings 40–42.

76. Fiske Kimball, *Jefferson, Architect,* drawings 35, 36, 38, 39, 62–64.

77. The Marquis de Chastellux, quoted in O'Neal, *Bibliographers,* p. 5.

78. Davis, *Intellectual Life,* p. 211; Nichols and Bear, p. 9.

79. Andrews believes it to be rivaled as a campus only by Frank Lloyd Wright's Florida Southern University project, p. 64. Also see Fiske Kimball, *Jefferson, Architect,* p. 74; William A. Lambeth and Warren H. Manning, *Thomas Jefferson as an Architect and a Designer of Landscapes* (Boston, 1913), p. 38.

80. Quoted in Fiske Kimball, *Jefferson, Architect,* p. 190, and in Nichols, p. 8.

81. Quoted in Nichols, p. 8, and in Fiske Kimball, *Jefferson, Architect,* p. 188. Kimball calls this plan new for an American university, p. 80.

82. I. T. Frary, *Thomas Jefferson: Architect and Builder* (Richmond, 1931), p. 52; Lambeth and Manning, p. 116. Whitehill, p. 176; Nichols, p. 9.

83. Fiske Kimball, *Jefferson, Architect,* p. 78, drawings 208, 209, 211, (pavilions), and the large, fold-out plan of the entire University; Nichols, pp. 8–9, drawings 23, 24, 25 (pavilions), 26 (total plan), 27 (Rotunda), 28 (serpentine wall); Lehmann, pp. 161, 171 (pointing out that Jefferson's Rotunda is two columns narrower and more graceful than the heavy looking Pantheon — photographs are supplied); the best source on the Rotunda is O'Neal, *Jefferson's Buildings at the University of Virginia: The Rotunda* (Charlottesville, 1960), pp. 2, 57–58; Plates VI, VII, VIII, IX, XI, XII, XIII, XIV.

84. Lehmann, p. 167.

85. Quoted in O'Neal, *Rotunda,* p. 1.

86. O'Neal, *Rotunda,* pp. 7, 12, 52; *Bibliographers,* p. 124.

Chapter Nine

1. *The Life of Thomas Jefferson,* I (Philadelphia, 1837), 90. Laudatory comments include those by Padover, *The Complete Jefferson* (New York, 1943), x; Lester J. Cappon, *The Adams-Jefferson Letters* (Chapel

Hill, N.C., 1959), pp. xlvii, xlix; Davis, *Intellectual Life,* p. 291. A dissenting opinion is in Max J. Herzberg, "Thomas Jefferson as a Man of Letters," *South Atlantic Quarterly,* XIII (1914), 324, 327.

2. *Papers,* I, xxvii, 193–98.
3. *Papers,* I, 495, 677ff; XVI, opp. p. 52, picture of the seal.
4. *Papers,* I, 133, 227, 242; VI, 340; *Writings,* VII, 95.
5. *Papers,* I, 132, 3–20; *Selected Writings,* pp. 176–80; 3ff.
6. *Selected Writings,* pp. 3, 51.
7. *Papers,* I, 122, 186, 195; XII, 356.
8. *Papers,* XI, 226; *Writings,* III, 263.
9. *Papers,* I, 134, 135; XI, 370; *Writings,* VII, 93; *Farm Book,* p. 54.
10. *Papers,* I, 124–25; II, 239.
11. *Papers,* VI, 350, 374.
12. *Papers,* X, 557; *Writings,* VI, 107.
13. *Writings,* X, 183 (1821); *Papers,* VIII, 637 (1785).
14. *Writings,* III, 102, 109, 110. See E. P. Tompkins, and J. Lee Davis, *The Natural Bridge and Its Historical Surroundings* (Natural Bridge, Va., 1939), *passim.*
15. *Papers,* II, 238.
16. *Papers,* XVIII, 350; V, 633; XI, 657; VIII, 241.
17. *Papers,* XIII, 269; VIII, 681; XI, 123.
18. *Papers,* X, 50; VIII, 233; XI, 251.
19. *Papers,* VII, 27, 108, 233; X, 557; *Writings,* VI, 119; IX, 231.
20. *Writings,* IX, 329; Marie Kimball, *Thomas Jefferson's Cookbook* (Richmond, 1949), pp. 1, 10; *Writings,* VII, 28; IX, 7; *Papers,* VIII, 239.
21. *Writings,* IX, 333; *Selected Writings,* pp. 684–85.
22. *Papers,* X, 443–53.
23. *Writings,* X, 396.

Chapter Ten

1. See Washington Irving, "The Reign of William the Testy," in *A History of New York* (1809), a satire of the Jeffersonian administration; Robert Frost, "The Black Cottage" (1914); Robert Penn Warren, *Brother to Dragons* (1953).
2. Assessments of Jefferson's reputation are Malone, *Jefferson the Virginian,* p. viii; Peterson, *The Jefferson Image in the American Mind* (New York, 1960), pp. 68, 379, 439; Mayo, *Myths and Men* (New York, 1963), pp. 61–83; Dixon Wecter, "Thomas Jefferson, The Gentle Radical," in Peterson, *Profile,* pp. 1–40; Walter B. Hendrickson, "Thomas Jefferson — Up from Slander," *Social Education,* VI (1954), 244–48; Brodie, "Jefferson Biographers and the Psychology of Canonization," *Journal of Interdisciplinary History,* II (1971), 155–71.
3. Some years ago I wrote these observations, to which I still subscribe:

Whatever American civilization is today is due in no small measure to what American Civilization was in the Age of Jefferson. No other era in our national past is so important as Jefferson's time in aiding our study of what we have been and what we have become. . . . A great deal is known about Jefferson through many excellent studies. His works are now being reprinted and newly edited. It seems we always expect a new book on Jefferson, and we get it without a long wait. . . . But as we think of Jefferson, and of his death in 1826, we realize his Age was not only one of beginnings, but of the end of something. . . . we sense perhaps the passing of a kind of giant who helped form the older American myth.

If those were the times that tried men's souls, there was at least no wanting for great men to meet the crises. But no more beyond the Age of Jefferson would the many-sided Man of the Enlightenment walk among us — no more Franklins, Websters, Rushes, Barlows, no Jeffersons. One manifestation, one almost mythic, one demigodlike figure representing what Jefferson once called "the American mind," was lost and cannot be recovered. This is in part the measure of how far American civilization today has moved away from the former time.

Midcontinent American Studies Journal, IX (1968), 5–6.

4. John Dewey, "The Moral Faith of the Declaration," in Ginsberg, *Casebook,* p. 162–65.

5. *Writings,* V, 367.

6. Carlyle C. Douglas, "The Dilemma of Thomas Jefferson," subtitled "He Wrote the Declaration of Independence but Failed to Practice What He Preached," *Ebony,* XXX (1975), 60–66.

7. *Selected Writings,* p. 705; *Papers,* IV, 265.

8. *Writings,* VII, 24, 100; IX, 425; X, 69, 231.

9. *Papers,* XVI, 179; *Writings,* VII, 22.

10. *Writings,* VII, 4; VIII, 22.

11. *Writings,* X, 391–92.

Selected Bibliography

PRIMARY SOURCES

BETTS, EDWIN M., ed. *Thomas Jefferson's Farm Book, with Commentary and Relevant Extracts from Other Writings.* Princeton: Princeton University Press, 1953. A transcription, augmented by letters and other data, of the detailed accounts of cash crops, the market, and related matters on Jefferson's plantations, including records of slave holdings.

______, ed. *Thomas Jefferson's Garden Book, 1766–1824, with Relevant Extracts from His Other Writings.* Philadelphia: American Philosophical Society, 1944. A transcription, augmented by letters and other sources, of Jefferson's records of foods raised for consumption on his plantations, tree planting and landscaping, with meteorological data. This is the best source for studying the moldboard plow.

______, and JAMES A. BEAR, JR., eds. *The Family Letters of Thomas Jefferson.* Columbia: University of Missouri Press, 1966. Presenting correspondence between Jefferson, his daughters, and his grandchildren, this collection is useful in studying how Jefferson's tone varied depending upon the age and the station of the person addressed.

BOYD, JULIAN P. *The Declaration of Independence: The Evolution of the Text, as Shown in Facsimiles of Various Drafts by Its Author, Thomas Jefferson.* Princeton: Princeton University Press, 1945. Reproduced in their original handwriting are such documents as George Mason's draft of the Virginia Bill of Rights, Jefferson's "first ideas" on the Virginia Constitution, Richard Henry Lee's resolution of independence, Jefferson's Rough Draft of the *Declaration,* other copies of the *Declaration* in Jefferson's hand, and the first printing of the *Declaration.* There are many helpful notes and passages of discussion which make this an indispensable research source on the *Declaration.*

______, et al., eds. *The Papers of Thomas Jefferson.* Princeton: Princeton University Press, 1950——. Over fifty vols. are projected; nineteen have appeared. This will eventually be the complete works of Jefferson — letters, architectural drawings, and documents of all kinds. The notes are meticulously done and are more detailed by far than those of any other edition. There are major and lesser essays placing many of the papers in historical context and relating them to biographical facts. Because the editing is refined and exemplary, the edition will form a scholarly monument to Jefferson, as well as function as one of the richest sources of American historical research.

BOYKIN, EDWARD, ed. *To the Boys and Girls, Being the Delightful, Little-Known Letters of Thomas Jefferson to and from His Children and Grandchildren.* New York: Funk and Wagnalls, 1964. With a helpful running commentary by the editor, and illustrations including portraits and artifacts, are selected letters to and from Jefferson; Martha (Patsy) and Mary (Polly), his daughters; and his grandchildren. The qualities of Jefferson as a father and grandfather are vivid in these samples.

CAPPON, LESTER J., ed. *The Adams-Jefferson Letters: The Complete Correspondence between Thomas Jefferson and John and Abigail Adams.* Chapel Hill: University of North Carolina Press, 1959. The once impaired friendship between the two men is made clear in the frankness and in the earnest tone of the letters. One of the most remarkable women of her time emerges as she exchanges, on equal terms, ideas on many subjects with Jefferson. Several keys to Jefferson's political philosophy are contained in these letters.

Calendar of the Correspondence of Thomas Jefferson. 3 vols. New York: Burt Franklin, 1970. Rpt. of 1894–1903 edn., U.S. Bureau of Rolls and Library. This useful, not yet obsolete listing of Jefferson's letters is for scholars interested in his private voices, for the correspondence is largely unknown to the public of his lifetime.

CHINARD, GILBERT, ed. *The Commonplace Book of Thomas Jefferson: A Repertory of His Ideas on Government.* Baltimore: Johns Hopkins Press, 1926. This is a transcript, with annotations, of Jefferson's notes on and abstracts of books he read, mostly when he was a student, with a few entries closer to the writing of the *Declaration.* Included is his abstract of Montesquieu's *Spirit of Laws,* of works of Locke and Kames, and of other largely political works among his early reading. As to how much can be inferred about Jefferson's choice of readings, however, it must be remembered that many of these must have been assigned by his tutors and professors who assessed his efforts by examining his notes.

———, ed. *Houdon in America: A Collection of Documents in the Jefferson Papers in the Library of Congress.* Introduction by Francis Henry Taylor. Baltimore: Johns Hopkins Press, 1930. After a brief life of Houdon and a discussion of his American visit and work, there appear several dozen letters, memoranda, and other documents from the years 1784–1825. These outline the Jefferson-Houdon relationship that brought the French sculptor to the United States to immortalize the new nation's heroes in statues and busts. A number of the entries remain in French; a few are translated. Most of Jefferson's, and all the documents of Adams, Franklin, Washington, Madison, Monroe, and others, are in English. Illustrations include photographs of busts of Franklin, Lafayette, and Jefferson, with the full-length Washington in the capitol at Richmond.

______, ed. *The Letters of Lafayette and Jefferson.* Baltimore: Johns Hopkins Press, 1929. Between 1781 and 1825 Lafayette and Jefferson exchanged a great number of letters, mostly in English. These and some documents in French (with translations), including Lafayette's *Declaration des Droits de l'Homme* (1789), are accompanied by extended notes.

______, ed. *The Literary Bible of Thomas Jefferson: His Commonplace Book of Philosophers and Poets.* Baltimore: Johns Hopkins Press, 1928; rpt. New York: Greenwood Press, 1969. Not to be confused with *The Jefferson Bible,* this book is unrelated to Jefferson's religious *tour de force.* From his days as a schoolboy and as a young man, here are notes gleaned (largely copied) from the leading writers of his time and from antiquity, which Jefferson was no doubt called upon to read by his instructors.

COMETTI, ELIZABETH, ed. *Jefferson's Ideas on a University Library: Letters from the Founder of the University of Virginia to a Boston Bookseller.* Charlottesville: University Press of Virginia, 1950. Late in his life Jefferson tried to make sure a sound quantity and variety of books would be available to his University students, and he turned to Boston, as America's leading *entrepôt* of books, for purchasing, as the letters here show.

DUMBAULD, EDWARD, ed. *The Political Writings of Thomas Jefferson: Representative Selections.* Indianapolis: Bobbs-Merrill, 1955. An introduction, a bibliography, and notes to the selections accompany the *Declaration,* his drafts of a Virginia constitution, *A Summary View,* the Kentucky Resolutions, many letters, and other documents, in whole or in part, from throughout his lifetime.

FOLEY, JOHN P., ed. *The Jeffersonian Cyclopedia: A Comprehensive Collection of the Views of Thomas Jefferson, Classified and Arranged in Alphabetical Order Under Nine Thousand Titles, Relating to Government, Politics, Law, Education, Political Economy, Finance, Science, Art, Literature, Religious Freedom, Morals, etc.* New York: Funk and Wagnalls, 1900. Here are thousands of quotations, primarily from the Ford edition, which represent Jefferson on a huge variety of subjects. A curious work, still useful for quick reference; uniquely catalogues a great American's thoughts.

FONER, PHILIP S., ed. *Basic Writings of Thomas Jefferson.* Garden City, N.Y.: Halcyon House, 1950. Based on the Lipscomb-Bergh and the Ford editions, arranged chronologically from 1774–1821 ("Major Writings Other Than Letters"), and 1760–1826 ("Selected Correspondence"), there appear over 800 pages of representative items.

Included are *A Summary View,* The *Declaration, Notes,* the inaugural messages, and dozens of other items, with many letters, and Jefferson's will.

FORD, PAUL LEICESTER, ed. *The Writings of Thomas Jefferson.* 10 vols. New York: G.P. Putnam's Sons, 1892–99. Basic; still a valuable and reliable research source (the best edition of *Notes*). The Ford edition is famous for careful editing and intelligent selection of materials, as well as for helpful notes. Until the Boyd-Princeton edition is finished, the scholar should turn to Ford for material not yet appearing in the new volumes.

KIMBALL, FISKE, ed. *Thomas Jefferson, Architect: Original Designs in the Coolidge Collection of the Massachusetts Historical Society, with an Essay and Notes.* New York: Da Capo Press, 1968. Introduction by Frederick Doveton Nichols. Rpt. of 1916 edn. The basic book of Jefferson's drawings and plans, a truly remarkable production of scholarship and judgment. Kimball's notes and attributions are still largely reliable, Nichols' introduction clarifying any shortcomings. A full description of each document is given; the reproductions of the drawings and plans are excellent. Here are Jefferson's elevations of Monticello, the capitol at Richmond, floor plans, the University designs, and numerous other sketches by America's early, though amateur, master architect. This is a huge book of high quality, a work of art in itself.

KITE, ELIZABETH S., ed. *L'Enfant and Washington, 1791–1792: Published and Unpublished Documents Now Brought Together for the First Time.* Baltimore: Johns Hopkins Press, 1929. Introd. J. J. Jusserand. A number of Jefferson's letters, letters of L'Enfant, official government documents, and other items follow a lengthy essay of introduction. Notes clarify L'Enfant's role in planning the District of Columbia at every turn. The L'Enfant plan is photographically reproduced.

KOCH, ADRIENNE, ed. *Great Lives Observed: Jefferson.* Englewood Cliffs, N.J.: Prentice-Hall, 1971. An introduction and running notes are helpful in establishing the context of the selections from Jefferson's writings, and assessments of others concerning Jefferson. The "Rough Draft" of the *Declaration, Notes,* letters, and other of Jefferson's documents appear. These are complemented by remarks by Chastellux, Abigail and John Adams, Hamilton, Madison, and other contemporaries; and by modern observers such as John Dewey and Dumas Malone.

———, and WILLIAM PEDEN, eds. *The Life and Selected Writings of Thomas Jefferson.* New York: Modern Library, 1944. Based on the Lipscomb-Bergh edition, this is the fullest and best one-volume anthology of writings from the hand of Jefferson. Reprinted complete are the *Autobiography,* to 1790 (with the *Declaration* and the author's account of its genesis); the *Anas* (his autobiography continued to 1809); the rarely reprinted *Essay on Anglo-Saxon; Notes;* other public documents; and over 200 letters from 1760–1826. A full index helps make this a fine research source.

LEE, GORDON C., ed. *Crusade Against Ignorance: Thomas Jefferson on Education.* New York: Teachers College, Columbia University, 1961. Chiefly letters (1776–1825), with some public documents, introduction, and notes, on the subject of education at all levels, formal and informal.

LIPSCOMB, ANDREW A., and ALBERT E. BERGH, eds. *The Writings of Thomas Jefferson.* 20 vols. Washington, D.C.: Thomas Jefferson Memorial Association, 1903. A major attempt at publishing Jefferson's writings, this edition is not as carefully edited as the Ford edition, though it contains more bulk, and is being rendered obsolete by the Boyd-Princeton edition.

MAYO, BERNARD, ed. *Jefferson Himself: The Personal Narrative of a Many-Sided American.* Charlottesville: University Press of Virginia, 1970. Rpt. of 1942 orig. Letters, parts of the *Autobiography,* illustrations, and editorial commentary trace Jefferson's entire life through his written opinions. This is the fullest "autobiography" available. A full index contributes to the book's utility for research.

NICHOLS, FREDERICK DOVETON, comp. *Thomas Jefferson's Architectural Drawings, Compiled and with Commentary and a Check List.* 2nd edn., rev. and enl. Boston: Massachusetts Historical Society; Charlottesville: Thomas Jefferson Memorial Foundation and University of Virginia Press, 1961. Expands upon Kimball by reproducing additional drawings, sketches, and plans (Monticello, the University, etc.). Descriptions and locations of 531 documents are given; the commentary includes a discussion of Jefferson's development as an architect.

O'NEAL, WILLIAM B. *Jefferson's Buildings at the University of Virginia: The Rotunda.* Charlottesville: University of Virginia Press, 1960. This excellent book reproduces Jefferson's designs for the Rotunda, pertinent plates from Palladio, and the 1822 Maverick Plan of the entire University. Parts of a good many letters and other documents are reprinted, tracing the development of the designs. An essay explaining the context of the project is helpful, as is the index.

PADOVER, SAUL K., ed. *The Complete Jefferson as Revealed in His Letters.* New York: Tudor, 1943. Selections, representative though far from "complete," from Jefferson's letters (180, 1760–1825), a memorial sampling at the 200th anniversary of his birth. Fully indexed.

______, ed. *Thomas Jefferson and the National Capital, Containing Notes and Correspondence Exchanged Between Jefferson, Washington, L'Enfant, Ellicott, Hallett, Thornton, Latrobe, the Commis-*

sioners, and Others, Relating to the Founding, Surveying, Planning, Designing, Constructing, and Administering of the City of Washington, 1783–1813, with Plans and Illustrations. Washington, D.C.: Government Printing Office, 1946. The lengthy title accurately describes this thorough and useful gathering.

PETERSON, MERRILL D., ed. *The Portable Thomas Jefferson.* New York: Viking, 1975. A fine anthology of Jefferson's writings, well selected, with a major essay of introduction by the editor. Notes accompany the documents, which include *A Summary View, Notes,* the *Declaration* ("Draft" and final), other public papers, and dozens of letters (1771–1826).

RANDOLPH, THOMAS J., ed. *Memoir, Correspondence and Miscellanies, from the Papers of Thomas Jefferson.* 4 vols. Charlottesville: F. Carr, 1829. The earliest basic printing of Jefferson's writings, now useful mainly to the antiquarian who would trace the evolution of Jeffersonian texts. A pioneering project, famous in its time (appearing so quickly after Jefferson's death), and still respected today.

ROCHE, O. I. A. *The Jefferson Bible, with the Annotated Commentaries on Religion of Thomas Jefferson.* New York: Clarkson N. Potter, 1964. Introduction by Henry Wilder Foote; Foreword by Donald S. Harrington. A newly typeset printing of Jefferson's "Bible" — his redaction of the New Testament, comprising his versions of the sayings of Jesus — is accompanied by a valuable photo-reproduction of the original volume wherein Jefferson pasted the selections he clipped from the Bible. There is a table of the (biblical) texts and an index of (gospel) extracts, as well as selected parts of letters and other Jefferson documents concerning religion.

VERNER, COOLIE, comp. *Mr. Jefferson Distributes His "Notes": A Preliminary Checklist of the First Edition.* New York: New York Public Library, 1952. A good scholarly pamphlet "to determine the disposition of the greater part of the first edition [1785] of Thomas Jefferson's *Notes on Virginia.*" Snippets of letters from Madison, Franklin, Adams, Lafayette, Buffon, and many others acknowledging receipt of gift copies of *Notes* trace Jefferson's distribution of the book from 1785–1787, and in a few instances in later years, with notations by the giver; editorial notes locate presently existing copies.

SECONDARY SOURCES

1. Books

BEAR, JAMES A., JR., ed. *Jefferson at Monticello: Memoirs of a Monticello Slave, as Dictated to Charles Campbell by Isaac; The Private Life of Thomas Jefferson, by Rev. Hamilton Wilcox Pierson* [recollections by Edmund Bacon, overseer]. Charlottesville: University

Press of Virginia, 1967. Here are two unique views of daily life at Monticello. Isaac's account (written 1847) extends from 1781–1824. This part of the book includes a remarkable photograph of Isaac, and genealogical tables of Isaac's family and of the Hemings family. Bacon's account (1862) covers the period 1806–1822. There are many detailed notes, commentary, and a full index — a truly fine editing job.

BECKER, CARL. *The Declaration of Independence: A Study in the History of Political Ideas.* New York: Vintage, 1942. Rpt. of 1922 edn. Pioneer study; still reliable. Versions of the *Declaration* are delineated; historical antecedents are traced; the style of the *Declaration* is discussed; an index is included.

BERMAN, ELEANOR DAVIDSON. *Thomas Jefferson Among the Arts: An Essay in Early American Esthetics.* New York: Philosophical Library, 1947. The sources of Jefferson's esthetic are explored, as is the alleged Hogarthian influence. There are chapters on painting, sculpture, architecture, gardening, music, rhetoric, and literature.

BINGER, CARL. *Thomas Jefferson, a Well-Tempered Mind.* New York: Norton, 1970. A popular biography, lacking in detail or depth of interpretation, but a good introduction to the subject, with many scholarly notations for a short book.

BOORSTIN, DANIEL J. *The Lost World of Thomas Jefferson.* Boston: Beacon Press, 1964. Rpt. of 1948 edn. A partly successful attempt to characterize Jefferson's philosophy as based on *a priori* assumptions reinforced by empirical data. The book is heavily annotated, and discusses such subjects as nature, the races, metaphysics, religion, and politics — all considered as aspects of Jefferson's philosophy.

BOWERS, CLAUDE G. *Jefferson and Hamilton: The Struggle for Democracy in America.* Boston: Houghton Mifflin, 1966. Rpt. of 1925 edn. With the two volumes below, a biography. All three volumes have good narrative style. *Jefferson and Hamilton* (centers on the 1790s) is solid on the social background and color of the milieu, but is melodramatic in delineating the good and bad characters of the political struggles of the era.

———. *Jefferson in Power; The Death Struggle of the Federalists.* Boston: Houghton Mifflin, 1936. Covers the presidential years. Pictures Jefferson as little less than a miracle worker; those opposing him, as virtual traitors.

———. *The Young Jefferson, 1743–1789.* Boston: Houghton Mifflin, 1945. The sense of chronology during Jefferson's formative years not carefully enough maintained.

BRODIE, FAWN M. *Thomas Jefferson, an Intimate History.* New York: Norton, 1974. The most thought provoking of all Jefferson biographies, clarifying Jefferson's private life. The controversial thesis that Jefferson and a slave woman, Sally Hemings, were in love over a long period of time is established. Jefferson, a widower, unable to live openly with the Black woman, clandestinely did so and fathered her children. No other historian or biographer has tried so earnestly and so objectively to resolve the nature of the association between these two people.

BROWN, STUART GERRY. *Thomas Jefferson.* New York: Washington Square Press, 1963. The best brief biography of Jefferson yet written. The chapter on Epicurus and Jefferson, though very short, is excellent.

BULLOCK, HELEN D. *My Head and My Heart: A Little History of Thomas Jefferson and Maria Cosway.* New York: Putnam's, 1955. Centering on Jefferson's years in Europe in the 1780s, the book explores in detail Jefferson's affair (he was then a widower) with a married woman artist. Whether there was sexual involvement is not clearly established. Many letters between the lovers are quoted.

CHINARD, GILBERT. *Thomas Jefferson, the Apostle of Americanism.* Ann Arbor: University of Michigan Press, 1964. 2nd edn., rev. (1929 orig.). Classic study of Jefferson's philosophy. Written by a scholar intimately aware of French thought, it controverts at every turn any notion that Jefferson formed his ideas under French influence; rather, the French philosophers reinforced what he already believed before going to France and before his reading of French works.

COMMAGER, HENRY STEELE. *Jefferson, Nationalism, and the Enlightenment.* New York: George Braziller, 1975. Largely a popular treatment of Jefferson and his time, this is nonetheless a good introductory treatment of the *Declaration,* "The Pursuit of Happiness" concept, and early American nationalism.

CRIPE, HELEN. *Thomas Jefferson and Music.* Charlottesville: University of Virginia Press, 1974. The best and fullest treatment of this specialized area. Fully documented and well illustrated, it carefully describes Jefferson's musical interests, especially his musicianship on the violin, and adds sections on the Monticello music collection, Jefferson's catalog of sheet music, and gives perhaps the final word on his ownership of musical instruments.

DAVIS, RICHARD BEALE. *Intellectual Life in Jefferson's Virginia, 1790–1830.* Chapel Hill: University of North Carolina Press, 1964. The standard study of the subject, an excellent treatment of the ideological milieu of Jefferson's time and place, showing the darkness Jefferson tried to bring light to, and the brighter aspects of southern society in the new nation. Sees Jefferson as "a prophet of manifest destiny."

DUMBAULD, EDWARD. *Thomas Jefferson: American Tourist, Being an Account of His Journeys in the United States of America, England, France, Italy, the Low Countries, and Germany.* Norman: University of Oklahoma Press, 1946. Based chiefly on Jefferson's letters and journal entries, this book delineates an active mind exploring the mores of people unfamiliar to him as a Virginia provincial. The subject explores economics, customs, the arts, inventions, and many other topics as he inquisitively travels, as a government representative, or as a private citizen.

FOOTE, HENRY WILDER. *The Religion of Thomas Jefferson.* Boston: Beacon Press, 1963. Orig., *Thomas Jefferson: Champion of Religious Freedom, Advocate of Christian Morals,* 1947. Very brief; tends to be superficial in its description of the "Christian" Jefferson. Stopping short of making him out to be orthodox, it rightly emphasizes Jefferson's "Christian" ethics in his *Bible* and in his "Unitarianism."

FRARY, I. T. *Thomas Jefferson, Architect and Builder.* Richmond: Garrett and Massie, 1931. A kind of companion piece to Fiske Kimball, *Jefferson, Architect,* with many photos, especially rare pictures of the Capitol. While not a very scholarly work, a valuable one in helping scholars visualize Jefferson's buildings.

GARRETT, WENDELL D., and JOSEPH C. FARBER. *Thomas Jefferson Redivivus.* Barre, Mass.: Barre Publishers, 1971. The finest gift-book, with many photos, relating to Jefferson; has a good brief biography. The pictures — many in color — make more vivid than any other book scenes where Jefferson either lived or visited: Shadwell, Tuckahoe, Williamsburg, the Wythe House, the Raleigh Tavern, Philadelphia, France, England, Italy and other foreign countries, various places in Virginia and, of course, Monticello.

GINSBERG, ROBERT, ed. *A Casebook on the Declaration of Independence.* New York: Crowell, 1967. Good collection of essays by several hands; outstanding ones listed below separately under Articles. Gathering, as it does, articles on various aspects of the subject by respected scholars, the anthology saves later researchers the time and labor of seeking out the items separately. An original essay by the editor is added. (The articles range from those contemporary to the *Declaration* to the very recent.)

HAWKE, DAVID. *Transaction of Free Men: The Birth and Course of the Declaration of Independence.* New York: Scribner's, 1964. A popular treatment of the background, inception, and influence of the *Declaration* on America. Stresses the American quality of Jefferson's thought.

HAZELTON, JOHN H. *The Declaration of Independence: Its History.* New York: Dodd, Mead, 1906. An accurate investigation of the (largely American) antecedents to the *Declaration,* and the American evolution toward it. Good review of contemporaneous (English and American) reactions to it, especially to the "created equal" concept.

HONEYWELL, ROY J. *The Educational Work of Thomas Jefferson.* New York: Russell and Russell, 1964. Rpt. of 1931 edn. An attempt at tracing Jefferson's position in the overall history of formal education in the United States. Appendices reprint Jeffersonian documents on education.

JONES, HOWARD MUMFORD. *Jeffersonianism and the American Novel.* New York: Teachers College, Columbia University Press, 1966. A pioneer study needing expansion by literary historians.

KIMBALL, MARIE. *Jefferson: The Road to Glory, 1743 to 1776.* New York: Coward-McCann, 1943. With the two volumes below, a good biography, fully documented, with illustrations. *The Road to Glory* treats the early years of Jefferson's unselfconscious rise to reputation in politics, with his growing interest in the arts and other areas.

______. *Jefferson: The Scene of Europe, 1784 to 1789.* New York: Coward-McCann, 1950. A fine treatment of Jefferson among the aristocrats and ideologues of France, including his travels and the Cosway affair.

______. *Jefferson: War and Peace, 1776 to 1784.* New York: Coward-McCann, 1947. Traces the years as governor and the problems caused by war and its aftermath.

KOCH, ADRIENNE. *The Philosophy of Thomas Jefferson.* Chicago: Quadrangle Books, 1964. Rpt. of 1943 orig. Tries to base Jefferson's philosophy on French thought, an invalid thesis (see Chinard, *Apostle,* above). The author's failure to follow chronology gives a false sense of the development of Jefferson's thought; the first fifty years of his life are virtually ignored.

LAMBETH, WILLIAM A., and WARREN H. MANNING. *Thomas Jefferson as an Architect and a Designer of Landscapes.* Boston: Houghton Mifflin, 1913. Two interesting monographs, still useful, though based on incomplete data. Jefferson drawings and documents are printed, but the authors are not clear as to the most important aspects of Jefferson's esthetic development in the two areas discussed.

LEHMANN, KARL. *Thomas Jefferson, American Humanist.* New York: Macmillan, 1947. One of the very best books on Jefferson, with a clear grasp of his philosophic position, fully documented. A number of illustrations enhance the text, which traces the rise of Jefferson's intellectual and esthetic questing as a young person, through "Mature Exploration" into Epicurean thought, to show the free ranging mind and creativity of the subject. "American Humanist" becomes a just description in these pages.

LEVY, LEONARD W. *Jefferson and Civil Liberties: the Darker Side.* Cambridge, Mass.: Belknap Press, 1963. A partially successful attempt to counterbalance Jefferson "worship," or whitewashing, by debunking. For example, it is maintained that Jefferson sanctioned prosecution of Federalist editors under the sedition laws, while pardoning Republican abuses. Slavery and other issues are also approached.

LINN, WILLIAM. *The Life of Thomas Jefferson, Author of the Declaration of Independence, and Third President of the United States.* Ithaca: Mack, Andrus and Woodruff, 1839. 2nd edn. A sample of how Jefferson's biographers looked at him in the years just after his death (original, 1834), it attempts to make the subject over into a nearly orthodox Christian, and to look aside from the slavery question.

MALONE, DUMAS. *Jefferson and the Ordeal of Liberty.* Boston: Little, Brown, 1962. With the volumes below, the biography *Jefferson and His Time.* This volume follows Jefferson to his first presidential term (1800).

______. *Jefferson the President: First Term, 1801–1805.* Boston: Little, Brown, 1970. The Louisiana Purchase is thoroughly dealt with, but "The Miscegenation Legend" (an appendix) attempts to defend Jefferson under the mistaken notion that to have been intimate with Sally Hemings he would have had to have dirtied himself.

______. *Jefferson and the Rights of Man.* Boston: Little, Brown, 1951. Jefferson emerges as a party leader in the 1790s.

______. *Jefferson the Virginian.* Boston: Little, Brown, 1948. Provides a full picture of Jefferson's formative years, to his departure for Europe in 1784. Includes a genealogy, an appendix on his flirtation with a friend's wife (before Jefferson's marriage, "The Walker Affair") and, as is true of all the volumes, an extensive bibliography.

MARTIN, EDWIN T. *Thomas Jefferson: Scientist.* New York: Collier, 1961. Excellent book, not only on Jefferson and science, but on the era in which he lived, experimented, and invented. The fullest, most intelligent treatment of the man who was at once a meteorologist, paleontologist, ethnologist, archaeologist, astronomer, chemist, geologist, botanist, inventor, sponsor of explorations, a dabbler in medicine and, of course, an agriculturist.

MAYO, BERNARD. *Myths and Men: Patrick Henry, George Washington, Thomas Jefferson.* New York: Harper and Row, 1963. Good brief review of Jefferson's fluctuating reputation, from utter neglect to an apotheosis into American mythology.

MOSCOW, HENRY, DUMAS MALONE, and the Editors of *American Heritage. Thomas Jefferson and His World.* New York: American Heritage, 1960. Primarily for adolescents, an excellent introductory book, with many illustrations. The text is simple, but the contemporaneous and modern pictures (many in color), make the subject vivid.

NICHOLS, FREDERICK D., and JAMES A. BEAR, JR. *Monticello.* Monticello, Va.: Thomas Jefferson Memorial Foundation, 1967. Intended as a guidebook to the house and grounds, this is far more; has an excellent description of Monticello, and numerous illustrations, including maps, floorplans, photographs of decor, of the narrow staircases, and other details. An intelligent text cogently describes the background and function of each room or section.

O'NEAL, WILLIAM B., ed. *American Association of Architectual*

Bibliographers Papers, Vol. VI. Charlottesville: University Press of Virginia, 1969. Subtitled "An Intelligent Interest in Architecture: A Bibliography of Publications about Thomas Jefferson as an Architect, Together with an Iconography of the Nineteenth-Century Prints of the University of Virginia." The bibliography, fully indexed, ranges from Chastellux on Jefferson and architecture (1786), through the nineteenth century, to Frank Lloyd Wright (1959) and entries as recent as 1968. A long "Iconography" section then, with copious illustrations, lists graphic picturings of the University, from the Maverick plan (1822) through the late nineteenth century.

———. *Jefferson's Fine Arts Library for the University of Virginia, with Additional Notes on Architectural Volumes Known to Have Been Owned by Jefferson.* Charlottesville: University of Virginia Press, 1956. The story of how Jefferson amassed a collection of books on the fine arts for the university is outlined, and the works are listed, "eighty-some titles and nearly two hundred volumes."

PADOVER, SAUL K. *Jefferson.* New York: Harcourt, Brace, 1942. A standard biography; laudatory in tone, but not excessively so, it somewhat defensively makes Jefferson out to be a Christian. A good bibliography includes items contemporaneous to Jefferson.

PETERSON, MERRILL D. *The Jefferson Image in the American Mind.* New York: Oxford Univ. Press, 1960. Fine treatment of the influence of Jefferson's thinking in American history; an assessment of him as a political symbol; a review of his changing reputation over the decades.

———. *Thomas Jefferson and the New Nation: A Biography.* New York: Oxford University Press, 1970. Excellent treatment, with some tendency to idealize, especially on slavery; paints a bleaker picture of Jefferson's late years as a reactionary than other biographers do. Deals with Jefferson fairly sternly on "states' rights."

———. *Thomas Jefferson: A Profile.* New York: Hill and Wang, 1967. Helpful, intelligent gathering of essays by several hands; some of the best discuss politics, architecture, commerce, the Hamiltonian struggle, and religion.

RANDALL, HENRY S. *The Life of Thomas Jefferson.* 3 vols. New York: Derby and Jackson, 1858. Though old-fashioned by modern scholarly standards, still a basic treatment. It printed for the first time some of his letters, and depended in part on interviews with still-living persons who knew Jefferson and who had visited Monticello.

RANDOLPH, SARAH N. *The Domestic Life of Thomas Jefferson, Compiled from Family Letters and Reminiscences by His Great-Granddaughter.* New York: Frederick Ungar, 1958. Introd. Dumas Malone, Rpt. of 1871 edn. Charming if at times inaccurate view of life at Monticello, written by a person whose tone is naturally laudatory, and who also largely avoids all controversial subjects. It was meant to provide an intimate view of Jefferson's private life, and in a limited sense does so. Prints letters not before made public.

ROSENBERGER, FRANCIS C., ed. *Jefferson Reader: A Treasury of Writings about Thomas Jefferson.* New York: Dutton, 1953. Reprints many articles, contemporaneous to Jefferson and after his lifetime (visits, attacks, poems, eulogies); a fine compendium of articles judiciously chosen, some of which are listed separately, below. It is possible to sketch opinion on Jefferson over nearly two centuries by consulting this book, a most useful, labor saving volume.

SCHACHNER, NATHAN. *Thomas Jefferson: A Biography.* New York. Thomas Yoseloff, 1964. 4th printing. One of the finest biographies (originally two volumes) yet written. Jefferson emerges as fallible, intellectual, and in many ways typically American. No attempt is made to soften his flaws or paint a portrait based on suppressed data, except for the Hemings question.

SOWERBY, E. MILLICENT. *Catalogue of the Library of Thomas Jefferson.* Washington, D.C.: Library of Congress, 1952–1959. 5 vols. A superb scholarly reconstruction of Jefferson's holdings. Many of Jefferson's annotations are included. A selection of 683 items pub. Washington, D.C.: Microcard Corp., 1968.

TUCKER, GEORGE. *The Life of Thomas Jefferson, Third President of the United States, with Parts of His Correspondence Never Before Published, and Notices of His Opinions on Questions of Civil Government, National Policy, and Constitutional Law.* 2 vols. Philadelphia: Carey, Lea and Blanchard; London: Charles Knight, 1837. Best, and fullest, of biographies before Randall. Recognizing Jefferson as a very controversial figure, the author attempts objectivity, and accuracy sufficient to leave his subject a fair place in history.

WEYMOUTH, LALLY, ed. *Thomas Jefferson, the Man, His World, His Influence.* New York: G.P. Putnam's Sons, 1973. Essays by several hands, on various subjects, some of which are listed separately, below. Included are discussions of the Enlightenment, the *Declaration,* economics, the arts, the press, and Jefferson's legacy. The book contains numerous excellent illustrations: extremely valuable sketches by Jefferson; photographs of his paraphernalia; portraits; buildings.

WILSTACH, PAUL. *Jefferson and Monticello.* 3rd edn., rev. Garden City, N.Y.: Doubleday, Doran, 1931. A popular biography, attempting to describe everyday life at Monticello.

WILTSE, CHARLES MAURICE. *The Jeffersonian Tradition in American Democracy.* New York: Hill and Wang, 1960. Rpt. of 1935 edn. Good on the background of the *Declaration,* on Jefferson's political and philosophic views, and on Jefferson and the law. In effect an "intellectual biography," still a valuable work.

2. Articles

BAKER, A. T., et al. "Independence: The Birth of a New America." *Time,*

["4 July 1776"] (May, 1975), pp. 5–13. In a special Bicentennial issue of *Time* magazine (Jefferson is pictured on the cover), a popular but sound treatment of the historical moment surrounding the *Declaration,* with a brief sketch of Jefferson, and many illustrations.

BAUGH, ALBERT C. "Thomas Jefferson, Linguistic Liberal." *Studies for William A. Read.* Ed. Nathaniel M. Caffee and Thomas A. Kirby. Baton Rouge: Louisiana State University Press, 1940. pp. 88–108. Shows Jefferson ahead of his time in recognizing linguistic phenomena as relative and fluctuating.

BECKER, CARL. "What Is Still Living in the Political Philosophy of Thomas Jefferson?" *Proceedings of the American Philosophical Society,* LXXXVII (1944), 201–10. In Peterson, *Profile,* pp. 41–60. Excellent, brief exposition of Jefferson's political thought, with an attempt to assess its twentieth century validity, especially on the subject of natural rights.

BLACK, R. M. "The Ethics of the Declaration of Independence." *Annals of the American Academy of Political and Social Science,* 2 (1891), 138–44. In Ginsberg, *Casebook,* pp. 78–82. The terminology of the *Declaration* is examined and explicated; the concept of "equality" is the key to Jefferson's radicalism.

BOTTORFF, WILLIAM K. "The Age of Jefferson." *Midcontinent American Studies Journal,* IX (1968), 5–7. Introduction to a special issue, "The Age of Jefferson" (seven articles on the era, some listed below), asserting that the Jeffersonian period is the key to American history.

BOYD, JULIAN P. "The Megalonyx, the Megatherium, and Thomas Jefferson's Lapse of Memory." *Proceedings of the American Philosophical Society,* CII (1958), 420–35. Charming article on Jefferson's mistaken attribution and on his honesty in admitting his error.

BRODIE, FAWN M. "The Great Jefferson Taboo." *American Heritage,* XXIII (1972), 48–57, 97–100. First and clearest working out of Jefferson's relationship to Sally Hemings. Full scholarly annotations.

______. "Jefferson's Biographers and the Psychology of Canonization." *Journal of Interdisciplinary History,* II (1971), 155–71. Fullest treatment of Jefferson's changing reputation. Reviews Malone's *The President,* and Peterson's *The New Nation* in an essay that takes into account many other biographies. All are found wanting, as the "inner man" has escaped his chroniclers.

______. "Thomas Jefferson's Unknown Grandchildren: A Study in Historical Silences," *American Heritage,* XXVII (1976), 28–33, 94–99. Establishes that Sally Hemings, a quadroon, was Jefferson's wife's half sister; Sally Hemings and Jefferson were together for thirty-eight years, had seven children; discusses each child who survived infancy; gives family tree down to the present.

BROWN, ROLAND W. "Jefferson's Contribution to Paleontology." *Journal of the Washington Academy of Science,* XXIII (1943), 257–59.

The *Megalonyx jeffersoni* briefly dealt with as Jefferson's only venture into paleontology.

BROWNE, CHARLES A. "Thomas Jefferson and the Scientific Trends of His Time." *Chronica Botanica,* VIII (1944), 361–424. Jefferson is shown to have been a careful, if not always correct, scientist, in the forefront of his time.

CHINARD, GILBERT. "Thomas Jefferson as a Classical Scholar." *The American Scholar,* I (1932), 133–43. In Rosenberger, *Reader,* pp. 140–48. Firmly shows Jefferson's grasp of classical languages and literary and philosophical works.

CLARK, AUSTIN H. "Thomas Jefferson and Science." *Journal of the Washington Academy of Science,* XXXIII (1943), 193–203. In Rosenberger, *Reader,* pp. 149–60. General survey of Jefferson's scientific interests.

DANA, WILLIAM F. "The Political Principles of the Declaration." *Harvard Law Review,* XIII (1900), 319–43. In Ginsberg, *Casebook,* pp. 102–26. A good, clear, short treatment of the Lockean influence on the *Declaration.*

DEWEY, JOHN. "The Moral Faith of the Declaration." *The Living Thoughts of Thomas Jefferson Presented by John Dewey.* New York: Longmans, Green, 1940. In Ginsberg, *Casebook,* pp. 162–65. An antitotalitarian document from the 1940s when Jefferson was decidedly in fashion.

DORFMAN, JOSEPH. "The Economic Philosophy of Thomas Jefferson." *Political Science Quarterly,* LV (1940), 98–121. Detailed study of the subject; makes Jefferson's ideal economic system "commercial-agrarian," guided by "a planter's logic."

DOUGLAS, CARLYLE C. "The Dilemma of Thomas Jefferson." *Ebony,* XXX (1975), 60–66. Special Bicentennial issue; asserts that Jefferson "failed to practice what he preached" about equality in the *Declaration.*

GINSBERG, ROBERT. "The Declaration as Rhetoric." *A Casebook on the Declaration of Independence.* New York: Crowell, 1967. Excellent article on a seldom approached subject, the persuasive elements, diction, tone, and other stylistic and rhetorical aspects of the *Declaration.*

GITTLEMAN, EDWIN. "Jefferson's 'Slave Narrative': The Declaration of Independence as a Literary Text." *Early American Literature,* VIII (1974), 239–56. Attempt at a close reading of parts of the *Declaration* as a literary work, wherein the original antislavery section becomes pivotal.

GRAMPP, WILLIAM D. "A Re-examination of Jeffersonian Economics." *The Southern Economic Journal,* XII (1946), 263–82. In Peterson, *Profile,* pp. 135–63. A good attempt at ending the overly simple view of Jefferson as an "agrarian." His policy evolved after 1806 toward protectionism (away from free trade) and manufacturing.

HAZELTON, JEAN HANVEY. "Thomas Jefferson, Gourmet." *American Heritage,* XV (1964), 20–21, 102–105. Centering on the White House years, a sketch of Jefferson's bent for *haute cuisine* after his French experience.

HENDRICKSON, WALTER B. "Thomas Jefferson — Up from Slander." *Social Education,* XVIII (1954), 244–48. A tracing of Jefferson's changing reputation from early positive (1800) and negative (1801) opinions, through Tucker and Randall in the nineteenth century, to his low point early in this century, to his peak in the 1940s.

HERZBERG, MAX J. "Thomas Jefferson as a Man of Letters." *South Atlantic Quarterly,* XIII (1914), 310–27. A rare discussion of Jefferson in literary terms; views the *Declaration* as not only political but as the chief literary work of the Revolution; the Adams-Jefferson correspondence also displays his literary skill.

HOWELL, WILBUR SAMUEL. "The Declaration of Independence and Eighteenth-Century Logic." *William and Mary Quarterly,* 3rd ser., XVIII (1961), 463–84. In Ginsberg, *Casebook,* pp. 194–215. Explains how Jefferson, fitting his logic into the context of the era, could use *a priori* thinking.

JUDGE, JOSEPH. "Mr. Jefferson's Monticello." *National Geographic,* CXXX (1966), 426–44. Featuring many color photographs (a narrow staircase, the coffee urn, the library, the dining room, the bedroom, etc.), a brief text introducing the reader to today's restored Monticello.

KALLEN, HORACE M. "The Arts and Thomas Jefferson." *Ethics,* LIII (1943), 269–83. In Peterson, *Profile,* pp. 218–42. Good introduction to Jefferson's decades long artistic expressiveness in language, music, and architecture, with some words on his opinions regarding other arts.

KIMBALL, FISKE. "Jefferson and the Arts." *Proceedings of the American Philosophical Society,* CXXXVII (1943), 238–45. In Rosenberger, *Reader,* pp. 193–207. Supplies some background as to the state of the arts in Jefferson's early environment; speaks of his violin playing and of his growing ideas on sculpture and painting.

______, and MARIE KIMBALL. "Jefferson's Curtains at Monticello." Rpt. from *Antiques* (1947), n.p. Charming three-page note on Jefferson as an interior decorator, and on his attention to details of design.

KIMBALL, MARIE. "Jefferson, Patron of the Arts." *Antiques,* XLIII (1943), 164–67. Sketch of Jefferson as collector and commissioner of artistic works.

KNOLES, GEORGE HARMON. "The Religious Ideas of Thomas Jefferson." *Mississippi Valley Historical Review,* XXX (1943), 187–204. In Peterson, *Profile,* pp. 243–60. Stresses Jefferson's early orthodoxy (Anglicanism), along with his disbelief in revelation and later unorthodox position ("Unitarianism").

LEVY, LEONARD. "Jefferson as a Civil Libertarian." In Weymouth, *Jefferson,* pp. 189–215. Jefferson, though flawed as a civil libertarian, yet did embody liberal ideals — he simply "reflected both traditions," able to revoke or abridge rights as well as insist on them.

LYND, STAUGHTON. "Beard, Jefferson and the Tree of Liberty." *Midcontinent American Studies Journal,* IX (1968), 8–22. Briefly asserts that Jefferson at first failed to understand the rise of political parties in the new United States (1790s). His famous figure of the tree of liberty being watered periodically with the blood of tyrants is from Bolingbroke.

MALONE, DUMAS. "Jefferson, Hamilton, and the Constitution." *Theory and Practice in American Politics.* Ed. William H. Nelson. Chicago: University of Chicago Press, 1964. In Peterson, *Profile,* pp. 164–77. In the Kentucky and Virginia Resolutions "Jefferson turned to the states because he had nothing else to turn to." He invoked states' rights only to protect human rights.

MARTIN, JOHN S. "Rhetoric, Society and Literature in the Age of Jefferson." *Midcontinent American Studies Journal,* IX (1968), 77–90. Good background article on the milieu of language in which Jefferson wrote; especially examines the first inaugural address and *Notes.*

MIRKIN, HARRIS G. "Rebellion, Revolution, and the Constitution: Thomas Jefferson's Theory of Civil Disobedience." *American Studies,* XIII (1972), 61–74. Jefferson, the most revolutionary voice of his revolutionary generation, never backed down on the theoretical right of revolution, even in face of a supposedly fixed Constitution. His thinking is the most relevant today.

MONTGOMERY, H. C. "Thomas Jefferson as a Philologist." *American Journal of Philology,* LXV (1944), 367–71. Brief mention of Jefferson's ethnological-linguistic interests.

PERRY, RALPH BARTON. "The Philosophy of the Declaration." *Puritanism and Democracy.* New York: Vanguard, 1944, pp. 123–30. In Ginsberg, *Casebook,* pp. 166–73. Admiration of Jefferson's concise style and underlying ethical position in the (theistically based) *Declaration.*

PETERSON, MERRILL D. "Thomas Jefferson and Commercial Policy, 1783–1793." *William and Mary Quarterly,* 3rd ser., XXII (1965), 584–60. In Peterson, *Profile,* pp. 104–34. Attempts to trace Jefferson's search for an American economic structure consonant with the revolutionary principles that began the new nation; centers on his "Report on the Privileges and Restrictions on the Commerce of the United States in Foreign Countries" (1791-1793). A well documented, reasonable account showing how his lead was not followed.

SCHLESINGER, ARTHUR M. "The Lost Meaning of 'The Pursuit of Happiness.' " *William and Mary Quarterly,* 3rd ser., XXI (1964), 325–27. In Ginsberg, *Casebook,* pp. 216–18. A provocative note on how the famous phrase may have meant "to pursue" as in the pursuit of law or medicine.

SHEEHAN, BERNARD W. "The Quest for Indian Origins in the Thought of the Jeffersonian Era." *Midcontinent American Studies Journal,* IX (1968), 34–51. Good view of the background of ethnological thought of the era in which Jefferson lived. His investigations of Indian origins, based on his extensive study of Indian languages, were more empirically careful than those of others.

SMITH, DAVID E. "Thomas Jefferson and Mathematics." *The Poetry of Mathematics and Other Essays.* New York: Scripta Mathematica, Yeshiva College, 1934, pp. 49–70. General view of Jefferson's interest in mathematics; sketches of his modest contributions.

TYLER, MOSES COIT. "The Declaration of Independence in the Light of Modern Criticism." *The Literary History of the United States.* New York: G. P. Putnam's Sons, 1897. I, 498–521. In Ginsberg, *Casebook,* pp. 83–101. "Modern," of course, is now very old-fashioned, but here a pioneering American literary historian assesses whether the *Declaration* shows "originality" (it does, especially in style; it is "a prose lyric").

VERNER, COOLIE. "Mr. Jefferson Makes a Map." *Imago Mundi,* XIV (1957), 96–108. Jefferson's 1786 map of Virginia, the best of its time, documents the westward movement. His only map (appended to *Notes*), it is reproduced.

WAYLAND, JOHN W. "The Poetical Tastes of Thomas Jefferson." *Sewanee Review,* XVIII (1910), 283–99. A notice of Jefferson's wide reading in poetry, and of his scrapbook of poetic clippings (many are Fourth of July odes), mostly from American newspapers and periodicals.

WECTER, DIXON. "Thomas Jefferson, the Gentle Radical." *The Hero in America.* New York: Scribner's, 1941. In Peterson, *Profile,* pp. 1–40. In the *Declaration* Jefferson was "the amanuensis of Americanism," but his historical reputation (whose ups and downs are traced) has not been secure.

WHITEHILL, WALTER MUIR. "Thomas Jefferson, Architect." In Weymouth, *Jefferson,* pp. 159–77. General review of Jefferson's architectural activities; stresses the French influence and that of Palladio.

WILSON, M. L. "Jefferson and His Moldboard Plow." *The Land,* III (1943), 59–64. Useful article tracing the evolution of the idea of a more efficient plow (1788–1798), the last and best of the old wooden implements, and the herald of the metal ones to come.

———. "Survey of Scientific Agriculture." *Proceedings of the American Philosophical Society,* LXXXVI (1942), 52–62. Outline of the state of the science of agriculture in Jefferson's time, with a few words on his position therein, stressing his plow.

WRIGHT, LOUIS B. "Thomas Jefferson and the Classics." *Proceedings of the American Philosophical Society,* LXXXVII (1944), 223–33. In Peterson, *Profile,* pp. 195–217. Because of his formal schooling, and his lifelong inclination, Jefferson was a profound student of Greek and Latin texts. He especially liked the "Roman historians and moralists."

Index